Browning's Roman Murder Story

Here be facts, charactery; what they spell
Determine, and thence pick what sense you may!
(3. 837–38)

Browning's
Roman Murder Story

A Reading of "The Ring and the Book"

RICHARD D. ALTICK
and
JAMES F. LOUCKS, II

The University of Chicago Press

CHICAGO & LONDON

Library of Congress Catalog Card Number: 68–14627

THE UNIVERSITY OF CHICAGO PRESS, CHICAGO 60637
The University of Chicago Press, Ltd., London W.C.1

To

ALBERT J. KUHN

who found us the time

Acknowledgments

The authors are deeply indebted to the administrative officers of the Ohio State University, its College of Arts and Sciences, and its Department of English, for releasing them from a portion of their academic duties and in other generous ways making possible the writing of this book.

For teaching him much that now appears in these pages, Mr. Altick wishes to thank the members of his graduate seminar in Browning over a period of more than a dozen years, and in particular Wilma O. Compton, Nancy Mason Dasher, Samuel W. Jones, and John H. Matthews, who wrote master's theses on *The Ring and the Book* under his supervision. The author of a fifth such thesis, which was followed by a doctoral dissertation on the poem, is named on the title page of this volume.

We are grateful to the university's Graduate School for purchasing for our use a Xerox copy of the manuscript of the poem in the British Museum, to Ida Mae Cornelius for her exemplary work as typist of the final draft, and to D. Alan Youel for helping with the proofs.

Contents

Contents   ix

I cannot help looking on [*The Ring and the Book*] as a sort of sublime "stunt." Its very individuality is enough to bar it from being really great—except in spots. Nine tenths of it is not poetry; nor is all of one tenth of [it] great poetry.

> EDWIN ARLINGTON ROBINSON in a letter of 1899;
> quoted, *Victorian Newsletter*, no. 23 (1963), p. 20

The Ring and the Book is a laborious and desperate attempt to find ultimate truth in the history of . . . a crime.

> JOHN HEATH-STUBBS, *The Darkling Plain* (1950),
> pp. xiii–xiv

. . . the book never comes to life for long. There is no real progress from one speech to the next, no internal development, because Browning has reduced all his complex material to a simple, external contrast between chivalry and chicane. . . . It was only a short step from *The Ring and the Book* to the tedious word-spinning of the poet's last twenty years.

> L. G. SALINGAR in *From Dickens to Hardy* (Pelican
> Guide to English Literature, vol. 6, 1958), p. 254

The trouble is, that this is no way to tell a story. There are some impressive parts (notably the Pope's concluding monologue), but a monologue to be effective must not go on and on, nor should it be bound up with other protracted monologues in a sequence that the reader has no dramatic reason for pursuing as a sequence.

> DAVID DAICHES, *A Critical History of English
> Literature* (1960), 2: 1007

I suppose that *The Ring and the Book* still has some claims to distinction.

> EDMUND WILSON, *The Shores of Light* (1952), p. 36

Introduction

When *The Ring and the Book* was published in 1868–69, it
was praised to the far side of idolatry. "We must," said a
normally restrained literary weekly, "record at once our conviction, not merely that 'The Ring and the Book' is beyond all
parallel the supremest poetical achievement of our time, but
that it is the most precious and profound spiritual treasure that
England has produced since the days of Shakespeare." [1] Few
poems, no matter what their strengths, can indefinitely sustain
so extravagant an initial recommendation, and, as our page of
epigraphs suggests, Browning's has proved no exception. Still,
present-day opinion generally holds that if it is not one of the
finest long poems of any age, it certainly marks the zenith of
Browning's powers, a judgment which in itself is no slight
praise. Whatever the poem's worth, however (the size of this
volume is a fair indication of our own estimate), it has never
been the subject of a wide-ranging analysis from a modern
critical point of view. This book, published as the poem
reaches its centennial, is the first full-length study of *The Ring
and the Book* as a work of literary art.

There is, of course, a large so-called literature on the poem,
reaching from A. K. Cook's learned *Commentary* and the
massive editions and translations of its source by Charles W.
Hodell and John Marshall Gest to scores upon scores of eulo-

[1] *Athenaeum*, no. 2160 (March 20, 1869), p. 399. The writer was
Robert Buchanan.

1

gistic essays, most of them many years old. But the modern
reader, accustomed to scrutinizing a poetic text for detail and
subtlety as well as for grand effect, cannot help feeling that one
of the richest and most complex of English poems has been
inadequately served by criticism. G. K. Chesterton's observation, made at a time when there was widespread confidence
that Browning's poetry was an open book whose full import
could be seized at a glance, still holds:

> It is sometimes curious to notice how a critic, possessing
> no little cultivation and fertility, will, in speaking of a
> work of art, let fall almost accidentally some apparently
> trivial comment, which reveals to us with an instanta-
> neous and complete mental illumination the fact that he
> does not, so far as that work of art is concerned, in the
> smallest degree understand what he is talking about. He
> may have intended to correct merely some minute detail
> of the work he is studying, but that single movement is
> enough to blow him and all his diplomas into the air.
> These are the sensations with which the true Browningite
> will regard the criticism made by so many of Browning's
> critics and biographers about *The Ring and the Book*.[2]

Whether or not Chesterton himself achieved a superior understanding of the poem as a whole is not at issue here, though
some of his comments on the subject come nearer to the
mark than does most criticism of the poem. What does concern
us is the belief that, since sound criticism must rest on comprehension, the claims of *The Ring and the Book* to a high place
in English poetry cannot be fairly examined until we determine what Browning actually proposed to do, and what he
did: what the poem, in short, is really like. This is our
purpose in an exploratory book which makes no attempt to be
either comprehensive or definitive but is meant simply to
suggest the grounds upon which future evaluation of the poem
may reasonably be based.[3]

[2] *Robert Browning* (London, 1903), pp. 162–63.
[3] A few recent writers have commented helpfully and sometimes
provocatively on certain aspects of the poem. Although we are occasionally indebted to their observations, the substance of their essays

Every rereading of *The Ring and the Book* widens one's awareness of Browning's virtuosity. Henry James's terms, in his essay "Browning in Westminster Abbey," serve well: "complexity and convertibility, . . . passion and ingenuity, irony and solemnity, the impressive and the unexpected." [4] The poem is massive, but it rewards the closest study, because Browning, in addition to being an architect on a gigantic scale, worked with astonishing care in little things. At whatever page we open it, we discover fresh evidence of the manifold artistic sources from which it derives its scope and power: new instances of Browning's seemingly inexhaustible gift of invention, his management of cunningly interwoven themes and nuances, his abounding humor and irony—all firmly controlled by a central conception. Chesterton was surely right: "It is exceedingly dangerous to say that anything in Browning is irrelevant or unnecessary. We are apt to go on thinking so until some mere trifle puts the matter in a new light, and the detail that seemed meaningless springs up as almost the central pillar of the structure." [5]

Virtually all sympathetic critics have dwelt upon the poem's grandeur, its nobility of thought and utterance. No one can deny it these qualities. But they are balanced, at the very least, by the spirit of comedy which presides over much of the characterization and permeates many of the images and allusions: a bold statement to make in view of the ritual solemnity with which the poem is ordinarily approached, but one we are confident we can sustain. The realism of Browning's character portrayal and *mise en scène,* likewise, though hardly overlooked by traditional criticism, has not hitherto been allowed the importance it actually possesses. The sense of concrete detail, of particular person, place, and time, is as strong here as anywhere else in Browning's work.

---

has not, for the most part, been absorbed into the present pages, not necessarily because of any disagreement but because so much of our own discovering has had to be covered in a limited space. See the Bibliographical Note, pp. 363–65.

[4] *English Hours* (Boston, 1905), p. 52. (First printed in *The Speaker,* January 4, 1890, pp. 10–12.)

[5] *Robert Browning,* p. 160.

That the comedy and realism of *The Ring and the Book*
have not received the attention their prominence claims is due
primarily to the assumption that the poem's only major interest is the sentimental splendor of the Pompilia-Caponsacchi
story, together with its judgment from the lips of the Pope.
This was the direction which criticism took from the beginning. A not untypical early comment ran, "The fascination of
the work is still so strong upon us, our eyes are still so spell-
bound by the immortal features of Pompilia (which shine
through the troubled mists of the story with almost insuffera-
ble beauty), that we feel it difficult to write calmly and
without exaggeration." [6] This excessive concentration upon
the tragic love story—their spontaneous and ineffaceable delight in it springing from what was both best and worst in the
Victorians' sensibility—became so deeply embedded in the
later nineteenth-century literary habit that it has not been
rooted out even from our own. Readers still are invited to
devote themselves to the three monologues of Caponsacchi,
Pompilia, and the Pope, which are the only parts usually
included in the anthologies where nearly all make their first,
and normally their only, acquaintance with the poem. The
result is that they form a totally distorted notion of its real
artistic character and its meaning. Unquestionably the narrative of purity in peril and chivalry in action is the poem's
motivating force, but in no sense is it the whole poem. On the
contrary, it is so thoroughly integrated into all that surrounds
it, much of which is neither sentimental nor splendid, that to
interpret it in isolation is to misunderstand the poet's intention
and to underestimate the true breadth of his art.

Only by giving equally serious attention to all twelve of the
books, therefore, can one grasp Browning's full design. This
means dealing equitably with great sections of the text which
critics from his day to our own have dismissed as irrelevant or
worse. Almost all readers, even those most favorably disposed
toward Browning, have groaned over the books of the two
lawyers, which they take to be mere tiresome burlesque rendered even less appealing by the copious interlarded Latin.

[6] *Athenaeum*, no. 2160, p. 399.

These monologues are, however, as germane to Browning's purpose as all the rest. Far from being mere overextended farce, they are compact of rhetorical and casuistical wit whose employment sheds much light, not merely on the character of the speakers, but on Browning's larger purposes. The advocates, along with their lay colleagues, the curbstone explicators of Books 2 and 3 and the supposedly "impartial" analyst of Book 4, receive in the present volume the same amount of attention previously given only to the three principals and the Pope. They deserve no less.

Early commentators on the poem, including John Addington Symonds in *Macmillan's Magazine* (January, 1869) and Swinburne (*Fortnightly Review*, May 1, 1869), suggested analogies between Browning's art and Balzac's. In *The Ring and the Book* we do indeed possess a *comédie humaine* of broad scope and vitality. It is a commonplace that Browning, in his canon as a whole, greatly expanded the subject matter of English poetry, embracing subjects hitherto reserved for the novel and the drama. The observation applies, above all, to *The Ring and the Book*, for in it he restored all of life to the accessible province of the poet working on a grand scale. If numerous portions of the poem suggest Renaissance religious art with its Madonnas and angels and saints with flaming swords (and it is only natural that they should, because the imagery owes much to Browning's absorptive wanderings through Italian churches and galleries), a like number suggest the populous canvases of Pieter Breughel the Elder or Hogarth with their superabundant movement and their Antaeus-like attachment to what Hazlitt called, in his essay on Hogarth's works, "the gross, material, stirring, noisy world of common life and selfish passion." Just as the tragic is here inseparable from the comic, so the mundane mingles with the cosmic. And lengthy though the poem is, it seldom falters, never is at rest; it teems with activity, physical, psychological, intellectual, even verbal—for the very tropes and allusions have a dynamism and continuity of their own. Its condition is that of romantic energy rather than of classic repose.

Long before the term acquired its modern critical vogue, one could speak with entire accuracy of the "world" of *The*

Ring and the Book. Carlyle, erstwhile master painter of a Paris
turbulent with revolutionary mobs, found its "curiously minute picture of Italian Society" one of its redeeming qualities;
and Henry James, the sensitive assayer of ambience, wrote
admiringly of "that breath of Browning's own particular
matchless Italy which takes us full in the face and remains
from the first the felt, rich, coloured air in which we live." [7]
We attend the opera at Arezzo and watch young canons-
about-town tossing comfits to attract ladies' eyes; we join the
sensation seekers at the church of San Lorenzo, where they
climb pillars and crowd into the organ loft, fighting for a
glimpse of the slaughtered Comparini couple; we are present by
anticipation at a birthday party for a bright little boy who
studies Latin, and in retrospect at the wedding, solemnized by
stealth, of a frightened thirteen-year-old girl and an ugly,
undersized man almost four times as old.

Browning realizes character as vividly as he does scene.
Although it is the principals of the story who naturally remain
most conspicuous in our memory, in a very true sense we know
some of the other characters, especially the comedians, better;
for, having room to stress their individuality (as he could not
with the Pope, for instance, because of the heavy measure of
didacticism which that speaker's monologue had to contain),
Browning achieves a Dickens-like particularity of character.
The subordinates, the walk-ons, even the men and women
glimpsed but momentarily in metaphors, parables, and allusions are delineated with a sharpness normally reserved in dramatic poetry for the chief personages. These supernumeraries
include people-in-the-mass, laughing at Guido in his poverty,
his cuckoldry, and his cowardice, and finally adopting him as
the hero of the moment when he is carted to his beheading;
churchmen from barefoot friars to wearers of the purple;
washerwomen liberally displaying their ankles as they bend
over a Roman cistern; bombastic lawyers and drawing-room
raconteurs; mendicants and Magdalenes. The *dramatis perso-*

[7] Carlyle is quoted in *William Allingham: A Diary*, ed. H. Allingham and D. Radford (London, 1908), p. 194; James's words are in
"The Novel in 'The Ring and the Book,'" *Quarterly Review*, 217
(1912) : 79.

nae are drawn not only from late seventeenth-century Italy but from classic myth, the Bible, and the treasury of proverb and folk legend. The fabled courtesan Phryne rubs shoulders with Judith, and Samson with Perseus; a flea-bitten monk slaves away in his cell over a reply to Fénelon for which his bishop will take credit (6. 321–28),[8] and a nobleman of the old school takes his daily exercise on a rack, "command[ing] the varletry stretch, strain their best, / While friends looked on, admired my lord could smile / 'Mid tugging which had caused an ox to roar" (8. 416–18). In character as in setting, the poem includes a multiplicity of societies, sacred and secular.

The Ring and the Book is baroque in many of its aspects: in its scale, intensity, vitality, emphasis upon illusion and transformation, and, not least, the vigorous, ventriloquial Browning style that is both his and not his but the various speakers'. By its very artistic qualities it captures the flavor of the period with which it deals. But perhaps its most emphatically baroque trait is its diversity of manner. Possessing attributes of several literary genres, the poem belongs to none. In its length, twelve-book scheme, and incidental devices it bears superficial resemblance to the epic. The formal Homeric simile is sometimes used, and the "O lyric love" invocation which concludes Book 1 recalls the ceremonial opening of the *Aeneid* and *Paradise Lost*. But the poem's matter lacks epic scope: the action is confined to Arezzo and Rome in a brief period of the late seventeenth century. The only epic action is Caponsacchi's rescue of Pompilia, and the only victory is the vindication, by a Pope thought to be in his dotage, of the fame of a Roman prostitute's illiterate daughter. The central subject, in fact, is a domestic plot of the sort which in the true epic is relegated to secondary importance and even used for comic relief. Nor does the language possess epic grandeur, except in certain exalted passages of philosophical commentary.

[8] All citations follow the text and line numbering of the first edition (4 vols., London, 1868–69), which are also followed by the Everyman and Oxford editions. Later editions during Browning's lifetime and some modern reprints have slightly different textual readings and line numbering because of Browning's revisions. See the Bibliographical Note, p. 363.

The Ring and the Book has some points of similarity to the novel, notably the deep interest in psychological revealment, change, and motivation. Yet it lacks immediate conflict: the characters are deliberately isolated (the sole occasion upon which all three protagonists meet is the brief encounter at Castelnuovo), and they are limited to describing only past events as they remember them. The plot is mainly in the past, and the situations represented in the successive monologues are but the aftermath of the important events. The story line, furthermore, is continually interrupted by recapitulations and digressions. In fact there are two narrative sequences—the events leading up to the murder (the past) and the events subsequent to it (the occasion of the poem)—and these not only are intertwined but involve much repetition.

Though it does, after a fashion, tell a story in verse (fortunately, however, not in the rhymed couplets Browning first chose! [9]), the poem belongs neither to the romantic genre of narrative poetry nor to the specifically Victorian one of the novel-in-verse. Yet it does embody some of the themes of romantic and Victorian narrative poetry (and drama): the elemental conflict of good and evil, the inquiry into the criminal mind, the exploitation of the abnormal and the grotesque. Elsewhere we detect traces of the romance, the morality play, the medieval story-cycle, and the novella.[10] Its broad eclecticism of literary manner is illustrated by lines suggestive of Byron—

> Pompilia chose to cloister up her charms
> Just in a chamber that o'erlooked the street,
> Sat there to pray, or peep thence at mankind
>
> (2. 809–11)

of Boccaccio—

> One merry April morning, Guido woke
> After the cuckoo, so late, near noonday,
>
> (2. 889–90)

[9] *William Allingham: A Diary*, p. 181.

[10] As, for example, the repeated pastiche in Book 1 of the style of chapter headings in Boccaccio and his descendants: "How Half-Rome found for Guido much excuse" (882), "How quality dissertated on the case" (942), "How Guido, after being tortured, spoke" (1015), "How the priest Caponsacchi said his say" (1075), and so forth.

and of Milton, as in the description of Guido's priestly pan-
der-brother as having an eye of "Scintillant, rutilant, fraternal
fire" (3. 359). In short, Browning's work cuts across many
genres and styles to produce a separate species of poetic narrative. But flavored though it is with reminiscences of still other
masterpieces from Ovid to *Othello*,[11] *The Ring and the Book* is
far from being merely derivative; it is *sui generis*, an original
and bold conception. Ezra Pound was entirely accurate when
he characterized it as "serious experimentation." [12]

The experimental device for which the poem is most famous
is the interplay of points of view through a series of individual
monologues.[13] Browning had already developed the dramatic

[11] The Renaissance atmosphere of the poem is intensified by various literary allusions and echoes, the most prominent of which are
the repeated reminiscences, in phrase and idea, of *Othello* (cf. 1. 774;
2. 1376–77; 3. 307, 1239; 4. 42, 1190; 5. 710, 1389, 1494–95, 1695; 6.
148, 1235–37, 2035; 7. 949; 8. 165; 10. 329–30; 11. 920). But the
similarities are not confined to atmosphere: there are more fundamental resemblances. Both poem and play deal with the fatal conflict of
innocence and evil. Their respective plots relate the intrigue of an
older man against his young and inexperienced wife, of whom he is
(or maintains he is) jealous—in both cases, unjustifiably so. He
murders her *honoris causa* (each husband makes much of the "honor"
which supposedly has been abused) and also because he is driven to
the deed by the taunts of onlookers. Both husbands are repeatedly
alluded to as devils. But Othello at least is a man of honesty and
courage, virtues to which Guido can lay no claim. Guido is, of course,
also strongly suggestive of Iago; and Browning himself was aware of
his villain's "Iago-qualities" (*Robert Browning and Julia Wedgwood:
A Broken Friendship as Revealed by Their Letters*, ed. Richard Curle
[New York, 1937], p. 175). On the whole the story and characters of
The Ring and the Book have more affinity to *Othello* than to Shelley's
The Cenci, despite Swinburne's efforts to draw parallels with the
latter (*Fortnightly Review*, n.s., 5 [1869]: 559–61).

[12] "How to Read" ("1928 or '27"), in *Literary Essays of Ezra
Pound*, ed. T. S. Eliot (London, 1954), p. 33.

[13] Browning is not the only literary artist to have grappled with
the problem of multiple points of view, though few others have had
his lofty purpose of achieving a philosophic synthesis through presenting numerous differing versions of the same events. His method was
anticipated, crudely and at considerable distance of time, by the
epistolary novel; and in his immediate age Wilkie Collins' *The
Woman in White* (1860) used several characters to narrate the story,

monologue as a means of incisive psychological revelation; what now remained was to link contrasting speeches, the more adequately to illustrate how prejudice obscures truth even in the minds of those who claim to be revealing it. In the course of doing so, he looks at a tiny episode of life ten different ways through the minds and eyes of nine highly idiosyncratic speakers, crowding the stage with types at once illustrative of specific nobility or folly and of universal human traits. Browning inserts the Jamesian density of specification into every speaker's thought and speech patterns. Ranging in manner from the systematic and studiedly rhetorical to nearly pure stream-of-consciousness, the monologues are compact of eclectic allusion and shifting metaphor which reflect scattered, fragmented experience recalled under stress and made coherent through the force of will.

To the descriptive power of each monologue—descriptive both of the speaker and of the life he sees—is added internal drama, for through the technique of the dramatic monologue Browning reveals the response of character to intense motivation. The speakers are in danger of exposure, in hope of advancement, in shock, in outrage, *in extremis;* whatever their situation, they are somehow trying to make a case. By so doing, six of the nine (Pompilia, Caponsacchi, and the Pope, who speak directly from their souls, are the obvious exceptions) reveal through their inconsistencies and prejudices and obsessions more of their hidden nature and unacknowledged motives than they intend their speeches to express. This drama of character and motive, played within the limits of the individual books, is expanded and rendered more complex by the total plan of the poem, which not only pits speaker against speaker, attitude against attitude, but involves constantly shift-

but in sequence, not covering and recovering the same ground. One thinks also of the chief principle of Pirandello's dramas, the varying estimates of "truth" held by several figures; and of Jakob Wasser-mann's *Der Fall Maurizius* (1928), which not only employs a fragmentary unfolding of the plot through the expression of varying points of view but like Browning's poem is based on an old criminal case and the documents pertaining to it (see *Modern Language Notes,* 48 [1933]: 16–17). In another medium, there is the example of the Japanese film *Rashomon.*

ing relationships between poet and speaker, between speaker and his audience, and between poet or speaker and reader. The poet's tone when speaking in his own person and his manipulation of the tone and arguments of the people he quotes, the placement of speakers in the scheme of the whole poem—these and similar matters of technique (all of them bearing on the speaker's engagement or distance, which determines his response to events, and so in turn the reader's) add complication to complication.

Given the poem's magnitude and complexity, the fact that it was composed in no more than three and a half years, with occasional long interruptions, surely entitles it to be called a tour de force. Browning said that he wrote it straight through, from beginning to end, never leaping ahead or doubling back. He seems, in the three morning hours he spent each day at his desk, to have written at great speed; the periodic progress bulletins he issued to his friends are wholly quantitative, as if he were proud above all of the sheer size the poem was acquiring. The line count rose steadily, from 8,400 in July, 1865, some eight or nine months after he is thought to have begun, to 16,000 in May, 1866, and finally to "somewhat exceeding 20,000" in July, 1867. It was, as he described it in mid-October of the latter year, an "exceedingly lengthy business." Did he keep rough working papers, outlines, and memoranda, as Dickens did when he wrote his novels? Or did he carry the whole scheme of *The Ring and the Book* in his head from beginning to end, including the thousands upon thousands of small details that echo, re-echo, expand, modify, and invert points already made? We do not know; but the latter assumption is the more likely. Whatever the truth, Browning's agile, endlessly inventive talent, combined with a preternaturally retentive memory and, perhaps, an absolute command of future developments, enabled him to perform a prodigy of artistic composition whose full dimensions are evident only after intensive study.[14]

---

[14] The history of the poem's composition can be reconstructed from Browning's letters and from the diaries, letters, and recorded conversations of his acquaintances; there is a good précis in William C.

The sheer length of the poem is one obvious reason why it has not enjoyed the painstaking line-by-line analysis that many shorter poems of its era have recently received. We have Dr. Johnson's word that none ever wished *Paradise Lost* longer than it is—and Milton's poem is only half as long as *The Ring and the Book*, to which the remark supposedly would be doubly applicable. In the nature of the case, it would be too much to expect that Browning was able to load every rift with ore; but there is abundant reason to be grateful for the riches the poem contains. He uttered no more than the simple truth when he remarked, in a letter to his Boston publishers, "It is the shortest poem, for the stuff in it, I ever wrote." [15]

DeVane's *Browning Handbook*, 2d ed. (New York, 1955), pp. 319–25. The lengthy interruptions are noted in *Browning and Julia Wedgwood*, p. 126. Browning's assertion that he wrote the poem straight through is in William Michael Rossetti's diary, printed in *Rossetti Papers 1862 to 1870* (London, 1903), p. 302; it is questioned by DeVane (*Handbook*, p. 330). The statement about the morning hours set aside for writing is found on the same page of the Rossetti source and in other books. A much more detailed record of progress-by-line-count could be compiled from various sources. The selected figures given here (8,400, 16,000, and 20,000) are from *Letters of Robert Browning*, ed. Thurman L. Hood (New Haven, 1933), p. 85 (cf. p. 351); *Dearest Isa: Browning's Letters to Isabella Blagden*, ed. Edward C. McAleer (Austin, Tex., 1951), p. 239; and *Rossetti Papers*, p. 302. The letter containing the "exceedingly lengthy business" phrase is in Hood's collection, p. 123.

[15] *Letters*, ed. Hood, p. 114.

One

"*Art May Tell a Truth Obliquely*"

THE POEM'S PURPOSE

I

The "square old yellow Book" (1. 33) upon which Browning happened one summer day in the Florentine flea market belongs among literary history's luckiest *trouvailles*. A collection of fortuitously assembled documents relating to a late seventeenth-century Roman murder case, it proved, in its complicated mixture of plain fact and ultimate mystery, to be the perfect stimulus for Browning's imagination and intellect. His immediate, delighted engrossment in its contents—chiefly printed pamphlets of legal and extra-legal argument with an addendum of manuscript—is preserved in the opening paragraphs of *The Ring and the Book*. One recalls (it takes some resolution not to quote extensively from Browning's vivacious narrative) how he made his way through the streets and then across the Arno to the Casa Guidi, his myopic eyes close to the volume. But, as he goes on to say, his attempts to share his excitement with others were at once rebuffed. Roman citizens whom he approached for further information "snickered" at his hopes: French invaders had, of course, burned all the old records, and in any event the story "tells / Against the Church, no doubt"? (1. 429–34.) No one else, it seemed, could find any interest in this record of a sordid crime and its aftermath. Carlyle's well-known dictum after *The Ring and the Book* was published, that it was "all made out of an Old Bailey story that might have been told in ten lines, and only wants forgetting," was foreshadowed by the response of Browning's wife, who, he told Julia Wedgwood, "never took the least interest in the

13

story, so much as to wish to inspect the papers." He could not even give it away. In the winter of 1860–61 he offered it to a minor novelist, Miss Ogle, and to one W. C. Cartwright, both of whom are remembered today only because they evidently were the first to turn it down. They were soon in distinguished company. Anthony Trollope, unlike Henry James, who came along too late, failed to see in it any possibilities for the novelist. Many years later Tennyson told William Allingham that Browning had offered it to him as well.[1] Presumably it was only after these repeated refusals that Browning decided to do something himself with the contents of the Old Yellow Book.

This, in barest outline, is what the "Old Bailey story" set in Rome and Arezzo in 1693–98 was about, as recited in the poem (the details are not necessarily faithful to the Old Yellow Book): Count Guido Franceschini, "poor, care-bitten, sorrow-sunk, / Little, long-nosed, bush-bearded, lantern-jawed, / Forty-six-years full" (4. 717–19) was the head of an old Aretine family fallen upon evil days, and himself a disappointed long-term seeker of preferment in the church. With the connivance of his brother Paolo, a priest, he married a thirteen-year-old Roman girl, Pompilia Comparini, upon whom her parents of the lower middle class had settled a substantial dowry. In addition, Pietro Comparini ceded his freehold property to Guido, and the remainder of his estate, a usufruct, was to pass at his death to Pompilia or her lawful heir. Accompanied by her parents, Pompilia and Guido took up residence at Arezzo, where the Comparini, discovering that the Franceschini's penury belied the representations earlier made of the family's wealth, alleged with great public outcry that Guido had been brutal to them and to Pompilia. The parents then returned to Rome, where Violante, the putative mother, re-

---

[1] Carlyle's dictum: *Letters of Dante Gabriel Rossetti to William Allingham, 1854–1870,* ed. George Birkbeck Hill (New York, n.d.), pp. 284–85; Mrs. Browning's lack of interest: *Browning and Julia Wedgwood,* p. 154; the offer to Miss Ogle and to W. C. Cartwright: W. Hall Griffin and H. C. Minchin, *The Life of Robert Browning* (London, 1910), p. 229; to Trollope: *William Allingham: A Diary,* p. 180; to Tennyson: *ibid.,* p. 326.

vealed that Pompilia was not her child but that of a washer-woman-prostitute from whom she had bought Pompilia before birth. The Comparini, arguing that the marriage contract was therefore invalid, sued to recover the dowry as well as to nullify Pietro's cession of his property to Guido. The court, while agreeing that Pompilia was not the Comparini's daughter, refused to interfere with Guido's possession of the dowry but at the same time directed Guido to hand Pietro's property back to him. Both sides appealed this verdict, and the appeals were still pending as the remaining events took place. Meanwhile Pompilia, who had been left with Guido at Arezzo, was alleged to have written to Paolo, reporting that her parents on leaving for Rome had urged her to find a helpful paramour-companion, burn down Guido's house, and return to Rome with Guido's money. It was undisputed that she went to the archbishop and the governor of Arezzo, as well as to a poor friar, begging protection against Guido's cruelty. They all turned her down, out of deference to Guido's rank.

Then, after four years of marriage, Pompilia fled Guido's house in the company of Giuseppe Caponsacchi, a young, personable priest of noble Aretine family. Nearing Rome, they stopped overnight at the Castelnuovo post house, where Guido overtook them. In the ensuing confrontation Pompilia, seizing Guido's sword, denounced him and fiercely defended her protector. Flourishing a sheaf of impassioned letters he claimed they had exchanged, Guido had the fugitive couple arrested and charged with adultery and flight. The Roman court found them guilty of these charges but gave them the lightest possible sentences, Pompilia to be cared for by the Convertite nuns, Caponsacchi to be "relegated" to the nearby Civita Vecchia, where he might think things over. Guido then instituted a divorce action against Pompilia, upon which the Comparini in turn began one against him on her behalf. Lawsuit thus continued to be heaped upon lawsuit. Eight months after leaving Arezzo, Pompilia, having been transferred from the Convertites' custody to that of the Comparini, gave birth to a boy, Gaetano. Back home, Guido, hearing the news, hired four peasants to accompany him to Rome. He traced Pompilia to the Comparini's house, where, having tricked Violante into

opening the door, he and his accomplices forthwith knifed all
three. His motive, he claimed in his subsequent defense, was
honoris causa, vindication of husband's honor; but he stood
also to gain the Comparini's money which would come to him
by way of the sole survivor, Pompilia's (and his?) child. The
Comparini died at once, but Pompilia, lingering four days,
told her version of events to a group of sympathetic listeners at
her bedside. Guido and his henchmen started back to Arezzo
but were caught, charged with murder, and brought to trial.
This trial, along with the subsequent appeal (based on privilege of clergy) from the judges' verdict of guilty, occasioned
the printing of many legal briefs and depositions and popular
pamphlets arguing the cause of one side or the other. It was
copies of these which a Florentine lawyer gathered into the
volume Browning was to pick up a century and a half later in
the Piazza di San Lorenzo.

Although the court's attention, like that of Rome at large,
was focused upon the triple murder itself, the whole sequence
of events leading up to the bloody climax was of course recalled in an attempt to fix the guilt. This history of a crime
involved a score of unanswered questions of deed, character,
and motive:

1. What was the Comparini's position in life before the
advent of Pompilia: were they poor or well off, contented or
dissatisfied?

2. What was Violante's purpose in acquiring Pompilia
from her natural mother?

3. What was her purpose in marrying Pompilia off to
Guido?

4. What (transferring question 1 to the other party) was
Guido's true history as head of his family and ineffectual
hanger-on at Rome—and what was his and his family's eco-
nomic and social situation at Arezzo at the time he treated for
Pompilia through Paolo?

5. What were his motives in marrying Pompilia? And
who took the initiative, he or Paolo?

6. What were the rights and wrongs of the first disturb-
ance at Arezzo? Were the Comparini actually abused? Or was

Guido the hapless victim of his unjustifiably vindictive and parasitic parents-in-law?

7. How did Pompilia behave at Arezzo after her parents' departure? Was she a meek, silent sufferer or a subtle schemer who moved to checkmate Guido? And did he, as some alleged, practice great cruelty upon her?

8. Was Pompilia's letter to Paolo a forgery? Whether or not it was (the question of Pompilia's literacy is much debated by various speakers), was it true in substance?

9. What were the implications of Pompilia's appeal to the Aretine authorities and their prompt rejection?

10. What was Guido's reaction to Violante's disclosure of Pompilia's origin?

11. What did the court's middle-of-the-road verdict concerning the dowry and Pietro's property imply about the rights and wrongs of the respective parties?

12. How did Caponsacchi get involved in the affair? What were his motives in communicating with Pompilia?

13. What were the motives and circumstances of the flight from Arezzo?

14. What was the meaning of Pompilia's defiance when Guido confronted her and Caponsacchi at Castelnuovo?

15. Why did Guido not kill them at once, when, having surprised them after their overnight stay at the inn, he had presumably clear proof of their guilt?

16. Were the letters Guido found in their possession genuine evidence that the pair were lovers, or were they forged and planted?

17. What interpretation should be made of the fact that the court found Pompilia and Caponsacchi guilty of adultery yet mitigated their punishment?

18. What motives led Guido to return to Rome following the birth of Pompilia's baby?

19. Why and how was Guido admitted to the Comparini's house, and why did he kill them?

20. Was the court right in rejecting Guido's plea that to kill a faithless wife is not culpable homicide but a stern and praiseworthy act of justice?

These were the principal mysteries which the records of the Franceschini case conveyed to Browning, the ever-curious inquirer into human motives. But as an early speaker in the poem demands, anticipating the impatient Carlyle: "What need of minute search into such springs / As start men, set o' the move?" (3. 862–63.) The question was one which Browning was uniquely equipped to answer by way of demonstration. For providential as his encounter with the Old Yellow Book was in the first place, no less fortunate was the fact that in the end, when others declined the gift, its contents were left for him to exploit; they were peculiarly suited to his temperament, experience, and reading of life. Although seemingly he did not at once realize its full potentialities (otherwise why should he have initially been so ready to part with it?), his taking up the Roman murder case was a perfect matching of man and material. From its recital of long-forgotten events and its evocation of long-dead characters could be fashioned a poem that would give expression to the whole gamut of his interests and ideas.

It is fairly clear what aspects of the Old Yellow Book stirred Browning's enthusiasm as he read his way home that first day. While he was writing the poem several years later, he customarily spoke of it merely as his "Roman murder story." A certain amount of depreciation may have been involved— Browning was not one to proclaim the philosophical ambitions of his work—but it is also true that the Old Yellow Book's subject, a multiple homicide, had much to do with Browning's laying out "eightpence English just" (1. 39) for the battered volume in the first place. For his was the age in England which George Orwell was to call "our great period in murder, our Elizabethan period, so to speak"; and Browning, like Tennyson and many other contemporary writers, was a connoisseur of the homicidal art. The author and publisher Kegan Paul, at a dinner party where murder was the topic of conversation, found Browning "acquainted with the minutest details of every *cause célèbre* of that kind within living memory." With his father, another enthusiast, the poet had discussed the details of such extensively debated cases as the Constance Kent

affair at Road in 1860.[2] Here, in this square collection of
ephemeral pleadings, was a vintage crime, complex and controversial, and left untouched since it was laid down in 1698.
One can almost envision Browning raising the chalice and, in
the manner of his poem "Popularity," praising God for a
miracle: "Thou . . . keep'st the good wine till now!" Although it was plain enough who had killed the Comparini, the
really important matters associated with the case—the secret
motives, the unexpressed hopes and fears and passions of the
characters—were left in doubt. To discover them was a task
most agreeable to a poet who had a strong interest in both
crime and human psychology. No matter if complete understanding was beyond reach, "Since, how heart moves brain,
and how both move hand, / What mortal ever in entirety
saw?" (1. 828–29.) One of the most fundamental of Browning's tenets was that relish for a quest was directly proportional
to the impossibility of full success.

Moreover, the very obscurity of the Franceschini case, a
onetime sensation that had been wholly forgotten with the
passage of some 160 years, especially recommended it. From
the outset of his career Browning, passing over the more
familiar materials of history, had made a specialty of retriev-
ing events and people from the dustiest pages of old folio
histories and encyclopedias—material unencumbered by later
commentary, hence completely malleable, available to the artist to make of it what he would.

The central episode of the Franceschini affair was an elopement, a deed which of course had special meaning to Browning. The story enabled him to treat at great length the theme of
a beleaguered woman and her chivalrous rescuer, and to re-
live, in a way, his own glorious adventure in 1846 as a
Perseus–St. George. While there is little overt resemblance
between Pompilia and Elizabeth Barrett, apart from their dark
hair and their pallor, it is likely that Pompilia is in some ways

[2] Orwell, "The Decline of the English Murder," *Shooting an Elephant* (London, 1950), p. 197; C. Kegan Paul, *Memories* (London,
1899), p. 338; *The Browning Collections* (catalogue of the Sotheby
sale) (London, 1913), p. 28.

a much idealized version of Browning's dead wife, or, perhaps more accurately, a substitute figure. The terms of the invocation at the end of Book 1 forge a strong implicit link between the women whom Caponsacchi and Robert Browning had rescued respectively from the marital prison at Arezzo and the invalid's couch in Wimpole Street.[3] And into the figure of the "soldier-saint" Caponsacchi (7. 1786), Browning worked the traits of stalwart moralism that constituted his ethical creed.

Individualist that he was, as impatient as Carlyle with the grand pretensions and the ineffectuality of human institutions, Browning saw in the Old Yellow Book ample evidence of the inadequacy of both organized religion and secular law. In an access of bitterness, the irony lying heavy in such words as "strength," "honest," and "brave," the Pope says:

> Since all flesh is weak,
> Bind weaknesses together, we get strength:
> The individual weighed, found wanting, try
> Some institution, honest artifice
> Whereby the units grow compact and firm:
> Each props the other, and so stand is made
> By our embodied cowards that grow brave.
>
> (10. 1491–97)

In no sense, Browning maintained, are institutions dependable guides to truth or instruments of justice. The blindness of church and law, their proclivity to err, indeed on occasion to do actual wrong, are the sum of all individual ecclesiastics'

---

[3] Quite probably there is significance in Browning's using the same associated words in connection with both the dedicatee of the poem—

> O lyric *Love*, half-angel and half-bird
> And all a wonder and a *wild desire*,—
> Boldest of hearts that ever braved the *sun*,
>
> (1. 1391–93)

and Pompilia,

> one *wide* glory of *desire*
> To incorporate the whole great *sun* it *loves*
> From the inch-height whence it looks and longs!
>
> (10. 1043–45)

and lawyers' human limitations. Far from serving their original and still official purposes, like all social systems religion and law have become the tools of men's self-interest.[4]

I I

But beyond the criticism of human institutions in *The Ring and the Book* lie much broader philosophical issues. The premise of the poem, stated perhaps oversimply, is Browning's belief that truth and good are, if not synonymous, correlative, as are their opposites, falsehood and evil; and that while man's truth (most especially, in problems of morality) is relative, God's truth is absolute. If the story of Guido, Pompilia, and Caponsacchi exemplifies the ceaseless conflict between good and evil, it is at the same time one long illustration of the struggle between truth and innocence on the one hand and error and guile on the other. The inseparability of these correlatives, and the doubtful willingness and capacity of finite human beings to recognize the truth and live according to God's law, form the poem's grand subject. Browning, to put it another way, has three topics: the limitations of human apprehension; the dramatic struggle between good and evil; and the justification of the Christian faith and of the inclusion of doubt in God's scheme of human existence.

Browning asserted that he "had mastered the contents, knew the whole truth / Gathered together, bound up in this book" (1. 117–18) by the time he reached home. "The whole truth," however, related only to the limited circumstances of the murder case; the far greater truth, embodied in his answers to the fundamental problems of metaphysics, morality, and religion they raised, was to be grasped only upon reflection. The implications of the story are hinted at nowhere in the Old Yellow Book's documents, whose argumentative authors had not the slightest tendency toward either philosophy or poetry. The speeches of those in the poem who recognize and express these philosophical meanings, the Pope and Fra

---

[4] On the "anti-social implications" of the poem, see E. D. H. Johnson, *The Alien Vision of Victorian Poetry* (Princeton, N.J., 1952), pp. 119–33.

Celestino, are Browning's inventions, and their ideas cannot
conceivably be attributed to the men who bore those names in
the Rome of 1698. They are the most immediate evidence of
the way Browning transformed the narrative of a crime into a
work of art. He took a mass of historical facts, many of them
disputed, and in the immemorial way of artists gave them new
form and additional substance, interpreting them in the light
of his whole view of life, man, and God. To the narrative thus
enlarged and deepened, he added a large body of commentary,
sometimes explicit (through the Pope, Celestino, and the hero
and heroine) but more extensively implicit.

This is the process Browning describes, not with perfect
clarity, in the famous gold-and-alloy image of Book 1. Like an
artificer, he says, he reshaped the materials he found, making
a gold ring (the poem) from a gold ingot (the "factual"
sources). The means by which he wrought is figured as the
goldsmith's alloy: the "Something of mine which, mixed up
with the mass [of historical fact], / Made it bear hammer and
be firm to file," the faculty which "fused my live soul and that
inert stuff" (1. 462–63, 469), "motions of mine / That quick-
ened, made the inertness malleolable / O' the gold [that] was
not mine" (1. 701–3). What Browning is describing obviously
is the poetic imagination. But in elaborating the metaphor he
constantly opposed the implication that he did anything to the
golden materials of the Old Yellow Book other than change
their shape. He added nothing, subtracted nothing; he was
merely the agent of reconstitution or, to adopt the other metaphor by which he describes his role, of resuscitation (1. 719).
He did not create; Elisha-like, he simply breathed fresh life
into what supposedly was dead (1. 760–72).[5] So he maintained.

---

[5] The nature of the creative—or, if we are forbidden the word, the
resuscitative—process is described with less ambiguity in the beginning of the lawyer Bottini's monologue. The passage (9. 86–108) is
too long to quote in full, but its gist is this: the artist, says Bottini,
hewing to a line familiar in the criticism of Horace and Longinus,
turns away from the "studies" he has made (the equivalent of the
documents in the Old Yellow Book, rough representations of fact
unmodified by art) and "buries him and broods / . . . On the inner

The discrepancy between his posture of self-effacing historian in Book 1 and his unquestionable practice of free poetic creation in the rest of the poem has perplexed most readers who are acquainted with his source.[6] Although he insists that in the poem he is dealing exclusively with "fact" and "truth" untouched by the imagination, he uses the very terms so inconsistently, sometimes apparently as synonyms and at other times seemingly as discrete terms, that his intended point becomes hazy indeed. But explanations are available. One is that he actually was, to a certain extent, the painstaking historian he represents himself as being. He inquired for more documents in Rome; from England, he asked his friend Frederick Leighton, the painter, to send him a description of the

---

spectrum, filtered through the eye"—the synthesizing faculty of imagination. The artistic product is not literally faithful to the factual details studied but is something greater and on a higher level of truth:

> the main central truth
> And soul o' the picture, . . .
> Not those mere fragmentary studied facts
> Which answer to the outward frame and flesh—
> Not this nose, not that eyebrow, the other fact
> Of man's staff, woman's stole or infant's clout,
> But lo, a spirit-birth conceived of flesh,
> Truth rare and real, not transcripts, fact and
> [therefore?] false.

Read in context, the passage conveys a quite different impression, though its substance is unaffected. It is part of a long, magnificently fatuous argument in which Bottini, on the surface at any rate a fool of the purest ray serene, fancies himself an artist at work on a painting of the Flight into Egypt; and its pompous and finally ludicrous extravagances, which often are nothing more than exaggerations of the poet's usual manner, tempt one to believe that Browning is here indulging in self-parody. It is well known—or should be—that Browning is capable of expressing wholly serious ideas through extravagant comedy such as burlesque.

[6] The latest canvassing of this perennial worry, a symposium in the *Victorian Newsletter*, nos. 15–17 (1959–60), failed to produce many new insights. See also Paul A. Cundiff, "The Clarity of Browning's Ring Metaphor," *PMLA*, 63 (1948) : 1276–82, and George B. Wasserman, "The Meaning of Browning's Ring-Figure," *Modern Language Notes*, 76 (1961) : 420–26.

church of San Lorenzo in Lucina, where the Comparini's man-
gled corpses had been displayed; and later still he was looking
for a contemporary map of the Arezzo-Perugia-Rome road to
verify the route of Pompilia's and Caponsacchi's flight. And so
he made at least the gestures of research. Again, his insistence
that he is not a creating but merely a reviving force can be
traced in some measure to convention. Browning is expressing
the humility a poet traditionally assumes when embarking on a
great enterprise; else what are epic invocations for?

This was not the only time in Browning's career that he felt
obliged to assert his adherence to history; many years earlier
he had similarly vaunted the historical fidelity of *Paracelsus.*
For—and this is probably the chief explanation—he was writing in a scientific, pragmatic era which required that art rest
on firm documentary props. "Romancing" was suspect; artistic "invention," uncontrolled by a sense of real life, was to be
avoided. To make their stories acceptable to readers who had
inherited strong puritanical or utilitarian biases against fiction, novelists had to assure the readers that the tales possessed
a solid basis of truth. In the prefaces to his various novels,
Dickens felt obliged to deny that his powers of invention had
overruled his sense of fact; one recalls especially his defense,
more vigorous than cogent, of Krook's death by spontaneous
combustion in *Bleak House* (1852–53).[7] At the time Browning
was transmuting the stuff of the Old Yellow Book into art,
Charles Reade was deriving novels and plays from his huge,
elaborately indexed scrapbooks of newspaper clippings and
pamphlets. George Eliot was asking Frederic Harrison (1866)
for guidance on legal points in *Felix Holt,* and a little later
(1868–69, the very years when *The Ring and the Book* was
published), in preparation for *Middlemarch* she was compil-
ing the political events of the Reform Bill years from *The
Times* and the *Annual Register* and assembling into a note-
book a mass of documentary evidence on the state of the
medical profession at that time. In his preface to *The Moon-
stone* (1868) Wilkie Collins assured his readers that he had

[7] On Dickens and "the critics of probability" see George H. Ford,
Dickens and His Readers (Princeton, N.J., 1955), chap. 7, esp. pp.
129–35.

"first ascertained, not only from books, but from living authorities as well," the probable results of the "physiological experiment" upon which the novel's climax hinges. (Eight years earlier, in the preface to *The Woman in White*, he had devoted a long paragraph to the pains he had taken to ensure that the correctness of every legal detail was vouched for by the profession.) At this time, also, the rigorously objective ideal of Ranke and his German school was beginning to be adopted by English historians. In the late sixties Stubbs, Freeman, and Gardiner and the developing Oxford and Cambridge groups of historians were transforming historiography from a vehicle of speculation and argument into a quasi-science that drew its strength from masses of primary data.

It is therefore not hard to understand the impulse behind Browning's preliminary assertions in *The Ring and the Book*, misleading as they are when compared with his actual practice.[8] But although he pays the expected deference to the positivistic ideal of "the fact untampered with" (1. 365), his true subscription is to the ideal of the older school of subjective, "romantic" historians, whose position had recently been set forth anew by Ernest Renan: "The imagination, which exclu-

[8] A passage in John Addington Symonds' diary, recording "a long talk" with Browning in Venice in November, 1888, is pertinent here. Presumably the statements and opinions are Browning's rather than Symonds'. The subject was "the treatment of stories in drama. The great thing is to penetrate the tale and squeeze out the whole truth and virtue—not to invent and add imaginative elements. . . . The 'Ring and the Book' is merely a faithful reproduction of the MS (which Browning means to leave to Balliol), worked out with imaginative effort to seize the real virtue of each part." (To the very end of his life, therefore, Browning clung to the patently false notion that he added nothing and invented nothing.) "Browning's method of dramatic narrative and psychological revivification," continued Symonds, ". . . is nicely invented to suit the imaginative conditions under which a poet who respects his subject, and who lives in sympathy with scientific history, can now work with satisfaction. Art becomes ancillary to science, to history, to fact, in this age. The artist dares not distort events and invent machinery. Query: whether art does not gain? Cerebration increases. It is easy to invent puppets and distort facts. It is difficult to penetrate real persons and to exhibit things." (*Letters and Papers of John Addington Symonds*, ed. Horatio F. Brown [London, 1923], pp. 214–16.)

sively erudite historians proscribe with so many anathemas, has often more chance of finding truth than a servile fidelity, content to reproduce the original accounts of chroniclers." [9]

Browning's conception of art based on history and directed toward high philosophical ends owes much to Carlyle, his master in this as in some other important respects. Carlyle's writings, both in the theory they express and in their actual method, anticipate what Browning set out to do in *The Ring and the Book*. Just as Carlyle had discovered in the chronicle of Jocelin of Brakelond, dealing with events in a twelfth-century Benedictine abbey, a wealth of larger truth bearing on God, man, eternity, and the condition of England in 1842, so did Browning discover in the records of a sordid murder case a transcendental truth: a parable of the ways of God to men and of the problems of faith and doubt which, Browning suggests, were essentially the same in the 1860's as they had been in the 1690's. *The Ring and the Book* might well have had as epigraph "Herr Sauerteig's" thesis that "History, after all, is the true Poetry; that Reality, if rightly interpreted, is grander than Fiction; nay, that even in the right interpretation of Reality and History does genuine Poetry consist." [10]

One Carlylean passage with especially striking relevance to *The Ring and the Book* occurs in the essay "On History" (1830):

> Nay, even with regard to those occurrences which do stand recorded, which, at their origin have seemed worthy of record, and the summary of which constitutes what we now call History, is not our understanding of them altogether incomplete; is it even possible to represent them as they were? The old story of Sir Walter Raleigh's looking from his prison-window, on some street tumult, which afterwards three witnesses reported in three different ways, himself differing from them all, is still a true lesson for us. Consider how it is that historical

[9] Translated from Renan's *Essais de morale et de critique*, 2d ed. (Paris, 1860) by Emery Neff, *The Poetry of History* (New York, 1942), p. 162.

[10] Carlyle's essay on Boswell, *Critical and Miscellaneous Essays*, Centenary ed. (New York, 1900), 3: 79.

documents and records originate; even honest records, where the reporters were unbiased by personal regard; a case which, were nothing more wanted, must ever be among the rarest. The real leading features of a historical Transaction, those movements that essentially characterise it, and alone deserve to be recorded, are nowise the foremost to be noted. At first, among the various witnesses, who are also parties interested, there is only vague wonder, and fear or hope, and the noise of Rumour's thousand tongues; till, after a season, the conflict of testimonies has subsided into some general issue; and then it is settled, by majority of votes, that such and such a "Crossing of the Rubicon," an "Impeachment of Strafford," a "Convocation of the Notables," are epochs in the world's history, cardinal points on which grand world-revolutions have hinged. Suppose, however, that the majority of votes was all wrong; that the real cardinal points lay far deeper: and had been passed over unnoticed, because no Seer, but only mere Onlookers, chanced to be there! . . . Men understand not what is among their hands: as calmness is the characteristic of strength, so the weightiest causes may be most silent. It is, in no case, the real historical Transaction, but only some more or less plausible scheme and theory of the Transaction, or the harmonised result of many such schemes, each varying from the other and all varying from truth, that we can ever hope to behold.[11]

[11] *Ibid.*, 2: 87–88. An interesting restatement of the same idea appeared closer to the time of *The Ring and the Book* in that explosive manifesto of liberal theology, *Essays and Reviews* (1860). In his essay "On the Study of the Evidences of Christianity" Baden Powell wrote (p. 106): "We look at all events, through the medium of our prejudices, or even where we may have no prepossessions, the more sudden and remarkable any occurrence may be, the more unprepared we are to judge of it accurately or to view it calmly; our after-representations, especially of any extraordinary and striking event, are always at the best mere recollections of our impressions, of ideas dictated by our emotions at the time by the surprise and astonishment which the suddenness and hurry of the occurrence did not allow us time to reduce to reason, or to correct by the sober standard of experience or philosophy."

In view of Browning's great exemplification of this very
idea—modified by his provision of a "Seer," the Pope, who
does discern "the real cardinal points" that everyone else
missed—there is much irony in Carlyle's curt dismissal of
what he took to be the only issue in the Franceschini matter:
"The whole is on a most absurd basis. The real story is plain
enough on looking into it; the girl and the handsome young
priest were lovers." [12] Of all the poem's first readers, Carlyle
was best equipped to appreciate its purpose. But while conceding that it was "a wonderful book, one of the most wonderful
poems ever written," [13] he failed to recognize that Browning
had performed a peculiarly Carlylean feat, an illustration on a
huge scale of Carlyle's fundamental beliefs concerning the
elusive nature of truth and the shadowiness of "reality."

III

Browning's imagination, so original and impatient of artistic precedent, set him on a difficult road as he developed his
conception of *The Ring and the Book*. The very singularity of
his raw material seems to have given extra stimulus to his
normal zeal for innovation: uncommon data (copious, vivid,
authentic, never before used—but also refractory) called for
uncommon treatment if they were to be transmuted into art in
a way that would serve Browning's lofty aim. "Art," he wrote
near the end of the poem—the word perhaps carrying the
extra suggestion of "craft"—"remains the one way possible /
Of speaking truth, to mouths like mine, at least." (12.
839–40.) Pure truth, unequivocally expressed, betrays its purpose:

> How look a brother in the face and say
> "Thy right is wrong, eyes hast thou yet art blind,
> Thine ears are stuffed and stopped, despite their length,
> And, oh, the foolishness thou countest faith!"
> Say this as silverly as tongue can troll—
> The anger of the man may be endured,

---

[12] *William Allingham: A Diary*, p. 207.
[13] *Letters of Rossetti to Allingham*, p. 284.

> The shrug, the disappointed eyes of him
> Are not so bad to bear—but here's the plague
> That all this trouble comes of telling truth,
> Which truth, by when it reaches him, looks false,
> Seems to be just the thing it would supplant,
> Nor recognisable by whom it left—
> While falsehood would have done the work of truth.
>
> (12. 841–53)

Profoundly aware of the weakening and distortion that meaning endures when transmitted through language and the sometimes dense, sometimes cynical medium of the human mind, Browning chose the method of indirection, which may in the end serve the truth more faithfully than outright statement: "Art may tell a truth / Obliquely, do the thing shall breed the thought, / Nor wrong the thought, missing the mediate word." (12. 855–57.) To achieve this seemingly paradoxical end he adopted the methods of paradox. Wishing to approach absolute truth, he spent most of his space illustrating relativism. Seeking to reach consensus, he showed his speakers in endless disagreement. Desiring to exalt the power of good, he showed evil (apparently) triumphing.

Of all literary forms, the dramatic monologue in which the nine speakers of *The Ring and the Book* are heard was best suited for Browning's special purposes. Its method is the very definition of indirectness, for it achieves its effects through exploiting the relation, often complicated and subtle, between the members of not one but two sets of speaker and audience. In the dramatic monologue the poet seeks to convey his ideas and attitudes to the reader not directly, as in the lyric, but obliquely, by means of an intervening communication between the monologuist and his listeners. What the reader, the ultimate beneficiary of this devious transaction, learns is the product of a dramatic situation contrived by the poet; and his response is governed by his estimate and comparison of the two speakers to whom he must listen—the poet (heard only by inference) and the monologuist, through whom the poet speaks but whose attitudes may or may not be the poet's. Unlike the speaker in the lyric, the monologuist is an avowedly fictitious creation, and while he may directly utter his creator's ideas, as does the lyric "I," more characteristically he is a figure from whom the poet stands at some distance, and even, sometimes, at the polar opposite.

The monologue aspires to the condition of drama without the prime dramatic advantage of conflict of character and idea through action or dialogue. The truth which art seeks cannot therefore be developed through the immediate confrontation of different viewpoints; on the contrary, in the ten dramatic monologues that comprise the main substance of *The Ring and the Book,* "truth" is under the exclusive control of one speaker after another, each of whom monopolizes our attention for periods ranging, in the first edition, from 1,547 lines (Book 2) to 2,425 (Book 11). If viewpoints other than the current speaker's are to be presented during his tenure of the stage, they must be introduced by him, through quotations or even quotations within quotations. The result is a double ventriloquism, a creation within a creation. The speaker in the monologue says (in his own person) what the poet wants him to say as a dramatically conceived character, and when he quotes someone else, he in turn, still under the poet's command, imposes his will on that person, who is *his* dramatically conceived character, and whose arguments and language (notably his metaphors) he frames in the way that serves him best. If misrepresentation, as in the choice of a particular dialectic path or weighted analogy, will help, he forthwith uses it. And in so doing, he additionally characterizes himself.

It is not easy to conceive a method of narration more capable of leading one away from the truth. In this series of dramatic monologues, which contain stories within stories and reveal (or imply) motives within motives, truth is wrapped in layer upon layer of possible misrepresentation, the exact amount and purpose of which it is constantly the reader's task to determine. Where is Browning being "straight" (speaking directly through his characters) and where ironic (having them speak at cross purposes to him)? To what degree does he sympathize with a character and to what degree reject him? At exactly what points in a given monologue may the speaker be assumed to be telling the truth? By what argumentative means does the speaker seek to persuade his hearers? To such questions concerning the relationship between the poet and speaker and between the speaker and his audience must be added similar questions relating to the reader's position vis-à-vis the other parties, for he too is an audience, his judgment being the final objective of the transaction the poet brings him to witness between the two fictional parties. He may, for instance, be more or less alienated in sympathy and values from the speaker, and indeed from the speaker's audience, so far as the latter's attitudes can be inferred. Or he may sympathize with one and not with the other, or he may feel deep emotional rapport with both speaker and audience, as Browning obviously wished his readers to identify themselves with Pompilia and with the devoted watchers at her bed. Whatever the situation, the reader is as much a target of the speaker's rhetorical strategy as is the reader's imaginary surrogate, the dramatic listener; and so he is the ultimate objective of the poet's own strategy as it works itself out through the speaker. What, in the last analysis, does Browning wish *us* to believe? The problem is that posed by most if not all of his dramatic monologues, but here it is immensely magnified and complicated.

Furthermore, several of the speakers employ the manifold devices of formal rhetoric, which in the popular view, whatever it may be in theory, is dedicated to obscuring truth by the use of artfully selected words and tropes. And upon the intensely "real," solid, specific universe of place and character—the poem's historical scene and action—Browning imposes a second universe, a fictitious one generated by the various speakers' lavish use of images to describe others. By this means each character in the poem is in a sense deprived of his identity and becomes a shadow-person, a construct of language, living in the midst of an inconstant penumbra of appearance which replaces, distorts, or modifies his true qualities.

The movement of the poem therefore seems persistently away from a core of sharply defined meaning. Yet the final effect, when we have grasped the real purposes of techniques which at first seem self-defeating, is the opposite: the whirlpool of words turns out to carry us into the heart of the mystery as Browning conceived it. What we take to be the diffuseness, the centrifugal scattering, the welter of conflicts, the fragmentation of character through discrepant imagery, are in fact the poem's crowning illusion. Nowhere in the world's literature, perhaps, is there a more extensive demonstration of what Coleridge called "unity in multiety."

The Ring and the Book consists of the simultaneous onward movement of a number of separate yet closely related and mutually illuminating themes and actions. Within the drama of the poem's language—for Browning uses language not only to convey meaning but to exemplify through its own action his view of the inadequacies and hazards of human communication—there are several distinguishable subdramas, as it were. One is made up of the various speakers' developing and related rhetorical strategies as they participate, one by one, in the long process of accusation and vindication. A second is the kaleidoscopic movement of allusion, in which a wide variety of biblical texts (especially) are subjected to repeated use and abuse by the speakers, the recurrence of the same texts or of the same scriptural characters in new circumstances providing additional continuity and tension. And a third is the equally kaleidoscopic movement of metaphor, which involves the same principle of repetition-within-diversity.

In later chapters it will be seen that these intellectual-verbal dramas provide several concurrent means by which the poem's major ideas are illustrated and implicitly commented upon. Leading themes of Christian doctrine; central moral and metaphysical concepts such as ethical relativism and the pervasiveness of deceit and illusion in the world; such issues as the supposed primacy of natural law over God's and the undermining of Christian faith by rationalism—all of these are subjected to widely different interpretations and put to varying strategic uses as they serve the purposes of the successive monologuists. Along with the ceaselessly conflicting interpretations of the motives and events in the Franceschini case, they add to the ever-tightening tension between viewpoints. But they are so managed that in the end the tension is resolved into a statement of Browning's own beliefs.

Nor is the drama confined to the stresses of the inner self

and to ideological conflict; for the poem is also composed of external situations and episodes. These are of two kinds, one within the other. The first are the actions which are represented in the monologues themselves (the knowing lectures of the bystanders, the appearance of Caponsacchi and Guido before the judges, Pompilia's deathbed, the lawyers' busyness as they prepare their cases, the Pope's solitary brooding). In each scene there is sufficient indication of locale, gesture, and interplay between speaker and auditors, physically present or only hypothesized, to warrant calling the ten interior books of the poem "dramatic monologues" in the term's most exact sense.[14] The content of these speeches, in turn, is a series of narrated actions and scenes—the Franceschini story itself, told and retold. Accompanying these are the small incidental actions which occur in the speakers' running repertory of pregnant illustrations—their anecdotes, analogies, and circumstantial figures of speech, most of which, far from being static pictures, are pulsing with life. The monologues thus are triply dramatic, not only in form but in content.

Of the two narratives that constitute the poem's outer framework and much of its substance, the first, the succession of events in the present that are represented or reported in the series of monologues (from Rome's excited gossip over the murders to Guido's execution), provides unbroken continuity. The other, consisting of the multiple versions of the anterior events, provides eventual unity, but by the indirect route of seeming (*only* "seeming") repetition.[15] The former narrative,

---

[14] Even in the speeches delivered in solitude, auditors are present *in absentia*, so to speak. Both lawyers zestfully anticipate the forensic fencing they would engage in were they to meet face to face in the courtroom, and the Pope is conscious of the judges who will measure the justice of his decision, the Roman people and God.

[15] Because modern reference works and other "authorities" insist on preserving the old misapprehension that the ten (*sic*) speakers of the poem tell the same story ten times over, it is worth a footnote to put the record straight. Each version of the Franceschini case is distinguished from all the rest by innumerable instances of distortion, emphasis, suppression, selection, abbreviation, and magnification. The variations of their respective accounts are, in fact, the principal means by which the speakers are distinguished from one another. But

once it is pieced together, proves a simple linear one; the latter is a more subtle manner of proceeding which merges a succession of linear accounts of the same events into new synthesis. Browning's aim, as he says at the conclusion of Book 1 (1348–64), is not the ordinary one, such as a novelist might adopt, of choosing a single aspect of a theme (in this instance, the Franceschini story) and "putting solely that / On panel somewhere in the House of Fame," portraying what he remembered from observation, not what he derived from poetic meditation. That would be as if a poet were to attempt to describe only one season, thus fixing in "cramped corpse-fashion" the progress and variety of the whole year.

> Rather learn and love
> Each facet-flash of the revolving year!—
> Red, green and blue that whirl into a white,
> The variance now, the eventual unity,
> Which make the miracle.
>
> (1. 1360–64)

In a world of uncertainty, relativity, and change, Browning's intention is to adopt many points of view, and, through an

---

this is not to say that there are as many different full narratives as there are speakers. Only the first speakers, the onlookers of Books 2, 3, and 4, offer fairly comprehensive narratives, beginning with the Comparini in their childless state. The next three, Guido, Caponsacchi, and Pompilia, recount only those portions of the story in which they have participated. There is, of course, a certain amount of overlapping among these three first-hand versions. In subsequent books Guido's lawyer, dispensing with a connected narrative entirely, devotes his monologue to a legalistic defense of his client's actions; Pompilia's lawyer confines himself to a fanciful biography of the murdered wife which is remarkable mainly for its irreconcilability with all the other accounts; and the Pope allots only a small portion of his long soliloquy to events as such. In his second monologue, similarly, Guido is concerned not with any consecutive retelling of episodes but with self-exculpation. In all ten books the stress is uniformly on those phases of the story which best aid each speaker's argument. For a systematic study of these differences, see Bruce R. McElderry, Jr., "The Narrative Structure of *The Ring and the Book*," *Research Studies of the State College of Washington*, 11 (1943): 193–233.

intuitive merging of all the separate, limited facets, to achieve a truth that is greater than their simple sum.

Browning's effort, then, despite the particularity of his method, is to reveal the timeless in the temporal, the universal in the individual, the abstract in the circumstantial—in short, to derive philosophy from crude earthly material by means that would, he hoped, appeal to the Victorian audience who read while they ran (1. 1379–82). Whether or not he could have achieved his ambition in smaller compass is a moot point; but the fact is that he used more than twenty-one thousand lines of blank verse. These gave him the maneuvering room he needed, but the poem's size did nothing to lighten either the artistic burden he laid upon himself or the challenge he presented to the reader, whose powers of comprehension (in both meanings of the word) and of retentiveness he mistakenly assumed to be as great as his own. In adopting so large a scale for his magnum opus, Browning further compounded for the reader the difficulty inherent in his decision to "tell a truth obliquely." That problem is twofold: first, the necessity of reading the poem simultaneously on the numerous levels just suggested—the concurrent dramas of language, idea, event, and psychological revelation; and second, the necessity of keeping steadily in mind the detailed exposition as it progresses and accretes on all levels.

The ideal method of reading *The Ring and the Book* would require the suspension of time or the adoption of an extra dimension. In a critical study restricted, like all books, to consecutive presentation, it is unfortunately necessary to examine more or less separately the individual threads that constitute the poem's design, so doing violence to a work one of whose chief distinctions is the coherence and simultaneity of its development. More occurs at once in the poem than it is possible fully to appreciate even after many rereadings or to demonstrate in an arbitrary series of chapters.[16] But having

---

[16] Although almost everything in this book can be said to illustrate the poem's "density"—the presence in any given passage of several closely integrated purposes, techniques, and effects—certain other elements which contribute to this density are not discussed, notably diction, phonetic qualities, rhythm, syntax, and punctuation. These

once been shown these threads, the reader may perhaps be able, on his return to Browning's pages, to perform the all-important synthesis for himself.

------

could well form the subject of a separate study, the nature of which is indicated in Park Honan, *Browning's Characters: A Study in Poetic Technique* (New Haven, Conn., 1961), chaps. 7 and 8. In chapter 9 Professor Honan minutely explicates and subjects to verbal analysis two short passages of the poem (5. 701–19 and 11. 433–54), revealing in small compass the profit to be had from a line-by-line examination of Browning's word choice and verse texture.

Two

"The Eventual Unity"

THE POEM'S DESIGN

I

Some of Browning's most thoughtful and sympathetic critics have asserted that *The Ring and the Book* lacks form. Henry James, for one, lamented the poem's "great loose and uncontrolled composition, [its] great heavy-hanging cluster of related but unreconciled parts." [1] What is ordinarily regarded as the "Gothic" structure of the poem seems at odds with the Jamesian ideal of artistic shape, but it is by no means as devoid of organization and control as the popular connotation of "Gothic" suggests. Not least among the poem's many wonders, indeed, is its superb architecture. Given its basic movement—the coalescence of partial truths into a transcendent Truth—the succession of the twelve books must be regarded as completely logical.

To understand the careful principles upon which book is laid upon book, it is necessary to review the poem's entire structure. Although the following pages contain what may seem at first glance to be mere skippable synopsis, it is not a bare summary such as can be found in, for example, DeVane's *Browning Handbook*. It contains many interpretations of the various speakers' characters and strategies, and of Browning's intention in certain of the monologues, which sometimes, as in the cases of Tertium Quid and Bottini, are drastically at variance with the received ones. This general view of *The Ring and the Book* is intended to serve not only as an explanation of

[1] *Quarterly Review*, 217 (1912): 69.

37

its design but also as necessary background for the analysis, in later chapters, of what we take to be the most important separate aspects of the poem's artistry and thought.

Book 1, "The Ring and the Book," is wholly introductory and, in the main, needs little discussion. Browning immediately introduces the gold-alloy figure which will recur all the way through this book and reappear at the very end of Book 12 to mark the closing of the poem it emblematizes. After narrating his discovery, purchase, and immediate perusal of the Old Yellow Book, Browning backs with humorous perversity into what is to prove the subject of his poem. He tells us, at some length, that the pleadings and other documents have to do with a certain Franceschini murder case, but only gradually and fragmentarily, as Book 1 proceeds, do we learn what the case involved. (We reach lines 383–87, for example, before we hear of Caponsacchi.) Instead of providing a straightforward narrative of earlier events to throw light on those immediately associated with the papers in the Old Yellow Book, specifically the trial for murder and the condemned man's subsequent appeal, Browning resumes the story of himself: how he fruitlessly sought further information in Rome, and how, standing on his Casa Guidi balcony on a sultry night with heat lightning falling silently from cloud to cloud, he projected himself in his imagination from Florence to Arezzo and Castelnuovo, envisioning the scenes that occurred there so long ago. During this reminiscence, further portions of the Franceschini case and its aftermath appear, but they have yet to be fitted together. The joining occurs only at lines 780–823, where Browning, suddenly turning businesslike, compresses the whole essential plot into a single verse paragraph. Then follows a series of previews, somewhat suggestive of the General Prologue to *The Canterbury Tales*, of the ten speeches to come—previews which might, with advantage to the reader, be moved to the heads of the books they respectively describe. Finally, Browning completes the statement of his artistic purpose which he had begun in the middle of this first book and then suspended, and rounds off the book with a moving, though syntactically tortuous, invocation and dedication to the memory of his wife.

Encircled by the "ring" of Books 1 and (prospectively) 12,

Books 2–11 contain the alleged facts of the Franceschini case as set forth and interpreted by nine speakers. The chief key to the poem's structure lies in the three triads (plus one additional monologue in which Guido reappears) into which these ten internal books are divided. The first triad (2–4) involves chiefly an exposition of the externalities, the events of the case; the second (5–7) shifts emphasis to character, and the third (8–10) to theme (the poem's great issues, such as truth, deceit, language, and religion). Thus there is a continuous upward progress toward a revelation of the ultimate significance of event and character.

In the first triad, designated as "Rome and rumour" (1. 943), three speakers, identified only as "Half-Rome," "the Other Half-Rome," and "Tertium Quid," voice opinions of the kind which, as one learns from the so-called "anonymous pamphlets" included in the Old Yellow Book, were current in the city as the murder case swept to its climax; these are the divergent views of the spectators. Here in particular, though the demonstration continues throughout the poem, Browning displays the principal reasons why men ordinarily are incapable of discerning, much less of expressing, the whole truth about any episode of human experience. Their vision is clouded by the "idols of the mind" which Bacon enumerated in the *Novum Organum* as the sources of human error. In the second triad, hearsay gives way to the inside testimonies of the three protagonists, Guido, Caponsacchi, and Pompilia. In the third, we move from the principals first to their professional advocates and then to the Pope, who in effect adjudicates the lawyers' conflicting claims. In the last of the monologues (Book 11), given additional prominence by its separation from the scheme of triads, Guido speaks again. Every one of the nine speakers asserts or implies that his own version of events and motives is the true one.

The poem's symmetry derives mainly from the patterning of the individual triads. At the base corners of each triangle are speakers who represent extreme opposites in point of view and line of argument, yet who also have some kind of affinity, such as equal social position or similarity of personal experience. At the apex of each triangle is a speaker who is superior to the other two in authority, either social or moral, and who speaks either in extension of the previous arguments or in opposition to them. In the first triad the two prejudiced witnesses, the diametrically opposed two Halves of Rome, give way to the "quality," the socially and (on the surface) intellectually superior Tertium Quid, who substitutes a posture of judiciousness and disinterestedness for the relatively unconcealed bias of his predecessors. In the next triad Guido and Caponsacchi, the first two speakers, though antagonists in the drama, are linked in that both are men of experience in human weakness: Guido has succumbed to his inner propensity to evil, while Caponsacchi, after a severe test of his priestly vows, has triumphed over it. Above them presides the saintly Pompilia, the quiet, self-effacing center of all the controversy and the very embodiment of innocence, who places in due moral perspective the characters of the two men. In the third triad it is the rival lawyers who provide the base. Both betray the causes they have been retained to defend, and in so doing reveal the extent of their ignorance—or deliberate neglect—of the true issues involved, which transcend the largely irrelevant questions they labor in their respective pleadings. Far above them broods the aged Pope Innocent XII, whose use of the intuitive powers available to all who abjure selfish interests in their search for truth is commentary enough on the blindness of the lawyers and their kind. Books 4, 7, and 10, the apex monologues, therefore are the pivotal arguments, each serving to illuminate the meaning of the two monologues that have immediately preceded it. They are emblematic—Tertium Quid, of compromising intellect; Pompilia, of uncompromised innocence; and the Pope, of uncompromising justice and surpassing insight. Together they embody Browning's opinions on the central moral themes of the poem.

II

The monologues of the first two onlookers represent the Roman populace's "feel after the vanished truth," the stone of fact that has disappeared into a pool:

Honest enough, as the way is: all the same,
Harbouring in the centre of its sense
A hidden germ of failure, shy but sure,
Should neutralize that honesty and leave
That feel for truth at fault, as the way is too.
Some prepossession such as starts amiss,
By but a hair's breadth at the shoulder-blade,
The arm o'the feeler, dip he ne'er so brave;
And so leads waveringly, lets fall wide
O' the mark his finger meant to find, and fix
Truth at the bottom, that deceptive speck.

(1. 848–58)

"The instinctive theorizing whence a fact / Looks to the eye as the eye likes the look" (1. 863–64)—this, to borrow Pompilia's words uttered much later, constitutes "the world's insight" (7. 1792).

Despite the implication of the name Browning gives him,[2] the first speaker, Half-Rome, represents the heavily dominant portion of public opinion (cf. 1. 276–94, 363, 1141–42; 11. 39 ff., 392). Meeting by chance an acquaintance outside the church of San Lorenzo, in which the bodies of the murdered Comparini are lying exposed to the gaze of sensation seekers, Half-Rome, buttonholing him with a fixity reminiscent of the Ancient Mariner, treats him to what purports to be an authoritative account of the events that resulted in the slaughter. It is (not least because it is the first detailed version we read) a fairly plausible story, redounding to Guido's credit. The speaker undoubtedly believes what he says. But in a surprise ending,[3] he reveals that he is the very antithesis of a detached

---

[2] Taken literally, the names "Half-Rome" and "the Other Half-Rome" are ill bestowed, since they suggest, erroneously, that each speaker, with his private reason for siding with Guido or Pompilia, typifies one-half of the Roman population. Arithmetic and elementary logic, if nothing else, would deny that distinction to both men. The speakers are representative not in respect to the specific sources of their biases but in the sense that, like all the rest of Rome, they are prejudiced in one way or another.

[3] In retrospect, however, the ending is not unprepared for, since Half-Rome intersperses his narrative with claims of a husband's rightful ascendancy over his wife and of his right to discipline her.

observer. Because, like Guido, he "keeps" a wife to whose window a certain man is in the habit of repairing, he uses the Franceschini story (and a casually displayed knife? [2. 67]) to convey a wholesome warning to the suitor through his auditor, who happens to be the suitor's cousin. Thus his disqualifying bias is revealed: it is inevitable that, having a marital situation analogous to Guido's, he should be Guido's partisan. His version of truth is invalidated by prejudice born of personal identification and sympathy.

The Other Half-Rome would appear to be a foil to Half-Rome, not only in name but in his prejudices and sympathies. A bachelor, he is understandably little concerned with the honor of husbands; his sympathies are with Pompilia, whom he envisions as a pure hapless flower of a girl lying on her deathbed, yet alive as if by miracle. Unlike the stern Half-Rome, he is a creature of deep sensibilities verging on the poetic (3. 1–90). He gives free play to these as he stands eulogizing Pompilia in the Piazza Barberini near Bernini's Triton fountain (and also near the hospital where she is dying). The reverence of his initial manner contrasts strikingly with the minatory tone that marked the end of the preceding speech. Again unlike Half-Rome, he appears to have no specific and constant auditor, and may be considered as delivering for the most part a long speech to an indeterminate audience, which is occasionally appealed to directly.[4]

But the obvious points of contrast with Half-Rome do not adequately describe his character and attitude. The Other Half-Rome, though plainly siding with Pompilia, is not the simple-minded, thoroughgoing sentimentalist implied in his opening lines. The bulk of his monologue is in fact an apparently judicious weighing of evidence on both sides, one which anticipates in form and technique the following speech of Tertium Quid, thus presaging the theme of the safe "middle course" which will reappear in a number of subsequent books. This judicious temper persists down to the last lines, where it

[4] But the evidence is uncertain. The allusions to "you" (lines 824–25, 838, 964, 1516) and "we" (lines 118, 812–13, 831–33) suggest the presence of an auditor. The pronouns, however, may simply represent the Other Half-Rome's rhetorical habit.

vanishes as he reveals that, like his predecessor, he is interested personally in the case, not because it happens to mirror
his own situation—it obviously does not—but because he is
nursing a long-standing grievance against the accused himself.
He cannot forgive an insult (whether real or imagined we are
not told) by Guido, who was co-heir of an estate administered
by the speaker.[5] Guido's objection to the Other Half-Rome's
performance of that trust has become a stain upon his honor
fully as malign as that which Half-Rome has represented Guido
to have suffered through his wife's elopement with the priest.
In effect, then, the emotional distance between the first two
speakers is not so great as the substance and the manner of
their diverging arguments would lead us to believe; and both
of them, for reasons that are unlike yet related, are prevented
from seeing the truth, even though they purport to reveal it.

For the apex monologue of the first triad the scene shifts
from the pavements of Rome to an aristocratic drawing room,
where a *soirée*, well populated by ecclesiastics, is in progress.
Half-Rome has led us to expect that Caponsacchi will be the
star entertainer,

> The hero of the adventure, who so fit
> To tell it in the coming Carnival?
> 'Twill make the fortune of whate'er saloon
> Hears him recount, with helpful cheek, and eye
> Hotly indignant now, now dewy-dimmed,
> The incidents of flight, pursuit, surprise,
> Capture, with hints of kisses all between.
>
> (2. 1452–58)

---

[5] In one line of the poem (4. 588) there is a hint—unless it be
merely a figment of Guido's rhetoric as relayed by Tertium Quid—that
in the early years of his marriage, specifically at the time when he was
involved in litigation over Pompilia's dowry, Guido expected an uncle
to die "and leave me his estate." It is interesting to speculate whether,
if the uncle did die and favor Guido in his will, Guido was in fact
cheated out of his legacy by the Other Half-Rome. If so, it is a
circumstance that would add irony to the latter's detestation of Guido
and substance to Guido's claim of honest penury. But we are no more
likely to learn the "fact" of the matter than we are to find out how
many children were born to Lady Macbeth.

But Caponsacchi is not present. Instead, the speaker here is a supercilious logic chopper whom Browning appropriately names "Tertium Quid": "neither this nor that / Half-Rome aforesaid; something bred of both: / One and one breed the inevitable three." (1. 912–14.) Although, like his alchemical namesake, Tertium Quid has elements of two other substances—the speakers preceding him—he is not a simple product derived from them but something quite different. He is the perfect drawing-room raconteur,

> some man of quality
> Who,—breathing musk from lace-work and brocade,
> His solitaire amid the flow of frill,
> Powdered peruke on nose, and bag at back,
> And cane dependent from the ruffled wrist,—
> Harangues in silvery and selectest phrase
> 'Neath waxlight in a glorified saloon
> Where mirrors multiply the girandole.[6]
>
> (1. 928–35)

Tertium Quid's predecessors, relatively simple in their approach to the Franceschini case, were candid in their respective views of the rights and wrongs. Tertium Quid's approach, on the contrary, is sophisticated and studiedly ambiguous: he sweepingly, scornfully rejects the emotional treatment favored by "reasonless unreasoning Rome" (4. 11).

> Indulge me but a moment[he begs his company]:
>   if I fail
> —Favoured with such an audience, understand!—
> To set things right, why, class me with the mob
> As understander of the mind of man!
>
> (4. 58–61)

---

[6] Although the setting requires "girandole" to be read as "branched candlestick," a second meaning is also apropos: revolving firework or catherine wheel, a fortuitous anticipation of the skyrocket at the opening of Book 12. Certainly the mirrors in the Roman drawing room reflect a spectacular display of pyrotechnic wit. In either case, the point is that Tertium Quid's arguments are as remote from the truth as the multiplied images in the mirror—reflections of reflections—are from the original object. The flickering candles of truth have become multiple illusions.

Instead of the shadowy bypaths of the mob, he takes the high
road of the intellect:

> You get a reasoned statement of the case,
> Eventual verdict of the curious few
> Who care to sift a business to the bran
> Nor coarsely bolt it like the simpler sort.
> Here, after ignorance, instruction speaks;
> Here, clarity of candour, history's soul,
> The critical mind, in short: no gossip-guess.
>
> (1. 920–26)

That Tertium Quid is critical and "judicious"—on the surface—is plain enough. But that he is "impartial," "objective,"
and "detached," as most commentators on the poem characterize him, is simply not true. The elaborate pretense of judiciousness and "candour" is only window-dressing to conceal a
thoroughgoing partisanship for Guido, one born of both personal and class sympathies. His actual prejudice is the more
culpable because it is everywhere disavowed. And his own
remark, in the middle of his speech, that "Guido lacks not an
apologist" (4. 700), is a monumental understatement. This is a
point so vital to the correct understanding both of Tertium
Quid's monologue and of the poem's whole rhetorical strategy
that, along with the speaker's exemplification of the self-
compromising middle course adopted by both church and law,
it must be explored in detail later (see pp. 136–42, 145–48).
But it should be noted here that through Tertium Quid, who is
entirely Browning's invention, the poet discredits logic and its
rhetorical uses by having him adopt it to defend Guido. The
end being morally repugnant—for Browning has made it clear
in the beginning of the poem (1. 544–660) that the Count is a
villain—Browning requires us to find equally repugnant the
means by which it is achieved, a one-man debate in which
pivotal points are developed by sophistry and casuistry. It was
not the only time in his career that he sought to bring rational
processes into disrepute by representing them as sophistry and
associating them with an unacceptable moral position.

The result of Tertium Quid's lecture, in any event, is most

unsatisfactory to him. His inconstant audience finally dissolves
completely:

> Her Excellency must pronounce, in fine!
> What, she prefers going and joining play?
> Her Highness finds it late, intends retire?
> I am of their mind: only, all this talk, talked,
> 'Twas not for nothing that we talked, I hope?
> Both know as much about it, now, at least,
> As all Rome: no particular thanks, I beg!
> (You'll see, I have not so advanced myself,
> After my teaching the two idiots here!)
>
> (4. 1632–40)

Both do, indeed, "know as much about it, now, at least, / As all
Rome"; but that is not saying very much. The chief result of
Tertium Quid's exquisite intellectualization of the issues is
that he propagates in elite circles the vulgar error of irrational
prejudice he so roundly condemns in the mob.

Thus Book 4, marked throughout by Tertium Quid's self-
interested pose of disinterestedness, provides a thematic climax
to the first triad, in which it is demonstrated how events can be
progressively misconstrued and truth *not* arrived at. Prejudice
born of identification with a participant, as in Book 2, or of
personal grudge, as in Book 3, beclouds the issues. But even
less effective a means to truth than bias, Browning would
say—in fact, a more insidious enemy of truth—is that adopted
by Tertium Quid, the one who trumpets most loudly and often
about his devotion to truth. Cold reason (or the posture
thereof), he demonstrates, can be as crippling as conscious
bias, not least when it is deliberately employed for self-
advancement. Tertium Quid emerges, ironically, as the most
thoroughly disqualified of the first three speakers with respect
to the search for truth.

I I I

In the next triad (books 5–7) hearsay evidence and attributed motives are supplanted by the testimony of the participants themselves—a development which encourages us, falsely

as it turns out, to believe that the full truth of all disputed matters is now in prospect. Guido speaks first. Fresh from the torture, he appears before ecclesiastical judges whose sympathies he tries to win by every available resource:

> Soft-cushioned sits he; yet shifts seat, shirks
>   touch,
> As, with a twitchy brow and wincing lip
> And cheek that changes to all kinds of white,
> He proffers his defence, in tones subdued
> Near to *mock-mildness* now, so mournful seems
> The obtuser sense truth fails to satisfy;
> Now, moved, from *pathos* at the wrong endured,
> To *passion;* for the natural man is roused
> At fools who first do wrong, then pour the blame
> Of their wrong-doing, Satan-like, on Job.
> Also his tongue at times is hard to curb;
> Incisive, nigh *satiric bites* the phrase,
> Rough-raw, yet somehow *claiming privilege*
> —It is so hard for *shrewdness* to admit
> Folly means no harm when she calls black white!
> —*Eruption* momentary at the most,
> Modified forthwith by a fall o' the fire,
> *Sage acquiescence;* for the world's the world,
> And, what it errs in, Judges rectify:
> He feels he has a fist, then folds his arms
> Crosswise and *makes his mind up to be meek.*
>
> (1. 954–74; italics supplied)

In a gambit already prepared for by Tertium Quid (4. 1529–32), he begins by assuring the judges that the dislocation of his shoulder blade and the damage to his backbone [7]

---

[7] Guido's back trouble provides an amusing minor motif in the poem. It naturally suggests his choice of imagery, not always to his comfort: he refers to "a master-stroke of argument / [That] will cut the spinal cord . . . ugh, ugh! . . . I mean, / Paralyse Molinism for evermore!" (11. 641–43.) The image stands for the unexpressed but mutually understood truth of the marriage agreement by which he obtained Pompilia: "The veritable back-bone, understood / Essence of this same bargain" (5. 500–501) ; "They [the Comparini] knew and

and hands during the law's late extortion of truth—his confession—are of no moment: his sojourn on the rack was luxury compared with the mental torture to which Pompilia, her parents, her lover, and the grinning populace of Arezzo had subjected him (5. 21–77).

His whole performance thereafter is, as the passage quoted has foretold, a shrewd *mélange* of casuistry, nervous jokes, flattery, false humility, emotional outbursts, and appeals to class sympathy. Despite the show of passion and pathos, his version of the story is, even more than that of Tertium Quid, one of the mind—calculated, intellectualized. The tactics of ingratiation which, adopted for different ends, marked the preceding monologue are Guido's in far greater measure. The juxtaposition of the two books therefore is artistically right, because each colors and illuminates the other. They are similar in viewpoint and method: both speakers are (or have been) seekers of preferment in the church; both address clerics as their audience, though the circumstances differ; and they argue repeatedly that noblemen like themselves are both gifted and privileged above the mob. Guido can in a way be regarded as a Tertium Quid under severe stress. His tone tempts one to believe that if he were not so desperately involved in the case, he could easily adopt Tertium Quid's ironic "detachment" as his own attitude toward it. In any case, the various points of affinity between the two emphasize the elements that disqualify both as witnesses to the truth.[8]

I knew where the back-bone lurked / I' the writhings of the bargain." (5. 510–11.) A further hint of the natural sympathy existing between Tertium Quid and Guido is contained in Tertium Quid's prior adoption of the metaphor. The mercenary considerations underlying the bargain, he says, were "The straight backbone-thought of the crooked speech" (4. 514). This association of backbone and marriage occurs also when Caponsacchi's bishop defines the easy terms of his marriage to the church: "Nobody wants you in these latter days / To prop the Church by breaking your back-bone." (6. 291–92.) In his second speech Guido shifts the image as he describes the mortal combat of fox and wolf as a symbol of man's innate propensity for evil: "the jaws enjoy / Their re-embrace in mid back-bone they break, / After their weary work thro' the foes' flesh." (11. 2313–15.)

[8] Some additional evidence of the underlying affinity between Guido and Tertium Quid is given below, pp. 136, 160 n., 301.

Of all Guido's strategic devices, the one which most conclu-
sively removes him from the reader's sympathy, whatever effect it may be presumed to have on his auditors, is his recurrent likening of himself to Christ. We are not unprepared for
it. We have already been told that he "folds his arms / Cross-
wise" as he confronts his judges and resolves to be meek (1.
973–74), and Tertium Quid has recalled that, with a minor
order or two in the church, he "clipped / His top-hair and thus
far affected Christ" (4. 404–5). On being offered a reviving
potion after his torture, he is both sarcastically surprised and
obsequiously delighted to find that it is good Velletri wine,
"not vinegar and gall" (5. 5) or (later) a "cup of bitterness"
(879) which "knocks at my clenched teeth" (903). He alludes
to his family's resemblances to "our Lord" in saintliness and
sacrificial poverty (156–64), to his "crown of punishments"
(83), to the indignity of being spat upon (1104, 1459); he
makes ready analogies between his conduct and that of the
church, the spouse of Christ (720–43). He portrays himself as
the good shepherd, a role, sanctified by Scripture and the
custom of early Christian art, which would inferentially cast
Pompilia, the lost lamb "Who once was good and pure . . . /
And lay in my bosom," as a sinner (1638–40). He recalls
how, after the court's decision sending Pompilia to the care of
the Convertite nuns and Caponsacchi to Civita Vecchia, he
traveled the road back to Arezzo as if it were the road to
Calvary, "station by station" (1257), each with its reminder
of his agony. He handily converts the Comparini's reputed lot
at Arezzo to a "stiff crucifixion by my dais" (532), they being,
by implication, the thieves and he the Christ. His return home
after prosecuting Pompilia and Caponsacchi was suggestive of
Christ's being laid in the sepulcher—a relatively plausible
analogy, considering what was undoubtedly the tomblike atmosphere of the Franceschini palace. (His sympathizer Half-
Rome has called it "the dark house" and specifically a sepulcher [2. 331, 470].) But there was no rest, no glory, even
there, for he had to endure a descent into the hell of gibes and
jests:

> [I] found myself in my horrible house once more,
> And after a colloquy . . . no word assists!

With the mother and the brothers, stiffened me
Strait out from head to foot as dead man does,
And, thus prepared for life as he for hell,
Marched to the public Square and met the world.
                                                    (5. 1269–74)

Toward the end of his monologue Guido recounts a mystical
vision, suggested by the birth of Pompilia's (and, for present
purposes, his) son at the Christmas season, in which the fate
of the Christ child appears as a prophecy of his own. As he
struggled "Nine days o' the Birth-Feast" against temptation,
reenacting the agony at Gethsemane,

I stopped my ears even to the inner call
Of the dread duty, heard only the song
"Peace upon earth," saw nothing but the face
O' the Holy Infant and the halo there
Able to cover yet another face
Behind it, Satan's which I else should see.
But, day by day, joy waned and withered off:
The Babe's face, premature with peak and pine,
Sank into wrinkled ruinous old age,
Suffering and death, then mist-like disappeared,
And showed only the Cross at end of all,
Left nothing more to interpose 'twixt me
And the dread duty,—for the angel's song,
"Peace upon earth," louder and louder pealed
"O Lord, how long, how long be unavenged?"
                                [Ps. 94:1–3, Isa. 6:11]
                                                    (5. 1596–1610)

Later, in a climactic exploitation of Christian idea and story,
Guido revives the image of his only-begotten son for the sake
of inviting still more sympathy for himself. The sole aim of his
life, he says,

is now to evoke life from death,
Make me anew, satisfy in my son   [Rev. 21:5–7]
The hunger I may feed but never sate,

Tormented on to perpetuity,—
My son, whom, dead, I shall know, understand,

.　　.　　.　　.　　.　　.　　.　　.　　.

Moulded into the image and made one,
Fashioned of soul as featured like in face.

(5. 1964–73)

In the sweet Utopia that will come into being when the balance
of justice is righted and husbands will once again reign Jeho-
vah-like in the effulgence of universal veneration,

Then will I set my son at my right-hand
[Acts 2:24–25, 34]
And tell his father's story to this point,
Adding "The task seemed superhuman, still
I dared and did it, trusting God and law:
And they approved of me: give praise to both!"
And if, for answer, he shall stoop to kiss
My hand, and peradventure start thereat,—
[John 20:20–29]
I engage to smile "That was an accident
I' the necessary process,—just a trip
O' the torture-irons in their search for truth,—
Hardly misfortune, and no fault at all."

(5. 2048–58)

Here Gaetano, the son, is inferentially Christ, and Guido is
both God (at whose right hand Christ sits) and not God (since
he himself refers to God, in whom he trusts). It is not every
blasphemer who can claim for himself not one but two divine
roles; but Guido is equal to the temptation, because it is
advisable for him now to alleviate the long-sustained emphasis
upon death by hopeful reference to everlasting life—his own
earthly life everlasting. (All that is missing from the picture is
the Holy Ghost, a somewhat surprising omission in view of
Guido's prefatory invocation of "the indivisible Trinity" [5.
121].) But in his concluding lines Guido reverts to the role of
the tortured and mutilated Christ for the sake of echoing his
all-forgiving "they know not what they do." Law, he implies, is
a system like the society which he both fears and flatters, and

systems must be indulged in their little formalities. Neither do
they know what they do.

Guido's justification of the murder of his wife Pompilia is
simple and, taken at face value, persuasive: by his account he
had been much sinned against, though never sinning. He was
constantly victimized by hypocritical institutions, especially
church and marriage, and misled by bad advice. Furthermore,
even as a dishonored husband, he acted with dignity, courage,
and restraint (all this in a land where tempers flare easily over
violations of domestic honor and where cuckolds are publicly
scorned). It is not surprising, therefore, that Guido's argument
is chiefly devoted to the careful rehearsal of his manifold
provocations and temptations, together with his saintly, nay,
Christlike forbearance.

Of Guido may be said what used to be observed of Milton's
Satan: as a dramatic character he almost steals the show. He is
at once a symbol of monstrous, unmitigated evil and an engaging comic figure; and Browning's triumph lies in his making
this dual nature credible. The enormity of Guido's pretending
to the role of a latter-day Christ, the sulphurous terms in which
he is denounced by the sympathetic speakers, and his horri-
fying self-revelation in his second appearance (Book 11) leave
no doubt that he is the devil incarnate. On the other hand, he
is also portrayed, in at least as great detail, as (in present-day
terminology) a comic anti-hero. Strikingly unhandsome, indeed contemptible in appearance and manner, this inexpert
schemer is also mean, cowardly, failure-prone. Many of the
situations in which he figures have their comic side: the penu-
riousness of his family, his inability to make headway in the
church, his Boccaccian May-December marriage, his Byronic
pursuit of his escaped wife and her friend the priest across the
Italian countryside, his discomfiture at Castelnuovo, his climactic ill-luck when his flight to Arezzo after the murders is
foiled by "the one scrupulous fellow in all Rome" (11. 1637).
The farcical nature of all this, as will be shown in chapter 9, is
constantly underscored by the ridicule heaped upon him by
the onlookers. And though the two roles of devil and comedian
are diametrically opposed, Browning firmly connects them by
describing Guido in a variety of metaphors drawn from the

whole intervening moral spectrum, terms which range from lamb to wolf, from patient ox to furious bull, from swan to snake, from cuckold to Antichrist. Altogether, the portrait, so masterly in its reconciling of incongruities, reflects a side of Browning's judgment of life which is seldom sufficiently recognized: if, as the story of Pompilia and Caponsacchi shows, the hand of God may be seen in the humble, unregarded events of everyday life, it is equally true that the Prince of Darkness may lurk there, so disguised as to be not fearful but comic. As a satanic character, Guido is the most human in literature, and, by that very fact, one of the most terrible.

Hard upon his final obsequious, forgiving words to his judges comes Caponsacchi's angry speech before the same tribunal, those "blind guides," as he calls them, "who must needs lead eyes that see! / Fools, alike ignorant of man and God!" (6. 1783–84.) He had been in their presence earlier, after his arrest at Castelnuovo. Brought back now as *amicus curiae*, he bitterly recalls their imperfectly concealed amusement at the scrape this spirited young priest had got himself into. While they smiled their indulgent smiles, Guido had been free to murder the "young, tall, beautiful, strange and sad" girl (6. 399) who was his wife and Caponsacchi's spiritual savior. As she lies dying in St. Anna's hospital, Caponsacchi recounts how her intolerable situation at Arezzo afforded him—a handsome, worldly scion of the church, a "coxcomb and fribble" (6. 87, 98, 340) who was destined for great things if he played his cards right—the means by which he could serve God and redeem his soul.

He recalls his tortured hovering between temptation and resolution in the days and nights before his instinctive decision to rescue her. In lines as reverberant with true passion as Guido's were filled with craft, he interprets his experience of self-sacrifice in religious terms: he was not only St. George slaying the dragon, but his namesake Joseph escorting a Madonna-like figure to safety from a murderous Herod. In the religious phraseology and imagery which color the latter portion of his narrative, their spontaneity contrasting with Guido's calculating use of biblical allusion, is foreshadowed the Pope's eventual interpretation of the priest's and Pompilia's

experience as possessing divine significance. Caponsacchi's
newly purified and heightened instinct assures him that the
experience has been wholly different from that which any of
the four preceding speakers were capable of imagining. The
"revelation" (6. 1866) has, in fact, been of ineffable importance, and so cannot be adequately expressed in temporal
terms:

> It seems to fill the universe with sight
> And sound,—from the four corners of this earth
>   [Rev. 7:1]
> Tells itself over, to my sense at least.
> But you may want it lower set i' the scale,—
> Too vast, too close it clangs in the ear, perhaps;
> You'd stand back just to comprehend it more:
> Well then, let me, the hollow rock, condense
> The voice o' the sea and wind, interpret you
> The mystery of this murder. God above!
> It is too paltry, such a transference
> O' the storm's roar to the cranny of the stone!
>   (6. 66–76)

Nevertheless the meaning of his experience, insofar as he is
able to define it, is limited; he can realize it only in terms of
his individual awakening. God, through Pompilia, has touched
an errant human being and revealed the transcendent claim of
spirit over flesh, a claim to which the response is virtuous
conduct and, if need be, decisive action. He has learned

> To live, and see her learn, and learn by her,
> Out of the low obscure and petty world—
> Or only see one purpose and one will
> Evolve themselves i' the world, change wrong
>   to right:
> To have to do with nothing but the true,
> The good, the eternal—and these, not alone
> In the main current of the general life,
> But small experiences of every day,
> Concerns of the particular hearth and home:

> To learn not only by a comet's rush
> But a rose's birth,—not by the grandeur, God—
> But the comfort, Christ.
>
> (6. 2085–96)

In his view, the miracle—not the least miraculous portion of
which has been his discovery that sublimity may reveal itself
in simple circumstances—involves him and Pompilia alone.
Through moral struggle, specifically the determination to redeem his soul from the temptations of an easy life in the
church by serving God through one of his imperiled children,
he was won divine grace.

Among the chief actors in this drama, Caponsacchi occupies the middle ground between the devils and the angels. His
resemblances to Guido, though largely fortuitous, are significant. Both men are from noble families; one is, the other has
been, a cleric whose ambiguous standing—each on a different
level—is the one certain thing about his recent life. Although
cast as adversaries through the agency of fate, both have
sought personal salvation—again on very different levels and
for different reasons—through Pompilia. Caponsacchi regards
the advent of Pompilia as an act of healing administered to his
sick and worldly soul, just as Guido under Paolo's persuasion
had earlier regarded marriage to Pompilia as the salvation of
his ailing worldly interests. And although both argue from
opposite rhetorical positions (Guido from studied humility,
Caponsacchi from righteous indignation) both have a nice
sense of personal honor. Caponsacchi is, then, *l'homme moyen
sensuel*, a fact perhaps most emphatically revealed in his having frequented "a certain haunt of doubtful fame" across from
Guido's palace—an allegation made by Half-Rome (2. 806–7)
and regretfully accepted by the Pope (10. 1201). Nor does his
transformation into a chivalric hero, illustrating Browning's
vital principle of moral growth, remove him from the middle
ground in the spectrum of the poem's characters. His instinct
as a man still provides for uncompromising retribution. Urging frightful eternal punishment for Guido, in a Dantesque
vision he sees Pompilia's vengeful husband slithering on the
edge of creation, there to meet an earlier outcast, Judas:

Kiss him the kiss, Iscariot! Pay that back,
That smatch o' the slaver blistering on your lip—
By the better trick, the insult he spared Christ—
Lure him the lure o' the letters, Aretine!
Lick him o'er slimy-smooth with jelly-filth
O' the verse-and-prose pollution in love's guise!
The cockatrice is with the basilisk!
There let them grapple, denizens o' the dark,
Foes or friends, but indissolubly bound,
In their one spot out of the ken of God
Or care of man, for ever and ever more!

                                               (6. 1944–54)

This ferocious outburst (there is much more to it) serves both
to heighten the effect of Pompilia's forgiveness of Guido in the
next book—unlike Caponsacchi, she is removed from ordinary
humanity, and so is capable of a magnanimity that is beyond
him—and, in its development of the Judas-betrayal theme, to
underscore the enormity of Guido's pretending to Christlike
martyrdom.

Caponsacchi, therefore, in his masculine dignity and his
righteous sense of outrage, his energy, and his chivalric mien,
represents the church militant in the manner of Spenser's Red
Cross Knight. A fallible human he may be, but it is through
such men that the Gospel is extended into the lives of ordinary
mortals who must apprehend divine truth through experience
rather than through the intellect. It is his action, after all,
which is the pivot of the whole drama.

"Then a soul sighs its lowest and its last / After the loud
ones." (1. 1076–77.) God's agent Pompilia, the frail Madonna
figure whom Caponsacchi has praised as in a litany, herself
speaks after being confessed.[9] Considering that she is dying

─────────

[9] The attending crowd about the dying Madonna figure suggests
the press of friends and neighbors who are seen congregating about St.
Anne's bed in pictures of the Nativity of the Virgin. Considering the
sordid obscurity surrounding Pompilia's own birth, it would patently
have been inadvisable for Browning to represent it, least of all with
any reference to scriptural or iconographic analogues. But the effect
that he had to forgo at the outset of Pompilia's life, he managed to
introduce at the end.

from multiple stab wounds and in addition is an ignorant girl, her eloquent 1,845-line monologue is the least realistic of all. Browning created her to exemplify every Christian virtue enumerated in the Sermon on the Mount. She is meek, all-loving, all-forgiving; she almost compulsively turns the other cheek. If Caponsacchi is the Red Cross Knight, she is Una. If he is the church militant, she is the great exemplar of Christian morality. Where he is vigorous and active, she is wrapped in innocent passivity; where he denounces the evil embodied in men like Guido, she finds it impossible to conceive of that evil, let alone recognize and least of all cope with it.

Pompilia reveals herself as a victim of villainy which most often took the form of deceit, though she does not call it by so harsh or particular a name. All she knows is that her whole life, down to the escape from Arezzo, was a series of visitations of falseness, of unreal episodes which she endured as if in a dream. To her, as to the Neoplatonists of whom she has never heard, evil is not a positive force but simply the absence of good—a blank rather than a palpable blackness. She bears no enmity toward Guido, who was, to her, no villain; whatever fault there was in their relationship, she implies (for she is too unsophisticated to put the notion into words), lay in man's fallen condition, or in the nature of a universe in which reality is constantly masked by appearance. In the course of her monologue the true, unbelievable measure of her inability to believe in malign motives is found in her concurrence, time after time, in the apologies of Guido's partisans and in Guido's own self-exculpation. He sinned, but out of ignorance or misapplied desire to do good: the same forgiveness she applies to the Comparini.

Her fatal experience of evil therefore left her soul unblemished. Indeed, the very improbability inherent in her remaining pure is part of Browning's design: she is the antithesis of fallen Eve. In her, Browning illustrates both the power for good inherent in the pure spirit—she was the divinely chosen means by which Caponsacchi's eyes were opened to true moral and religious values—and the mystic affinity that leads good instinctively to recognize and cling to good. Her instantaneous sense of Caponsacchi's worth, contrasted with her comprehen-

sive ignorance of the evil that environed her, shows how deep
may call unto deep and goodness evoke response where evil
fails. And Caponsacchi's great deed, complementing and re-
paying her own, was to rescue her from a temporal world of
illusion and deceit, of falseness called reality, and yet to preserve her innocence:

> Therefore, because this man restored my soul,
> All has been right; I have gained my gain, enjoyed
> As well as suffered,—nay, got foretaste too
> Of better life beginning where this ends—
> All through the breathing-while allowed me thus,
> Which let good premonitions reach my soul
> Unthwarted, and benignant influence flow
> And interpenetrate and change my heart,
> Uncrossed by what was wicked,—nay, unkind.
>
> (7. 1667–75)

In addition, Caponsacchi helped her save life, her own and her
unborn child's—life being an inestimably precious gift of God
to be preserved at all costs. "Through such souls [as Caponsacchi's] alone," she says as she finishes her testimony, "God
stooping shows sufficient of His light / For us i' the dark to
rise by. And I rise." (7. 1843–45.) In the sinful, heedless
Rome of 1698, the miracle of the Assumption is symbolically
reenacted.

   In this second triad as compared with the first, the relationship among the books is inverted. It is the first book of the
three, not the last, that portrays cunning reason at work, albeit
behind a façade of emotion. Against this background of Guido's slippery self-defense, the twin speeches of Caponsacchi
and Pompilia, ennobled by their sincerity, unconscious pathos,
and self-abnegation, vindicate the pure natural instinct—not
the debased and misapplied instinct invoked by Tertium Quid
in his apologia for Guido and then by Guido himself—as the
way to such a degree of spiritual truth as is accessible to
human beings. If we come closer to truth in their books, it is
because in them cold rationality has no place and the heart in
communion with God speaks. Intuition as a means of vision is
not clouded by personal prejudice, as in the two Halves of

Rome. Instead, the value of its function when undefiled is shown by the selfless experience of Caponsacchi, who sacrificed his churchly career for Pompilia (and found his soul in the process), and of Pompilia, who sacrificed her fame among men for her unborn child and for the possibly redeemable soul of her husband. But, like Caponsacchi, Pompilia cannot grasp the broader significance of what she has been through; hence, as her monologue concludes this movement of the poem, the ultimate truth is still to seek.

IV

How far it is still to seek becomes apparent at once, as Browning descends to the stage of law and church. In this, the third triad of books (8–10), truth is subjected to the inquiry not of casual bystanders nor of participants but of representatives of august institutions. The first two of these representatives, like the judges before whom Caponsacchi has appeared, have eyes and see not; as individual men they devote themselves to the manipulation of language and logic and the narrow self-seeking that to Browning invalidate human law as a means to truth. The third speaker, the Pope, proves that association with a human institution does not necessarily entail abuse of the tools of mind and tongue, callousness, or service to self. Although the deficiencies of the church in general may be fairly typified by the nest-feathering clergymen who populate the poem, a rare individual man, gifted with the wisdom and humane vision denied the generality, may rise above the institution within which he works.

After the long-sustained seriousness and elevation of the Caponsacchi and Pompilia books, Browning now indulges himself and his readers in an equally long farcical entertainment. He privately called the lawyers who are the speakers in Books 8 and 9 "buffoons," and his letters leave no doubt that his personal opinion of lawyers at large was as low as that expressed in the poem.[10] These two monologues are comedy of

[10] See, for example, *Browning and Julia Wedgwood*, pp. 146, 153, 163–64.

many colors and qualities: literary and legal burlesque, intellectual and verbal wit, and extravagant rhetoric. As human portraits they are at once simplified and subtle. From one angle the concentration on and exaggeration of one or two psychological traits remind us of the "humors" characters created by Ben Jonson and Dickens; from another, the distortion of the characters' thought patterns by physical or psychosexual drives anticipates Freud.

The lawyers, whose mission, as Browning wryly puts it, is to "teach our common sense its helplessness" (1. 1107), live in a mental world in which the uncontested facts of the Franceschini case are regarded merely as inconvenient, but easily superable, embarrassments to their sophistical and rhetorical flights. Their pleadings are a "leash of quibbles strung to look like law" (12. 379), a "spiritual display, / Proud apparition buoyed by winged words / Hovering above its birth-place in the brain" (8. 390–92): nothing so dull as an attempt to separate the rights from the wrongs of the case and thus serve the ends of truth and justice. "Anything, anything to let the wheels / Of argument run glibly to their goal!" (9. 471–72.) Both lawyers thrive on difficulties which they go to great lengths to discover and complicate. Far from contesting arguments damaging to their causes, they let them stand. What they want is "scope / Not for brute-force but ingenuity, / Explaining matters, not denying them!" (8. 313–15.)

Because in the Roman courts no allowance was made for personal confrontation, the lawyers are confined to written briefs. The defense counsel, Dominus Hyacinthus Archangelis, is forced to conjecture just how his wily opponent will argue. Despite his confidence that he can accurately anticipate the other's moves, he guesses wrong, for his rival, Doctor Johannes-Baptista Bottinius, turns out to raise none of the charges and "aggravations" Arcangeli so elaborately answers on behalf of his client. Having in hand Guido's confession as well as "the luck o' the last word, the reply" (8. 246), Bottini the Fisc deliberately ignores the issue of Guido's guilt, which needs no further proof, to devote his pleading to a much more attractive subject, Pompilia's alleged wrongdoings. Both advocates, impelled by their great conceit to choose the grounds most hospitable to arguments that will display their rhetorical finesse, waste their energies and unquestionable talents coping with imaginary issues and, what is worse, making concessions ruinous to their respective clients' causes.

As character foils, one obvious contrast between the lawyers is that of the rotund *vs.* the orotund. The first lawyer to speak, Guido's defender Arcangeli, is a fat, visceral, engaging figure whose relish for the good things of life provides an immediate contrast with the poem's grim atmosphere and tragic theme, just as his domestic contentment contrasts with the miseries of his client's married life. In the midst of the extremes of passion that dominate the case in which he is professionally involved, his personal formula for happiness is the golden mean: "Just so much work as keeps the brain from rust, / Just so much play as lets the heart expand, / Honouring God and serving man." (8. 54–56.)

Although an enthusiastic and, as he is pleased to admit, skillful man of law, his mind is not on his work as he sits in his office, "Rubs palm on palm, rakes foot with itchy foot" (1. 1154), and roughs out his defense of Guido, "First fashion of a speech; the chick in egg" (1. 1126). His thoughts constantly tug him toward the imminent birthday dinner of his eight-year-old son Hyacinth, upon whom he lavishes affection as boundless as the store of diminutives into which he fondly twists the boy's given name. (The touching vision of father and son with which Guido wound up his first defense before the judges doubtless owed a bit to his lawyer's coaching; would that Arcangeli were as solicitous for Guido's neck as he is for Cinuzzo's tender throat in this cold weather! [8. 280–81]) "Ah, boy of my own bowels, Hyacinth," he rhapsodizes,

> Wilt ever catch the knack,—requite the pains
> Of poor papa, become proficient too
> I' the how and why and when—the time to laugh,
> The time to weep, the time, again, to pray,
> And all the times prescribed by Holy Writ?
> Well, well, we fathers can but care, but cast
> Our bread upon the waters!
>
> (8. 1457–63)

The curly-pated lad is appointed to follow Papa in his profession, and to be a good lawyer one must be a good Latinist; to his father's delight, he is showing much promise, for he has already finished Caesar and "verges on Virgil" (8. 78). The numerous passages in which Arcangeli translates his legal Latin into the vernacular, phrase by phrase, neatly associate his professional and paternal concerns, suggesting as they do that indispensable adjunct to elementary Latin studies, the interlinear pony or—a word he uses in other connections— "trot." [11]

As the imagery of the bread upon the waters suggests, Arcangeli's thought processes and language, realistically presented in an interior monologue which borders on true stream-of-consciousness, are dominated by his savory expectations of the birthday dinner and his worry that things may not be going smoothly in the kitchen at home. Anxiety lest Gigia the cook not garnish the fried liver with minced herb, first manifested in lines 117–18, turns up again in lines 541–47, ironically revived by his sententious rhetorical question to the judges: Should man "live for the low tastes alone, / Mean creeping cares about the animal life?" (8. 539–40.) As he "wheezes out law and whiffles Latin forth," the Ovidian

---

[11] Although it is quite possible to skip the interlinear Latin in these speeches—the English is a dependable enough guide to the sense—the reader does so at the risk of some loss, for Browning is not above playing sly tricks with the text. For instance, as Cook (*Commentary*, p. 178) points out, in the lines Arcangeli cites from Horace (8. 1796–98) only "baccis" (pearls) occurs; the preceding "mammis" is a Freudian addition.

In the combination of doting father, son, and Latin lies autobiography, for at the very time Browning was writing the poem he was coaching his son Pen for his Oxford matriculation. Arcangeli's high hopes for his boy's future career must be a reflection of Browning's. Unfortunately Pen, unlike Hyacinth, had no studious inclinations and squandered his time ("Pen, truce to further gambols!" [8. 474]), so that he not only failed to qualify for Balliol—his father's dream—but, having gained admission to Christ Church, was dropped from that college's rolls after only a year. In view of Pen's unsatisfactory performance at Oxford and in later life, this high-spirited study of a father's delight in his son's fair prospects must in time have made bitter reading for Browning.

quips and Ciceronian cranks with which he sprinkles his pages are "A-bubble in the larynx while he laughs, / As he had fritters deep down frying there" (1. 1151–59). In the midst of exuberant consonance and alliteration occurs a culinary verb: "Let law come dimple Cinoncino's cheek, / And Latin dumple Cinarello's chin" (8. 64–65)—and for the rest of the soliloquy (as we shall note in detail in chapter 9) the motif of dietary delight prevails. "Feed me with food convenient for me!" Arcangeli cries, echoing the letter, though not the spirit, of Agur's wish (8. 1778; cf. Prov. 30:1, 8); but the *pièce de résistance* that night will be lamb fry, and by this time the course of the poem's imagery has firmly established Pompilia as the sacrificial lamb. "Bottini, burn your books, you blazing ass!" cries Arcangeli as he tosses his papers into a pigeonhole and heads home. "Sing 'Tra-la-la, for, lambkins, we must live!'" (8. 1804–5.)

In defending Guido, Arcangeli faces virtually insuperable difficulties. All he can do in the circumstances is offer arguments in extenuation or mitigation, but he excels in these. To be sure, he deliberately jettisons some of his strongest points (for instance, the alleged illegality of a nobleman's confession made under torture) for the sporting sake of increasing the odds against him. But he valiantly pursues the argument that vindication of one's marital honor is justified by the laws of nature, man, and God. Since the legitimacy of the end is not questioned, any means by which it can be attained is lawful. This is the argument the historic Arcangeli used, and some of the applications, ludicrous as they may strike us, cannot be attributed to Browning; they are found, advanced in all seriousness, among the pleadings in the Old Yellow Book. But Browning, a talented hand at intellectual comedy, improved on some and invented still others, with the result that Arcangeli cuts a ridiculous figure as he prepares Guido's defense against Bottini's anticipated attack. His personality is wholly comic; his argument too, though based on the precepts of classical forensics, is comic in its machinery if not in its conclusions. It is the ingenuity, not the cogency or the morality of his arguments that evokes admiration. He cites authority for *honoris causa* ranging from the bees (at least, he says, of the "nobler

sort") to the church fathers. In a master stroke he uses the
accomplices' confession that, when Guido failed to pay them,
they had planned to kill him on the way back to Arezzo, as a
stone to kill two birds. On the one hand it is proof that Guido's
murder of Pompilia and the Comparini was motivated only by
lofty desire to preserve honor, money being furthest from his
mind at this time; and on the other hand it is proof that the
thugs were mercenaries who killed without malicious intent
and therefore were guiltless of murder (8. 1593–1622). There
is also winning impudence in Arcangeli's aside, of course not
incorporated in his brief, that had not Guido confessed to the
triple murder, the lawyer would have pinned it on Caponsacchi, who committed it while Guido was on his way from
church to tell Pompilia he had forgiven her (8. 363–80).

But these intellectual gymnastics hardly promote the
discovery of truth. Arcangeli's purpose is solely to win his
case. He hungers for the applause Rome has for a brilliant
lawyer who gets his client off despite heavy odds; he relishes
the prospect of Bottini's discomfiture as his fumbling stupidity
is exposed to general laughter; and he looks forward to a stiff
fee, including the pearls, once Violante's, that will make a
necklace to adorn his wife's bosom. After all, while he shows
little interest in Guido as a person, he does sympathize with
Guido's cause. He too is a married man, revering the sanctity
of the home (though admittedly he seems to have no such
cause for apprehension as Guido maintains he had). And
Guido's appetite for the money he would receive through
Pompilia's son Gaetano, though not to be conceded in the
argument for his defense, strikes a responsive chord in the
lawyer who cherishes the hope that the "hale grandsire's" will
contains generous provision for Giacinto. The boy's inheritance might be augmented by codicil if his father could

> but coax the good fat little wife
> To tell her fool of a father of the prank
> His scapegrace nephew played this time last year
> At Carnival.

                                                    (8. 1780–83)

If the truth of the Franceschini affair is rendered more
remote by the professional vanity of Guido's lawyer, it is

totally obscured by the rhetorical extravagances of the prosecuting attorney.[12] Physically and temperamentally Bottini is Arcangeli's opposite. The well-fed Arcangeli scorns him as a "lean-gutted hectic rascal" (8. 224), and we discover him to be, in addition, a pompous courtroom Chanticleer (1. 1203–4) who rehearses his florid oratory in the solitude of his small office, or "studio" as Browning calls it, fitting the setting to the man (1. 1202). Unlike Arcangeli's draft, his is a "full-grown speech,"

> some finished butterfly,
> Some breathing diamond-flake with leaf-gold fans,
> That takes the air, no trace of worm it was,
> Or cabbage-bed it had production from.
>
> (1. 1167–71)

Pathetically, Bottini is a musician doomed to muteness; for his oration must be confined to paper. He cannot deliver it, as he would wish, in a courtroom crowded with a hushed and rapt multitude, including "fifty judges in a row" (9. 7).

> Clavecinist debarred his instrument,
> He yet thrums—shirking neither turn nor trill,
> With desperate finger on dumb table-edge—
> The sovereign rondo, shall conclude his *Suite*,
> Charm an imaginary audience there,
> From old Corelli to young Haendel, both
> I' the flesh at Rome, ere he perforce go print
> The cold black score, mere music for the mind.
>
> (1. 1209–16)

Though, like Arcangeli, he is an enthusiastic Latinist, he venerates the language primarily as a repository of hothouse flowers of speech and story. Classic myth and models of oratorical splendor are to him what lamb fry is to his opponent; and as he gorges himself at the Ovidian-Ciceronian feast, hapless truth is sacrificed before his preposterous declamation.

A bachelor, Bottini finds a somewhat arid substitute for familial affections in his vaunted devotion to the maternal

[12] In respect to both verbosity and salaciousness, the figure of Bottini may owe something to Il Dottore of the *commedia dell'arte*.

figure of the law—a loyalty which provides an instructive counterpart to Guido's earlier sycophantic eulogies of law and her faithful servants and at the same time a dissent from Arcangeli's unlawyerlike opinion that law does not adequately serve man's needs. This filial allegiance poses a serious problem for Bottini, one that is as formidable to him as the existence of Guido's confession is to Arcangeli. His venerated Lex Mater, passing judgment on the adultery suit after the episode at Castelnuovo, has already decided that Pompilia is not without blame. Since he obviously cannot question that decision, he must make the best of it in Pompilia's behalf by simultaneously acknowledging her possible guilt and asserting her relative blamelessness—or maintaining that whatever sins she committed were motivated by ignorance, fear, and feminine weakness.

It is a most agreeable challenge. Stimulated by the latter excuse, the prurience which is soon revealed as a dominant element in his character leads him to turn what should be "The last speech against Guido and his gang, / With special end to prove Pompilia pure" (1. 1217–18) into what amounts to a prosecution of the injured wife for chronic inchastity. We

> Hear law, appointed to defend the just,
> Submit, for best defence, that wickedness
> Was bred of flesh and innate with the bone
> Borne by Pompilia's spirit for a space,
> And no mere chance fault, passionate and brief.
>
> (12. 580–84)

Bottini welcomes every charge that Guido's partisans have made against her, with emphasis on her alleged sexual intrigues, and when these prove to offer insufficient scope for his powers of rebuttal he devises more outrageous ones of his own. His way with these charges, whether real or invented, is masterly. First he denies them, *pro forma;* then he takes them up, almost lovingly, and—for the sake, he says, of argument—treats them as if true. Having done so, with particular recourse to the *reductio ad absurdum,* he concludes that each allegation is false, or exaggerated, or simply ridiculous. But while such a procedure may win tactical victories, in the long run it leads to strategic disaster, for each initial concession does such damage to Pompilia's reputation that no amount of subsequent sophistry can repair it. After all the fireworks have died away, the image of Pompilia which persists is not that of an innocent victim of a vicious husband's cruelty but that of a splendid wanton.

Bottini adopts his aberrant strategy, he maintains, not because any of the accusations leveled against Pompilia are necessarily true but because by demolishing them he will add luster to her pure image and so prove her a saint (9. 1395–98). Whatever the result, there is considerable method in the lawyer's seeming madness, a method that becomes evident only when we realize that his strategy, like Arcangeli's, is dictated by the precepts of the classical rhetoricans. However far he overreaches himself, he is, at bottom, a serious and extremely talented forensic artist. This consideration is so important that it must be given careful attention later on (chapter 6).

The two lawyers are, in more than one respect, counterparts of the two Halves of Rome. Arcangeli takes Guido's part at the bar of law, just as Half-Rome, also a married man, did in the marketplace; Bottini and the Other Half-Rome, bachelors and men vulnerable in their respective ways to the appeal of womanly beauty, are naturally inclined toward Pompilia. But whereas the sidewalk oracles formulated their versions of truth through emotional prejudice, the two lawyers produce theirs primarily through casuistry. Browning uses them to resume, extend, and expose the idea first embodied in Tertium Quid's monologue. Like him, they are not disinterested seekers after truth. To them intellectual analysis and pleading are means to an end, and the end is not truth but some form of private gain. Nor have they any personal concern for their clients; Guido and Pompilia are merely pawns in a court case, straw figures without a life of their own. In such a manner does Browning further discredit reason as the way to truth. The lawyers' cynical misuse of its powers reduces the search for truth to nothing more than an intellectual frivolity.

But now the farce is over; let the curtain fall. The remainder of this drama is performed on other stages. In Book 10, the climax of the third triad of books as it is the philosophical climax of the entire poem, Pope Innocent XII conducts his wintry rumination over the court records brought before him by Guido's appeal from the death sentence. With Bottini's slaughter of Pompilia's reputation, our hopes for the triumph of truth have faded almost into nothingness, and as the new book begins there seems no prospect they will revive. The Pope is eighty-six years old, a man whom "the popular notion," as he himself says, "class[es] . . . / One of well nigh decayed intelligence" (10. 1245–46). His "chafing loose-skinned large-veined hand with hand" (1. 1245) inevitably recalls Arcangeli's habit of rubbing palm on palm (1. 1154). And like both lawyers, he immediately consults precedent, now in a ponderous history of the Papacy. For guidance as he meditates Guido's fate he reviews the protracted ancient controversy over whether a ninth-century Pope, one Formosus, was a true vicar of Christ or an impostor. Is this apparently senile Pope, then, to be nothing more than a superficially spiritualized version of the lawyers, appealing to dubious authority and equally incapable of perceiving the true issues underlying the Franceschini case? His humility as he presently closes the volume of history suggests otherwise; he may, after all, possess a degree of wisdom denied the rest. "Which of the judgments was infallible? / Which of my predecessors spoke for God?" (10. 150–51.) The Pope emerges as that rarity, a man ready to admit that he lacks the delusion of certainty. Nor does he pretend to the sort of judiciousness to which Tertium Quid, however speciously, laid claim, because he is to pronounce on a profound moral issue in which disinterestedness can have no place.

Instead, he applies to the rights and wrongs of the Franceschini affair the peculiarly incisive intuition he has acquired through longevity, further sharpened by the imminence of death. More than one Browning commentator has called him "a Protestant Pope." He claims no special access to truth by virtue of his office, but his humble awareness that the whole truth is withheld from men enables him fully to discern whatever portion is vouchsafed from heaven. In addition, he is the first to recognize that the question of Guido's guilt and Pompilia's and Caponsacchi's innocence cannot be resolved by natural or human law, as the lawyers tried for the most part to do, or by cold ratiocination. Hence, he proceeds to apply God's law as he understands it; and this means reviewing the case with a mind inspired and guided by the highest and noblest emotions of which man is capable. The issue, however, is never in doubt: from the outset he unhesitatingly rejects Guido's appeal.

The Pope's soliloquy bears to the speeches of the two lawyers the same relationship that Tertium Quid's bore to those of the two Halves of Rome. But the import of this triad is inverted. Tertium Quid sought, he said, to resolve the contradictions of the two opposing factions of emotion-heated public opinion by applying calm, judicious reason; but far from achieving truth, he merely rationalized society's bias in favor of Guido. The Pope resolves the more blatant contradictions of the lawyers, those professional sophists, by applying emotion, but emotion of a sort infinitely more pure and exalted, and therefore more efficacious, than any known in the Roman streets, salons, or law offices. His truth-finding faculty is of the same nature as Pompilia's and Caponsacchi's, but while theirs was necessarily limited by their youth and their involvement with each other, his is rendered more penetrating by age and self-abnegation and more comprehensive by the absence of earthly passion. The Pope sees the Roman murder case as Browning wishes us to see it—as a kind of morality play, with characters representing the forces of good and evil, truth and error, in conflict; and with implications far exceeding the mere guilt, innocence, or fate of several individual human beings.

V

When Guido speaks again, in Book 11 (which lies outside the triads but is indispensable to the climactic argument of the poem), he promptly substantiates the Pope's judgment. Revealing his true bestial self, he argues that, having fallen from his niche in the hierarchy of being, he deserves to be free to act according to the ethic of his present station. Stripped of his title and family name, he is the archetypal "natural man"

(1. 961), a creature to whom the earthly life, dedicated to feral rapacity and crass self-indulgence, is all. Here the Guidonian amorality, glimpsed from time to time in Book 5, is fully seen for what it is, not merely the aberration of a single human being but a disease to which the whole race is susceptible. Because Browning has taken pains to depict Guido, in the midst of his diabolic nature, as being at the same time an all too recognizable specimen of the common run of humanity, clothing his cynicism and Godlessness in plausible common sense, the point is clear enough. Guido is a mirror of what all men have it within themselves to be unless they are redeemed by Christianity and thenceforward remain firm in the faith. By offering a final picture of depravity, his speech provides a black background against which the remembered radiance of Pompilia's and Caponsacchi's purity becomes all the brighter, as well as an immediate proof of the Pope's conviction that in this world evil is always present to challenge the children of God.

Guido is the third major character to be seen facing death. The respective preparations of Pompilia, the Pope, and Guido might be said to constitute a nineteenth-century treatise on the *ars moriendi*. Pompilia was serene, her composure complete as she welcomed God's reaching hand. The Pope, old and shrewd in the ways of the world as she was young and naïve, had examined his conscience and found it clear: in condemning Guido, he had simply been the instrument of God's justice. But while the Pope knew neither the day nor the hour of his passing (though he might reasonably expect it to be soon), to Guido death is imminent, and he fights it with every resource at his command. It is a lurid and harrowing scene.[13] Cowering

---

[13] Browning's device of the return appearance made possible the most artistically successful unmasking of any villain in Victorian literature, not least because Guido accomplishes it with no outside aid. His would-be confessors are present, but, unlike (for instance) Micawber stage-managing the undoing of Uriah Heep, they are not agents. They simply stand by, appalled, while Guido condemns himself out of his own mouth.

It might be added that the dramatic setting of Book 11 was much to the taste of Browning's audience. The Victorians inherited from their fathers in the romantic age a strong predilection for prison

and screaming in his cell, Guido faces a cardinal and an abbot
who have come to receive his last confession. This "confession" takes a mixed form, part diatribe, part frantic chatter.
Hatred, accusation, defiance, self-extenuation, even attempts
at bribery pour from him. As a commentary on the Pope's
somber but not wholly despairing view of the present age as
one of religious complacency shading into doubt, Guido
portrays himself, a ruthless egoist and hedonist, as the only
honest man in a world of hypocritical "believers" who are, in
fact, as cynical and unchristian as he. When, at an especially
shocking outburst (11. 605–6), one of his auditors tries to
stop his mouth with a crucifix, it is evident that Satan is almost
literally present in the cell; the priest works

> his best with beads and cross to ban
> The enemy that comes in like a flood
> Spite of the standard set up, verily
> And in no trope at all, against him there.
>
> (1. 1303–6)

Sometimes Guido seems to be speaking from the depths of
hellish conviction. "Lucidity of soul," he says—Browning here
demonstrating how even the devil can quote Matthew Arnold—"unlocks the lips." (11. 159.) But at other times he
suggests that his very obduracy has been staged: "All's but a
flourish, figure of rhetoric! / One must try each expedient to
save life" (11. 851–52); "I thought you would not slay impen-
itence,— / Teazed first contrition from the man you slew."
(11. 2229–30.) At least once we overhear him giving himself
a cue, as it were: "Now for a burst of gratitude! / There's
some appropriate service to intone, / Some *gaudeamus* and
thanksgiving-psalm!" (11. 1846–48.)

Although normally it is difficult if not impossible to distin-

---

scenes, especially those in the very shadow of gallows or guillotine.
Fagin in the death cell helped make young Dickens' fortune, just as
Eugene Aram, similarly situated, contributed to Bulwer's early literary fame. And as Margaret Maison points out (*The Victorian Vision*
[New York, 1961], p. 92), certain Victorian evangelical novelists
were distinguished by "a fondness for the horrors of the condemned
cell." The ex-evangelical George Eliot, it will be recalled, used it as
the setting for the climactic scene of *Adam Bede* (1859).

guish sincerity from show in this wild speech, Guido's con-
summate hypocrisy is unmistakable in the passages in which
he resumes from his earlier monologue his insistence that his
fate is analogous to Christ's. In his recollection of the legal
ordeal through which he has passed—

> This path, twixt crosses leading to a skull
>   [Matt. 27:33]
> Paced by me barefoot, bloodied by my palms
> From the entry to the end

—the spears of "affront, failure, failure and affront" were
thrust into his side (11. 1768–71). He imagines himself nailed
to the cross and mocked by the Pope:

> "Save yourself!"   [Matt. 27:39–40]
> The Pope subjoins—"Confess and be absolved!
> So shall my credit countervail your shame,
> And the world see I have not lost the knack
> Of trying all the spirits,—yours, my son, [1 John 4:1]
> Wants but a fiery washing to emerge
> In clarity! Come, cleanse you, ease the ache
> Of these old bones, refresh our bowels, boy!"
>   [Phil. 1:20]
>   (11. 1784–91)

And when he speaks of his belated resolve to act decisively
regardless of the cost—a resolve that brought death to the
Comparini—he uses imagery reminiscent of the Last Supper:

> I, like the rest [his accomplices], wrote "poison"
>   on my bread;
> But broke and ate:—said "those that use the sword
> Shall perish by the same;" then stabbed my foe.
>   [Matt. 26:52]
>   (11. 2003–5)

In this horrific inversion of the Eucharist, Guido portrays
himself as breaking the bread of death which is to be distributed to the Comparini and to that suddenly militant wife
who at Castelnuovo challenged him at sword-point.

In this monologue, then, Browning adds one more dimension to his study of truth. What is claimed to be truth, it now appears, varies not only from man to man: within a single man it changes with the passing of time, and even in the course of a single hour's tirade. Guido's accents and manner are alternatively those of Christ and Satan. Assertions, denials, contradictions tumble over one another in frantic confusion; and a close comparison with his earlier speech reveals how often he now suppresses or evades the charges he cited and met then. All these differences render terribly ironic his repeated claim that he is changeless and unchangeable. At bottom, however, the truth of Guido's inner character reveals itself as indeed constant: from the moment of birth he has been, as the Pope decided, a man of unmitigated evil, whom no amount of beneficent opportunity and example could swerve from his black course.

Finally the "frightful Brotherhood of Death," all in black, torches aflame and crucifix grounded (1. 1307–17), gather crow-wise outside the cell door. "My first true word"—this is line 2418!—"Is—save me notwithstanding!" And in a last awful appeal he calls upon his Madonna-wife to intercede:

> Don't open! Hold me from them! I am yours,
> I am the Granduke's—no, I am the Pope's!
> Abate,—Cardinal,—Christ,—Maria,—God, . . .
> Pompilia, will you let them murder me?
>
> (11. 2422–25)

The concluding line not only emphasizes the irony of his ultimate dependence upon the woman whom he himself has murdered, but suggests one further association with Christ ("My God, my God, why hast thou forsaken me?" [Matt. 27:46]).

It is too sentimental and melodramatic to suppose, as some have done, that Browning implies that Guido, in so addressing Pompilia, has come to a last-second realization of her spiritual nobility and therefore, the scales of evil torn from his eyes, stands a chance of being saved. Browning's intention can be read clearly enough in his preview of Book 11:

While life was graspable and gainable, free
To bird-like buzz her wings round Guido's brow,
Not much truth stiffened out the web of words
He wove to catch her: when away she flew
And death came, death's breath rivelled up the lies,
Left bare the metal thread, the fibre fine
Of truth, i' the spinning: the true words come last.

(1. 1275–81)

The ultimate desperate attempt he makes to save his life is the
final measure of the man. The "truth" revealed is not so much
in the words themselves as in what they tell of the speaker—the utter evil of a man who does not hesitate, in the
shadow of death, to beg aid from the very one he has despised
and wrought upon.

What remains is by way of epilogue, the closing of the ring.
Book 12 is short and miscellaneous—a tension-relaxing montage which draws together loose threads of plot, allows several
characters to reappear, and in its last pages recapitulates the
meaning of all that has gone before. The book almost inevitably is anticlimactic in part, a fact suggested at the outset
by the fine image of the rise and fall of a rocket, emblematiz-
ing the spectacular but ephemeral blaze of a deed that enabled
God's truth momentarily to appear in the heavens above a
dark, uncomprehending world. Anticlimactic too are the episodes which, we learn, followed the scene in Guido's cell. His
execution was the occasion of a true Roman holiday. Bright
little Hyacinth had, as a special treat, an excellent vantage
point from which to view the unfortunate result of his father's
defense of Guido. And in the midst of the festive spirit,
circumstances and Guido's penchant for role-playing extended
into one more scene the ironies of the parallel between his
story and that of Christ. For Guido's progress through the
streets to the place of execution was implicitly a *via crucis*
(12. 138–66), and the site of the execution itself, the Place of
the People, was a Calvary where, with his accomplices dan-
gling "on either side" as the Pope had ordered (10. 2112),
Guido "harangued the multitude beneath," begging "for-

giveness on the part of God" (12. 167–89). The report does not specify whether the pardon was begged for Guido's sins or for those of his executioners. But with the stroke of Mannaia (the guillotine) Guido's sanctity—or, at the least, his factitious glamour—vanished. When the executioner held up his severed head, the mob discovered the features of a common criminal, not those of a martyr whom there had already been an incipient movement to canonize. And life went on, unaffected by the sublime illustration of divine will and love which the murder case provided. Bets were paid; Arcangeli briskly prepared for new cases ("Serve them hot and hot!" [12. 326]) which failed to materialize, his prospective clients being fed up with the law's caprices; and Bottini, having, as he is confident, vindicated Pompilia's fame, reports that he has accepted a brief from the Convertite nuns who wish to brand her a harlot in order to receive her estate—a commission for which he is uniquely and admirably prepared. His pro-Pompilia argument can be used, almost as it stands, as proof of the nuns' contention that she was unchaste.

In the letter announcing this felicitous turn of events Bottini encloses a portion torn from a newly printed sermon preached by Pompilia's Augustinian confessor—a "long-winded" paragraph, so he says, for whose language and substance he has only impatient contempt. But the fragmentary sermon (12. 459–642) contains a summary interpretation of the late happenings in Rome which actually is more succinct and to that extent more eloquent than the Pope's own. Finally Browning adds his own short homily on art as "the one way possible / Of speaking truth, to mouths like mine, at least" (12. 839–40), and the ring is closed. From the chaotic, ambiguous materials of the Old Yellow Book—the asseverations and lies, the half-truths, sophistries, evasions, rumors, and sudden fugitive veracities—the indirectness of Browning's art has fashioned a circle of transcendent, universal truth.

Thus *The Ring and the Book*, while it lacks the sort of unity that is supplied by a continuous development of plot and the presence of a central, controlling intelligence, has an adequately solid and symmetrical structure imposed on it by its philosophical preoccupations. We know how the story ends as

early as Book 1; Browning goes out of his way to avoid any
suggestion of suspense in the ordinary meaning of the term.
Even in Book 10 the question of whether the Pope will or will
not reject Guido's appeal, which might supply dramatic tension, is answered almost at the outset. We do not learn until
the climax in Books 10 and 11, however, what the story means.
The manifold conflicts of truth and error, of good and evil are
developed gradually, and it is only when we stand back to
regard the completed poem from a certain distance that we
realize how carefully Browning has interwoven and balanced
his themes. In particular, we observe how, in successive books,
the two opposing faculties, intellect and intuition, are placed
in ever-changing contrast. In each book, from Half-Rome to
the Pope, one or the other is exemplified, but never twice in
the same form, and usually with an admixture of the other.
The two Halves of Rome, Tertium Quid, Guido in his first
monologue, and the two lawyers illustrate the operation of
error in the world, either through emotion debased by self-
interest or through casuistry. But they are interrupted by the
books of Caponsacchi and Pompilia, whose perceptions,
though imperfect, are accurate as far as their scope allows, and
they are crowned by the book of the Pope, toward whose
monologue those of the spiritual lovers had been pointing. The
elemental conflict of intuitive truth *vs.* reasoned falsehood has
been sustained throughout.

V I

The scheme of triads most aptly describes the grouping of
the monologuists and the hierarchy of their thematic and
dramatic relationships. Surrounding these are Book 1 ("The
Ring and the Book") and 12 ("The Book and the Ring"),
which are nearly perfect complements, as the symmetry of
their titles implies. Together they suggest the encompassing of
the book of history and human drama, with its error and
groping, by the ring of artistic truth.

But there are at least two other instructive ways of viewing
the poem's structure. If we conceive of it as a circle divided
into twelve arcs, each representing a book, we realize that

Browning positioned the various books so that each has, as an opposite number, one which either complements or reinforces it. If Books 1 and 12, the farthest separated in the text but adjacent when the symbolic ring is closed, join to provide the thematic and ideological frame of the poem, then Books 6 and 7, arcs opposite them and therefore the farthest removed, together comprise the heart of the narrative. Here we have the focus of the whole controversy, in the relationship of Pompilia and Caponsacchi, whose flight to Rome has precipitated the vengeance of Guido. These monologues offer the only first-hand accounts of the love affair and elopement; yet, while they are not factually inconsistent, they are, as we have seen, poles apart in tone and emphasis. Nor is either account comprehensive or objective. Both wife and priest utter the truth only of immediate experience, often inchoate, often unconscious, and in no way ideologically interpreted. It is this immediacy of report, free of abstract speculation, that makes Books 6 and 7 stand in especial contrast to Books 1 and 12.

Ranged on either side of these paired arcs is a series of four matched monologues (2–5, 8–11), each series finding its culmination in speech by Guido. Each of the individual books also has an exact rhetorical and thematic counterpart. Perhaps even more important, each speaker's character, tastes, and mannerisms find either parallel or ironic contrast in those of his opposite number. The pro-Guidonian Half-Rome (2) and his counterpart Arcangeli (8), both married men, argue from the principle of *honoris causa* as applied to the married state and build their respective arguments on a careful tracing of Guido's agonized footsteps along the paths of chicanery, deceit, and contumely, often reminding us of Guido's noble station. The Other Half-Rome (3), the first pro-Pompilia speaker, is, as we find in his last lines, just as much concerned about honor of a kind as his predecessor Half-Rome; but his rhetorical approach, in keeping with his subject, is far different. In fact, he foreshadows the character and approach of Bottini (9), who is his opposite figure. In contrast to those who speak immediately before them, both are bachelors with well-developed tastes for the beauty (and pathos) of a woman dying before her prime. Subordinating Guido to Pompilia, they attempt—and fail—to write a new legend of Pompilia's sainthood. Their failure is due to a common inclination to view her as they view other women. Failing to see her for what she is (an avatar of sanctified innocence), both persist in substituting for her true character an imaginative rendering of the mistress of their own repressed desires. Both speakers attempt to see Pompilia aesthetically. While the Other Half-Rome likens Pompilia to flowers, birds, and other natural objects with attributes of beauty, Bottini often represents her in artistic terms: she is variously a model for a painting, a precious cut stone, and so on. The two aesthetic treatments are neatly complementary, and are in marked contrast to the impassioned directness of Caponsacchi, who, when he does see Pompilia in metaphorical terms, regards her as a martyr or *Mater Dolorosa*—as a suffering human being, not an *objet d'art*.

Together, the speakers of Books 2 and 3 represent the emotional approach to the case which may be expected in men who for one reason or another—sympathetic identification with the accused or a grudge against him—cannot view it with detachment. In contrast, their conjoined opposites, the lawyers of Books 8 and 9, are supposedly detached by virtue of their professional roles; yet this disinterestedness is not untinged by varying degrees of personal involvement resulting from the uxoriousness of Guido's counsel and the libidinousness of Pompilia's. The difference between Books 2–3 and 8–9 therefore is not absolute but rather one of emphasis.

Tertium Quid (Book 4), as the third of the speakers, contrasts not only with the previous two but stands directly antipodal to the Pope, his counterpart. In moral matters the one is a relativist, the other an absolutist. Although both represent "higher authority," they differ markedly in character as well as in their approaches to truth. Whereas Tertium Quid purports to reveal the real truth by judiciously weighing all arguments, the Pope strips away all the fripperies of debate, regarding logic as an instrument of deception, not of revelation; he seems, in fact, to be denouncing Tertium Quid's very method in his disparagement of intellectualism and his own exercise of intuition. And whereas Tertium Quid exploits the elasticity of language, its ambiguity and equivocation, the Pope is straightforward, clear, and uncompromising in his every pronouncement.

The counterpart of Book 5, the villain in disguise, of course is Book 11, the villain unmasked. Guido thus is seen both before and after the Pope's judgment. No contrast in the poem is more vivid than the extreme change in the man's outward character. Gone are the politic devotee of *noblesse oblige,* the faithful churchman, and the long-suffering husband self-portrayed in Book 5; revealed is the depraved wolf whose self-image matches the heinousness of his crime. Passion replaces articulate persuasion; desperation replaces cynical affability.

The symmetrical ring structure, then, provides a useful and revealing pairing of characters. Viewing the poem in this way also permits us to note the regular procession of rhetorical modes. To adopt the terminology of Aristotle's *Rhetoric,* Half-Rome's argument for Guido depends heavily on *ethos* (good character, high station, noble lineage, honorable deeds), while the Other Half-Rome uses *pathos* in delineating Pompilia, and Tertium Quid relies upon *logos* (the intellectual and ratiocinative) to persuade his blasé audience. Guido, as we might expect, uses all three modes of persuasion in his first defense. The pattern thus established is then repeated: Caponsacchi fiercely affirms the honor of Pompilia (*ethos*) and argues that he himself has been saved; Pompilia's deathbed confession is replete with unconscious *pathos;* and the two lawyers consciously manipulate *logos* in their legal infighting. The Pope's speech resembles Pompilia's, in that like her he is not trying to persuade but only articulating the truth as he sees it; if he argues from any particular principle, it is from a more comprehensive *pathos,* that of the human condition in general. Guido's final speech completes the cycle by again employing all three modes of persuasion indiscriminately.

There is still another way of seeing the structure of the poem as a whole. With respect to the discovery of the hard core of truth which Browning posits in Book 1, the books follow a cyclic movement approximating an inward and elliptical spiral. In this progression, Books 2 and 3 (the two

Halves of Rome) pass by the central truth at roughly the same
distance, though at opposite angles. Book 4 (Tertium Quid) is
much farther removed, and Book 5 (Guido) is at apogee. At
this point the tendency is reversed, Books 6 and 7 (the lovers)
coming markedly closer to the truth than did the Halves of
Rome, but still at a distance imposed by their limitations of
knowledge. With Books 8 and 9, however, the earlier outward
movement is resumed as Browning places the speeches of the
issue-muddying lawyers immediately after Pompilia's. They
are at least as far removed from the truth as Guido was on the
opposite side of the orbit. But with the book of the Pope the
tendency is once more reversed; at this point the course of the
poem comes the closest yet to truth. Then follows, in Book 11,
what appears to be a violent retrograde movement; but in this
final speech of Guido's there is, in fact, a measure of awful,
undeniable truth. As the poem ends, Celestino's sermon in
Book 12 redirects the movement even nearer the center.

The spiral concept therefore illustrates one of the poem's
chief points: that, in the relativistic sphere of human existence, no man is vouchsafed a direct vision of the truth. One
can skirt around it, or drive toward it, but none of the
speakers may apprehend truth in its utter purity and whole-
ness. The self-seeking gain by retreating away from truth's
light into the penumbra of deception, and even the most sincere and altruistic are capable of discerning only partial light:
speakers whose nature and insight place them on or near the
axis of vision, the purest perception of truth that man is
capable of. The Pope and Celestino, though denied direct
contact with incandescent truth, at least see into its heart from
a short distance. Pompilia and Caponsacchi reside just off this
axis because they have only limited apprehension of the numinous quality of their experience.

It is fortunately unnecessary to have to choose among these
three interpretations of the structure of *The Ring and the
Book*. They do not conflict, and our understanding of Browning's purpose and our admiration of his command of the
principles of large-scale poetic art are equally enhanced if we
keep all three in mind as we read. To remove any single book,

as impatient readers often recommend, or to revise their order would be to destroy the effect of Browning's meticulous planning. In the largest dimensions of its structure, as in the multitudinous smaller details, the form of *The Ring and the Book* is inseparable from its meaning.

Three

"Our Human Testimony False"

THE WORLD'S ILLUSION

I

"So, British Public," wrote Browning in a passage which sums up the metaphysical burden of the poem,[1]

> learn one lesson hence
> Of many which whatever lives should teach:
> This lesson, that our human speech is naught,
> Our human testimony false, our fame
> And human estimation words and wind.
>
> (12. 831–36)

We have an instinctive yearning toward truth, but it seldom gets us very far, "feeling as we are wont / For truth, and stopping midway short of truth, / And resting on a lie" (1. 742–44). For man is doomed to imperfect knowledge. The perfect truth that resides in God, says the Pope, "existent somewhere, somehow, as a whole," is

> Here, as a whole proportioned to our sense,—
> There, (which is nowhere, speech must babble thus!)
> In the absolute immensity, the whole
> Appreciable solely by Thyself,—
> Here, by the little mind of man, reduced

---

[1] As we begin to describe the leading ideas of the poem, it may be well to emphasize that they are, almost without exception, intellectual commonplaces. Browning's originality resides in the fresh expression he gives to these familiar metaphysical, ethical, and religious attitudes, not in the ideas themselves.

To littleness that suits his faculty,
Appreciable too in the degree.

(10. 1315–22)

The evidence upon which man forms his judgments, Browning
says in his own person—and Celestino echoes him at the end
of the poem (12. 606–7)—is "No dose of purer truth than man
digests, / But truth with falsehood, milk that feeds him now, /
Not strong meat he may get to bear some day" (1. 830–32).

To Browning, this invincible ignorance, or at best half-
knowledge mixed with error, is a proof of God's mercy, for if
the ineffable truths were not stepped down to the level of man's
capacity they would be unbearable. The care of "the angel of
this life" is "lest men see too much at once" (1. 594–95).
"Sun-suffused, / A cloud may soothe the eye made blind by
blaze." (10. 1644–45.) The ultimate truth is

> reduced to suit man's mind,—
> . . . truth reverberate, changed, made pass
> A spectrum into mind, the narrow eye,—
> The same and not the same, else unconceived—
> Though quite conceivable to the next grade
> Above it in intelligence,—as truth
> Easy to man were blindness to the beast
> By parity of procedure,—the same truth
> In a new form, but changed in either case.

(10. 1389–97)

The "plague of squint" is everywhere (1. 879). No two
people see the same events in the same way: "One calls the
square round, t'other the round square." (4. 36.) As the monologues of the two Halves of Rome illustrate, truth is beheld
only through the refraction of bias. Man guesses at the shape
and size of the sunken pebble of truth by the indirect evidence
of its splash and the "rush and ripple" of the water into which
it has been cast. His "feel after the vanished truth," though
honest enough, contains "A hidden germ of failure" which
"neutralize[s] that honesty" and misguides the "feel for
truth." A prejudice, diverting his aim initially "by but a hair's
breadth at the shoulder-blade," results in its falling wholly
wide of the mark, "that deceptive speck" of truth at the pool's
bottom (1. 839–58). The onlookers' versions of the Frances-

chini case, in short, typify the error common to all men. "So
we are made," says Pompilia, rendered preternaturally wise by
the world's failure to recognize Caponsacchi's nobility,

> such difference in minds,
> Such difference too in eyes that see the minds!
> That man, you misinterpret and misprise—
> The glory of his nature, I had thought,
> Shot itself out in white light, blazed the truth
> Through every atom of his act with me:
> Yet where I point you, through the chrystal shrine,
> Purity in quintessence, one dew-drop,
> You all descry a spider in the midst.
> One says, "The head of it is plain to see,"
> And one, "They are the feet by which I judge,"
> All say, "Those films were spun by nothing else."
>   (7. 918–29)

Inability or unwillingness to discern truth, no matter how
plainly presented, is regrettable enough; but far worse, because it is an inveterate instrument of evil, is man's practice of
deception—his exploiting, for selfish ends, the limitations of
knowledge and the discrepancy between appearance and reality that are the conditions of earthly existence. In *The Ring
and the Book* falsehood is the form that evil most characteristically takes. Greed is Guido's motive, but the lie is his chosen
tool. The events of the poem illustrate many varieties of lie,
trick, and deliberate ambiguity. The "pretentious hate / Of
plain truth" which the Other Half-Rome attributes to Guido
and his family (3. 523–24) is almost universal. "There is no
monopoly / Of lies and trick i' the tricking lying world," as
Guido, according to the Pope, has discovered; the entire hierarchy of creation plays the game, each level to its degree (10.
575–88). It is, above all, the game of the devil, that "Lord of
Show" (6. 1820) who typically "pays . . . his liegeman, brass
for gold" (3. 1463).[2] The practice of deception, as Caponsac-

---

[2] In order to underscore the identification of Guido with Satan,
Browning later has Caponsacchi refer to Guido's paying his double-
duty maidservant—"his light-of-love / And lackey-of-lies"—with
"rank brass coin" (6. 608–10).

chi is wont to say, is wreathed in "smoke from hell" (6. 2). There is fitting symbolism in his recollection that, as he was about to answer Pompilia's call, the possibility of entrapment was "a certain ugly cloud-shape, goblin-shred / Of hell-smoke hurrying past the splendid moon" (6. 923–24). With good reason, as the Pope reviews the heaped-up lies and forgeries that are the "evidence" in the case he must decide, does he exclaim: "Why then, / Craft to the rescue, craft should supplement / Cruelty and show hell a masterpiece!" (10. 643–45.)

By their very nature, lies have some of the same apparent qualities as truth; and among these, ironically, is their ability to be transmuted. If truth, distorted in transmission either by accident or by intention, becomes falsehood, so by the reverse process falsehood may be turned into truth. Although Pompilia, the very symbol of truth, realizes that "wormy ways" are a poor substitute for the path of goodness and openness (7. 669–73), she nevertheless finds some justification, admittedly beyond her understanding, for lies as a possible instrument of the divine will. She asserts that "such as are untrue / Could only take the truth in through a lie" (7. 1196–97): lies, in a world of deceitful men, have become the common currency of language, but they may also prove the chance vehicle of truth.[3]

---

[3] One illustration of the way good may spring from evil design is found at the moment of Pompilia's decision: "Tell Caponsacchi he may come!" she orders the servant employed to compromise her. "But," replies the woman, "do you know that I have bade him come, / And in your own name?"—as part, that is, of Guido's campaign to compromise Pompilia (7. 1358–71).

Cf. the note on "Lying and Equivocation" which Newman added to the second edition of the *Apologia pro vita sua*. It begins: "Almost all authors, Catholic and Protestant, admit, that *when a just cause is present*, there is some kind or other of verbal misleading which is not sin." Charles Kingsley used, as epigraph for his pamphlet which called forth the *Apologia* ("What, Then, Does Dr. Newman Mean?"), a statement taken from Newman's *Sermons on the Theory of Religious Belief*: "It is not more than a hyperbole to say, that, in certain cases, a lie is the nearest approach to truth." One is tempted to believe that Browning's thoughts on this subtle subject were affected by its appearance in the Kingsley-Newman controversy. See p. 130, n. 1.

An unwitting casuist, subtle beyond her years, she maintains further that Violante's lie about her parentage was unreal, for Violante thought

> real lies were—lies told
> For harm's sake; whereas this had good at heart,
> Good for my mother, good for me, and good
> For Pietro who was meant to love a babe.
>
> (7. 306–9)

Such an argument places her in incongruous alignment with her nominal defender, Bottini, who elaborately excuses her alleged campaign of "feigned love, false allurement, fancied fact" (9. 526) on the ground that, though it may not have produced positive good, as Pompilia supposes Violante's deceit was intended to do, it forestalled a greater evil. And Guido, for his part, defends pretended love as a legitimate substitute for true love:

> if there's no love prompts it,—love, the sham,
> Does twice the service done by love, the true.
> God bless us liars, where's one touch of truth
> In what we tell the world, or world tells us,
> Of how we like each other?
>
> (11. 1387–91)

But any attempt to justify lying on ethical or pragmatic grounds is vitiated either by Pompilia's naïveté or by the casuistry of cynics like Bottini and Guido. The fact is that the murder of the Comparini is the climactic product of a long series of events each of which has been characterized by some form of lying, trickery, or ambiguity. Pompilia enters life under the shadow of Violante's lie regarding her origin (which is, in any case, obscure: who was her father?). Her birth, allegedly to Violante, is "a sleight of hand" (2. 226), and Violante's subsequent contriving of Pompilia's fraudulent marriage is "a new trick" to add fresh life to the old one (2. 251–53). The marriage is marked by a double deception, the Comparini falsely putting Pompilia forth as a legitimate heir and Guido claiming to own considerably more than an ancient name. The wedding itself, according to Browning's version (not that of the historical documents), is "clandestine" (2.

380). After the Comparini's disillusioned return to Rome, they receive from Pompilia a letter which may or may not be a forgery.[4] The course of events by which Caponsacchi is drawn into Pompilia's service is "tenebrific" (3. 789). Were the love letters attributed to Pompilia and Caponsacchi genuine or forged? In the next phase of the action, Pompilia bears a child whose paternity, like her own, is in doubt; the ambiguity that has cursed her life is now transmitted to a new generation. Within two weeks, Guido knocks at the door of the Comparini's house and gains admission by a ruse. To the very end, therefore, the poem's actions are attended, often dominated, by some form of deceit or uncertainty.

To the evilly inclined, the necessary existence of doubt in the world provides chance after chance not only to win something at others' expense but to excuse their own villainy. The basis of Guido's first defense is that he was the victim of lies on the part of others or of honest doubts on his own part; since the world is notoriously a place of illusion, he could scarcely be blamed for acting on the basis of misinterpreted appearance. Did not the Roman court, pronouncing on the fugitive Pompilia and Caponsacchi, imply that her fear of Guido's cruelty, and Caponsacchi's belief that her life was in danger, were sufficient reason for their flight, even though the fears were groundless? Did it not also allow that the love letters and the elopers' supposed intimacy during the journey could likewise bear innocent explanation (5. 1180–1210)? Such au-

---

[4] The complication of falsehoods and suppression of truth that has marked the story down to this relatively early point is epitomized in the lines Violante's confessor at Rome speaks to her:

> Your husband who, no partner in the guilt,
> Suffers the penalty, led *blindfold* thus
> By love of what he *thought* his flesh and blood
> To alienate his all in her behalf,—
> Tell him too such contract is null and void!
> Last, he who *personates* your son-in-law,
> Who with *sealed eyes* and *stopped ears*, tame
>   and mute,
> Took at your hand that bastard of a whore
> You *called* your daughter and he *calls* his wife,—
> Tell him, and bear the anger which is just!
>   (3. 589–98; italics supplied)

thoritative recognition that things may not be what they seem
and that no one should be punished for confusing appearance
and reality, Guido seeks to have applied to his own case.
"Humanity pleads that though the wife were true, / The priest
true, and the pair of liars true, / They might seem false to one
man in the world!" (11. 887–89.) This is the basis upon
which Tertium Quid defends Guido's failure to act at
Castelnuovo:

> He has the first flash of the fact alone
> To judge from, act with, not the steady lights
> Of after-knowledge,—yours who stand at ease
> To try conclusions: he's in smother and smoke,
> You outside, with explosion at an end:
> The sulphur may be lightning or a squib—
> He'll know in a minute, but till then, he doubts.
>
> (4. 1184–90)

Thus uncertainty may be used either to palliate a deed or to
rationalize culpable inaction.

In his second speech, Guido shifts the emphasis, but at no
cost to his sedulously created self-image of injured virtue. He
retains from his first defense whatever alibis he deems still
useful. He clings to the argument that, as a cuckolded husband, he was "horn-blind" (11. 916). He is the victim of other
people's devotion to deception, beginning with the scheming
Comparini, whose "life had been a lie" (11. 879), and ending
with his present auditors' anxiety that he "Keep up the jest, lie
on, lie ever, lie / I' the latest gasp of me," for the sake of
proving that he is penitent (11. 414–15). But where formerly
he laid principal stress on his being the victim of falsehood, he
now portrays himself, more emphatically than before, as the
past and present guardian of truth. He confesses—with sarcasm as far as Pompilia is concerned, but in utter seriousness
as regards himself—that "I'm my wife outright / In this
unmanly appetite for truth" (11. 170–71); "stick[ing] /
Still to the truth" he will "declare with my last breath, / I die
an innocent and murdered man" (11. 417–19).

For all his claims to be telling the whole truth, Guido's final
speech is laden with the contradictions and self-betrayals that

reveal the full extent of his duplicity. He admits that he has been a wolf in sheep's clothing (11. 1174–84). But he assumed his "sheepskin-garb" (11. 443) initially, he says, at the urging of the church, which put a premium on falsehood: "Inasmuch as faith gains most" by way of pleasure and avoidance of pain, "feign faith!" (11. 772.) "You as good as bade me wear sheep's wool / Over wolf's skin, suck blood and hide the noise." (11. 824–25.) But when, obedient to this advice, he played the wolf and thereby thrust himself beyond the pale of Christian decency, the church

> forced me choose, indulge
> Or else renounce my instincts, still play wolf
> Or find my way submissive to the fold,
> Be red-crossed on the fleece, one sheep the more.
> (11. 820–23)

Complacent in their own hypocrisy, churchmen yet were unwilling to concede Guido the same privilege, even though the passions they urged him to suppress—thirst for blood revenge upon an errant wife—were far more creditable than those in which they themselves indulged while officially deploring them (11. 1498–1517).[5] Nonetheless, while denouncing others' advice to pretend to be what he was not, he traces the ruin of his marriage to Pompilia's refusal to play a role herself. She "would not begin the lie that ends with truth, / Nor feign the love that brings real love about" (11. 1428–29). Seemingly

---

[5] The law, too, encourages deceit. The ambiguity of its several decisions is extensively canvassed by several speakers, whose reactions to them provide one of the most ample touchstones to their respective biases (see below, pp. 133–34, 148–49). The courts, in their easygoing attitude toward truth, "allowed [Violante's] cheat for fact," "let the tale o' the feigned birth pass for proved" (2. 735–38). "That self-same machine, that very law / Man vaunts, devised to dissipate the gloom, / Rescue the drowning orb from calumny," says Celestino, by the "marvellous perversity of man" proved wholly inadequate and inept, and truth was saved only by divine intervention (12. 575–79). The pun on "lawyers" and "liars" in the same book (656–57) quietly sums up Browning's estimate of the role the law plays in a world where falseness is rampant.

he does not recognize the contradiction, for he offers Pompilia's fault as a part of his apologia.

Especially throughout his second monologue, as has been noted, it is impossible to distinguish fully between the true Guido and the actor playing a desperate role. He is an "ambiguous creature" (10. 1226), the most equivocal of all in the poem. And the very fact of his ambiguity is, when all its implications are considered, the most damning count against him. We have already stressed his basic dualism: he repeatedly likens himself to Jesus Christ but in reality is Satan. He recognizes that his is a mixed nature, but one that does no discredit to him; too late, he says, he (who had believed the saying, "A man requires a woman and a wife") discovered that he has a "woman-side" (11. 162, 168). But the true aspect and meaning of his duality are revealed by the Pope, in an excoriating figure appropriate to the Naples-born pontiff who has a taste for littoral images (9. 372–73; cf. 10. 1439–49). Guido is an "ambiguous fish," a soldier crab which, when cornered after his scavenging takes him far from his protective shell, pleads, "But the case out yonder is myself!" (10. 485–509.)

Guido's ambiguity has its partial reflection in Caponsacchi. Just as Guido hovered " 'Twixt flesh and fowl" (5. 361) on the fringe of the church, so Caponsacchi necessarily had a double role within it. His tonsure was hidden by his rich dark-brown curls (7. 911).

> Mingling each its multifarious wires,
> Now heaven, now earth, now heaven and earth at once,
> Had plucked at and perplexed their puppet here,
> Played off the young frank personable priest;
> Sworn fast and tonsured plain heaven's celibate,
> And yet earth's clear-accepted servitor,
> A courtly spiritual Cupid, squire of dames
> By law of love and mandate of the mode.
>
> (1. 1019–26)

It was a role which, in retrospect, saddens the Pope:

> this youth prolonged though age was ripe,
> This masquerade in sober day, with change

> Of motley too,—now hypocrite's-disguise,
> Now fool's-costume: which lie was least like truth,
> Which the ungainlier, more discordant garb
> With that symmetric soul inside my son,
> The churchman's or the worldling's,—let him judge,
> Our Adversary who enjoys the task!
>
> (10. 1129–36)

Ironically, just as sheep's clothing concealed Guido the wolf, Caponsacchi's clerical garb also was an instrument of dissimulation: the "fribble and coxcomb" (6. 340) masqueraded as a priest.

Nor did the two men masquerade only in a manner of speaking. In the course of the events that the poem narrates they actually went through parallel changes of clothes for the sake of disguise. Caponsacchi, preparing to escort Pompilia beyond Guido's reach, had "flung the cassock far, / Doffed the priest, donned the perfect cavalier" and had become

> Paris in correct costume,
> Cloak, cap and feather, no appointment missed,
> Even to a wicked-looking sword at side,
> He seemed to find and feel familiar at.
>
> (2. 999–1009)

Overtaking him at Castelnuovo, Guido hoped to find that the priest was "In serge, not silk, with crucifix, not sword"; instead, to his dismay, "the grey innocuous grub, of yore, / Had hatched a hornet, tickle to the touch, / The priest was metamorphosed into knight" (4. 1156–59). In a succeeding episode Guido, hearing of the birth of a son to his wife, "Donned the first rough and rural garb I found" (5. 1565), "a clown's disguise" (6. 2001) in which to achieve his purpose.[6] Each assumed costume, as a matter of fact, was more faithful to its wearer's character than his habitual garb.

[6] Guido's disguise was compounded when, hurrying out of Rome after performing the murders in his rural garb, he sought to fob himself off on the incorruptible frontier official as a duke, not a mere count (11. 1634). Exaggeration seemingly ran in the family: when the Franceschini arms were designed, the furze sprig that figured in the family legend was enlarged into a tree (11. 2159).

But Guido's disguise was adopted for an evil end, Caponsacchi's for a noble one. As fate had it, the priest's exercise in deception was a direct consequence of his having for the first time come to grips with the evil implicit in a practice which hitherto had appealed to him merely as an amusing pastime and possible battle of wits. At first, more or less out of habit, he engaged Guido in a cat-and-mouse game; but in the end he refused to be lured into a situation in which, craftier than Guido, he would have the satisfaction of turning the tables on him (6. 548–56). Pompilia's tragic beauty put a new light on Guido's machinations to entangle her with the priest. For the first time, Caponsacchi realized how incompatible deception was with life's serious purpose, even if it was the intending deceiver who would be deceived. Yet he donned the costume of cavalier for the journey because the necessity of saving Pompilia took priority over any scruples arising from his new-found ethical principle. In a sense, his act had the nature of a justified lie. The remainder of Caponsacchi's story, as he tells it, comprised a battle against the forces of falsehood that threatened Pompilia and all she symbolized.

I I

The ironies so far noticed, however, are much surpassed by the one resulting from Bottini's handiwork as he portrays Pompilia as an antagonist worthy of her husband's guile. A skilled dissembler, possessed of "melting wiles, deliciousest deceits, / The whole redoubted armoury of love" (9. 231–32), she was, says Bottini, experienced in the tactics of amorous war games from earliest youth. When Guido's cruelty stirred her to action, she was by no means without resources. Taking the vigorous initiative, she wooed Caponsacchi with the only gift worthy of a celibate priest:

> the lady here
> Was bound to proffer nothing short of love
> To the priest whose service was to save her. What?
> Shall she propose him lucre, dust o' the mine,
> Rubbish o' the rock, some diamond, muckworms prize,

> Or pearl secreted by a sickly fish?
> Scarcely! She caters for a generous taste.
>
> (9. 507–13)

Hence, for the sake of "escape from death," she employed the
classic stratagems, not overlooking the Petrarchan oxymoron:
"She burns, he freezes,—all a mere device / To catch and keep
the man may save her life, / Whom otherwise nor catches she
nor keeps!" (9. 540–42.) And so through the entire course of
flirtation, capitulation, and elopement. But her "sole permitted
weapon," Bottini asserts, was employed in a good cause (9.
430–35). Adopting his opponent's argument that the end justifies the means, he describes Pompilia as having used the
weaponry of feminine wiles solely in behalf of clearly perceived purposes. Her wits served her even when Guido burst
into the Comparini's house.

> to the last Pompilia played her part,
> Used the right means to the permissible end,
> And, wily as an eel that stirs the mud
> Thick overhead, so baffling spearman's thrust,
> She, while he stabbed her, simulated death,
> Delayed, for his sake, the catastrophe,
> Obtained herself a respite, four days' grace,
> Whereby she told her story to the world.
>
> (9. 1415–22)

Her deathbed statement disclaiming all sin was a cunning lie,
as, in view of the manifold discrepancies between it and his
version of events, Bottini is bound to regard it. But even here
the assumption of virtuous guile suffices for explanation: she
fabricated her tale of unsullied innocence, he says, both to
save her lover's name (9. 1464–71) and to forestall Guido's
plea that he was avenging adultery. "O splendidly mendacious!" (9. 836.)

Thus Bottini's whole case, like so much of Guido's, depends
on the willingness of his world-wise auditors to believe in the
deceptiveness of appearances. Pompilia's tragedy was that
every human action is capable of at least two interpretations,
and hers were always interpreted the wrong way. But the

premise of Bottini's argument, that Pompilia had a perfect genius for ambiguous conduct, has already been undercut by her own monologue, which stresses that far from adding to the world's store of deception, she has been its constant victim—the very claim, we recall, that Guido had made for himself two books earlier.

According to Pompilia, her marriage was shadowed from the beginning, when her deceiving foster-mother was herself deceived by Paolo's smooth speech, though only because she wished, for Pompilia's sake, to believe him. "Instead of piercing straight / Through the pretence to the ignoble truth," Violante saw a way of rescuing the girl from the consequences of past falsehoods:

> I, whose parents seemed such and were none,
> Should in a husband have a husband now,
> Find nothing, this time, but was what it seemed,
> —All truth and no confusion any more.
>
> (7. 326–37)

But truth, when it appeared, was not at all what she had been led to expect. To her, "cavalier"—the term Violante optimistically applied to Guido—meant the figure of St. Michael as he was pictured in a beloved tapestry in their home, a "slim young man / With wings at head, and wings at feet, and sword / Threatening a monster" (7. 390–92).[7] Instead, her intended husband proved to be old, undersized, "Hook-nosed and yellow in a bush of beard, / Much like a thing I saw on a boy's wrist, / He called an owl and used for catching birds" (7. 394–98). Here appearance by no means belied reality, but Pompilia was too innocent to know. After all, a repulsive

---

[7] Later Pompilia specifically identifies the warrior as St. Michael (7. 1215–18), but his accouterments suggest Perseus or Mercury instead. Perhaps he is an assimilation figure of the sort that often results from Browning's habit of making cross-referenced or coalesced metaphors. The transference of the attributes of a mythological figure to a Christian one is certainly faithful to Renaissance practice. The Pope notes how the church "was wont to turn each Venus here / . . . Into Madonna's shape" (10. 1117–20) as a thrifty means of putting pagan statues to holy uses.

doctor, "so lean, so sour-faced and austere," once came to treat her,

> dripped a drop or two
> Of a black bitter something,—I was cured!
> What mattered the fierce beard or the grim face?
> It was the physic beautified the man.
>
> (7. 417–22)

But Pompilia's hope ultimately proved illusory: Guido the physician administered an infinitely more bitter medicine.[8] The two were married hastily, secretly; Pompilia was "cloaked round, covered close, / I was like something strange or contraband"; she mistook the purpose of her trip to the church, fancying "we were come to see a corpse"; the priest waiting at the altar proved to be Paolo, "not our parish friend"; and at the necessary moment Guido emerged from "behind the altar where he hid." As the "silent and scared" girl emerged from the church, "the rain had stopped, / All things looked better" (7. 428–58). But only "looked"; for Pompilia at once was forced to conceal the truth from Pietro by acting the role of the still unmarried girl. The fruits of deception, temporarily delayed, would soon ripen; the comfort found in Guido's absence for the next three weeks was illusory (7. 474–75).

The cruelty to which Guido subjected Pompilia at Arezzo is defined by the sufferer herself simply as his trying to force her to act a lie—an account which provides useful perspective on both Guido's preceding version and Bottini's later one. Guido

---

[8] The true physician turned out to be Caponsacchi, whose ministrations were recommended, ironically, by Margherita, Guido's maidservant:

> The imposthume at such head,
> One touch, one lancet-puncture would relieve,—
> And still no glance the good physician's way
> Who rids you of the torment in a trice!
>
> (7. 1145–48; cf. 2. 1206)

It is equally ironic that the role of St. Michael later is assumed in the poem's metaphorical movement by both Guido (11. 2096–97)—thus substantiating Pompilia's original identification—and the true cavalier, Caponsacchi.

attempted to make her behave as "a coquette, / A lure-owl posturing to attract birds" (7. 677–78), and to respond to the letters allegedly sent by Caponsacchi. In her innocence, she did just the opposite, "thwarting Guido's true intent."

> He ought not to have wished me thus act lies,
> Simulate folly, . . .
>
> .   .   .   .
>
> To make me and my friend unself ourselves,
> Be other man and woman than we were!
>
> (7. 695–708)

Into this black world of deception, actual and advocated, "sprang the young good beauteous priest" (1. 586). In one sublime moment white erased black, and the blank that Guido's evil had made of her life since they arrived at Arezzo—a memoryless abyss of unreality—was succeeded by the reality of God's truth, of which Caponsacchi was the unconscious messenger and champion. Now, at last, by divine grace she was herself able to distinguish truth from delusion. She had once seen through the gibberings of a madman who thought he was Pope Sixtus VI and the reigning Pope Innocent was Lucifer in disguise; now she pierced the falsehoods alleged about Caponsacchi (7. 1163–86). At Castelnuovo her sudden strength sprang from that same confidence: " 'Twas truth singed the lies / And saved me, not the vain sword nor weak speech!" (7. 1640–41.) The shadows of the deceptions which formerly environed her disappeared, and now, in her dying hours, like Caponsacchi she dedicates herself to uttering the truth she has learned through trial:

> my last breath shall wholly spend itself
> In one attempt more to disperse the stain,
> The mist from other breath fond mouths have made,
> About a lustrous and pellucid soul.
>
> (7. 932–35)

Giving final evidence that she has been enabled to tell the real from the false, she declares, "Marriage on earth seems such a counterfeit, / Mere imitation of the inimitable: / In heaven we have the real and true and sure." (7. 1824–26.)

I I I

All the other characters in the poem are somehow involved in the practice or allegation of disguise, pretense, or double identity.[9] While it may not be true that, as Browning says Livy wrote, Arezzo was "Founded by Janus of the Double Face" (12. 811), certainly that most suitable of divinities presides over the poem. Even the Pope does not escape the accusation of being something other than what he seemed: Guido maintains that, by turning down his appeal, the Pope has disabused men "of our strange conceit / Of the angel in man's likeness, that we loved / And looked should help us at a pinch" (11. 59–61).

The "part-man part-monster" Guido (1. 1294), not surprisingly, is surrounded by relatives and servants who in various ways reflect his duplicity and hybrid nature. The Pope condemns Paolo as

> This fox-faced horrible priest, this brother-brute
> The Abate,—why, mere wolfishness looks well,
> Guido stands honest in the red o' the flame,
> Beside this yellow that would pass for white,
> This Guido,[10] all craft but no violence,
> This copier of the mien and gait and garb
> Of Peter and Paul, that he may go disguised,
> Rob halt and lame, sick folk i' the temple-porch!
> Armed with religion, fortified by law,
> A man of peace, who trims the midnight lamp
> And turns the classic page—and all for craft,
> All to work harm with, yet incur no scratch!
>
> (10. 879–90)

[9] Even incidental objects occasionally have multiple aspects, though not necessarily with any deception implied. Thus, in a kind of visual pun, the "paper toque" the boy Hyacinth is to wear at his birthday party (8. 1752) not only represents his father's professional headgear but suggests, as well, the tall hat of a chef.

[10] "Guido" occurs in the manuscript as well as in the printed text. But surely the context requires "Paolo"?

His brother Girolamo, similarly, is

> nor wolf nor fox,
> But hybrid, neither craft nor violence
> Wholly, part violence part craft: such cross
> Tempts speculation—will both blend one day,
> And prove hell's better product?
>
> (10. 897–901)

Guido's maidservant Margherita not only is "part-messenger / Part-mistress" (6. 553–54)—"Most of us have two functions in his house," she says (6. 522)—but also is "a masked muffled mystery" as she delivers the letter to Caponsacchi (6. 506) and "would personate the wife" (6. 554) in the scene which Guido devises to ensnare Caponsacchi.[11]

The Comparini also are capable of pretending, of being mistaken for what they are not, and of being deceived. On her visit to the hovel where Pompilia's prospective mother does business, "A woman who professed the wanton's trade / Under the requisite thin coverture, / *Communis meretrix* and washer-wife" (2. 561–63), Violante is mistaken first for the woman's procurer and then, in a violent revision, for "Madonna's self" (4. 159–63). Taking Pompilia to be married by a priest (*"perhaps* Abate Paolo" [3. 455]), Violante is disguised both figuratively and literally. She

> fairly wrapped herself
> In her integrity three folds about,
> And, letting pass a little day or two,
> Threw, even over that integrity,
> Another wrappage, namely one thick veil
> That hid her, matron-wise, from head to foot,
> And, by the hand holding a girl veiled too,

---

[11] The Franceschini's taste for revising reality to suit their private ends survived Guido's death and Paolo's prudential exit from Rome. Browning reports that their sister won from the Aretine authorities a fresh "public attestation to the right / O' the Franceschini to men's reverence" (12. 781–87). By exacting a vote of confidence in the very aftermath of Guido's bloody deed, the family made a further, and peculiarly gratuitous, contribution to the sum of human error.

> Stood, one dim end of a December day,
> In Saint Lorenzo on the altar-step.
>
> (3. 442–50)

Having been informed by the excited Violante, in terms too
elegant for his limited brain, that Pompilia has been identified
as "the Hesperian ball / Ordained for Hercules to haste and
pluck," Pietro rubs his eyes, "Look[s] very wise" and proceeds for enlightenment to the loafers assembled at the Boat-
fountain. They are delighted to tell him that

> Hercules was just the heir
> To the stubble once a corn-field, and brick-heap
> Where used to be a dwelling-place now burned.
> Guido and Franceschini; a Count,—ay:
> But a cross i' the poke to bless the Countship? No!
>
> (3. 384–401)

Gullible but well-meaning in some versions, the Comparini are
quite the opposite in others. After their revelation of her
illegitimacy, says Guido, Pompilia should have denounced
them as "fiends, who drop disguise and glare revealed / In
your own shape, no longer father mine / Nor mother mine!"
(5. 788–90.)

Both lawyers, by the character of their profession as well as
by natural inclination, play roles. Bottini is distinguished both
by his theatrical manner and by his dual nature. He is, says
Browning, a "composite" creature.

> Odds of age joined in him with ends of youth.
> A man of ready smile and facile tear,
> Improvised hopes, despairs at nod and beck,
> And language—ah, the gift of eloquence!
>
> (1. 1174–79)

The "outside man" is a curious mixture: "Blue juvenile pure
eye, and pippin cheek, / And brow all prematurely soiled and
seamed / With sudden age, bright devastated hair." (1.
1197–99.) His rival Arcangeli portrays him as a "pale-haired
red-eyed ferret which pretends / 'Tis ermine, pure soft
snow from tail to snout" (8. 225–26). Beneath the surface

generally suggestive of innocence smolders, as we are given much reason to know, the hidden fire of the sensualist.

Incidental physical settings, accessories, and situations add their share of "casual ambiguity" (9. 704). The damage done by the crowd come to view the Comparini's bodies in the church of San Lorenzo reveals that what looked like porphyry was actually "wooden work / Painted like porphyry to deceive the eye" (2. 94–95; cf. 6. 313–16). A nobleman, according to Guido, paid the value of a whole farm for a painting by Pietro of Cortona which "probably / His scholar Ciro Ferri may have retouched" (5. 488–89), the sly implication being that the picture was not a genuine work of the master.[12] After the execution, Arcangeli writes a Janus-faced letter to his Florentine correspondent ("old fox" [12. 292]), one sober side for display to clients, the other, more confidential, for the reader's private edification. The public message refers reverently to "His Blessed Memory / Count Guido Franceschini now with God" (12. 241–42), whereas privately Arcangeli remarks, in a quite different vein and with a jocose play on Caponsacchi's name, that "Somebody's thick headpiece . . . was bent / On seeing Guido's drop into the bag" (12. 299–300).[13] At Castelnuovo Pompilia mistakes the "reddening white" of sunset for the "whitening red" of daybreak (3. 1189–91). Part of

---

[12] Another form of "retouching"—ghost-writing—is not unknown in the church of *The Ring and the Book*. The Archbishop at Arezzo has written a "masterly" attack on Molinism, assisted by "somebody [who] could help / And touch up an odd phrase in time of need, / (He, he!)" (6. 360–64), and he keeps "a heavy scholar cloistered up, / Close under lock and key" writing an anti-Fénelon polemic for him (6. 321–24). A peasant's son rose to ecclesiastical preferment by writing another anti-Molinist attack and dropping it on the desk of a Cardinal "Who, deep in thought and absent much of mind, / Licensed the thing, allowed it for his own" (5. 205–6). And Arcangeli, implying that ghost-writers can be useful at the very pinnacle of the church, stresses the Pope's need for one in order to make his position clear on the Franceschini case. The lawyer, in the interests of little Giacintino's future, is not loath to offer his services (8. 104–15).

[13] The pun, which is also found at 2. 1249, may have an oblique reference to the apocryphal story of Judith and Holofernes, alluded to by Bottini (9. 567–73). Judith deposited the Assyrian general Holofernes' head in a sack after detaching it from his person (Jth. 13).

Guido's strategy in bending Pompilia to his will, so he says, was harmless bluster, which unsympathetic observers wrongly interpreted as cruelty:

> threatening, talking big,
> Showing hair-powder, a prodigious pinch,
> For poison in a bottle,—making believe
> At desperate doings with a bauble-sword,
> And other bugaboo-and-baby-work.
>
> (5. 947–51)

His was only a "poor lathen dagger," no murderous Bilboa sword (5. 849–50). The "pitch" that Aretines noticed on Pompilia's limbs—alluding to the story of Hesione's daubing pitch on herself to "elude the purblind monster" (9. 976)— actually, says Bottini, was nothing more than the bruises left by her savior Caponsacchi's "more than duly energetic" gripe (9. 1002–6).

A biblical case of mistaken identity, that of Rachel, Leah, and Jacob, is the basis of Paolo's argument in a letter to Guido, warning him that he has no grounds for his contemplated suit for divorce (5. 1309–22; see below, p. 209). In another ingenious adaptation of an inherited story, Bottini recalls the tale of Peter, John, and Judas, wayfarers faced with the problem of having but one starveling fowl to satisfy three hungry stomachs. They agree that the man who dreams the happiest dream will get the fowl. Judas reports that he "dreamed I dreamed; and in that mimic dream / (Impalpable to dream as dream to fact)" he saw himself stealing down to the inn kitchen and eating the fowl. He cheerfully renounces the prize, which his companions, struck with sudden horrid suspicion, discover belongs to him both in theory and in fact, as the dreamer of the happiest dream: he has been beforehand, and eaten it just as he "dreamed" he did (9. 1040–1106). The double illusion is tied to a double cross—an assocation symbolic of a great deal of the moral meaning of *The Ring and the Book*.[14]

[14] Elsewhere, other cases of mistaken identity or interpretation are referred to. Bottini cites Mary Magdalene's mistaking Jesus for a gardener (9. 936–39), and earlier he suggests that Guido was wrong

I V

If the world of the poem is one of illusion, it is equally one of change. Man's existence, we learn, is marked by ceaseless instability of forms and appearances. In the climactic passage of Book 1 Browning stresses at once the incompleteness, the complexity, the relativity, and the changeability of human knowledge. A view of life which fails to take account of them is no more natural or faithful than an arrested-motion photograph:

> See it for yourselves,
> This man's act, changeable because alive!
> Action now shrouds, now shows the informing thought;
> Man, like a glass ball with a spark a-top,
> Out of the magic fire that lurks inside,
> Shows one tint at a time to take the eye:
> Which, let a finger touch the silent sleep,
> Shifted a hair's-breadth shoots you dark for bright,
> Suffuses bright with dark, and baffles so
> Your sentence absolute for shine or shade.
> Once set such orbs,—white styled, black stigmatized,—
> A-rolling, see them once on the other side
> Your good men and your bad men every one,
> From Guido Franceschini to Guy Faux,
> Oft would you rub your eyes and change your names.
>
> (1. 1364–78)

Thus ambiguity of character and appearance is inseparable from change: sometimes the white shows, sometimes the black,

---

in thinking Pompilia a serpent when she really was an eel (9. 392–93). The Pope at one point imagines himself making a false diagnosis and consequently treating for "a frenzy-fit, / A falling-sickness or a fever-stroke" a patient who, it turns out after he has died, was actually bitten by a serpent (10. 242–55).

as the man turns or as the beholder shifts his position. Witness the continual shift in the appearance of the Franceschini case as speaker after speaker tells his tale. Only in the accounts of the heroic pair, Caponsacchi and Pompilia, can essential agreement be found, and even here some events, vividly perceived at the time, are recollected only as blurs because of the physical or emotional exhaustion which attended either the experience or the remembrance, or both (cf. 6. 1179; 7. 1566).[15] And Caponsacchi's own account underwent alteration between his earlier testimony before the court and the narrative reproduced in the poem. As he says, "I' the colour the tale takes, there's change perhaps; / 'Tis natural, since the sky is different, / Eclipse in the air now." (6. 1646–48.)

The vicissitudes of truth in a world populated by the blind, the biased, and the mendacious are foretold by a series of linked images in Book 1 in which Browning recounts the fate of man's knowledge of the Franceschini case and his own intervention to restore the lost truth. When the murderers were caught and brought to justice, good (truth) initially triumphed over evil (falsehood). But at once the daybreak of truth was clouded by the "world's bystanders" (1. 642) and their ill-informed versions of what had happened. At length, but again only for a moment, truth prevailed with the wise judgment of the Pope. As the years passed, however, new lies crowded into the memory of the case, and then the memory itself became like a pillar of a ruined temple, which proved to be sandstone, not granite, and was worn away by "time's tooth" until only its "entablature, / . . . no bigger than a book," remained (1. 666–72). Now the "entablature"—sole remaining fragment of what was once the Franceschini affair in all its detail—is transformed into the book it resembles: the "square old yellow book" Browning found in a jumble of second-hand oddments, the detritus of the past. From the book (represented earlier in Book 1 by a gold ingot—a square

---

[15] Guido claims sympathy on the strength of a like emotional blackout en route. "I have no memory of our way," he says of his traveling Romeward with his hirelings, bent on Pompilia's death (5. 1568).

block of precious metal) he finally fashions a ring, his poetic
imagination filling the silences of history. The transmutation
of entablature into book, and then of book into ring, is a
symbolic anticipation of the theme of change which pervades
the rest of the poem.

Instances of reversal and instability occur again and again.
Guido's moral façade, as has been noted, undergoes a bewildering variety of changes in both his monologues. The rela-
tions between Caponsacchi and the judges, as well as their
very demeanors, are reversed in the interval between their two
confrontations. At Caponsacchi's second appearance, "the accused of eight months since"

> Now is grown judge himself, terrifies now
> This, now the other culprit called a judge,
> Whose turn it is to stammer and look strange,
> As he speaks rapidly, angrily, speech that smites.
>
> (1. 1063–70)

Tertium Quid's audience is in a continuous state of flux as he
dissertates on the case. One conspicuous element in the confrontation scene at Castelnuovo is the fickleness of the onlookers, whose sympathies shift from Guido to Pompilia as
she stands in Caponsacchi's defense. But perhaps the most
mordant commentary on the human creature's changeability is
the aptly named Convertites' and Bottini's readiness to
"volte-face and chop, change sides" (12. 713) when the former discover that Pompilia, "who seemed so poor, proves
rich" (10. 1506). In view of this altered situation, "The kiss
turns bite, / The dove's note changes to the crow's cry. . . .
They unsay / All the fine speeches,—who was saint is whore."
(10. 1508–9, 1522–23.) Bottini, whose line of argument in
Pompilia's "defense" has seemed to give much color to the
nuns' new position, welcomes the opportunity to befoul in
earnest the name he has (in his own estimation) just finished
"sainting." He has already made a good start.[16]

---

[16] Even characters who merely occur in analogies manifest the
same ambiguity of appearance or action. The "Swiss guard off duty"
to whom the guillotine is compared is "both gay and grim" (11.

Caponsacchi's agonized vacillation of mood and purpose, as he weighs his respective duties toward the church and toward Pompilia, reflects the alternation of night and day. "I' the grey of dawn" outside the Pieve, he finds assurance that his obligation is to the church (and, as he listens, the church's imagined tone changes from "quip" to "scrannel voice"). He obeys.

> So, I went home. Dawn broke, noon broadened, I—
> I sat stone-still, let time run over me.
> The sun slanted into my room, had reached
> The west. I opened book,—Aquinas blazed
> With one black name only on the white page.
> I looked up, saw the sunset.
>
> (6. 1022–27) [17]

He repairs to his stall, reads his office, returns home, sits in the dark. "Again the morning found me, . . . / So the day wore." But when it is again evening, his mind is made up and he presents himself beneath Pompilia's window (6. 1034–64). Meanwhile, by a kind of symbolic sympathy, Pompilia is witnessing the same alternation of light and dark:

> No pause i' the leading and the light! I know,
> Next night there was a cloud came, and not he:
> But I prayed through the darkness till it broke
> And let him shine. The second night, he came.
>
> (7. 1458–61)

208–9), and a soprano who is all the rage in the current Roman season is

> dressed up like Armida, though a man;
> And painted to look pretty, though a fright,—
> He still made love so that the ladies swooned,
> Being an eunuch, "Ah, Rinaldo mine!
> But to breathe by thee while Jove slays us both!"
>
> (11. 1411–15)

[17] Earlier (6. 500–501) it had been Pompilia's smile, not her name, that "kept glowing out of" the page of the *Summa:* another incidental example of transformation.

When he speaks,

> I felt that, the same loyalty—one star
> Turning now red that was so white before—
> One service apprehended newly: just
> A word of mine and there the white was back!
>
> (7. 1467–70)

Caponsacchi's achievement, rendered more heroic by this en-
veloping atmosphere of change, is that his uncertainty is at last
vanquished by confidence.

A remarkable number of images suggest fluctuation of judgment or vision. All the leading speakers, by their occasional
use of what in a cinematic age would be called the "dissolve,"
reveal in their metaphor-making their awareness of life's instability. When he condemns Guido's hypocrisy and cruelty toward the Comparini, the Pope employs a formal epic simile:

> As when, in our Campagna, there is fired
> The nest-like work that lets a peasant house;
> And, as the thatch burns here, there, everywhere,
> Even to the ivy and wild vine, that bound
> And blessed the hut where men were happy once,
> There rises gradual, black amid the blaze,
> Some grim and unscathed nucleus of the nest,—
> Some old malicious tower, some obscene tomb
> They thought a temple in their ignorance,
> And clung about and thought to lean upon—
> There laughs it o'er their ravage,—where are they?
> So did his cruelty burn life about,
> And lay the ruin bare in dreadfulness.
>
> (10. 619–31)

And in one of the poem's most deftly managed images, quoted
on page 50 above, Guido describes his own vacillation before
the murders in concurrent terms of shifting picture and song.
The Holy Infant's face and halo at first obscured Satan's face,
but soon, as if infected by what lay behind,

> The Babe's face, premature with peak and pine,
> Sank into wrinkled ruinous old age,

> Suffering and death, then mist-like disappeared,
> And showed only the Cross at end of all. . . .
>
> (5. 1603–6)

Fifty lines later, the metaphorical opposition thus initiated of Christ and Satan concludes with a dramatic new twist, the reintroduction of Violante as the true villain. When Guido knocked at the door,

> Violante Comparini, she it was,
> With the old grin amid the wrinkles yet,
> Opened: as if in turning from the Cross,
> With trust to keep the sight and save my soul,
> I had stumbled, first thing, on the serpent's head
> Coiled with a leer at foot of it.
>
> (5. 1655–60)

The image is both stable and dynamic: the physical attributes of "wrinkled ruinous old age" are a constant, but their possessor varies with the course of the figure.

The most frequent reminder of flux, however, is the constant shift of metaphorical appearance that all the main characters undergo throughout the poem, a phenomenon which will receive separate treatment in chapter 8. But this is the place to note the number of metaphors which individually represent transformations of character. The Other Half-Rome's report of Guido's complaint at Castelnuovo is a notable example of what occurs, usually in smaller compass, at many other places. The shift of attributes transforms Pompilia from a caressable, though deceitful, lamb into a railing shrew;

> The past
> Took quite another shape now. She who shrieked
> "At least and for ever I am mine and God's,
> Thanks to his liberating angel Death—
> Never again degraded to be yours
> The ignoble noble, the unmanly man,
> The beast below the beast in brutishness!"—
> This was the froward child, "the restif lamb
> Used to be cherished in his breast," he groaned—
> "Eat from his hand and drink from out his cup,

> The while his fingers pushed their loving way
> Through curl on curl of that soft coat—alas,
> And she all silverly baaed gratitude
> While meditating mischief!"—and so forth.

(3. 1293–1306)

Natural and unnatural history, mythology, and popular lore all assist in depicting the changeability of human character or appearance. Pompilia, a "fragile egg, some careless wild bird dropped," hatches into a finch, according to her sympathizer the Other Half-Rome (3. 215–17)—or, beginning as a cuckoo's egg laid in his nest, hatches into a cockatrice, according to Guido (5. 655–57). Bottini sees her as a dove whose molting has brightened her "dingy feathers" into silver and gold (9. 1231–32), and the Pope envisions her as a "poor trampled worm" from which "springs up a serpent" (10. 698–99). She herself remembers a childhood fancy in which she was Daphne in a tapestry, transformed into a tree (7. 193–96). Caponsacchi is a "hornet" hatched from a "grey innocuous grub" (4. 1157–58), an "Apollos turned Apollo" (2. 794), an athlete in the Roman arena changed into a medieval knight (10. 1140–65). Pietro and Violante, says Guido, were

> two ambiguous insects, changing name
> And nature with the season's warmth or chill,—
> Now, grovelled, grubbing toiling moiling ants,
> A very synonym of thrift and peace,—
> Anon, with lusty June to prick their heart,
> Soared i' the air, winged flies for more offence.

(11. 1260–66) [18]

The one metaphor which repeatedly unites the closely associated ideas of false appearance, unsubstantiality, evanescence, and futility is that of a bubble. In a sense, the whole

---

[18] The same mutation motif is found in the description of Bottini's oration as a "finished butterfly" metamorphosed from a worm in a cabbage bed (1. 1168–71), in Half-Rome's assertion that the Comparini's family life was a "cabbage-plot / . . . turned fools'-paradise" (2. 254–55), and in Bottini's derisive remark that Celestino's "Noah's-dove that brought the olive back, / Is turned into the other sooty scout, / The raven" (12. 723–25).

poem is dominated by the memorable first image of Guido as a "bloated bubble" ("star supposed, but fog o' the fen, / Gilded star-fashion by a glint from hell") which is rolled, a "starlike pest[ilence]" to Rome, "And stationed . . . to suck up and absorb / The sweetness of Pompilia" (1. 544–58). All the succeeding allusions to a bubble necessarily are colored by our recollection of that terrible expanded image. Henceforth the bubble usually has its traditional symbolism of the vanity of earthly pride and possessions. Guido, we are told, had discovered the futility of ambition long before the Comparini did: "That bubble, they were bent on blowing big, / He had blown already till he burst his cheeks, / And hence found soapsuds bitter to the tongue." (2. 454–56.) Events at Arezzo proved how fruitless it was to barter the cherished family honor for "something with value of another sort." Guido testifies he has spent

> fifty years in guarding bubbles of breath,
> Soapsuds with air i' the belly, gilded brave,
> Guarded and guided, all to break at touch
> O' the first young girl's hand and first old fool's purse!
>
> (5. 441–52)

In the condemned cell, he recognizes that if he were freed, one more stroke of the capricious fortune which has repeatedly victimized him would make his life unbearable:

> The popular sympathy that's round me now
> Would break like bubble that o'er-domes a fly—
> Pretty enough while he lies quiet there,
> But let him want the air and ply the wing,
> Why, it breaks and bespatters him, what else?
>
> (11. 1811–15)

But there are also those who hold the bubble of fame in contempt. Caponsacchi, in his own way, has reconciled himself to the loss of reputation which must follow from an uncomprehending world's beholding a priest involved with a married woman: "If so my worldly reputation burst, / Being the bubble it is, why, burst it may." (3. 1353–54.) Significantly,

Celestino employs the same image at the climax of his sermon: [19]

> Fame,—that bubble which, world-wide
> Each blows and bids his neighbour lend a breath,
> That so he haply may behold thereon
> One more enlarged distorted false fool's-face,
> Until some glassy nothing grown as big
> Send by a touch the imperishable to suds,—
> No, in renouncing fame, the loss was light,
> Choosing obscurity, the chance was well!
>
> (12. 635–42)

The action of time upon illusions results often in bitter discovery of reality: the bursting bubble is an emblem of disillusionment. If the narrative of *The Ring and the Book* is, as we have said, one long series of deceptions, it contains an equally long series of discoveries—piercings of illusions, discreditings of falsehoods, and resultant glimpses of truth. Disillusionment, Guido argues, is the common lot of man and the age-old subject of comedy. Recalling the Comparini's outrage when they found that his ramshackle palazzo, which they had expected to find a sybarites' paradise, was in fact a thriving outpost of hell, he appeals

> to Plautus, Terence, Boccaccio's Book,
> My townsman, frank Ser Franco's merry Tales,—
> To all who strip a vizard from a face,
> A body from its padding, and a soul
> From froth and ignorance it styles itself,—
> If this be other than the daily hap
> Of purblind greed that dog-like still drops bone,
> Grasps shadow, and then howls the case is hard!
>
> (5. 559–66)

There is grim but apt irony in the poem's final moment of discovery, for Guido himself provided the last occasion of

---

[19] Derided by Bottini, of all people, as "ampollosity" (12. 643)— Browning's coinage, says Cook (*Commentary*, p. 271), from the Italian *ampollosità*, which in turn stems from the Latin *ampullari*, "to use inflated language."

disillusionment. When the executioner showed the Count's severed head to the expectant populace, who had been encouraged to believe he was "Youngish, considering his fifty years, / And, if not handsome, dignified at least," they found that "Indeed, it was no face to please a wife!" (12. 190–96.)

Whatever his views might have been at this moment, such stripping away of illusions is, as Guido maintained, a staple of comedy. Rude confrontations of illusion with reality have their undeniable humor. But in *The Ring and the Book*, as in life, they are at least as often the stuff of tragedy. No comedy resides in Pompilia's discovery, before she and Guido had cohabited a month, that he was "a devil and no man" (5. 612–13). What is found behind the veil of appearance is, on the whole, less likely to evoke laughter than sheer horror.

If, as all these instances of change and undependability together suggest, impermanence is a condition of existence, what hope can men cling to? To Browning, mutability can be countered by spiritual mastery, by man's dedicated approach while still in the flesh to the source and symbol of all permanence. Abiding, unshakable judgment—the ability to pierce behind the noisy conflict of prejudice and rumor and false appearance—is to be found only in men of integrity and wisdom; men, that is, who have toiled, dared, and loved their way to God. Both Pompilia and Caponsacchi are, at the outset, victims of change and uncertainty. But from the moment of their meeting—the great spiritual epiphany of the poem—hesitation ceases, and ignorance gives way to steady vision: "no change / Here, though all else changed in the changing world!" (7. 1414–15.) And this new state they discover is prophetic of the life to come, of "the gloriously-decisive change, / The immeasurable metamorphosis / Of human clay to divine gold" (10. 1614–16) that occurs at the moment of final judgment. Transformation to pure spirit that is forever impervious to change, says Browning, is the promise Christianity offers to those who would escape the flickering shadows of the mutable world of men.

Four

The "Filthy Rags of Speech"

LANGUAGE AS DECEPTION

I

To Browning, language is at once a product, symbol, and instrument of illusion and deception. It is the most inadequate as it is the most treacherous of intellectual tools. The attenuation and distortion which meaning undergoes between speaker and hearer is all too familiar a mark of man's fallen state. So declares the Pope, his mind wearied, his spirit dismayed by his long examination of the legal papers accompanying Guido's appeal—"Pleadings and counter-pleadings, figure of fact / Beside fact's self" (10. 215–16) in which language has turned meaning into a mere travesty of truth. But when the Pope and all other men are finally called before God, human speech will no longer impede nor conveniently becloud instant and complete communication.

> None of this vile way by the barren words
> Which, more than any deed, characterize
> Man as made subject to a curse: no speech—
> That still bursts o'er some lie which lurks inside,
> As the split skin across the coppery snake,
> And most denotes man! since, in all beside,
> In hate or lust or guile or unbelief,
> Out of some core of truth the excrescence comes,
> And, in the last resort, the man may urge
> "So was I made, a weak thing that gave way
> To truth, to impulse only strong since true,
> And hated, lusted, used guile, forwent faith."

112

> But when man walks the garden of this world
> For his own solace, and, unchecked by law,
> Speaks or keeps silence as himself sees fit,
> Without the least incumbency to lie,
> —Why, can he tell you what a rose is like,
> Or how the birds fly, and not slip to false
> Though truth serve better? Man must tell his mate
> Of you, me and himself, knowing he lies,
> Knowing his fellow knows the same,—will think
> "He lies, it is the method of a man!"
> And yet will speak for answer "It is truth"
> To him who shall rejoin "Again a lie!"
> Therefore this [1] filthy rags of speech, this coil
> Of statement, comment, query and response,
> Tatters all too contaminate for use,
> Have no renewing: He, the Truth, is, too,
> The Word. We men, in our degree, may know
> There, simply, instantaneously, as here
> After long time and amid many lies,
> Whatever we dare think we know indeed
> —That I am I, as He is He,—what else?
> But be man's method for man's life at least!

(10. 348–81)

Despite all its weaknesses, however, language remains the primary way of learning what lies beyond our immediate preception; "For how else know we save by worth of word?" (1. 837.) Language, with its inherent resistance, is a necessary means of stepping down the voltage of pure incandescent truth to the dull red glow tolerable to man. And so through the whole hierarchy of being. Just as the ultimate truth is reduced to suit the varied intelligences of the orders of creation, so must occupants of the various levels be reached by language appropriate to their stations. Arcangeli couches this far-reaching truth in a homely metaphor:

> We must translate our motives like our speech
> Into the lower phrase that suits the sense

---

[1] Both the manuscript and the first edition read "this," despite the obvious lack of grammatical agreement.

> O' the limitedly apprehensive. Let
> Each level have its language! Heaven speaks first
> To the angel, then the angel tames the word
> Down to the ear of Tobit: he, in turn,
> Diminishes the message to his dog,
> And finally that dog finds how the flea
> (Which else, importunate, might check his speed)
> Shall learn its hunger must have holiday,—
> How many varied sorts of language here,
> Each following each with pace to match the step,
> *Haud passibus aequis!*
>
> (8. 1498–1510)

Guido, too, maintains that language is necessary to put the sensed into the more accessible form of the heard:

> God breathes, not speaks, his verdicts, felt
> not heard,
>
> .   .   .   .
>
> Justinian's Pandects only make precise
> What simply sparkled in men's eyes before,
> Twitched in their brow or quivered on their lip,
> Waited the speech they called but would not come.
>
> (5. 1771–84)

His argument here, though containing a solid pebble of truth, obviously is adapted to his situation: it occurs as he advances his contention that natural instinct, as formalized by man's law, justifies his conduct. Pursuing the argument further in the same speech, Guido maintains that the very act of putting moral principles and penalties into the words of the law distorts their intent, chiefly by mitigating the latter's severity. As a result, the punishment allowed by the formal code is too lenient for the deed, and justice requires action, even violence, on the part of the injured one to restore and put into effect the spirit of law's decrees where the letter is ineffectual. In his murder of the Comparini, therefore,

> I have heightened phrase to make your soft
> speech serve,
> Doubled the blow you but essayed to strike,

Carried into effect your mandate here
That else had fallen to ground: . . .

. . . .

[I] have simply . . .
Blackened again, made legible once more
Your own decree, not permanently writ,
Rightly conceived but all too faintly traced.

(5. 1990–99)

The inherent weakness of language well serves those who would impugn, for their own ends, institutions reared on linguistic foundations—church, law, and politics.

Language is a means of obliterating moral distinctions and degrees: it "goes as easy as a glove / O'er good and evil, smoothens both to one" (1. 1180–81). Language also is the chosen camouflage of the hypocrite, or, to use the hypocrite's own euphemism, the "decent wrappage" for motives that are best left unexpressed. Of this truth, the brilliantly specious defense of the marriage contract, offered by Tertium Quid in Guido's behalf and then by Guido himself, is the most memorable example in the poem. Tertium Quid explains:

There was a bargain mentally proposed
On each side, straight and plain and fair enough;
Mind knew its own mind: but when mind must speak,
The bargain have expression in plain terms,
There was the blunder incident to words,
And in the clumsy process, fair turned foul.
The straight backbone-thought of the crooked speech
Were just—"I Guido truck my name and rank
For so much money and youth and female charms."—
"We Pietro and Violante give our child
And wealth to you for a rise i' the world thereby."
Such naked truth while chambered in the brain
Shocks nowise: walk it forth by way of tongue,—
Out on the cynical unseemliness!
Hence was the need, on either side, of a lie
To serve as decent wrappage: so, Guido gives
Money for money,—and they, bride for groom,
Having, he not a doit, they, not a child

Honestly theirs, but this poor waif and stray.
According to the words, each cheated each;
But in the inexpressive barter of thoughts,
Each did give and did take the thing designed,
The rank on this side and the cash on that—
Attained the object of the traffic, so.
The way of the world, the daily bargain struck
In the first market! Why sells Jack his ware?
"For the sake of serving an old customer."
Why does Jill buy it? "Simply not to break
A custom, pass the old stall the first time."
Why, you know where the gist is of the exchange:
Each sees a profit, throws the fine words in.

                                              (4. 508–38)

For his part, Guido urges that the arrangement was a mere
matching of *quid pro quo,*

Mere rank against mere wealth—some youth beside,
Some beauty too, thrown into the bargain, just
As the buyer likes or lets alone. I thought
To deal o' the square: others find fault, it seems:

.   .   .   .

I am charged, I know, with gilding fact by fraud;
I falsified and fabricated, wrote
Myself down roughly richer than I prove,
Rendered a wrong revenue,—grant it all!
Mere grace, mere coquetry such fraud, I say:
A flourish round the figures of a sum
For fashion's sake, that deceives nobody.
The veritable back-bone, understood
Essence of this same bargain, blank and bare,
Being the exchange of quality for wealth,—
What may such fancy-flights be? . . .

.   .   .   .

They knew and I knew where the back-bone lurked
I' the writhings [2] of the bargain, lords, believe!

                                              (5. 475–511)

[2] "Writhings" provides an ingenious connection between the written
flourishes spoken of earlier (note the implicit pun on "writings")

The Pope's verdict on such sophistry is curt and bitter: "All say good words / To who will hear, all do thereby bad deeds / To who must undergo; so thrive mankind!" (10. 517–19.)

The double intention so easily available in language also is observable in another kind of "marriage contract" which figures in the story. Religious vows, semantically distorted, smooth the path of the unrighteous. "Thou foolish boy!" smiled the bishop to whom Caponsacchi protested that he could not, as a weak, unworthy man of flesh, "engage to keep such vow inviolate":

> Clear up the clouds and cast thy scruples far!
> I satisfy thee there's an easier sense
> Wherein to take such vow than suits the first
> Rough rigid reading. Mark what makes all smooth,
> Nay, has been even a solace to myself!
> The Jews who needs must, in their synagogue,
> Utter sometimes the holy name of God,
> A thing their superstition boggles at,
> Pronounce aloud the ineffable sacrosanct,—
> How does their shrewdness help them? In this wise;
> Another set of sounds they substitute,
> Jumble so consonants and vowels—how
> Should I know?—that there grows from out the old
> Quite a new word that means the very same—
> And o'er the hard place slide they with a smile.
>
>   (6. 269–89) [3]

In addition to being a deceptive but attractive husk to conceal ignoble motives and a device to circumvent spiritual

---

and the often-iterated image of a snake, with its suggestions of slipperiness. Both "back-bone" and "writhings" are naturally suggested to Guido by his late sojourn on the rack.

[3] To show that the letter of language may divert attention and energy away from its spirit, the Pope refers to an actual contemporary occurrence in China, when a raging dispute between Jesuit and Dominican missionaries as to the proper Chinese name for God required the dispatch of a papal legate to the scene to "compose the difference" (10. 1590–1603). So, he says, a potentate may fume over some trivial infringement of his territory while whole cities are being destroyed by plague or famine.

truth, language lends itself to the execution of wily schemes—and to diverse misinterpretations of their import. Witness the discrepant accounts of the form and therefore the purpose of the password Guido used to gain admittance to the Comparini's house. Did he, as a wronged but still hopeful husband, intend to put Pompilia's innocence to a final test? Or did he speak the password simply to gain entrance without resorting to force? Were the exact words simply "Giuseppe Caponsacchi," as Half-Rome insisted (2. 1431)—the prompt opening of the door thus proving that Caponsacchi was an expected visitor, however illicit? Or were they, as the Other Half-Rome asserted, "A friend of Caponsacchi's bringing friends / A letter"? (3. 1598–99.) Or were the words (Tertium Quid this time) "Friends with a letter from the priest your friend"? (4. 1372.) Guido himself says the "predetermined touch for truth" which he used on the advice of his putative guardian angel was "What welcome for the wanderer? Open straight—/ . . . to Caponsacchi!" (5. 1629–33.) Whatever the formula, Pompilia reveals that she was by no means unprepared to respond to the cry. "It was the name of him I sprang to meet / When came the knock, the summons and the end. / 'My great heart, my strong hand are back again!' " (7. 1808–10.) So, ironically, Guido's alleged suspicions were well founded, though for reasons he would be incapable of understanding. In any event, interpretation of this climactic scene depends largely on the multiple implications a word or phrase can possess, and on its user's true motives in employing it. Purpose in the use of language can be as ambiguous as the words themselves.

Once in a while, however, language put to the purposes of trickery accidentally serves a good cause, just as outright lies may. Written communications are the instruments by which Guido schemes to compromise his wife and Caponsacchi. He conducts a ghost correspondence between the two, Pompilia's incoming share of which is necessarily read to her by Guido's tool, Margherita. Caponsacchi, annoyed yet inexplicably attracted by the letters he receives from Pompilia (actually of course from Guido), sends peppery replies, culminating in the promise that he will appear beneath her window. Margherita reads these also to Pompilia, but puts another construction on his words, making of them a plain invitation to adultery and elopement: "the agent put her sense into my [i.e., Caponsacchi's] words, / Made substitution of the thing she hoped, / For the thing she had and held, its opposite." (6. 1807–9.) But as Caponsacchi discovers when he first speaks to Pompilia, both sets of letters—Guido's forged ones, which Margherita had read as they were written, and Caponsacchi's genuine ones, which she had misquoted or misconstrued—had an effect upon Pompilia wholly unlike that intended in either case, and yet, again ironically, still serving Guido's aim. Caponsacchi's letters, both the fabricated and the genuine ones, had joined to arouse her hopes in her desperate plight:

> It cannot be she [Margherita] says the thing you mean;
> Such wickedness were deadly to us both:
> But good true love would help me now so much—
> I tell myself, you may mean good and true.
>
> (6. 735–38)

Out of this confusion of words, written and then misreported or misinterpreted for quite different purposes, sprang an unarticulated message from Caponsacchi to an inarticulately receptive Pompilia. "The spark of truth was struck from out our souls." (6. 1814.) As she explains to him when he comes:

> Friend, foolish words were borne from you to me;
> Your soul behind them is the pure strong wind,
> Not dust and feathers which its breath may bear:
> These to the witless seem the wind itself,
> Since proving thus the first of it they feel.
>
> (7. 1418–22)

False written and false spoken words in this instance precipitate a meeting of pure souls; language, normally an instrument of deception, has unintentionally provided the auspices of true communication. It takes the intervention of God, however, to bring about such a happy consequence; and the dramatic splendor with which Browning invests this rushing together of sympathetic spirits implies his belief that it was accomplished in spite of language rather than with language's assistance.

Words were present, but inoperative, when he "Recognized her, at potency of truth" and "she, by the crystalline soul, knew me" (6. 932–33).

The symbolic nature of language leads to the assumption that words are but "dust and feathers" or in Guido's phrase "mere wind" (11. 1491),[4] possessing only token significance. In one more respect, therefore, speech illustrates and deepens the universal contrast between shadow and substance. As she rides from Arezzo to Castelnuovo, Pompilia is so enveloped by her undefinable sense of the blessedness of the flight that "speech became mere talking through a sleep," empty of intention or coherence (3. 1138). In the cause of deceit, the language of the marriage service is reduced to a travesty of the spiritual essence it purports (but fails) to convey. To the frightened Pompilia it becomes unintelligible gabble: when she is brought to church, the priest "opened book, / Read here and there, made me say that and this, / And after, told me I was now a wife" (7. 445–47). And a measure of the indifference with which churchmen treat the sacred words when more urgent matters are on their minds is found in Canon Conti's use of the liturgy as mere punctuation for his whispered message to Caponsacchi at vespers:

> *In ex-cel-sis—*
> All's to no purpose: I have louted low,
> But he saw you staring—*quia sub*—don't incline
> To know you nearer . . .
>
> .   .   .   .
>
>   but there's the wife:
> Spare her, because he beats her, as it is,

---

[4] The difference between the children of light and the children of darkness in respect to their attitudes toward communication is epitomized in the contrast between Guido's use of "wind" and that of Pompilia, quoted just above. To Pompilia, "the pure strong wind" emblematizes true, uncorrupted communication, the "soul" behind the words—with a side allusion, perhaps, to the mystical voice of God as heard in the whirlwind at Pentecost (Acts 2:1–13). To Guido, however, the wind represents nothing more than the futility of words. By this cynical limitation, he inferentially rejects Pompilia's belief in the intuitive conveyance of meaning.

> She's breaking her heart quite fast enough—*jam tu*—
> So, be you rational and make amends
> With little Light-skirts yonder—*in secula*
> *Secu-lo-o-o-o-rum*. Ah, you rogue!
>
> (6. 438–49)

Words originally laden with powerful meaning can be weakened by repetition and abuse; men (to adopt an observation the Pope makes in another connection) become "too obtuse / Of ear, through iteration of command, / For catching quick the sense of the real cry" (10. 1197–99). This well-known fact of experience is illustrated by the vicissitudes of the word "truth," which is (of all words!) the poem's sorriest semantic casualty. It and the adjective "true" together occur some 317 times; and though they allude to the great theme of *The Ring and the Book* they are so abused that not the least suspenseful element in the poem is their struggle for survival as tokens of clear meaning. Already in Book 1 "truth" is necessarily used in so many ironic contexts that its dignity begins to be corrupted. Half-Rome, says Browning, will narrate his version of the Franceschini story "All for the truth's sake, mere truth, nothing else!" (1. 881), and the courts will "pump up and pour apace / Truth in a flowery foam shall wash the world" (1112–13). The more the succession of speakers—notably the three onlookers and Guido ("Now for truth!" [5. 120])—protest they are exhibiting the truth, all the while betraying their disqualification for the mission, the more suspect the word becomes. Its fate is like that of Caponsacchi's name in Pompilia's confused consciousness:

> That name had got to take a half-grotesque
> Half-ominous, wholly enigmatic sense,
> Like any bye-word, broken bit of song
> Born with a meaning, changed by mouth and mouth
> That mix it in a sneer or smile, as chance
> Bids, till it now means nought but ugliness
> And perhaps shame.
>
> (7. 1329–35)

The Pope temporarily rehabilitates "truth" by the vehemence with which he condemns hypocrisy and evasiveness. But the process of debasement is resumed in Guido's second defense, during which the reckless alternation of denial and asseveration places the word, and the concept, in more desperate danger than ever. Only at the last minute is its worth again proclaimed, when in his sermon Fra Celestino declares that, however abused it has been in the minds and mouths of men, truth is so precious a gift that God has miraculously intervened to vindicate its integrity—though, he adds, such occasions are rare.

In this ceaselessly talkative world resounding with accusation, explanation, extenuation, equivocation, and fabrication, a recurrent symbol of falsehood and evil, or at the very least, of inane argument, is noise—language reduced to confusion and unintelligibility. The "voices we call evidence," says Browning, are "uproar in the echo" (1. 833–34); the lawyers "wrangled, brangled, jangled" (1. 241), though only on paper; Guido and Pietro, in their suits and countersuits, "din / And deafen, full three years, at each long ear" of Judge Tommati (8. 265–66). The "Arezzo noise and trouble" (7. 1658) are loud, protracted, and, to Guido in particular, infuriating. Indeed, in his account of the various kinds of torture he has undergone, Guido's subjection to incessant noise is as much intended to evoke sympathy as is his experience of the rack or the more exquisite pain of being a known cuckold. The Comparini, discovering they had been cheated, shook Arezzo with their "hubbub," "hue and cry," "whimpering and wail," "a perfect goose-yard cackle of complaint." They resumed the "old noise" when they returned to Rome, and "clapped wing and crew / Fighting-cock-fashion" when they disclosed Pompilia's true origin (11. 1190–1209); and their triumphant noise found echo in the mighty chorus of ridicule the Aretines directed at Guido (5. 1306).[5]

---

[5] Guido is not the only sufferer. Pompilia too is distracted by noise, which she associates with hell (2. 691–93; 3. 1151). "Why," she asks on her deathbed, "should ill keep echoing ill, / And never let our ears have done with noise?" (7. 651–52). At the same time, quiet, the antithesis of noise, is at least twice associated in her person with innocence. When she and Violante, returning from the hasty wedding, are greeted by Pietro's genial questions about their absence, "Vio-

Nowhere in the poem is it suggested that any speech quoted is a product of divine inspiration; the closest God seems to come to guiding a character's language is when the deacon appointed to be Formosus' *advocatus diaboli,* who has been able only to speak "stammeringly forth / With white lips and dry tongue," is finally "emboldened by the Spirit" (10. 50–58). While human speech does, to some poor degree, serve as a vehicle for human transactions, it is totally useless in numinous matters, for which the unspoken Word of God alone suffices. A telling statement of the case can be derived from Bottini's boast, "I, it is, teach the monk [Celestino] what scripture means, / And that the tongue should prove a two-edged sword" (12. 707–8), modified in the light of its source in Hebrews (4:12): "For the word of God is quick, and powerful, and sharper than any two-edged sword." Man's tongue is indeed a treacherous two-edged sword—it can cut in behalf either of truth or of falsehood—but God's Word is infinitely stronger. " 'Twas truth singed the lies / And saved me," exclaims Pompilia as she recalls her sword-brandishing at Castelnuovo, "not the vain sword nor weak speech!" (7. 1640–41.) She might equally well have said "of" rather than "nor."

Much that transcends our material existence is in the realm of thoughts that lie too deep for words, as Pompilia in effect tells Caponsacchi at their first meeting. Later, troubled yet exalted by the first stirrings of her pregnancy, she says, "Why should I doubt He will explain in time / What I feel now, but fail to find the words?" (7. 1760–61.) Caponsacchi finds her silence more moving than any language as they ride toward Castelnuovo: "At times she drew a soft sigh—music seemed / Always to hover just above her lips / Not settle,—break a silence music too." (6. 1196–98.) What appears to be— and is formulated in words as being—a routine lovers' elopement,

---

lante gave my hand a timely squeeze, / Madonna saved me from immodest speech, / I kissed him and was quiet, being a bride." (7. 469–71.) And when the Comparini return to Rome, Guido "could begin make profit in some sort / Of the young bride and the new quietness" (2. 529–30). The suggestion of Keats's "Thou still un-ravish'd bride of quietness" is plain.

the logical consequence of a mundane affair, emerges as an ineffable experience, the meaning of which is evident only to the Pope, who plainly asserts the inadequacy of language to characterize it. Such an act is best revered in silence by those who can feel; to the rest, the miracle degenerates into mere spectacle. The lesson of it all is best summed up by the humble Celestino:

> who trusts
> To human testimony for a fact
> Gets this sole fact—himself is proved a fool;
> Man's speech being false, if but by consequence
> That only strength is true.
>
> (12. 601–5)

I I

To demonstrate *in extenso* his view of human speech as treacherous and subject to endless abuse, Browning uses the dramatic form which for its effect relies most heavily upon language to the exclusion of other means. Lacking physical action and the intellectual tension provided by give-and-take with other voices, the monologue requires that the single speaker, dedicated to justifying his past thought and deeds and interpreting those of others, entrust his whole case to the verbal art of persuasion. Although it is never heard, the presence of some sort of audience requires each speaker to employ a certain amount of verbal strategy, which must always be allowed for as we assess his words. Because Guido's appearance before the judges and later before the Cardinal and the Abate is literally a matter of life and death, he avails himself of every possible means of conciliating them, no matter what the cost to truth. Caponsacchi, who has nothing further to lose, can afford to be bluntly candid before the same auditors— candor is itself a kind of strategy—and he is. Other speakers, conscious of their listeners' lack of sympathy or receptivity, use various subterfuges such as casuistry, evasions, outright lies, or contrived rhetorical displays. In some instances (the lawyers and the Pope), the monologue may lack an immediate audience and thus the speech really amounts to a soliloquy. But only the Pope really addresses himself alone, for both lawyers speak, by anticipation, to the judges whom their arguments are intended to sway. The strategy employed when the audience is merely assumed and its responses hypothetical is quite different from the one required by the physical presence of an auditor, implicitly reacting to the statements made.

If, therefore, the search for the truth of the Franceschini affair itself is an arduous one, no less difficult (and stimulating) is the task of filtering out the true intent of some of the speakers—and in the upshot, Browning's own—from the rhetorical distortion by which that master dramatist of disputed motives makes them becloud it. (Pompilia, Caponsacchi, and the Pope are the obvious exceptions.) Browning, it is true, provides help of a sort by offering his own reading of events and characters in Books 1 and 12, and the reader rightly approaches the poem through this entrance and leaves it through that exit. But the preliminary character sketches in Book 1 prove to be not wholly trustworthy representations of the various monologuists' prejudices and rhetorical approaches. The Other Half-Rome is no mere sentimentalist, nor is Tertium Quid simply an intellectual fop; as we shall presently see, both are astute and subtle rhetoricians. Browning also provides help of another sort in his role of dramatist rather than commentator. When his angle of vision sharply differs from that of the speaker, he seeks to communicate his own values, the ones readers are intended to accept, by having the speaker (as in Books 4, 5, 8, 9, and 11) discredit himself unawares through revealing a fatal bias or moral myopia in the very course of speaking. But much more subtle, and in the long run more effective, is his conveyance of his own values through the dialectic and rhetoric of each character. It is not so much what the speakers say as the precise manner in which they choose to say it that ultimately defines their character and purposes and so, by inference, the poet's intention.

The speakers in this poem have at their disposal three large categories of language resources. The first is rhetoric in the more limited sense of argumentative strategy and the adoption of the classical oratorical devices ("formal" rhetoric). The

second is allusiveness, the use and often the distortion of
familiar inherited story material and quotations; a device
which, strictly speaking, is an ancillary element of formal
rhetoric but which in these monologues is a principal determinant of tone and a significant key to character. The third is
figurative language, which, lavishly though it is used in this
poem, is always controlled by Browning's dramatic and psychological intention; it is never mere embellishment. All three
classes are embraced, of course, by the term "rhetoric" in its
larger, Aristotelian meaning, of all devices of language directed to persuasive ends. And through their combined use
every speaker in the poem tries, deliberately or unconsciously,
to elicit a response that involves at once his listener's mind, his
feelings, and his sensory imagination.

The conscious rhetoricians are the contentious or forensic
speakers (the two Halves of Rome, Tertium Quid, Guido, and
the lawyers), bent on proving their cases by whatever means
are available. They are rhetoricians in the pejorative sense the
word had acquired long before Browning's age, and their
misuse of logic and unscrupulous manipulation of feeling
through the skillful selection and arrangement of words illustrate why rhetoric, hallowed instrument of argument though it
was from Plato's time down into the Renaissance, had come
into such disrepute. The cynicism with which it could be
employed by men bent upon perverting or obscuring truth is
suggested by the way the poem's rhetoricians expose their
awareness of what they are doing. The lawyers are always
consciously shaping their language for tactical ends. Half-
Rome, indulging in an imaginative reconstruction of what
Guido (here called "Guido's angel") thought as he knocked at
the Comparini's door, pulls himself up short with "here's rhetoric and to spare!" (2. 1422.) And Guido, after reciting in
detail his numerous aches consequent to his vigil-torture, inter-
rupts himself:

> But I curtail the catalogue
> Through policy,—a rhetorician's trick,—
> Because I would reserve some choicer points
> O' the practice, more exactly parallel—
> (Having an eye to climax) with what gift,

> Eventual grace the Court may have in store
> I' the way of plague—my crown of punishments.
>
> (5. 77–83)

Even in Book 11, where he argues with a ferocity that often mounts to hysteria, Guido still is aware that his pleadings are "voluble rhetoric" (174).

In each of the ten speeches, the superimposed patterns of formal rhetoric, allusion (especially to Scripture), and metaphor provide a self-contained and systematic body of commentary on both character and moral idea. Deliberately deceptive use of the arts of language is, for Browning, an unfailing mark of those who move in varying degrees of moral darkness; the more conscious facility one has with language, it appears, the more tempted he is to put it to ulterior use. The undoubted eloquence of Pompilia, Caponsacchi, and the Pope, on the other hand, owes nothing to calculated *eloquentia*. They play no games with language. All three, for instance, use figures of speech more sparingly than do most of the others, and when they do, their figures are employed in their clearest sense, with no hidden twists. And though Pompilia and Caponsacchi sometimes quote others' images characterizing them, they seldom clothe themselves on their own authority in the borrowed raiment of metaphor. They present themselves as they are, not as they would wish to be seen if their moral integrity did not suffice to justify them. The guile and frequency with which Guido meanwhile hides his true character under plausible rhetoric supply an accurate measure of the difference between the children of darkness, who move and are moved by the letter (which St. Paul says finally kills), and the children of light, who live by the spirit.

The same distinction can be made in respect to the specific rhetorical technique of quoting others' purported statements. Although we have no way of knowing what those absent speakers really said, the fidelity with which their ideas and attitudes are reported may confidently be inferred from the reporter's character. It is hardly to be expected that any of the poem's deliberate persuaders would be faithful to the actual words and intention of someone whom he alleges he is quoting, when accuracy might in many instances damage his own case and misrepresentation, on the other hand, would strengthen it. We may take it as a working principle that if they are not downright fictitious, the quotations Tertium Quid and the lawyers, for example, incorporate into their speeches are astutely amended versions of what was actually said. In the mouths of the altruistic and absolutely honest Caponsacchi and Pompilia, by contrast, the represented speech of others, while not necessarily a verbatim report, may always be relied upon as faithful to the spirit of the speakers quoted.

Because language is flexible and men bent on mischief are inventive, the abuse of language's power over others normally results in a thickening of the error which pervades human life. But that very flexibility and that very inventiveness sometimes join to produce poetic justice; for time after time, in those welcome intrusions of the antic spirit by which the poem is lightened, the rhetoricians overreach themselves. Their dialectic backfires or proves to contain its built-in rebuttal, and their biblical and mythological allusions and their metaphors, so carefully selected and shaped for a particular end, sometimes prove to possess a logic whose implications, if followed out, hoist the speakers with their own petard. Guido, for example, uses the image of "Lucifer . . . falling to find hell" (5. 1046) as a means of evoking sympathy for himself when he recites the trials brought upon him by his wife and Caponsacchi; but the fact that Lucifer is often said (by Milton, for example) to have been Satan in his prelapsarian state has the inadvertent effect of supporting the repeated identification of Guido as the devil.

Browning, it cannot be sufficiently stressed, is always in control of his characters' verbal operations, and with a sure sense of irony he repeatedly lets language wreak its vengeance upon its abusers.[6] For his point is the one with which this

---

[6] By an extension of the same technique, Browning achieves further irony by arranging for a speaker's image to be sabotaged in advance by someone else. Thus the Other Half-Rome says of Guido as he returned from his futile years courting preferment at Rome,

> he was slipping into years apace,
> And years make men restless—they needs must see

chapter began: the gift of speech, however susceptible it is to
human misuse and however inadequate for the expression of
numinous truth, nevertheless comes from God. Right speaking,
as Cicero asserted and Quintilian echoed, springs from moral
strength; and even though one is not perfectly strong or perfectly articulate, if his intentions be sincere, Browning implies,
his tongue will somehow speak truth. Unfortunately the world,
if the microcosm provided by *The Ring and the Book* is any
guide, is inhabited for the most part by men of another sort.

> Some certainty, some sort of end assured,
> Sparkle, tho' from the topmost beacon-tip
> That warrants life a harbour through the haze.
>
> (3. 284–88)

If we turn back to Book 1, we discover the same image of a bea-
con—but this time it lures a boat to destruction (1190–95), a fact
which, to those who remember it, naturally affects the tendency of the
image in Book 3. A suppressed detail may serve the same end. One
thinks of Guido's image in Book 5:

> When I find
> That pure smooth egg which, laid within my nest,
> Could not but hatch a comfort to us all,
> Issues a cockatrice for me and mine,
> Do you stare to see me stamp on it?
>
> (654–58)

The interest of these lines does not consist merely in its typifying the
intersection image with which the poem abounds—in this case, com-
bining the pure egg of 3. 64 and elsewhere with the cockatrice found
at three other places (1. 171; 6. 1950; 12. 538). In ancient lore it is a
snake that hatches the egg from which the cockatrice emerges; thus
the logic of the metaphor has Guido accidentally referring to himself
as a serpent. Other examples of subverted metaphor are given on pp.
258–59, n. 14 and pp. 259–60.

Five

"The Middle Way"

TERTIUM QUID AND ETHICAL RELATIVISM

I

The ambiguity and the inherent deceptiveness of language are by no means an isolated concern in *The Ring and the Book;* they are inseparable from the equally fundamental issue of ethical relativism. The nexus between the moral middle course and its linguistic equivalent is brought into focus in the poem's third monologue, that of the supercilious drawing-room sophist, Tertium Quid. His speech, freighted with contrived balances and antitheses, with marshaled argument and counterargument, epitomizes the middle way, that safe, broad path designed to facilitate its practitioner's survival in the complex world of the ambiguous and the inscrutable.[1] The great dra-

---

[1] The thematic emphasis on the "middle way" as the chosen official ground of church and law—the refuge, as Browning sees it, of timorous and hypocritical arbiters of justice—was perhaps immediately inspired by Newman's *Apologia pro vita sua* (1864), which recalled public attention to a central Tractarian concept, the *Via Media.* Often misinterpreted as a judicious golden mean, the proposed *Via Media* was really a compromise which would place the Church of England between submission to papal authority on the one hand and total freedom from church law on the other. Thus the movement was at once an effort to regain disaffected members and to eliminate "errors" generated by both Roman and reformed churches. This obviously unworkable idea was repudiated in the *Apologia* as a paper theory. But its recrudescence in Newman's pages, just as *The Ring and the Book* was taking shape, leads one to conjecture that Browning was turning the idea over in his mind and finding it, in the light of his strongly Protestant background, increasingly repugnant. His reaction to a specific, timely application of the middle course colored, or

matic irony implicit in Tertium Quid's speech, and indeed in those of the poem's other relativists, is that such a path becomes, in terms of the absolute moralism of the Pope, the broad way to destruction.

"Will you," as the Other Half-Rome says, "go somewhat back to understand?" (3. 964)—namely, to his own monologue, which immediately precedes Tertium Quid's. For in retrospect Tertium Quid's balancing act has been quietly anticipated by what is on the surface a speech markedly opposed in method and tone. At the beginning of Book 3 the quasi-religious imagery of birds and plants which coalesces in the figure of Pompilia seems to warrant Browning's statement in the preview that to this speaker she "seemed a saint and martyr both" (1. 909), to the exclusion, supposedly, of her more earthly qualities. But as the Other Half-Rome says very early, virtually pre-quoting Tertium Quid, "Truth lies between" (3. 83), and he tends toward the less celestial view of her as a quite human victim of inhuman cruelty. The real question is not whether she is a Madonna figure or simply a murdered Roman girl-wife but, assuming the latter, whether it was "a flower or weed" that was "ruined" (3. 84–85).[2] Undoubtedly he is committed to her side; but as he proceeds with his narrative he is torn between all-out emotional advocacy of Pompilia and the intellectual attraction of balanced alternatives. Nor is it a simple question of polarities. He is not happy with either emotion or intellect in its pure state, but instead tends constantly to qualify them and if possible to reconcile them. The erratic course of his monologue illustrates the trou-

---

intensified, his deep-seated distrust of the whole concept. Whether Browning actually read the *Apologia* is unclear, but he was certainly familiar with its ideas. He told Julia Wedgwood of discussing the book with a friend (*Browning and Julia Wedgwood*, p. 12) and, as Miss Wedgwood wrote him in September, 1864, "All the Reviews are busy with Newman's *Apologia*" (*ibid.*, p. 73).

[2] Perhaps only by accident, the question is symbolically foreshadowed in the fortuitous selection of battered volumes that flanked the Old Yellow Book when Browning found it at the Florentine stall: "the fond tale / O' the Frail One of the Flower, by young Dumas" and "The Life, Death, Miracles of Saint Somebody, / Saint Somebody Else, his Miracles, Death and Life" (1. 77–81).

ble awaiting the man who attempts to apply the judicious
approach to a matter involving strong feelings, who is reluctant to be dominated by either the head or the heart.

The emotional outburst which occupies the first hundred
lines or so of the Other Half-Rome's speech identifies him as
Pompilia's unreserved adorer. Then, calming down, he reveals
himself also as an apparent devotee of the golden mean. In his
description of the Comparini's situation in Rome, which
should be carefully compared with the preceding description
by Half-Rome, he lays great stress upon the near-paradisiacal
happiness the couple enjoyed as a result of their intermediate
social and moral position:

> Nor low i' the social scale nor yet too high,
> Nor poor nor richer than comports with ease,
> Nor bright and envied, nor obscure and scorned,
> Nor so young that their pleasures fell too thick,
> Nor old past catching pleasure when it fell,
> Nothing above, below the just degree,
> All at the mean where joy's components mix.
>
> (3. 120–26)

Husband and wife were perfectly matched, each compensating
for the other's deficiency: Pietro was "acquiescent and recipi-
ent," Violante "stirring striving," the two together balancing
"Quietude, enterprise, craving and content, / Which go to
bodily health and peace of mind." Only one "fatal germ"
spoiled their otherwise perfect contentment, the lack of a child
which, according to the Bible, completes the union of man and
woman (3. 127–54). Pietro's acceptance of Violante's subsequent deception was the act of a merely "foolish," not evil,
man (3. 190)— foolishness lying comfortably midway between virtue and vice.

The Other Half-Rome's seeming approval of the Comparini,
his denial of any culpable intent in them, is thus formulated in
specific terms of moderation and balance. Nevertheless, his
tone has been colored by a faint but unmistakable irony. He is
not really as committed to the ideal of the golden mean as he
first appears to be, for in the next portion of his speech he

attributes the same argument from the middle ground to
Paolo, treating for Pompilia in behalf of his brother Guido.
The Franceschini, says Paolo, were (like the Comparini) not
so rich as vulgar *arrivistes*, whose one measure of value is
money, would desire. On the other hand, they were not so poor
as they would be if they lacked the possibility, indeed the
certainty (the "if" of line 280 becomes the "when" of line
292), of a cardinal's bounty redeeming their fortunes. Poverty, after all, is relative: "Guido *for his rank* was poor." (3.
355.) Moreover, Guido himself, as a man of moderation,
wished only that the hoped-for bounty would "Irrigate far
rather than deluge near, / Go fertilize Arezzo, not flood
Rome" (3. 293–94). Paolo's whole reputed argument, in fact,
with its disastrous consequences for the Comparini whose
character and conduct the Other Half-Rome has just defended
in the same terms, thrusts into question the validity of the
sweetly reasonable approach to motives. If moderation is indeed a virtue, it can also rationalize a multitude of vices.

The Other Half-Rome's true valuation of the golden mean
becomes clearer when he reviews the successive court decisions, products of "the middle course the sage affect" (3.
671), for these actually were more beneficial to Guido than to
Pompilia. The Roman verdict on the charge of adultery and
flight was a masterpiece of compromise. "A middle course,"
the court is imagined as declaring, "is happily open yet." (3.
1380.)

> "To all men be our moderation known!
> Rewarding none while compensating each,
> Hurting all round though harming nobody,
> Husband, wife, priest, scot-free not one shall 'scape,
> Yet priest, wife, husband, boast the unbroken head
> From application of our excellent oil."
>
> (3. 1395–1400)

The Other Half-Rome's contempt for such shilly-shallying is
unequivocal: "That's Rome's way, the traditional road of law;
/ Whither it leads is what remains to tell" (3.
1417–18)—namely, the murder of Pompilia and the Compa-

rini by a villain who "took the middle course / Rome taught him" (3. 711–12). Where, then, are the advantages of the golden mean so revered by "the sage"?

But this rejection of the moderate course where crucial moral decisions are involved does not affect the Other Half-Rome's strong tendency to analyze and weigh rather than to plunge precipitately toward an unreasoned conclusion. Despite his adoration of Pompilia, he is extraordinarily reluctant to render judgments. He evinces a tentative, empiricist attitude (arguing from probabilities) that often verges on the cynical. The allegedly "innocent love" between wife and priest is, to him, a notion which "frankly outsoars faith: / There must be falsehood somewhere" (3. 906–7). He offers equally probable alternatives:

>   For her part,
> Pompilia quietly constantly avers
> She never penned a letter in her life.
>
> .   .   .   .
>   . . . All extemporized
> As in romance-books! Is that credible?
> Well, yes: as she avers this with calm mouth
> Dying, I do think "Credible!" you'd cry—
> Did not the priest's voice come to break the spell:
>
> .   .   .   .
>   . . . he, calm, constant then as she is now,
> For truth's sake did assert and reassert
> Those letters called him to her and he came,
> —Which damns the story credible otherwise.
> Why should this man,—mad to devote himself,
> Careless what comes of his own fame, the first,—
> Be studious thus to publish and declare
> Just what the lightest nature loves to hide,
>
> .   .   .   .
> —I say,—why should the man tell truth just here
> When graceful lying meets such ready shrift?
> Or is there a first moment for a priest

> As for a woman, when invaded shame
> Must have its first and last excuse to show?
>
> (3. 907–42)

He does entertain the possibility of the whole adventure's being a miracle, but this appears only as a fanciful alternative to a more "probable" or realistic interpretation; and if, as he later speculates, the priest and wife came together "as when star and star must needs go close / Till each hurts each and there is loss in heaven" (3. 1050–63), there remains his earlier assertion that "men are men" and "our man the Canon here / Saw, pitied, loved Pompilia" (3. 880–82).

But we finally recognize that this emphasis on the "tenebrific" passages of the narrative (3. 789), with the consequent weighing of alternatives, is simply the method the Other Half-Rome's natural inclination leads him to adopt as he argues in Pompilia's behalf. His case for her derives its attractiveness from his open-minded eagerness to consider adverse arguments as well as those in her favor. Intellectual moderation—reasonableness, objectivity—offers a valid mode of pleading, even if its application to moral issues (as practiced, for instance, by the court) falls far short of justice.

Yet would his commitment to Pompilia be as strong as it is if it resulted only from rational analysis directed, however irrationally, by an inherent temperamental weakness for visions of suffering womanhood? Browning implies that it would not, for in the surprise ending of the monologue he provides a much more explicit additional source for the Other Half-Rome's bias, his grudge against Guido. There is no absolute conflict between intellectual moderation as a general practice and vindictiveness in special circumstances: a reasonable attitude may be augmented, not necessarily invalidated, by an incidental irrational motive. And in any event, the ending seems to have been dictated both by Browning's Victorian penchant for melodramatic effects and by his craftsman's desire to balance the equally sensational surprise ending of Book 2. Both speakers are prejudiced on personal grounds, but for different reasons and with different results.

I I

Akin to the Other Half-Rome in "judiciousness" is Tertium
Quid, that cynical, resourceful exponent of casuistry as a way
to truth. But whereas the former's adoption of a rational
attitude evidently was sincere and his use of it honest, Tertium
Quid's are wholly strategic, for under the politic guise of an
adherent to the disinterested middle way, he energetically
defends Guido's cause. The tendency of his speech, indeed, is
the opposite of the Other Half-Rome's. That speaker's commitment was clear at the outset, and only as his monologue
progressed was his original simple partisanship complicated
by intellectual reservations. Tertium Quid's commitment, on
the other hand, is betrayed only covertly, through the dissembling cloud of assumed neutrality, until the truth of his position is suddenly exposed at the very end.

There is good enough reason why he should side with
Guido. He has, even more than Half-Rome, an identification of
interests with the Count. This "man of quality" (1. 928), who
clings to the fringe of society and the church convinced that
his position deserves improvement, is bound to sympathize
with the nobleman Guido Franceschini, who also clung long
and desperately. Tertium Quid, however, has at least won
entrée into a salon frequented by cardinals, whereas Guido
never got further in the church than being assigned to hold his
master the cardinal's horses. In spite of this disparity between
their respective fortunes, Tertium Quid and Guido are linked
by their common thirst for preferment. (If the indifferent
response of his card-playing, yawning auditors is any sign,
however, Tertium Quid's prospects are hardly more hopeful
than Guido's proved to be.)

More important, Tertium Quid's self-interest requires that
he accommodate his argument to the class sympathies of his
audience, and these, obviously, are on Guido's side. "Quality,"
Browning remarked in the poem's prologue, "took the decent
part, of course; / Held by the husband, who was noble too."
(1. 276–77.) As Guido's lawyer will later assert with satisfaction,

> that society of Rome,
> Hath so obliged us by its interest,
> Taken our client's part instinctively,
> As unaware defending its own cause.
>
> (8. 744–47) [3]

But both reason and the society which nominally venerates it shrink (in theory at least) from extremes, and Tertium Quid's method before this audience must be to appear to maintain intellectual and moral equipoise. His calculated shaping of syntax and selection of other grammatical and rhetorical devices are the most obvious of his tactics. In their contrived symmetry the very opening lines of his speech prophesy his insistence on the balanced middle course:

> True, Excellency—as his Highness says,
> Though she's not dead yet, she's as good as stretched
> Symmetrical beside the other two;
> Though he's not judged yet, he's the same as judged,
> So do the facts abound and superabound:
>
> .   .   .   .
>
> To hear the rabble and brabble, you'd call the case
> Fused and confused past human finding out.
> One calls the square round, t'other the round square.
>
> (4. 1–5, 34–36)

Twice, in interesting counterparts to the Other Half-Rome's treatment of the saving element of compensation in the Comparini's moral nature and conduct, he palliates their "sin" by

---

[3] Abstractly, Guido's case does embody several questions of class: whether a nobleman ought to have to undergo torture, or be permitted to take the law into his own hands, or be exempt from public exposure. But nowhere is it suggested that Roman society might with equal reason have sided with Caponsacchi. His dignity of lineage, after all, surpassed Guido's; and to such an audience as this, as to his judges (cf. the opening lines of Book 6), his elopement with Pompilia would have seemed little more than a peccadillo. Furthermore, such a salon was the predestined setting for a courtly priest like Caponsacchi, "the authority / For delicate play at tarocs, and arbiter / O' the magnitude of fan-mounts" (6. 348–50). His social graces, already well developed in the drawing rooms of provincial Arezzo, would in happier circumstances have found much fuller scope here.

calling attention to their subsequent reformation and to the
healing effect of time:

> Moreover, say that certain sin there seem,
> The proper process of unsinning sin
> Is to begin well-doing somehow else.
> Pietro,—remember, with no sin at all
> I' the substitution,—why, this gift of God
> Flung in his lap from over Paradise
> Steadied him in a moment, set him straight
> On the good path he had been straying from.
>
> (4. 284–91)

> healthy minds let bygones be,
> Leave *old crimes* to *grow young and virtuous-like*
> I' the sun and air; *so time treats ugly deeds:*
> They take the natural blessing of all change.
> There was the joy o' the husband silly-sooth,
> The softening of the wife's old wicked heart,
> *Virtues to right and left,* profusely paid
> If so they might *compensate the saved sin.*
>
> (4. 238–45; italics supplied)

Tertium Quid's adherence to the ideal of moderation is further
suggested by his avoidance of really decisive language.
Whereas Half-Rome had made a point of describing the Comparini's poverty in explicit terms, Tertium Quid, again somewhat in the manner of the Other Half-Rome, dilutes the facts:

> This Pietro, this Violante, live their life
> At Rome in the easy way that's far from worst
> Even for their betters,—themselves love themselves,
> Spend their own oil in feeding their own lamp
> That their own faces may grow bright thereby.
>
> .   .   .   .
>
> Meantime their wick swims in the safe broad bowl
> O' the middle rank,—not raised a beacon's height
> For wind to ravage, nor swung till lamp graze ground.
>
> (4. 70–86)

Many of Tertium Quid's transitional devices, intended primarily to involve his audience, also help make him appear

uncommitted, tentative, and judicious. He is preternaturally willing to leap to the other side, or to qualify (or abandon) any point, ostensibly in the interest of clarity and justice. Explaining Violante's "crime," he pauses to say, "Is so far clear?" with apparent solicitude for the audience's understanding; but a moment later he characteristically reverses his field: "I thought as much. / But now, a question." (4. 227–33.) His concern for clarity proves factitious, however, for he can seem "moderate" only if his own argument remains ambiguous and stops short of final judgments. Thus, his disappointment is only assumed as he says,

> You see so far i' the story, who was right,
> Who wrong, who neither, don't you? What, you don't?
> Eh? Well, admit there's somewhat dark i' the case,
> Let's on—the rest shall clear, I promise you.
>
> (4. 314–17)

His pose of tentativeness appears again after his account of the marriage: "Now, here take breath and ask,—which bird o' the brace / Decoyed the other into clapnet? Who / Was fool, who knave? Neither and both, perchance." (4. 505–7.) And again,

> I anticipate however—only ask,
> Which of the two here sinned most? A nice point!
> Which brownness is least black,—decide who can,
> Wager-by-battle-of-cheating! What do you say,
> Highness? Suppose, your Excellency, we leave
> The question at this stage, proceed to the next.
>
> (4. 628–33)

But beneath this show of objectivity and moderation Tertium Quid's argument is as heavily weighted in Guido's favor as is that of Half-Rome. His ostentatious care to let both sides speak is more than canceled out by his unequal apportionment of space. Only about 470 lines are allotted to points in favor of Pompilia and the Comparini, while some 850 are devoted to Guido's side; and the former passages include arguments which, while superficially favorable to Pompilia and her foster parents, prove on closer inspection to add further substance to Guido's case. In addition, while Tertium Quid enhances his pose of detachment by reiterating that he is disinterestedly citing the claims of partisans on both sides, he sabotages the arguments of Pompilia's defenders by using loaded terms, most of which betray his class consciousness and are intended to appeal to that of his auditors. The Comparini and their partisans are variously "dolts and fools," "selfish worthless human slugs," "simpletons," "rabble and brabble," "mob," "plebs," "commonalty," "cits" (a term Guido will himself use [5. 416]), "gnats," "two hateful faces," "selfish beasts." Violante is a "household sheep"; the eloped pair are "the pair of saints"; and Pompilia is referred to as Medusa and—disdainfully—as a "pet lamb."

Such disparagement is not applied to Guido, whom Tertium Quid normally describes as a tired, harassed nobleman trying against heavy odds to uphold, or restore, the family honor, and in his acute but undeserved poverty sending the family retainer to chaffer in the market for "the lamb's least leg" (4. 362). When it is time for a point against Guido to be presented, Tertium Quid offers adverse judgments only through represented speech, from which he can dissociate himself. It is Caponsacchi who is made to call him "a man of guile" and a "born coward" (4. 1091, 1093), and Guido's anonymous detractors who label him a "stock-fish" (4. 1147) for meekly appealing to law instead of taking manly revenge.

Tertium Quid's statement of the case against Guido is further undermined by frequent qualifiers or disclaimers. Argument after argument in behalf of the Comparini and, later, Pompilia and Caponsacchi is discredited as soon as it is introduced: "The mob,—now, that's just how the error comes!" (62); "The gnats say . . ." (563); "So say the Comparini" (573); "If, as is said . . ." (687); "'tis said" (767); "This, they say . . ." (769); "They also say . . ." (787); "Whose fault or shame but Guido's?—ask her friends" (850); "But then this is the wife's—Pompilia's tale . . ." (851); "Then, look into his [Caponsacchi's] own account o' the case!" (966); "And there's his story: what do you say to it[?]" (1008); "But then on the other side again,—how say / The pair of saints?" (1043–44); "She had prayed—at least so people tell you now" (1425). Only the "mob," never to be trusted, is cited in behalf of the Comparini, Pompilia, and Caponsacchi, who are not to be trusted either. Meanwhile the pro-Guido arguments are presented respectfully for the most part, with no such sarcasm or irony.[4] And it is noteworthy that Tertium Quid regularly sees to it that in each phase of the exchange of argument Guido's "friends" are heard last; with each Guidonian rebuttal the debate conveniently moves on to a new issue.

The extent to which Tertium Quid overlooks or plays down many facts militating against Guido or in Pompilia's favor can be appreciated only by a systematic comparison of his version of the story with the Other Half-Rome's, whose "judiciousness" has the opposite tilt. In addition, he seizes upon point after point alleged against Guido and, conceding its factual accuracy, converts it to the Count's advantage. Thus, although it is true that the Comparini had just grievances after the mutual cheat of the marriage contract was exposed, so did Guido; and he was the innocent victim of a lie (the Comparini's [4. 624–25]), while the Comparini's misfortune was that Guido had told the truth (4. 354). Again, although Guido was charged with having sought revenge upon Pompilia, the converse was true. Her life, argues Tertium Quid, anticipating the great theme of her own lawyer, was all of a pattern—that of deceit and double-dealing. Even her deathbed confession (reproduced as Book 7), which the church is bound to accept as true, is really a protracted lie accusing Guido of cruelty and denying her own guilt. Behind this confession, now made

---

[4] Here again, recollection of the Other Half-Rome's technique gives us a means of more clearly understanding Tertium Quid's strategy. At first glance, both speakers operate in the same way. But in the course of his long canvass of arguments and counterarguments, the Other Half-Rome avoided the weighted terms that Tertium Quid uses so freely. Note the former's choice of neutral verbs: "Pompilia . . . avers" (3. 908) ; "she avers" (919) ; "whether, as Guido states the case . . ." (1052) ; "Wife and priest alike reply" (1117) ; "She says" (1121) ; "The priest says" (1171) ; "Guido's tale begins" (1203)—and so forth. The only conspicuously loaded interpolation is in line 1112: "the accusers shriek." The difference between the Other Half-Rome and Tertium Quid in this small but significant respect is a good measure of their relative honesty.

public, stands (he insists, without evidence) a second and
private one: a confession that the first was untrue (4.
1479–83).

Where twisting the facts is insufficient for his purpose,
Tertium Quid contorts logic with equal facility. Defending
Pompilia's "adoption" by Violante, he says sardonically,

> Why, moralist, the sin has saved a soul!
> Then, even the palpable grievance to the heirs—
> 'Faith, this was no frank setting hand to throat
> And robbing a man, but . . . Excellency, by your leave,
> How did you get that marvel of a gem,
> The sapphire with the Graces grand and Greek?
> The story is, stooping to pick a stone
> From the pathway through a vineyard—no-man's-land—
> To pelt a sparrow with, you chanced on this.
>
> (4. 255–63)

He goes on to argue that, since the gem was valueless to the
peasantry, "Excellency" had a better claim; by analogy, Pompilia, being highly valued by the Comparini (as an heir),
belonged more properly to them than to her own mother, a
mere harlot. "If he [Pietro] accepts it why should you
demur?" (4. 283.) Casuistry again proves serviceable as he
justifies the lying and equivocation on both sides, most notably
in connection with the explicit and implicit terms of the marriage contract discussed above (pp. 115–16). With his fine
sense of balance he is aesthetically pleased by this *quid pro
quo* exchange of falsehood; his disappointment lies in the
fact—the root of all the ensuing mischief as he sees it—that
"One party had the advantage" (4. 551) and upset the precar-
ious balance. Completely amoral, he excuses all such chicanery, and accounts for its occasional exposure, on the easy
ground that such is the way of the world.

Repeatedly Tertium Quid pauses to demand judgments; not
that he really wants his audience to decide, but such pauses are
part of his rhetorical campaign of nominally engaging the
company. In addition, these gestures of debate without the
debating spirit may rouse them from their inattention and

prevent their always imminent departure: "How suits here /
This with the other alleged motive, Prince?" (915–16);
"Duke, note the knotty point!" (930); "Highness, decide!
Pronounce, Her Excellency!" (1113); "Make it your own
case,—you who stand apart!" (1175); "Come! / Are you not
staggered?—pause, and you lose the move!" (1193–94); "If
the case be clear or turbid,—you must say!" (1212); ". . .
let's see clearly from this point!" (1214); "Is it settled so far?
Settled or disturbed, / Console yourselves: 'tis like . . ."
(1280–81). But they never respond, as, indeed, they should
not; for to do so would be to spoil the effect of Tertium Quid's
pseudo-dialectic, in which thesis and antithesis alternate in
unending succession, with only illusory synthesis. Perhaps
their apathy is an additional sign that society has already
settled on Guido's side and that this coruscating display is
superfluous. But they would not be so inattentive if they realized what Tertium Quid was really doing; for he manipulates
them unconscionably, partly for the sake of potential reward,
partly to have some mordant fun at their expense. At the same
time that he flatters them aloud, he ridicules them under his
breath. As he becomes more and more conscious of their deaf
ears, he grows increasingly bold. His annoyance and his contempt for the assembled nobility and ecclesiastics prompt him
to walk another tight rope between opposed goals. He vents his
own contempt for them even as he uses their consciousness of
rank to cultivate their favor; and even as he tries to conciliate
them he slashes at them, both as individuals and as representatives of society and church, through various *ad hominem*
arguments and innuendoes.

These repeated gibes may seem to be mere devices intended
to flap his listeners to attention and assist the argument, but
they are actually cynical and dangerous, for he continually
refers from the facts of the case to analogues in the lives of
present company or their peers. Hardly anyone among Tertium Quid's listeners seems immune from the thrusts of his
malicious wit, driven accurately home by his acquaintance
with Roman gossip. Defending in his usual back-handed manner the Comparini's right to call Pompilia their child even
though it meant living a lie, he says,

> Why, thou exact Prince, is it a pearl or no,
> Yon globe upon the Principessa's neck?
> That great round glory of pellucid stuff,
> A fish secreted round a grain of grit!
> Do you call it worthless for the worthless core?
> (She don't, who well knows what she changed for it!)
>
> (4. 307–12)

Even without the parenthetical aside, the innuendo is clear
enough; but when we recall that Pompilia's real mother, a
child of the Roman streets, "trafficked her virginity away /
For a melon and three pauls at twelve years old" (4. 183–84),
the innuendo is compounded by slander. The erring Prin-
cipessa and Pompilia's mother were sisters under the skin:
bargained seduction, whatever the price agreed upon, is a great
social leveler. Later, justifying (as Bottini will also do) Pompilia's reputed delinquency, Tertium Quid draws another analogy from high society, this one a scandal which easily dwarfs
the mere elopement of an Aretine wife with a priest:

> How could a married lady go astray?
> Bless the fools! And 'tis just this way they are blessed,
> And the world wags still,—because fools are sure
> —Oh, not of my wife nor your daughter! No!
> But of their own: the case is altered quite.
> Look now,—last week, the lady we all love,—
> Daughter o' the couple we all venerate,
> Wife of the husband we all cap before,
> Mother o' the babes we all breathe blessings on,—
> Was caught in converse [5] with a negro page.
> Hell thawed that icicle. . . .
>
> (4. 867–77)

Adultery, Tertium Quid implies, is common among dissatisfied
wives of all social classes. The implication has a double effect:
it contributes to the running argument—if so high born a lady
stoops to folly, anyone of lower rank can all the more easily be

[5] In "criminal conversation," i.e., adultery. Guido seems to allude
to the same tidbit of gossip (5. 1153–61), although he prudently
attributes it to the writer Sacchetti and clothes it in a parody of
Sacchetti's manner.

presumed to do so—and it serves as one more reminder to the nobility that its sexual morality is not, after all, too remote from that of the plebs.[6]

It is just as well for Tertium Quid that these barbs miss their targets—or seem to (because it is possible that they have indeed struck home, but the victims discreetly conceal the fact). Nevertheless, the lack of response stirs him to anger: neither of his campaigns—to win advancement or, failing that, to get under his listeners' skin—has evidently succeeded. This personal, immediate frustration intensifies his unconfessed sympathy with Guido. As he reaches the climax of his suavely reasoned narrative of Guido's tribulations, the mask of disinterestedness begins to slip. "Offence and flight, one fact judged twice / By two distinct tribunals,—what result?" (4. 1507–8.) At Arezzo the sentence was life imprisonment for Pompilia; at Rome, "remitting with a smile / To her father's house, main object of the flight!" (4. 1518–19.) Tertium Quid pictures Guido as finally growing furious at "this discrepancy of judgments" (4. 1521). Up to now, like Tertium Quid, Guido has willingly employed the weapons of reason, but to no avail. "He flourishes wit and common sense, / They fail him,—he plies logic doughtily, / It fails him too." (4. 1550–52.) Tertium Quid's identification with Guido finally bursts into the open; both are frustrated victims (Guido in the past, Tertium Quid

---

[6] One more *ad hominem* innuendo is possibly detectable when Tertium Quid recalls that the zealous policeman Patrizj, after helping capture Guido, died of a fever:

> A warning to the over-vigilant,
> —Virtue in a chafe should change her linen quick,
> Lest pleurisy get start of providence.
> (That's for the Cardinal, and told, I think!)
>
> (4. 1411–14)

Might not the "warning" be read, more clearly, "overheating in pursuit of amorous business may bring on a chill"? A tiny bit of supporting evidence for this interpretation is found in Guido's monologue, when he is positing the unlikely event of his being a *cavaliere servente* summoned by "some friend's wife" to rescue her: "I might have fired up, found me at my post, / Ardent from head to heel, nor feared catch cough." (5. 678–84.)

at this moment) of a much-touted reasonableness which, in a
crisis, fails to serve their personal ends.

The inadequacy of wit, common sense, and logic to bring
Guido justice, says Tertium Quid, turned him into a "furious
bull." This metaphor, to be sure, he first attributes to Pompilia's faction; but in the very next paragraph he unconsciously
narrows still more the distance between Guido and himself by
adopting the "bull-similitude" as his own. He argues, for the
first time with genuine heat, that if Guido did turn enraged
bull, he had abundant provocation: "Do you blame a bull?"
(4. 1559–79.) For the moment, Tertium Quid deserts his
carefully assumed position of neutrality and allows passion
ascendancy over reason, effectively denying his basic premise
that the judicious intellect is all-sufficient. We recall the sarcasm with which he had earlier dismissed Caponsacchi's assertion that his recognition of his duty toward Pompilia came in
an intuitive flash:

> the truth was felt by instinct here!
> —Process which saves a world of trouble and time,
> And there's his story: what do you say to it,
> Trying its truth by your own instinct too,
> Since that's to be the expeditious mode?
>
> (4. 1006–10)

In the end, the scorned "expeditious" mode proved for Guido
to be the inevitable one. The rational and balanced legal mind,
the very judiciousness of which Tertium Quid has been so
blatant an exponent, by failing to render him justice—i.e., to
provide him with the revenge for which he thirsted—forced
him to take the law into his own hands.

But quickly sensing he has gone too far, Tertium Quid
retreats again into the safe twilight zone of moderation and
balance. In a kind of coda to the monologue, arguing that
"Each party wants too much, claims sympathy / For its object
of compassion, more than just" (4. 1583–84), he shows only
contempt for those who insist on absolutes. His obvious meaning is that what is "just" involves by definition a compromise.
Why, he asks, must Pompilia be called an angel, Guido a
devil? If these extremes are insisted upon, "Why, here you

have the awfulest of crimes / For nothing! Hell broke loose on
a butterfly!" Thus again does Guido benefit from Tertium
Quid's laudable attempt to see things levelly; Guido is thereby
rescued from monsterhood. "Why, he's a mere man—/ Born,
bred and brought up in the usual way." (4. 1600–4.) In this
retraction from extremes, Guido becomes "mere man," fallible
but noble, while Pompilia falls, a somewhat tarnished angel.
Devil and angel alike are restored to the middle ground of
earth—and earthly judgment. When so reasonable a posture
has been achieved, Tertium Quid is justified in expecting that
the matching tentativeness of his next proposal will distract
attention from its true audacity:

> What if a tragedy be acted here
> Impossible for malice to improve,
> And innocent Guido with his innocent four
> Be added, all five, to the guilty three,
> That we of these last days be edified
> With one full taste o' the justice of the world?
>
> (4. 1612–17)

The ensuing logic provides a final evidence of Tertium Quid's
scale of values which places him on Guido's side: "He is noble,
and he may be innocent." (4. 1624.) Although this judgment
is actually part of an argument against the vulgar use of
torture irons on noblemen, it has a wider application: nobility
certain, innocence possible; hence exonerate the man, since
"presumptive guilt is weak / I' the case of nobility and privilege" (4. 1627–28).[7]

---

[7] Now that we have seen how Tertium Quid's argument works, it is
instructive to compare it with the course of the Other Half-Rome's.
Although on first reading they seem to proceed on parallel but widely
separated lines that will never meet, in reality their paths converge
and even cross. While the Other Half-Rome speaks from an admitted
pro-Pompilia bias but during most of his monologue treats the case
with the instruments of rational analysis, Tertium Quid uses the same
instruments—proclaiming his total objectivity—but is secretly biased
in favor of Guido. Near the end, Tertium Quid's "reasoned" statement
gives way to an impassioned *ir*rational statement, analogous to the
Other Half-Rome's opening irrational praise of Pompilia. In the very
last lines both speakers return to their original positions, the Other

Whatever semblance of moderation and balance Tertium
Quid has managed to recover in the last lines is, however,
rendered futile by his prior endorsement of the "bull simili-
tude." But the failure of the ethical middle course has, in fact,
been evident throughout his brilliant demonstration of its presumed virtues. With him the golden mean implies a leveling of
good and evil, a meeting of angel and devil on common
ground, a refusal to recognize absolutes. He is entrapped in
the relativism which is attractive to the thinker but repugnant
to moralists such as the Pope—and Browning. And the condemnation of relativism which Browning accomplishes
through Tertium Quid's portrait is deepened by the latter's
ruthlessness and hypocrisy. He has it both ways: he appears
humble while heaping scorn on his audience and he appears to
be an objective reporter while actually slanting the argument
toward his forechosen side.

At the same time, the exposure of the inadequacies of law
(however fallacious the argument by which it is accomplished
in Tertium Quid's monologue) serves to expand and clarify the
variegated commentary on human law encountered in the two
preceding books. Law is the middle course institutionalized,
an instrument of both reason and reasonableness; but it is also
relativity sanctified. Its middle-of-the-road verdicts may
outrage or they may please, depending on how they are read
and whose ox is gored. The Other Half-Rome's righteous anger
over law's "moderation," which prevented it from rendering
decisions unequivocally favorable to Pompilia, was anticipated by Half-Rome's indignation stemming from its failure to
tip its scale wholly on Guido's side. "Thus," said Half-Rome in
recounting the verdict on the Comparini's attempt to repossess
their property and Pompilia's dowry,

> Was justice ever ridiculed in Rome:
> Such be the double verdicts favoured here
> Which send away both parties to a suit

Half-Rome with a burst of vindictive feeling inversely equivalent to
his opening panegyric and implying, perhaps, a certain enraged-bull
feeling of his own, Tertium Quid with a resumption of his judicious
pose, the "logic" of lines 1621–31.

> Nor puffed up nor cast down,—for each a crumb
> Of right, for neither of them the whole loaf.
>
> (2. 747–52)

He ironically quotes Law as praising herself for the temperance of her later decision on Pompilia's and Caponsacchi's guilt, in which absolutes, adoption of which would require the court to call for severe punishment, were replaced by a comfortable relativity. "Here's troublesomeness [says Law], scandal on both sides, / Plenty of fault to find, no absolute crime: / Let each side own its fault and make amends!" (2. 1170–72; cf. 3. 1395–1400, quoted above, p. 133.) Caponsacchi was sent to "some place not too far / Nor yet too near, midway twixt near and far" (2. 1178–79) and Pompilia received an equally mild rebuke. Guido too was accommodated: "See, what a double load we lift from breast!" (2. 1207.) But, as Half-Rome goes on to remark in his own person, Guido's portion of justice was shamefully less than he deserved.

Guido's view of the law's inadequacies is, in essence, a politic restatement of Tertium Quid's, although instead of stressing the desperation induced in him by the court's delicately poised verdict, he reads that decision as a vindication of his conduct (5. 1177–81). But at the same time, he blames the law for ordering too light a punishment for the crime. This ambivalent attitude contrasts with Caponsacchi's undisguised outrage that the law dealt "so ambiguously as gave / Guido the power to intervene" (6. 1855–56). Indeed, both the central male figures in the poem, as Caponsacchi observes, acted outside law, Caponsacchi above it because law did not protect Pompilia enough, Guido circumventing it because it protected her too much. Where moral absolutes are involved, law is unqualified to pronounce judgment or specify punishment. Whether both sides or neither is pleased by a verdict, there remains the question of whether true justice has been served.

Meanwhile, law is an always available means by which human beings may confirm themselves in error. It reinforces their prejudices by making possible multiple interpretations of single events; in the general gray of the court's decisions, onlookers may discern the particular specks of black or white which support their preconceptions. It is a ground where universal principles of truth and error, of good and evil, are comfortably compromised, a refuge for all the morally ambiguous creatures of the world—the Comparini, Guido and his brothers Paolo and Girolamo, and Tertium Quid—the "elaborated product" (1. 916) of the society in which merges the worst of two worlds, the secular and the ecclesiastical. The Pope's judgment on the Comparini applies to them all. However equivocal their own natures, there is nothing ambiguous in the fate that God's law, taking over when man's law defaults,[8] visits upon them:

> So they keep the middle course,
> Slide into silly crime at unaware,
> Slip back upon the stupid virtue, stay
> Nowhere enough for being classed, I hope
> And fear. Accept the swift and rueful death,
> Taught, somewhat sternlier than is wont, what waits
> The ambiguous creature. . . .
>
> .   .   .   .
>
> . . . Go!
> Never again elude the choice of tints!
> White shall not neutralise the black, nor good
> Compensate bad in man, absolve him so:
> Life's business being just the terrible choice.
>
> (10. 1220–37)

[8] But in the upshot of the Franceschini case man's law, it must be admitted, does not default. Whatever its earlier shortcomings as an arbiter of justice, it forthrightly condemns Guido the murderer to death, a verdict which the Pope merely confirms.

Six

"Here's Rhetoric and to Spare!"

THE LAWYERS AND CLASSICAL ORATORY

I

After the three principal figures in the Franceschini affair have testified, each pleading a case far removed from Tertium Quid's middle road where right and wrong are muddied into moral neutrality, the two lawyers come forward. They are worthy successors to Tertium Quid, who would have made a skillful advocate had he not chosen another route to potential reward. Like him, they are totally negligent of the real meaning, the final human values, that lie behind the legal proceedings. Neither Arcangeli nor Bottini would have raised an eyebrow over Tertium Quid's amazing assertion, alluding to the night the Comparini were murdered, that "The only one i' the world that suffered aught / By the whole night's toil and trouble" was the police officer who died of a fever caught while pursuing Guido and his accomplices (4. 1405–10). Arcangeli has no concern for his client as a person, nor does Bottini give the slightest indication that Pompilia's death is to be lamented.

But putting aside the lawyers' callousness: if the stakes in the Franceschini case were not so high—not merely the deliverance of justice in this particular instance of human cruelty and defamation, but, as Browning expands the issue, the vindication of divine truth in a world of sin and error—the forensic duel of Books 8 and 9 would be almost wholly comic. And even despite the somber background, the monologues that constitute this legal comedy are abundantly entertaining. In adopting the lines of argument actually found in the Old Yellow Book and then grossly inflating and extending them,

151

Browning applies the method of caricature to reason and rhetoric.

Puffed-up asses Arcangeli and Bottini unquestionably are. It does not matter how far Guido's or Pompilia's fame is sacrificed so long as the lawyer's own is enhanced, preferably with an accompanying exposure of his rival to ridicule. "Better we lost the cause," thinks Arcangeli, "than lacked the gird / At the Fisc's Latin, lost the Judge's laugh!" (8. 216–17.) But neither advocate is, at base, professionally irresponsible. The pleadings are technically well wrought, and their extravagances should not be permitted to obscure the essential seriousness of the lawyers' purposes; they well know that their interest is served only by winning their cases. Dismaying though their habit of gratuitous and damaging concession, for example, may be, the device itself is a perfectly sound tactic, especially useful in difficult cases to preclude an opponent's dwelling on uncomfortable issues. In these lawyers' practice the device usually misfires, but the fault lies in their reckless use of it, not in any defect in the theory. They are handicapped not by any deficiency, but rather a surplus, of ingenuity.

Arcangeli and Bottini obviously have studied and profited well from the rhetorical treatises of Aristotle, Cicero, and Quintilian.[1] Their tactics are traditional and conventional: the argument that the end justifies the means; the use of concession to stave off argument, or to gain an unforeseen advantage, or to appear reasonable; the use of probabilities, including the greater-less argument; arguing without reaching a conclusion (or reaching a specious conclusion); begging the question or the point to be proved; reasoning from false, irrelevant, superadded, or suppressed premises; and the crafty construction or

---

[1] There is no question that Browning was well acquainted with formal rhetoric. Besides the abundant internal evidence of the poem, we have the fact that his library contained various volumes on the subject: the complete works of Aristotle, including the *Rhetoric, Topica,* and *De sophisticis elenchis;* Plato's *Works, Dialogues, Republic,* and *Sophistes;* and Isocrates' *Orationes et epistolae* (cf. Bottini's reference [9. 1571] to Isocrates' *Panegyric*). See *The Browning Collections* (catalogue of the Sotheby sale), *passim.*

unnecessary embellishment of an argument to hide its true purpose. In combination the two advocates represent the complete orator as delineated by the ancient lawgivers of the rhetorical art. Arcangeli emphasizes *logos*, or the ratiocinative; Bottini favors *pathos*, the appeal to the emotions and the senses; and both adopt *ethos*, the third of Aristotle's persuasive types, as they argue the essential honor of the client. (Bottini's application of this, of course, turns the whole concept upside down, predicating Pompilia's honor on her very dishonor.)

Although there is not space in this book for an exhaustive study of the two lawyers' orations from the viewpoint of classical rhetoric,[2] what follows will at least reveal that the lawyers are not mere buffoons, as most critics, following Browning's own misleading term, have considered them. If the results of their employment of the rhetorical weapons inherited from antiquity are scarcely what morality and justice require, it is not because the lawyers have failed to con their guidebooks and apply the lessons which, they are assured on the highest authority, point the way to winning a debate.

I I

The case Arcangeli must plead has hardly a circumstance in its favor; it is what Cicero would have termed "a difficult case," one which "has alienated the sympathy of those who are about to listen to the speech." [3] Not only has Guido confessed: the judges themselves may be presumed to have a certain bias against him, for by taking summary revenge against the Comparini he has been flagrantly in contempt of the court, which had already decided his suit for adultery against Pompilia and Caponsacchi and in whose technical custody Pompilia remained at the moment Guido took the law into his own hands.

[2] A systematic analysis of the subject is found in James F. Loucks, II, " 'The Filthy Rags of Speech': A Study of Robert Browning's Use of Classical Rhetoric in Books VIII and IX of *The Ring and the Book*" (M.A. thesis, Ohio State University, 1965).

[3] *De Inventione*, trans. H. M. Hubbell (Cambridge, Mass., 1949), p. 41.

If he is to conciliate the judges, therefore, Arcangeli realizes that he cannot afford to dwell on the events leading to the crime. He must, like the wily fox he imagines himself to be (8. 300–306), lead his audience across country, through the briars of prickly logic, down bypaths which lead into the fox's home ground: "excuse, / . . . for who did the killing-work" (8. 448–49). What his argument lacks in pertinence to the central issue must be made up in novelty:

> Safer I worked at the new, the unforeseen,
> The nice bye-stroke, the fine and improvised,
> Point that can titillate the brain o' the Bench
> Torpid with over-teaching, by this time!
>
> (8. 259–62)

To divert the judges' attention from Guido's all too evident guilt, therefore, Arcangeli seizes upon less embarrassing and more pliable issues, principally that of the right, indeed the sacred duty, of a husband to punish the wife who has dishonored him. It is true that as a Franceschini, Guido had little honor left, if honor is measured by wealth and the other signs of rank; his family's latest impoverished scions had had to scratch for their fortunes in the church. Nor is Guido himself a very attractive client to defend on such lofty grounds as "defense of honor." He has been "A common hack-block to try edge of jokes" (8. 1670) in Arezzo, because of his disastrous May–December marriage, his ugliness, and his boorish behavior. Nonetheless, Arcangeli will insist upon portraying Guido as a nobleman whose sullied family name could be cleansed only by drastic action. As he does so, the notion of honor, like "truth" as it moves through the poem, is debased almost beyond saving. Much of the ironic humor in Book 8 resides in the way Arcangeli blandly construes as deeds in defense of honor the sins of avarice, cruelty, and blood lust.

Honoris causa, then—its social importance, its implications, and its especially urgent applicability to Guido's case—replaces Guido's guilt as the central issue. No matter if it can be proved that Pompilia was an utterly faithful wife; since the law holds that reasonable doubt is sufficient motive for action, the question before the judges is not whether Gui-

do's suspicions were justified but simply whether he had them
(8. 424–35).

Cheerfully flying in the face of doctrine, despite the fact
that the judges are priests, Arcangeli submits that honor is
"the supreme good" (8. 583), "the life and soul of us" (8.
476),

> a gift of God to man
> Precious beyond compare,—which natural sense
> Of human rectitude and purity,—
> Which white, man's soul is born with, brooks no touch.
>
> (8. 458–61)

Honor—really overweening pride—may react, like the sensitive human eye, to "a gesture simulating touch, / Presumable
mere menace of such taint,—/ This were our warrant for
eruptive ire" (8. 468–70). If honor is everything, then even a
feint in the direction of dishonor evokes justifiable wrath.[4] Nor
can the vengeance "be too excessive, too extravagant: / Such
wrong seeks and must have complete revenge" (8. 477–78).
One extreme (complete honor) justifies another (complete
revenge), a fallacy Arcangeli will later use in refuting the "six
aggravations" of the crime.

Having begged the question that honor is supreme, to demonstrate its universality Arcangeli cites one authority after
another which, he says, prove that throughout creation the
protection of honor is both instinctive and—for reasonable
creatures—dictated by logic itself. He parades before his auditors all manner of beasts, noting as they pass into Honor's Ark
that all who wive ("at least the nobler sorts") also feel the sting
of hurt honor. Take the bee, he says as he commences his bes-
tiary; even it feels a "hatred of immodest act" (8. 499).

---

[4] The necessity is urged by the device *dicaeologia* (*purgatio*): the
accused was at the mercy of a force beyond his control. Guido, says
Arcangeli, was driven mad by a faithless wife. In addition, the lawyer
adopts the ancillary line, recommended by Quintilian (*Institutes* 7. 4.
9), that the act was done in the interests of the state, law, or other
institution: the murders were a service to law and to society (8.
882–84).

> Only cold-blooded fish lack instinct here,
> Nor gain nor guard connubiality:
> But beasts, quadrupedal, mammiferous,
> Do credit to their beasthood.
>
> (8. 507–10) ⁵

Moving on to the "quadrupedal" beasts, he finds a paradigm in a virtuous elephant,

> Who seeing much offence beneath his nose,
> His master's friend exceed in courtesy
> The due allowance to that master's wife,
> Taught them good manners and killed both at once,
> Making his master and all men admire.
> Indubitably, then, that master's self,
> Favoured by circumstance, had done the same
> Or else stood clear rebuked by his own beast.
>
> (8. 513–20)

With the rigor of the logician, he insists it follows that a human being who takes no vengeance for insulted honor falls lower in the scale of being than the animals: he "is a brute, / . . . nay, . . . / Much more irrational than brutes themselves" (8. 526–29).

> If a poor animal feel honour smart,
> Taught by blind instinct nature plants in him,
> Shall man,—confessed creation's master-stroke,
> Nay, intellectual glory, nay, a god,
> Nay, of the nature of my Judges here,—

---

[5] Later the Pope will defend Pompilia's decision to flee Arezzo on the same ground of the irresistible natural instinct observable throughout creation. She accepted the obligation laid upon her, he says,

> to save the unborn child,
> As brute and bird do, reptile and the fly,
> Ay and, I nothing doubt, even tree, shrub, plant
> And flower o' the field, all in a common pact
> To worthily defend that trust of trusts,
> Life from the Ever Living.
>
> (10. 1074–80)

The solemnity of this use of the argument from nature helps expose, in retrospect, the speciousness of Arcangeli's pleading.

> Shall man prove the insensible, the block,
> The blot o' the earth he crawls on to disgrace?
> (Come, that's both solid and poetic)—man
> Derogate, live for the low tastes alone,
> Mean creeping cares about the animal life?
>
> (8. 531–40)

If brute instinct requires one to wreak vengeance, the obligation to do so is magnified many times by virtue of man's
possession of intellect. This variant of Aristotle's *a fortiori*
argument (*Rhetoric* 1379ᵇ15) is suspect, as Arcangeli knows:
reason is not a higher form of passion, but its opposite. He is
therefore well advised to forestall the judges' scrutiny of his
logic by the magnificent touch of hyperbole in which the
rhetorical order of climax elevates them above the gods.

From the hierarchical argument provided by the great
chain of being, he proceeds to the chronological, moving from
pagan to Christian times.

> If this were done of old, in a green tree,
> Allowed in the Spring rawness of our kind,
> What may be licenced in the Autumn dry,
>
> [Luke 23:31]
>
> And ripe, the latter harvest-tide of man?
> If, with his poor and primitive half-lights,
> The Pagan, whom our devils served for gods,
> Could stigmatise the breach of marriage-vow
> As that which blood, blood only might efface,—
> Absolve the husband, outraged, whose revenge
> Anticipated law, plied sword himself,—
> How with the Christian in full blaze of day?
> Shall not he rather double penalty,
> Multiply vengeance, than, degenerate,
> Let privilege be minished, droop, decay?
>
> (8. 552–65)

These highly charged rhetorical questions assume that as civilization advances, the severity of the penal code, written or
unwritten, increases. It takes some audacity to parade such a
notion before priests, because Scripture demands that, far
from multiplying vengeance, man leave it to God. But Arcangeli, like Bottini later on, is not above playing fast and loose

with both theology and the Bible. (The bogus doctrinal and textual authorities he cites in behalf of his pleading that honor is the supreme Christian good will be examined below, pp. 187–90.) No doubt, like Tertium Quid, he enjoys having a risky game with his auditors. For, again introducing (or inventing) a scriptural analogue, Arcangeli now seeks to evoke pathos, "Full measure, pressed down, running over" (6. 1767), by comparing Guido to Samson, who bore blindness, imprisonment, cruel punishment, and hard labor without complaint, but cried out in huge rage "when he found himself, i' the public place, / Destined to make the common people sport." (8. 645–46.) Guido therefore has inferentially been on a divine mission, the implicit parallel with the suffering Christ adding to the enormity of the suggestion; but before any comment can be offered from the bench on the dissimilarity of Guido and Samson, Arcangeli tightens his control of the forensic situation by indignantly asking, "Are these things writ for no example, Sirs?" (8. 656.) What can the court reply: yes or no?

Although he has proved to his own satisfaction that Judeo-Christian morality affirms the necessity of preserving honor unblemished, Arcangeli still must face the fact that a considerable body of Christian doctrine has quite the opposite tendency, of forbearance and mercy rather than summary revenge. As one might by this time expect, he turns this conflict of law and law to advantage. Appealing to the judges in histrionic despair (the device *anacoenosis*), he asks directions out of the maze:

> —Where do I find my proper punishment
> For my adulterous wife, I humbly ask
> Of my infallible Pope,—who now remits
> Even the divorce allowed by Christ in lieu
> Of lapidation Moses licensed me?
> The Gospel checks the Law which throws the stone,
> The Church tears the divorce-bill Gospel grants,
> The wife sins and enjoys impunity!
>
> (8. 708–15)

The contradictions can easily be resolved by a return (among the nobility) to "primitive revenge" as the "natural privilege of man" (8. 718–21). But an obstacle remains: the new secular law—manners induced by civilization—forbids such revenge. The wronged husband in modern Italy is in a dilemma reminiscent of the kind for which Tertium Quid had so exquisite an appreciation. If he obeys society's (Arcangeli does not add "Christianity's") injunction to "Be patient and forgive" instead of raising a hue and cry, he invites the scorn of the onlookers: "he's presumed a—foh!" (8. 751–55.) But if, as a law-abiding citizen, he takes his case to court, he receives no satisfaction. Arcangeli, mindful of the necessity of tact, does not say this in so many words; he merely remarks that the present tribunal has more important business to occupy it than the wrongs suffered by the Guidos of the world: "You sit not to have gentlemen propose / Questions gentility can itself discuss." (8. 759–60.) Thus adeptly, without risking offense to the court, does Arcangeli try to remove Guido from their jurisdiction. The cuckold, particularly if he has the advantage of being noble, is far better off taking his own cuckoldry by the horns (8. 782–89).[6]

Growing bolder, Arcangeli argues that law must bear some responsibility for Guido's crime.

> My lords, my lords, the inconsiderate step
> Was—we referred ourselves to law at all!
>
> .   .   .   .
>
> My lords, we rather need defend ourselves
> Inasmuch as for a twinkling of an eye
> We hesitatingly appealed to law,—
> Rather than deny that, on mature advice,
> We blushingly bethought us, bade revenge
> Back to the simple proper private way
> Of decent self-dealt gentlemanly death.
> Judges, there is the law, and this beside,
> The testimony! Look to it!
>
> (8. 800–801, 836–44)

This line of defense, the "neglect of a better course of action," is borrowed from Aristotle, who declared it fallacious (*Rheto-*

---

[6] This argument has been closely anticipated by Arcangeli's lay colleague, Half-Rome (2. 1505–24).

ric 1400[b]1–4). To this Arcangeli adds the closely connected
point that Guido unjustly faces punishment because, though
his action was licit enough, he did not perform it in a manner
agreeable to law.

> Each punishment of the extra-legal step,
> To which the high-born preferably revert,
> Is ever for some oversight, some slip
> I' the taking vengeance, not for vengeance' self.
> A good thing done unhandsomely turns ill;
> And never yet lacked ill the law's rebuke.
>
> (8. 803–8)

Assisted by the ambiguity of the word "ill," Arcangeli has
quietly substituted the aesthetic criterion for the moral. The
law in effect is second-guessing Guido by maintaining that
before acting he should have thought of a graceful, and therefore legally acceptable, way of doing his good deed. Witness
the decision in the Sicilian case of one Leonardus who was
condemned for turning ravening dogs upon his faithless wife.
"Why? For the murder? Nay, but for the mode! / *Malus
modus occidendi*, ruled the Court, / An ugly mode of killing,
nothing more!" (8. 819–21.)

"An ugly mode of killing": there's the rub. If only Arcangeli could prove that Guido dispatched his wife in the "simple
proper private way / Of decent self-dealt gentlemanly death"!
(8. 841–42.) Unfortunately, the attendant circumstances were
neither proper, decent, nor gentlemanly, as Arcangeli (erroneously) expects Bottini to point out. Arcangeli's lengthy refu-
tation of his opponent's anticipated charges in this connection
shows him at his sophistical best. In a reprise of Tertium
Quid's harping on the middle course,[7] he imagines Guido's

---

[7] Guido's alleged violation of the golden mean—or what Half-Rome
delicately called his "natural over-energy" in killing three instead of
one (2. 1534)—is of course not a charge on which Tertium Quid
would have wished to dwell, considering his own vaunted dedication
to that ideal. But in a number of respects Tertium Quid's speech
directly anticipates Arcangeli's; the lawyer, for example, repeats his
rankling-wound figure (8. 997–1001) and insists on the inadequacy of
the "reason-check" in the face of "fury" and "despair" (8. 599–605).
Here once again, though indirectly, Tertium Quid's sympathy for
Guido's cause is illustrated.

accusers conceding that a husband may slay his wife with impunity,

> "But why the innocent old couple slay,
> Pietro, Violante? You may do enough,
> Not too much, not exceed the golden mean:
> Neither brute-beast nor Pagan, Gentile, Jew,
> Nor Christian, no nor votarist of the mode,
> Were free at all to push revenge so far!"
>
> (8. 857–62)

The answer, he implies, is obvious: the real fault was not Pompilia's but her parents'. In a comic "parable of the recovered purse" he establishes the Comparini as the felons and Guido as "the over-ready to help Law" because he has, in one master stroke, squared his own private accounts along with those of law (8. 872–99). Even if the Comparini be proved guiltless, Arcangeli admits with studied insouciance, "Ours the mistake. Is that a rare event?" (8. 903.) This alleged peccadillo is merely the capital crime for which Guido is being tried!

The following charge, that Guido was at fault both in not killing Pompilia when he surprised her with Caponsacchi and then in killing her when he did, is dealt with at least as cleverly. How can a conscientious murderer win? At Castelnuovo absolute proof of Pompilia's guilt was lacking, and "husband sure should let a scruple speak / Ere he slay wife,—for his own safety, lords!" (8. 1005–6.) When, finally convinced of her dereliction, he did kill her, the circumstances in which he did so are proof of his undiminished scrupulousness. He lingered for over a week in Rome before finally knifing her, because it was Christmas time:

> Is no religion left?
> No care for aught held holy by the Church?
> What, would you have us skip and miss those Feasts
> O' the Natal Time, must we go prosecute
> Secular business on a sacred day?
>
> (8. 1073–77)

The argument is so audacious as almost to preclude reply. And, indeed, Arcangeli's rhetorical questions trap his auditors in a familiar dilemma (conflict of abstract moral and religious scruples with a circumstantial case) from which there is only one seemly escape.

Resuming the "manner of doing" argument, Arcangeli copes with the six "aggravations" of the crime itself which seem to deepen Guido's guilt: the use of paid accomplices, the use of illegal weapons, the place of the murder (the home of the victims), the use of disguise, the fact that Pompilia was then under the protection of the court, and the affront the deed presented to the majesty of the law. Arcangeli deals with these with unequal success. Sometimes the overworked plea that the end justifies the means seems still to serve; sometimes, rather weakly, he dismisses the charge as irrelevant; sometimes, notably in the case of the charge that Guido manifested his contempt of the court, his ingenuity wholly fails him. But there is winning impudence in his assertion that Guido should not be held responsible for the overenthusiasm of his accomplices, who stabbed not wisely but too well, and in his defense of Guido's performing the murders in the Comparini's home on the ground that he had the good taste not to make a public spectacle of this necessary discharge of private business.

For all the comedy in Arcangeli's impossible case and his absurd lines of argument, it must be admitted that his rhetorical escapes have been agile and cunning. Retracing his evasive paths, we realize that he has done all he could to palliate and excuse Guido's brutal crime by insisting on the defendant's nobility and on the essential virtue and unselfishness of his mission. He has continually shifted the name of the crime itself down the scale (the device *remotio criminis*). It began as "Our murder,—we call, killing—. . . a fact / Confessed, defended, made a boast of: good!" (8. 309–10.) But as he "Makes logic levigate the big crime [into] small" (1. 1153), repetition of the word "murder" is accompanied by reductive terms such as "abnormal act" and "secular business" (8. 853, 1077). He liberally uses another Ciceronian device, the "retort of the charge," to place the real blame on the Comparini, who, if we are to believe his allegations, provoked the act. And time after time, using the device *comparatio*, he compares Guido's crime to the provocation (which was dire), and contrasts Guido's probable punishment (execution) with the merciful remission accorded other men of noble rank, hoping that his judges will see the inequities residing in an unfavorable judgment. All these maneuvers have the blessing of Cicero.[8]

Arcangeli's vaunted emphasis on logical discourse gives way in his peroration to the *pathos* we all feel for a wronged man. In quasi-religious tones the lawyer tells the judges that Guido, who without honor is as good as dead, may yet be resurrected by an all-gracious court (8. 1629–39). His motive, after all, was not a selfish but a social one, to prevent the spread of "infamy," that disease feared by the nobler among us. He performed the act—which was really a ritual sacrifice—as a priest, in order to provide Rome with an example: no dishonest wife shall with impunity bring "opprobrium" on her husband and upon the holy institution of marriage. How then can Rome fail to rehabilitate its last honorably angry man?

I I I

Arcangeli's rhetoric has been a product chiefly of his legal wit, and it has been directed at what he assumes to be the judges' taste for such a display. Bottini's, by contrast, is a polished Ciceronian rhetoric based on manipulation of language itself, which he uses to evade or becloud reason. This one of Arcangeli's predictions, at any rate, turns out to be accurate:

> —I see him strain on tiptoe, soar and pour
> Eloquence out . . .
>
> .   .   .   .
> He'll keep clear of my cast, my logic-throw,
> Let argument slide.

(8. 239–44)

His appeal is to his auditors' emotions, not to their higher ones (for, cynic that he is, he is convinced that men are lacking in the nobler qualities of love and magnanimity), but to those shallower feelings which are most susceptible to sensuous words artfully woven. To him content is always subordi-

---

[8] *De inventione*, p. 237.

nate to form, and persuasion works through aesthetics, not ethics. Bottini is guided therefore by the rhetorical principle of *enargia*, or vivid representation in words of sense experience. Unlike Arcangeli, whose strategy has precluded setting detailed action and scene before his audience, Bottini will devote nearly his whole speech to the description of the supposed actions, words, instincts, and feelings of Pompilia.[9] His rhetorical aim is to win the judges by satisfying their human craving for the dramatic and the sensational—he uses the historical present throughout, a practice that heightens the fatuity of his manner—and by concentrating on this racy, vivid fiction he manages utterly to ignore the fundamental issue.

Unfortunately, the restriction of pleadings in the Roman court to written and printed documents denied Bottini the orator's advantages of *eloquentia* (elocution) and *actio* (delivery). "Had I God's leave," he says to himself,

> how I would alter things!
> If I might read instead of print my speech,—
> Ay, and enliven speech with many a flower
> Refuses obstinately blow in print
> As wildings planted in a prim parterre.
>
> (9. 1–5)

Nevertheless, he manages to embellish his oration with a colorful variety of figures of speech. His monologue is, in fact, an extensive florilegium of the devices of classical rhetoric.[10]

[9] Aristotle *Rhetoric* 1417[a]7 ff.: "The defendant will make less of the narration. He has to maintain that the thing has not happened, or did no harm, or was not unjust, or not so bad as is alleged. . . . The narration should depict character; to which end you must know what makes it do so. One such thing is the indication of moral purpose. . . . Again, you must make use of the emotions." It will be noted that this is Aristotle's advice to the *defendant*, not the prosecutor; the latter, of course, is Bottini's assigned role, which enables him to make full use of narration with all its dramatic advantages. The fact that he also adopts, in part, the strategy Aristotle specifically recommends for the other side (the minimizing of guilt, the emphasis on motive and emotions) underscores the point made earlier (p. 66), that his argument assumes Pompilia to be the defendant in the case. Thus he makes the most of two opposing rhetorical roles.

[10] Bottini's florilegium includes nearly all the species enumerated in the guidebooks to classical rhetoric. A small selection gives some

Under such a cover of extravagant language Bottini shifts
the grounds of his argument from the factual to the qualita-
tive, from the question of Guido's guilt to that of Pompilia's
behavior and motive: Was she pure? What caused her to act
as Guido and his partisans maintain she did? From the outset
Guido is removed from the dock and Pompilia, in a sense,
substituted.

> No further blame
> O' the man and murder! They were stigmatized
> Befittingly: the Court heard long ago
> My mind o' the matter, which, outpouring full,
> Has long since swept, like surge i' the simile
> Of Homer, overborne both dyke and dam,
> And whelmed alike client and advocate:
> His fate is sealed, his life as good as gone,
> On him I am not tempted to waste word.
> . . . my purpose holds,—which was and is
> And solely shall be to the very end,
> To draw the true *effigiem* of a saint,
> Do justice to perfection in the sex,—
>
> .   .   .   .
>
> By painting saintship I depicture sin,
> Beside the pearl, I prove how black the jet,
> And through Pompilia's virtue, Guido's crime.
>   (9. 1386–1411)

Why not? Bottini suspects that the court is wearied of Guido;
furthermore, since Guido has confessed, all that remains for
the prosecutor is the luxury of heaping coals on Guido's head
by exonerating Pompilia. Bottini's "full cup" indeed "runs
o'er" (9. 148), for he assumes that his celibate listeners share

---

idea of their variety: *paralipsis* (*occupatio*) (168–74), *auxesis*
(208–9), *hypozeugma* (227), *parison* (228), *epanorthosis* (229–30),
syllepsis (235–38), *anaphora* (261–68), *paranomasia* (338–42), *er-
otema* (*interrogatio*) (424–31), *polyptoton* and *synoeciosis*
(1486–87), *anadiplosis* (1499–1500). In certain passages the devices
come thick and fast. In lines 403–8, for example, can be found
epanalepsis, ecphonesis, ploce (*traductio*) and *polyptoton,* as well as
the familiar rhetorical question; and in 410–20 we find *antimetabole,
prosopopoeia, epanorthosis, meiosis,* and *gradatio* (climax).

his own bachelor's proclivity for contemplating errant womanhood. They would rather entertain lubricious fancies about a
woman than hear logical arguments about a man. And so,
under strict rhetorical guidance, he titillates their imagination
with a long series of courtly-love images and selected allusions
to pastoral idylls and erotic literature.[11]

But there are also more subtle motives for Bottini's concentration on Pompilia as a fallible woman. Such strategy permits
him to slip into the relativism of which he is perhaps a more
dedicated exponent even than Tertium Quid. His gnomic
"Grime is grace / To whoso gropes amid the dung for gold"
(9. 550–51) sums up his whole philosophy. Time after time he
avoids the absolute in favor of the conditional, as in his
distinction between conduct that is proper before marriage
and that which befits the married state:

> toys, permissible to-day, become
> Follies to-morrow: prattle shocks in church:
> And that curt skirt which lets a maiden skip,
> The matron changes for a trailing robe.
>
> (9. 1182–85)

Moral perfection such as he finds in Pompilia's dying speech
has no place in the relativism of law, which deals with the
probabilities of human nature, not with exceptions. Neither
the image she herself presents of a poor, harassed, bewildered
child-bride nor that of saint and martyr delineated by Caponsacchi recommends itself, he assumes, to these sophisticated
ecclesiastical judges. But in the safe, credible middle ground
resides Pompilia the voluptuous, cunning, acquiescent woman,
the very type of the sex, whose wantonness, as Bottini will
describe it, comports with man's normal experience—or fan-
tasy—of woman; and so he will present this figure to them in all

---

[11] It is noteworthy, but not surprising, that although Bottini has the
world's treasury of erotic story at his fingertips, when the drift of his
rhetoric requires mention of a decorous author he cannot think of a
single one. "Avaunt—," he imagines Pompilia crying, "Be burned, thy
wicked townsman's [Aretino's] sonnet-book! / Welcome, mild hymnal
by . . . some better scribe!" (9. 1201–3.) By attributing the lapse to
her, Bottini thriftily converts his own deficiency into another evidence
of her supposed character.

its vivid fleshliness. Only in his closing statements does he refer to Pompilia's sainthood, as climactic rhetorical strategy would seem to require if nothing else did. But by that time the idea of sainthood as he uses it has acquired the same dubious color as Guido's honor, and in view of all the sins and misdemeanors that Bottini has already imputed to Pompilia, it is obvious that this belated praise is but perfunctory.

Awareness of his rhetorical strategy, therefore, especially as it is directed by his personal inclinations and sanctioned by his sense of realism, makes it easier to understand why Bottini, with what seems at first to be sheer perversity, concedes almost all the damaging allegations made against Pompilia by others and, most numerously, by himself.

> Grant the tale
> O' the husband, which is false, for proved and true
> To the letter,—or the letters, I should say,
> The abominations he professed to find
> And fix upon Pompilia and the priest,—
> Allow them hers—for though she could not write,
> In early days of Eve-like innocence
> That plucked no apple from the knowledge-tree,
> Yet, at the Serpent's word, Eve plucks and eats
> And knows—especially how to read and write:
>
> .   .   .   .
>
> So she, through hunger after fellowship,
> May well have learned, though late, to play the scribe:
> As indeed, there's one letter on the list
> Explicitly declares did happen here.
> "You thought my letters could be none of mine,"
> She tells her parents—"mine, who wanted skill;
> But now I have the skill, and write, you see!"
> She needed write love-letters, so she learned,
> "*Negatas artifex sequi voces*"—though
> This letter nowise 'scapes the common lot,
> But lies i' the condemnation of the rest,
> Found by the husband's self who forged them all.
> Yet, for the sacredness of argument,
> For this once an exemption shall it plead—
>
> .   .   .   .

> Concede she wrote (which were preposterous)
> This and the other epistle,—what of it?
> Where does the figment touch her candid fame?
>
> (9. 443–75)

In the process of conceding that Pompilia *might* have learned
to read and write, Bottini makes such an improbable case for
her instant literacy (*reductio ad absurdum*) as to undermine
Arcangeli's serious argument.

In other passages employing *concessio*, Bottini grants that
Pompilia was guilty of the action charged but then builds an
elaborate casuistical argument, recalling Arcangeli's similar
defense of Guido's conduct, that she had to do it. It is over
these episodes, nearly all of them sexual, that Bottini seems to
linger more than the strict necessity of his argument requires.
By depicting her as a Magdalene, a sinner-saint (that is, a
saint "Who sinned not in the little she did sin" [9. 1487]
because her sins were committed in a good cause), he can
satisfy his libidinousness and yet finally limn her as a saint by
contrasting her with Guido. His argument, in sum, is based on
his (and supposedly the judges') estimation of the weaknesses
of the flesh. It is simply impossible for him to conceive of any
person, least of all a nubile young woman with a "flawless
form" (9. 195), as being morally beyond reproach.

Bottini's *exordium* begins with the flattery so often recommended by the classical authorities. Then he states his cause
indirectly, through an *allegoria* or conceit about an artist
commissioned to paint the flight of the Holy Family (9.
17–85). He has labored long on the "preliminary sketches"
(i.e., inquiry into fact), but intends only to present the finished painting to his judges: [12]

> Exactly so have I, a month at least,
> Your Fiscal, made me cognizant of facts,

---

[12] Bottini dispenses with "facts" as swiftly as Arcangeli did, in his
anxiety to have greater room for fanciful argument.—The careful
"detailism" (G. H. Lewes's word) which Bottini initially attributes to
his painter-self conceivably alludes to the Pre-Raphaelite penchant
for the same technique.

> Searched out, pried into, pressed the meaning forth
> Of every piece of evidence in point,
>
> .   .   .   .
>
> But shall I ply my papers, play my proofs,
> Parade my studies, fifty in a row,
> As though the Court were yet in pupilage
> And not the artist's ultimate appeal?
> Much rather let me soar the height prescribed
> And, bowing low, proffer my picture's self!
> No more of proof, disproof.
>
> $\qquad\qquad\qquad\qquad\qquad$ (9. 132–60)

Supported by his use of the epic invocation and simile, the implication is that he proposes to work on the grand scale. But finding the task too great—an early hint that his reach will sometimes exceed his grasp—he backs farther and farther away from the epic mode, settling instead for the pastoral idyll and the more salacious portion of Greek legend:

> (I leave the family as unmanageable,
> And stick to just one portrait, but life-size.)
> Hath calumny imputed to the fair
> A blemish, mole on cheek or wart on chin,
> Much more, blind hidden horrors best unnamed?
> Shall I descend to prove you, point by point,
> Never was knock-knee known nor splay-foot found
> In Phryne? (I must let the portrait go,
> Content me with the model, I believe)—
> —I prove this? An indignant sweep of hand,
> Dash at and doing away with drapery,
> And,—use your eyes, Athenians, smooth she smiles!
>
> $\qquad\qquad\qquad\qquad\qquad$ (9. 163–74) [13]

—At which point Bottini's implicit stage direction obviously calls for a tableau.

[13] Bottini, who is an authority on legends of bad women, must have particular regard for Phryne, one of antiquity's loveliest courtesans, because it was in the course of defending her on a charge of impiety that the Attic courtroom orator Hyperides (389–322 B.C.) staged one of his most spectacular forensic triumphs. Having expended much verbal argument to no avail, as a last resort Hyperides bade his client

Bottini's oration proper combines the traditional *narratio, divisio, confirmatio,* and *refutatio.* Not surprisingly, he opens it with a sensuous portrait of an earthly Ovidian mistress, replete with all the feminine wiles.

> First, infancy, pellucid as a pearl;
> Then, childhood—stone which, dew-drop at the first,
> (An old conjecture) sucks, by dint of gaze,
> Blue from the sky and turns to sapphire so:
> Yet both these gems eclipsed by, last and best,
> Womanliness and wifehood opaline,
> Its milk-white pallor,—chastity,—suffused
> With here and there a tint and hint of flame,—
> Desire,—the lapidary loves to find.
> Such jewels bind conspicuously thy brow,
> Pompilia, infant, child, maid, woman, wife—
> Crown the ideal in our earth at last!
>
> (9. 199–210)

In this *blason,* or encomiastic portrait, he invokes the lapidary art to define Pompilia's character: she embodies the ambiguity as well as the loveliness of the opal (both she and the jewel are the more desirable for their apparent impurities). Like the lapidary, Bottini will use his skill to reveal the subsurface flashes—of natural desire—beneath the apparent whiteness of her chastity. To shift metaphors, Pompilia will be painted an off-white, after the manner of an El Greco, and will appear true white only because she is set off starkly against the dark umber of the surrounding world.

Momentarily resuming the role of epic poet, Bottini begins

---

expose her body before the judges, who were thereupon won over. There are distinct suggestions of Hyperides in Bottini's character. The Greek too was a master of ingenious argument which circumvented the letter of the law; he specialized in defending clients from the demi-monde; and he wasted no love on his courtroom rival, who happened to be Demosthenes. On the other hand, it is Arcangeli, not Bottini, who shares Hyperides' excessive love for food; and unlike Bottini, Hyperides was noted for the studied simplicity of his rhetorical style. Some of Hyperides' orations, lost during the Revival of Learning, were recovered in Egyptian papyri in 1847. See [F. G. Kenyon], "Hyperides and the New Papyri," *Quarterly Review,* 178 (1894) : 531–52.

in medias res: "As Flaccus prompts, I dare the epic plunge—
/ Begin at once with marriage." (9. 217–18.) It is to his
advantage—a comparison with Tertium Quid is useful
here—to gloss over the marriage bargain, since it calls the
Comparini's motives into question. Ironically, his argument
from this point onward parallels that of his opponent Arcangeli; both rest on the primacy of natural law and on analogies
with the conduct of beasts and of figures in human history.
Whereas Arcangeli argues the husband's right of revenge
thereby, Bottini argues from natural evidence that each creature is true to its kind: "lamb and lamb, / How do they
differ? Know one, you know all / Manners of maidenhood."
(9. 220–22.) Using the figure *taxis* (assigning to each subject
its proper adjuncts), he reasons that Pompilia would therefore
be unnatural if she made no use of woman's proper endow-
ments:

> Prepare to find that, lamb-like, she too frisks—
> O' the weaker sex, my lords, the weaker sex!
> To whom, the Teian teaches us, for gift,
> Not strength,—man's dower,—but beauty, nature gave,
> "Beauty in lieu of spears, in lieu of shields!"
> And what is beauty's sure concomitant,
> Nay, intimate essential character,
> But melting wiles, deliciousest deceits,
> The whole redoubted armoury of love?

Bottini's reading of life assumes that the lovelier a woman, the
more prone she is to "vernal pranks, dishevellings / O' the
hair of youth that dances April in, / And easily-imagined
Hebe-slips" (9. 224–35).

Bottini next moves Pompilia from maidenhood to wifehood.
In unmistakable strains of the epithalamium, he announces
that the old frisks are at an end; marriage signalizes the
turning from youthful promiscuity to sober monogamy.

> For lo, advancing Hymen and his pomp!
> *Discedunt nunc amores,* loves, farewell!
> *Maneat amor,* let love, the sole, remain! [14]

---

[14] "Love" has two quite different senses here (the device *antanacla-
sis*): the loves are lovers, while love becomes an abstract essence—

> Farewell to dewiness and prime of life!
> Remains the rough determined day: dance done,
> To work, with plow and harrow!
>
> (9. 239–44)

Appropriately, she is no longer a lamb but a beast of burden—a heifer not yet used to the yoke of marriage:

> heifer brave the hind?
> We seek not there should lapse the natural law,
> The proper piety to lord and king
> And husband: let the heifer bear the yoke!
> Only, I crave he cast not patience off,
> This hind; for deem you she endures the whip,
> Nor winces at the goad, nay, restive, kicks?
>
> .   .   .   .
>
> Therefore, I hold a husband but inept
> Who turns impatient at such transit-time,
> As if this running from the rod would last!
>
> (9. 251–75)

Descending from the animal to the vegetable kingdom, Bottini argues that the plant-wife can scarcely be blamed for anomalous growth under adverse conditions:

> But what if, as 'tis wont with plant and wife,
> Flowers,—after a suppression to good end,
> Still, when they do spring forth,—sprout here, spread there,
> Anywhere likelier than beneath the foot
> O' the lawful good-man gardener of the ground?
> He dug and dibbled, sowed and watered,—still
> 'Tis a chance wayfarer shall pluck the increase.
>
> (9. 290–96)

Because the husband(man) has pruned his plant's growth too closely, it is only the more probable (and in accordance with natural law) that the plant would send forth runners outside the garden wall.

---

ironically suggesting an expansion rather than a restriction of sexual activity. Bottini is later to marvel at the democratic impartiality with which she distributed her favors.

After a slight change of garb, Pompilia emerges as a flower, in a reversal of the traditional metaphor of woman-flower-chastity (cf. Paolo's "Lily of a maiden, white with intact leaf" [3. 365]). Again he argues on the ground of subject-adjuncts, gracefully yielding the single most destructive point against his client.

> The lady, foes allege, put forth each charm
> And proper floweret of feminity
> To whosoever had a nose to smell
> Or breast to deck: what if the charge be true?
>
> (9. 298–301)

By what better means, he demands, could such a flower realize her true nature? If she is faithful to her nature, then the apparent sin, when carefully scrutinized, is really virtue misinterpreted. Assuming the charge of wholesale adultery to be true,

> The fault were graver had she looked with choice,
> Fastidiously appointed who should grasp,
> Who, in the whole town, go without the prize!
> To nobody she destined donative,
> But, first come was first served, the accuser saith.
>
> (9. 302–6)

For her magnanimity, implies Bottini, she ought to be praised, not censured; she was simply a good hostess, as befits the wife of a nobleman: "One chalice entertained the company." He heaps blame on Guido for misconstruing "such bounty in a wife":

> Which butterfly of the wide air shall brag
> "I was preferred to Guido"—when 'tis clear
> The cup, he quaffs at, lay with olent breast
> Open to gnat, midge, bee and moth as well? [15]

. . . .

[15] The Other Half-Rome earlier envisioned Pompilia as "a light tuft of bloom. . . . / . . . toyed with by butterfly or bee" (3. 244–45).

Bottini's sardonic allusion to the "chalice" which "entertained the company" contrasts with another likening of Pompilia to a sacramen-

> . . . charm of cheek,
> Lustre of eye, allowance of the lip,
> All womanly components in a spouse,
> These are no household-bread each stranger's bite
> Leaves by so much diminished for the mouth
> O' the master of the house at supper-time:
> But rather like a lump of spice they lie,
> Morsel of myrrh, which scents the neighbourhood
> Yet greets its lord no lighter by a grain.
>
> (9. 311–26)

Bottini now retracts the argument, using the device *paramo-logia* (concession to gain an unforeseen advantage). "Concede we there was reason in his wrong," must not Pompilia be praised for having renounced "lavish bounty" in favor of discrimination? "She laudably sees all, / Searches the best out and selects the same." (9. 328–37.) Fallaciously arguing from opposites (indiscriminateness *vs.* selectivity) he maintains that since Pompilia's wonted promiscuity merited Guido's reproach, her new fastidiousness ought to merit his approval. What if the man chosen be a well-favored priest? The fact is a tribute to her taste in men:

> Priest, ay and very phoenix of such fowl,
> Well-born, of culture, young and vigorous,
> Comely too, since precise the precept points—
> On the selected levite be there found
> Nor mole nor scar nor blemish, lest the mind
> Come all uncandid through the thwarting flesh!
>
> (9. 350–55)

---

tal object. Caponsacchi, recalling his reverential treatment of the young fugitive, avers,

> I never touched her with my finger-tip
> Except to carry her to the couch, that eve,
> Against my heart, beneath my head, bowed low,
> As we priests carry the paten
>
> (6. 1617–20)

—a striking illustration of the facility with which Browning uses similar imagery for wholly different purposes in different contexts.

This "levite," Caponsacchi, has just been depicted as patiently
waiting his turn with Pompilia. " *'Constans in levitate,'*—Ha,
my lords? / Calm in his levity,—indulge the quip!— / Since
'tis a levite bears the bell[e] away." (9. 340–42.)

Bottini next borrows from Arcangeli the familiar line which
he later delights in repeatedly casting in his opponent's teeth:

> permit the end—permit therewith
> Means to the end!
> How say you, good my lords?
> I hope you heard my adversary ring
> The changes on this precept: now, let me
> Reverse the peal!   (9. 516–21) [16]

To crush crime (the threat of murder) Pompilia may use "all
efficacious means" (9. 425). And what means, supposing
again that the charge of adultery be true, are more efficacious—and more proper to woman—than seductive wiles?

> "With horns the bull, with teeth the lion fights,
> To woman," quoth the lyrist quoted late,
> "Nor teeth, nor horns, but beauty, Nature gave!"
> Pretty i' the Pagan! Who dares blame the use
> Of the armoury thus allowed for natural[?]
>   (9. 427–31)

If "natural" (appropriate to animals) then right, argues Bottini, as had Arcangeli before him, though for a different end.
He concedes that Pompilia "somewhat plied / Arts that allure,
the magic nod and wink" (9. 435–36), but only, at first, to
save Guido from perdition and later herself from his cruelty.
Caponsacchi's celibacy notwithstanding, Pompilia is bound to
offer love as a fit reward for rescuing her (9. 507–9):

> licit end
> Enough was the escape from death, I hope,

---

[16] Another change has already been rung by Pompilia, who, in her
innocence, often happens to echo the chief tenets of her persecutors:
"What o' the way to the end?" she cries, alluding to her elopement,
"—the end crowns all." (7. 1648.) Here she anticipates Bottini's very
line of defense—but of course Bottini's definition of the means and
ends involved is not hers.

> To legalize the means illicit else
> Of feigned love, false allurement, fancied fact.
>
>   (9. 523–26)

And just as her deceit was dedicated to a high cause, so she was honor bound to keep her generous promises. Hence, the "nocturnal entertainment" and "midnight meetings" in the palace were merely Pompilia's prepaid reward to Caponsacchi for future services (9. 553–65).

From the assumption that the natural instinct for self-preservation justifies any deed (*dicaeologia:* excuse through dire necessity) Bottini proceeds to what can only be described as his crowning labor of lust: the detailed account of the love that came to Pompilia and Caponsacchi or, to join him in applying the names adopted in the love letters found in the Old Yellow Book, Amaryllis and Myrtillus. He can argue her innocence in this amorous sport, for like flirtation earlier, adulterous love to her is only a means, which is allowable if the end is. And if love, with all its dainty devices, is allowable, then Pompilia's mendacity must also be excused: "Worst, once, is best now: in all faith, she feigns: / Feigning,—the liker innocence to guilt, / The truer to the life is what she feigns!" (9. 543–45.) Intentionally freighted with paradoxes, the purport of which is that Pompilia's seeming guilt is really innocence adopting the garb of sin in order to remain pure (free from Guido's taint), this passage figures forth Bottini's own philosophy that artifice is somehow "the truer to the life." He is now equipped to answer the critics of Pompilia's reputation: her feigning has been so true to life that those easily deceived by appearance are disposed to condemn her. Indignantly challenging his audience, he asks,

> Would such external semblance of intrigue
> Demonstrate that intrigue must lurk perdue?
> Does every hazel-sheath disclose a nut?
> He were a Molinist who dared maintain
> That midnight meetings in a screened alcove
> Must argue folly in a matron—since
> So would he bring a slur on Judith's self,

> Commended beyond women that she lured
> The lustful to destruction through his lust.
>
> (9. 561–69)

Hiding the tenuousness of his Pompilia-Judith analogy behind imputations of heresy to his critics, Bottini once again has it both ways. On the one hand, probability argues that adultery did occur; on the other, there is reasonable doubt of Pompilia's guilt. Linking Pompilia with Judith (both are women with a mission) is a happy stroke; for, having introduced the legendary woman, Bottini argues *a fortiori* to show that Pompilia was more virtuous than Judith, the very type of activist feminine virtue. The device *litotes* (expressing a thought by denying its contrary), with its repetition of negatives, works well for Bottini until he presses the biblical parallel too far:

> Pompilia took not Judith's liberty,
> No faulchion find you in her hand to smite,—
> No damsel to convey the head in dish,
> Of Holophernes,—style the Canon so—
> Or is it the Count? If I entangle me
> With my similitudes,—if wax wings melt,
> And earthward down I drop, not mine the fault:
> Blame your beneficence, O Court, O sun,
> Whereof the beamy smile affects my flight!
> What matter, so Pompilia's fame revive
> I' the warmth that proves the bane of Icarus?
>
> (9. 570–80) [17]

Picking himself up undamaged and unabashed after this abortive flight, Bottini reviews with ever-increasing relish the

[17] In the apocryphal story, no mention is made of Judith's using her sex to lure Holofernes; Browning is perhaps echoing Friedrich Hebbel's tragedy *Judith* (1841), in which this added touch does occur. Nor does the dish Bottini specifies appear in the original story. His introduction of it indicates that he is confusing Judith with Salome, an error often committed by Renaissance painters but especially suitable to Bottini, who thereby is enabled to visualize two seductive murderesses (or accessories to murder) for the price of one. Judith's sword, an iconographic symbol of her virtue, is noticeably absent from Bottini's portrait of Pompilia in the role (cf. the second line of the quotation).

events that led up to the elopement. Ridiculing those who deplore the lovers' departure in the dark of night, he ironically suggests the alternative—Pompilia and Caponsacchi boldly marching down the sunlit street, flags flying and drums beating (9. 613–14). The allegation that Pompilia, "Who not so much as knew what opiates mean" (9. 640), administered one to Guido that night is "a fable"; but it is precisely such fables that stimulate him to his best apologetic efforts. The merciful deed, had it occurred, would have been another mark of her wifely solicitude.

> Therefore shall the lady's wit
> Supply the boon thwart nature baulks him of,
> And do him service with the potent drug
> (Helen's nepenthe, as my lords opine)
> Shall respite blessedly each frittered nerve
> O' the much-enduring man: accordingly,
> There lies he, duly dosed and sound asleep,
> Relieved of woes, or real or raved about.
> While soft she leaves his side, he shall not wake.
>   (9. 621–29)

Proceeding to the next felonious act Pompilia is alleged to have performed on that busy night, her stealing Guido's money and jewels to finance the junket to Rome, Bottini once more assumes fiction to be fact, and then argues again that any object ought to be put to its proper use:

> What fitter use
> Was ever husband's money destined to?
> With bag and baggage thus did Dido once
> Decamp,—for more authority, a queen!
>   (9. 653–56) [18]

---

[18] The same strategy is later used to justify her wielding her husband's sword against him. Since Guido chose to threaten in such a fashion rather than use words of mild reproof or conciliation, she had no choice.

> he must needs prefer the argument
> O' the blow: and she obeyed, in duty bound,
> Returned him buffet ratiocinative—
> Ay, in the reasoner's own interest,

As he develops the narrative of the journey toward Rome, the mud and dirt along the way acquire a moral connotation. The "long and devious road" they traveled (9. 719) was, it appears, not only sinuous but sinful. Bottini's casuistry has never been more brilliant than now, when he uses it to palliate any physical contact, intentional or accidental, real or imagined, that may have occurred between wife and priest. Caponsacchi is in low spirits as they ride along; there is "tedium," Bottini argues unconvincingly, in "a prolonged jaunt / In a close carriage o'er a jolting road, / With only one young female substitute" for the seventeen elderly canons who were his preferred company. What more effective way to raise his spirits than "a kiss / Sagely and sisterly administered"? The driver testified that "The journey was one long embrace"—a lie, of course, but even if he had seen what he "supposed a vulgar interchange of love, / This was but innocent jog of head 'gainst head," only a "casual ambiguity, no harm / I' the world to eyes awake and penetrative" (9. 666–705). Even so:

> Say, she kissed him and he kissed her again! [19]
> Such osculation was a potent means,
> A very efficacious help, no doubt   [Ps. 41:6]
>
> .   .   .   .
>
> [Which] kept the priest her servant to the end.
>   (9. 708–15)

> For wife must follow whither husband leads,
> Vindicate honour as himself prescribes,
> Save him the very way himself bids save!
>   (9. 908–14)

For the accompanying farcical analogy in illustration, see below, p. 252.

[19] Note how the single "sisterly" kiss of lines 677–78 is multiplied (one for each occasion when Caponsacchi felt an "incipient scruple" [681]) and finally stretched into "one long embrace" which lasted the whole journey (691). The process is the reverse of that observed in Arcangeli's speech (above, p. 162), in which he employed diminution. A similar tendency, recalling Falstaff's facile enlarging of the band of highwaymen, is found in Caponsacchi's escalation of the number of men ranged against Pompilia at Castelnuovo from six (Half-Rome's figure [2. 1039]) to twelve (6. 1547).

The climax of the narrative is reached in what must be the most audacious sexual scene in Victorian literature. Only a poet confident of his reputation for unintelligibility would have dared print such lines. When the fugitives reach the inn at Castelnuovo, Pompilia is as tired as the phrase (Matt. 26:41) Bottini applies to her condition: "Spirit is willing but the flesh is weak, / Pompilia needs must acquiesce and swoon." (9. 732–33.) In the next thirty-odd lines, Bottini insists no fewer than ten times that she remains asleep throughout what ensues. Caponsacchi, on the other hand, is most certainly conscious and active; he bears her to her couch, "unguarded save / By her own chastity" (9. 736–37), which by this point in Bottini's account is, of course, a highly undependable attribute. The rhetorical ascent to climax (*gradatio*) carries Caponsacchi—and Bottini—to the inn's bower of bliss:

> Nay, what and if he gazed rewardedly
> On the pale beauty prisoned in embrace,
> Stooped over, stole a balmy breath perhaps
> For more assurance sleep was not decease—
> "*Ut vidi*," "how I saw!" succeeded by
> "*Ut perii*," "how I sudden lost my brains!"
> —What harm ensued to her unconscious quite?
> For, curiosity—how natural!
> Importunateness—what a privilege
> In the ardent sex! And why curb ardour here?
> How can the priest but pity whom he saved?
> And pity is how near to love, and love
> How neighbourly to unreasonableness!
> And for love's object, whether love were sage
> Or foolish, could Pompilia know or care,
> Being still sound asleep, as I premised?
> Thus the philosopher absorbed by thought,
> Even Archimedes, busy o'er a book
> The while besiegers sacked his Syracuse,
> Was ignorant of the imminence o' the point
> O' the sword till it surprised him: let it stab,
> And never knew himself was dead at all.

> So sleep thou on, secure whate'er betide!
> For thou, too, hast thy problem hard to solve—
> How so much beauty is compatible
> With so much innocence! [20]

(9. 741–66)

While Pompilia "rosily is lost" in solving the riddle of her own innocence and before she springs up "in the garb of truth . . . / . . . Thalassian-pure" (9. 889–91)—that is, in the state in which Venus emerged from the sea [21]—Bottini busies himself preparing his formal rebuttal of the various charges against her (*refutatio*, 9. 767–1503). Fate has dealt him what a less self-assured advocate would regard as a low blow: in her deathbed "talk, chatter and gossipry" (9. 1430), reproduced in Book 7, she

> Falsified all I have adduced for truth,
> Admitted not one peccadillo here,
> Pretended to perfection, first and last,
> O' the whole procedure—perfect in the end,
> Perfect i' the means, perfect in everything,
> Leaving a lawyer nothing to excuse,
> Reason away and show his skill about!

(9. 1434–40)

" 'How reconcile' gasps Malice 'that with this?' " (9. 1444)—his own confident version of her gloriously sinful life? But Bottini is no more embarrassed by her protestations of purity than Arcangeli was by his client's admission of guilt. He has a genius for salvaging gain from apparent disaster. Actually, he maintains, her dying "babble" (9. 1431) was a tissue of cunning lies; if she had not been blessed with friends and an expert lawyer to set the record right, "Far better had Pompilia died o' the spot / Than found a tongue to wag and shame the law, / Shame most of all herself" (9. 1449–51).

[20] The compatibility of Pompilia's *guilt* with her innocence was a problem which, according to Caponsacchi, earlier occupied the court when it was confronted with the disputed love letters (6. 1735–36).

[21] Cook (*Commentary*, p. 191) cites other explanations of the term, including the supposition that the god of virginity was named *Thalassio*. Our interpretation, however, seems more consistent with the view we take of Bottini's character.

But though she lied, she (wily to the end) had taken the
precaution of confessing and receiving absolution beforehand,
so as to escape the guilt of lying. In explaining her subterfuge,
Bottini adopts the style of the church casuists:

> The sacrament obliterates the sin:
> What is not,—was not, in a certain sense.
> Let Molinists distinguish, "Souls washed white
> Were red once, still show pinkish to the eye!"
> We say, abolishment is nothingness
> And nothingness has neither head nor tail
> End nor beginning;—better estimate
> Exorbitantly, than disparage aught
> Of the efficacity of the act, I hope!
>
> (9. 1495–1503)

In one bold stroke, Bottini has avoided the tiresome necessity
of reconciling his "defense" of Pompilia with her own apologia and at the same time has triumphantly established what he
has, in face of all the presumptive evidence, been arguing all
along, her purity: for with her absolution, all her sins, including the lies she had not yet uttered, were canceled. It is not
every lawyer who can establish his client's sinfulness and her
innocence at the same time.[22]

[22] Tertium Quid likewise has not been abashed by Pompilia's
assertion of complete innocence; the "private" confession (which,
differing from Bottini, he places after the "public" one) covers the
discrepancy:

> "Confession," cry folks—"a confession, think!
> Confession of the moribund is true!"
> Which of them, my wise friends? This public one,
> Or the private other we shall never know?
> The private may contain,—your casuists teach,—
> The acknowledgment of, and the penitence for,
> That other public one, so people say.
>
> (4. 1477–83)

It is her husband who is truly discommoded by the fact that Pompilia
lived to offer her own story on her deathbed,

> not at judgment-seat
> Where I could twist her soul, as erst her flesh,
> And turn her truth into a lie,—but there,
> O' the death-bed, with God's hand between us both,

Although more is to come, notably Bottini's efforts to instruct the court in its duty (9. 1504–22) and his concluding use of an analogy between law and wine to show that nothing remains stable in this world of time and circumstance though the ingredients be the same (9. 1543–59), it is fitting that we leave him with that *coup de maître* most vivid in our memory.

What have the sophistries of Tertium Quid, Arcangeli, and Bottini proved? Simply that mere glibness or cleverness in logical disputation, governed by self-seeking motives, obscures, not reveals, truth. The three use reason and language not to reveal truth but to obscure it; to justify not the good but the evil; and to serve themselves, not their fellow men. They reject honestly rational confrontation in favor of sophistry, casuistry, and the unscrupulous use of emotive language and allusion. No wonder, then, that the Pope will reject out of hand "this coil / Of statement, comment, query and response" of which the lawyers' speeches serve as prime examples. Like leprous rags which must be burned, the legal arguments are "Tatters all too contaminate for use" (10. 372–74). The Pope would agree with Plato in the *Gorgias* that "there is no need for rhetoric to know the facts at all, for it has hit upon a means of persuasion that enables it to appear, in the eyes of the ignorant, to know more than those who really know." [23]

> Striking me dumb, and helping her to speak,
> Tell her own story her own way, and turn
> My plausibility to nothingness!

(11. 1681–87)

Bottini's argument that a precautionary prior confession absolves one from a subsequent sin recalls Arcangeli's invoking benefit of clergy to remove Guido from the jurisdiction of the temporal court: he "Has taken minor orders many enough, / Shows still sufficient chrism upon his pate / To neutralise a blood-stain" (1. 261–63).

[23] *Gorgias,* trans. W. C. Helmbold (Indianapolis, 1952), p. 18.

Seven

"Poke at Them with Scripture"

THE DRAMA OF ALLUSION

I

The lawyers also play a leading role in what is probably the crowning irony in this poetic study of language and error: with them, as with the other conscious rhetoricians—the effete worldling Tertium Quid, who seldom alludes to the Bible, is an exception—Scripture serves as an ever-ready vehicle for the twisting and hiding of truth. In their blindness to the things that matter, Browning shows men exploiting as a means to their narrow ends not only language in general but in particular the Word of God. In the rhetoricians' speeches the incessant mishandling of biblical language, incident, and image offers a large-scale study of casual blasphemy, or, to put it in the mildest terms, sheer indifference to the great source of Christian faith and hope.

The use and misuse of scriptural material, indeed, is a sure key to all the principal speakers' characters and intentions. To Caponsacchi, Pompilia, and the Pope (hereafter to be called the literalists in respect to biblical quotation) the Bible has only its true function of conveying the divine message. Having nothing to hide and nothing to gain from duplicity, they use biblical language and allusion with the reverence and directness, the fidelity to accepted meaning, that mark the children of light. For this reason little attention need be given to their employment of biblical allusion, frequent and tonally effective though it is. No distortion of meaning, no crafty purpose, is ever in question.

184

But to the casuists and the other pleaders, whom we shall call the ironists, the Bible, especially when misquoted or otherwise amended, provides an abundance of laws, codes, and analogies to be invoked as specious extenuation. To Guido, it supplies precedent for inhumane treatment of a wife, as well as a copious garner of pathetic parallels to his own situation. His argument that his deed merits the blessing of St. Peter and the pardon of the Pope typifies the method:

> Oh, if men were but good! They are not good,
> Nowise like Peter: people called him rough,
> But if, as I left Rome, I spoke the Saint,
> —"*Petrus, quo vadis?*"—doubtless, I should hear,
> "To free the prisoner and forgive his fault!
> I plucked the absolute dead from God's own bar,
> And raised up Dorcas,—why not rescue thee?"
>
> [Acts 9:40–41]
(11. 324–30)

In this merging of a canonical miracle of St. Peter with a legend told by St. Ambrose,[1] Guido has two simultaneous roles. He is a self-styled Christ, the Pope therefore being Peter; and he is also the prisoner whom the Pope ought, with the miraculous power of his forebear Peter, to release. As Guido goes on to say, "If Innocent succeeds to Peter's place, / Let him think Peter's thought, speak Peter's speech!" (11. 332–33)—especially when the speech is dictated by Guido.

If they detect this kind of chicanery, the ecclesiastical judges are in no position to deplore it. The practice of their clerical colleagues suggests that distortions or imitations of the sacred text have everyday utility in dealing with the ignorant commonalty. Interceding for Guido, the Archbishop at Arezzo tries to persuade Pompilia to yield to her husband:

---

[1] St. Peter, fleeing Nero's persecution, met Christ on the Appian Way, inquiring "*Domine quo vadis?*" On hearing the answer "*Venio iterum crucifigi*" he returned to Rome to be martyred (Cook, *Commentary*, p. 241). Note the inversion of roles in Guido's version, Christ (Guido) interrogating Peter.

The rod were too advanced a punishment!
Let's try the honeyed cake. A parable!
"Without a parable spake He not to them." [Mark 4:34]
(8. 819–21)

His homemade parable, faintly resembling Christ's allegory of
the barren fig tree (Matt. 21:19), is strictly *ad feminam,* and
is backed by no discoverable Christian teaching. It advises
Pompilia of the dangers of being a "restif fig" which, if it
refuses to yield its delectable pulp to the "fig-pecker, / The
bird" (Guido), is eaten by "three hundred thousand bees and
wasps" (e.g., the lustful Canon Girolamo).[2] "Therefore go
home, embrace your husband quick! / Which if his Canon
brother chance to see, / He will the sooner back to book
again." (7. 831–46.)

Whatever their own views on the misapplication of the
Bible for argumentative ends, the very fact that the judges
hearing the Franceschini case are churchmen would recommend, if nothing else did, the liberal use of scriptural allusion
by Guido and the two lawyers. "It's hard," complains Arcangeli:

[2] Cf. 9. 313 ff., in which, according to Bottini, Pompilia "lay with
olent breast / Open to gnat, midge, bee and moth." In choosing the
fruit for his improvised parable, the Archbishop gets into trouble:

> There was a ripe round long black toothsome fruit,
> Even a flower-fig, the prime boast of May:
> And, to the tree, said . . . either the spirit o' the fig,
> Or, if we bring in men, the gardener,
> Archbishop of the orchard—had I time
> To try o' the two which fits in best: indeed
> It might be the Creator's self, but then
> The tree should bear an apple, I suppose.
>
> (7. 822–29)

Although most of this must be presumed to be an unheard comment to
himself, it is reported by Pompilia, who, being illiterate, has to rely
on men of God to interpret the Scriptures for her. On one hand, the
Archbishop is betraying a solemn trust; but on the other, he is a
winning comic figure. He is not the only character, incidentally, who
loses control of his metaphors. Bottini (above, p. 177) and Half-
Rome (2. 443–44) are also victims of their rhetorical ambitions.

> you have to plead before these priests
> And poke at them with Scripture, or you pass
> For heathen and, what's worse, for ignorant
> O' the quality o' the Court and what it likes
> By way of illustration of the law.
>
> (8. 1736–40)

The first necessity, then, is to "ecclesiasticize" one's argument. But it is not decorum and rhetorical strategy alone which require it; for the reverence with which men react to even the smallest biblical phrase has the potential power to suspend the critical intelligence. In the circumstances, then, it would be most surprising if defendant and professional counsel did not liberally avail themselves of doctrinal and textural support, suitably touched up, for their respective cases.

The lawyers, with their variegated ingenuity and unscrupulousness, claim our attention first. Arcangeli is proud of his ability to reinterpret the divine message so profitably, using his talent to

> yield
> The Lord his own [Word] again with usury,
> [Matt. 25:14 ff.]
> A satisfaction, yea, to God Himself!
> Well, I have modelled me by Agur's wish,
> "Remove far from me vanity and lies,
> Feed me with food convenient for me!"
>
> [Prov. 30:1, 8]
> (8. 1773–78)

The lawyer inferentially is the "good and faithful servant" who employs his talent well: being usurious with the Word, he adds words of his own by way of interest!

The long passage in which Arcangeli impudently derives the rationale for *honoris causa* from natural law and Gospel exhibits the full range of his cleverness. The argument is based upon a begged question: "That Honour is a gift of God to man / Precious beyond compare." (8. 458–59.) There is no scriptural warrant for such an assumption. Although St. Peter urges, "Honour all men. . . . Honour the king" (1 Pet. 2:17), the word is of course used in a meaning wholly differ-

ent from that in which Arcangeli uses it; and in any event
honor, taken in its highest and purest sense, is one gift man
can offer to God, especially by willingly sacrificing his own:
"And they departed from the presence of the council, rejoicing
that they were counted worthy to suffer shame for his [Jesus']
name" (Acts 5:41); "Blessed are ye, when men shall revile
you, and persecute you, and shall say all manner of evil against
you falsely, for my sake" (Matt. 5:11). But having thus announced a patently unchristian doctrine, Arcangeli proceeds to
use it to justify Guido's vengeance: "This were our warrant for
eruptive ire / 'To whose dominion I impose no end.'"
(8. 470–71; cf. Ps. 145:13.) From this point, Arcangeli
repeatedly and often humorously inverts Christian teachings, relying on a surface resemblance between his "texts" and
the originals, as in his argument, "If this [husband's venge-
ance] were done of old, in a green tree, / . . . What may be
licensed in the Autumn dry . . . ?" (8. 552–54), where the
words of Christ are torn altogether out of context to justify the
very violence that Christ deplored ("For if they do these things
in a green tree, what shall be done in the dry?" [Luke
23:31]).

He next marshals some coined fragments of "Scripture" to
testify "that Honour is the supreme good." First he quotes
"Saint Jerome" at some length and then follows quickly with
some snatches of "Saint Gregory" (8. 583–98). As causes of
vengeful fury, he names (wisely deciding in this case not to
stray too far from the original, inasmuch as he is citing chapter and verse)

> the place, the memory, *vituperii,*
> O' the shame and scorn: *quia,*—says Solomon,
> (The Holy Spirit speaking by his mouth
> In Proverbs, the sixth chapter near the end)
> [Prov. 6:34–35]
> —Because, the zeal and fury of a man,
> *Zelus et furor viri,* will not spare,
> *Non parcet,* in the day of his revenge,
> *In die vindictae,* nor will acquiesce,
> *Nec acquiescet,* through a person's prayers,

> *Cujusdam precibus,—nec suscipiet,*
> Nor yet take, *pro redemptione,* for
> Redemption, *dona plurium,* gifts of friends.
>
> (8. 610–21)

But the passage in the King James Bible—we must believe this version was standard Writ in Rome in 1698—reads: "For jealousy is the rage of a man: therefore he will not spare in the day of vengeance. He will not regard any ransom; neither will he rest content, though thou givest many gifts." Arcangeli suppresses "jealousy" and translates *zelus* instead as "zeal"—a genial euphemism for Guido's murderous rage.

Judicious retranslation now gives way to deliberate misquotation. Arcangeli cites the Vulgate in support of his argument that Christ himself had a quick temper where his honor was threatened:

> Are these things writ for no example, Sirs?
> [1 Cor. 10:11]
> One instance more, and let me see who doubts!
> Our Lord Himself, made up of mansuetude,
> Sealing the sum of sufferance up, received
> [Ezek. 28:12]
> Opprobrium, contumely and buffeting
> [Matt. 26:67]
> Without complaint: but when He found Himself
> Touched in His honour never so little for once,
> Then outbroke indignation pent before—
> *"Honorem meum nemini dabo!"* "No,
> My honour I to nobody will give!"
>
> (8. 656–65)

That the alleged quotation is scarcely Christlike is obvious; he who habitually ate with publicans and sinners was not one to put an excessive price on honor. But the text Arcangeli cites is not even in the New Testament; it is found in Isaiah 42:8 (Vulgate): *"Ego Dominus, / Hoc est nomen meum; / Gloriam meam alteri non dabo."* Here God speaks, defending not *honorem* but *gloriam* (that is, his being the Godhead). Neither Jesus nor honor, in any sense, figures in the quotation Arcangeli cites.[3]

In the lines that follow, Arcangeli takes similar liberties with the words of St. Paul:

> We find Saint Paul
> No recreant to this faith delivered once: [Jude 1:3]
> "Far worthier were it that I died," cries he,
> *Expedit mihi magis mori,* "than
> That any one should make my glory void,"
>   [1 Cor. 9:15]
>
> *Quam ut gloriam meam quis evacuet!*
> See, *ad Corinthienses:* whereupon
> Saint Ambrose makes a comment with much fruit,
> Doubtless my Judges long since laid to heart,
> So I desist from bringing forward here—
> (I can't quite recollect it.)
>
>   (8. 671–81)

The sheer comedy of the ad lib which falls flat when St. Ambrose's sage comment fails to materialize is likely to divert attention from Arcangeli's slight but effective amendment of the Pauline text. St. Paul says, in connection with his zeal for Christ, "For it were better for me to die, than that any man should make my *glorying* void." [4] With one sly touch, the removal of the gerund ending, Arcangeli transmutes Paul's

[3] Recalling this passage of Arcangeli's pleading, the Pope comments, "Right of Him [Christ], just as if pronounced to-day!" (10. 1987.) The mistake may be evidence of the aged Pope's failing memory, but it also suggests the psychological assumption underlying the lawyers' deliberate distortion of Scripture. As time passes, familiar passages may seem to ring true in the human memory, even though they are subtly altered. The Pope, like lesser mortals, responds to the sound rather than the exact sense or the actual context of the quotation. That he is taken in by Arcangeli is both a tribute to the lawyer's skill and a mark of the Pope's human fallibility. He is trapped unawares into endorsing an unchristian idea.

[4] Italics supplied. A. K. Cook cites the right passage (1 Cor. 9:15) but misses the point. " 'My glory,' " he says, "should be 'my boast' . . . and St. Paul's boast is that while preaching the gospel he has not lived 'of the gospel'!" (*Commentary,* p. 170.) But this unnecessarily supposes that Browning was also levying from 2 Cor. 9:3, where "boasting" does occur. The former passage suffices, for in quoting it

selfless worship of Christ into vainglory. One has only to recall the apostle's words in Galatians 6:14 ("God forbid that I should glory save in the cross of Jesus") to realize how far Arcangeli has distorted Paul's intent.

But the lawyer's exploitation of St. Paul's authority still is not at an end. Much later in his argument, Arcangeli, seeking to extenuate Guido's having disguised himself before his crime, urges the judges,

> Read to thy profit how the Apostle once
> For ease and safety, when Damascus raged,
> Was let down in a basket by the wall,
> To 'scape the malice of the governor   [Acts 9:24–25]
> (Another sort of Governor boasts Rome!)
> —Many are of opinion,—covered close,
> Concealed with—what except that very cloak
> He left behind at Troas afterward? [5]
>
> (8. 1322–29)

With such a barrage of "Revelation old and new" (8. 684) does Arcangeli invoke Christian precedent, most of it

---

Arcangeli silently amends St. Paul's "glorying" to "glory"—a rather different matter. Browning may have been struck by the discrepant inflections of the word in the King James Version ("glorying") and the Vulgate-Douay ("glory"); Arcangeli cleverly opts for the Vulgate's *"gloriam meam"* to underscore his persistent linkage of honor with Christian teaching.

[5] Cook (*Commentary*, p. 175) remarks, "The 'many' who held this opinion forgot that the apostle asked for the cloak he left at Troas some thirty years after his escape from Damascus." Cf. 2 Tim. 4:13: "The cloak that I left at Troas with Carpus, when thou comest, bring with thee." But Cook neglects the possibility that Browning is here, as in several other passages (see below, pp. 330–34), obliquely alluding to what he took to be the profitless and impertinent skepticism of the higher (biblical) critics. Browning, with his tenacious memory, may be recalling an apposite passage in defense of the Bible as the revealed word of God in Coleridge's *Confessions of an Inquiring Spirit* (London, 1853), pp. 116–17: "If after all this, and in spite of all this some captious litigator should lay hold of a text here or there—St. Paul's *cloak left at Troas with Carpus*, or a verse from the Canticles, and ask: 'Of what spiritual use is this?'—the answer is ready:—It proves to us that nothing can be so trifling as not to supply an evil heart with a pretext for unbelief."

highly questionable, for precipitate revenge and flight. Even when not openly alluding to the Bible, he adopts its tone and even its phraseology.

> Our case is, that the thing we lost, we found:
>   [cf. Luke 15:6]
> The honour, we were robbed of eight months since,
> Being recoverable at any day
> By death of the delinquent. Go thy ways!
> Ere thou hast learned law, will be much to do.
>   [cf. Matt. 9:13]
>   (8. 1048–52)

The most audacious—and at the same time, the most blasphemous—of the allusions remain the clear-cut scriptural borrowings. During the next phase of his argument, for example, Arcangeli adapts the words of Christ to a wholly alien situation, that of Pompilia's alleged adultery. "Foxes have holes, and fowls o' the air their nests; / Praise you the impiety that follows, Fisc? / Shall false wife yet have where to lay her head?" (8. 1301–3.) The biblical original is: "And Jesus saith unto him, The foxes have holes, and the birds of the air have nests; but the Son of man hath not where to lay his head" (Matt. 8:20). The inevitable recollection of these words, together with their ironic use here, has a rhetorical effect far greater than the equivalent amount of unallusive language, especially when one realizes the extent to which Pompilia, the "false wife," and Christ are elsewhere, on a more serious level, compared. Despite Arcangeli's jocular tone, the image of the suffering Christ is superimposed on that of the dying Pompilia.

Such poking and prodding with a conveniently revised version of Scripture continues to the very end of Arcangeli's speech. In his highly charged peroration, for example, he herds the judges into the fold of the indulgent. In a circumstantial *ad hominem* appeal, he avers he is merely

> Seeking corroboration from thy nod
> Who art all justice—which means mercy too,
>   [Mic. 6:8]

In a low noisy smoky world like ours
Where Adam's sin made peccable his seed!
(8. 1433–36)

Arcangeli's brand of mercy, of course, involves exculpation of Guido, so that the latter's crucified honor, "buried fathom-deep / In infamy, *in infamia*, might arise, / *Resurgeret*, as ghosts break sepulchre!" (8. 1637–39.) Christ's promise, *Resurgam* (Matt. 27:63), is artfully transposed into the promise of Guido's earthly resurrection. Not only here, but at nearly every crucial point in his argument, Arcangeli's deft employment of scriptural associations, which both distance and lend a vague aura of sanction to the events in question, is surprisingly effective in lessening the cruelty and horror of Guido's criminality.

Bottini's allusions to Scripture, though fewer than his rival's, are no less consonant with his own rhetorical method and even more indicative of the man. Unconscious, of course, of the true extent to which he will supply it, he considers the time ripe for some comic relief. His story of the hungry apostles and the lone chicken—a parable, apocryphal to begin with, which he remodels closer to his immediate requirements—is specifically chosen to "recreate / The gravity of my Judges" (9. 1018–19). And whereas Arcangeli uses biblical citations chiefly as authority for his arguments, Bottini chooses them for their descriptive power, heightening it by the sensual overtones he gratuitously adds.

Describing the calm at Arezzo after the departure of the Comparini, he rhapsodizes,

He hath attained his object, groom and bride
Partake the nuptial bower no soul to see,
Old things are passed and all again is new, [2 Cor. 5:17]
Over and gone the obstacles to peace.

. . . .
. . . Every storm is laid,
And forth from plain each pleasant herb may peep,
Each bloom of wifehood in abeyance late:
(Confer a passage in the Canticles.) [Cant. 2:11–12]
(9. 280–89)

Pompilia-as-plant is now free to grow luxuriantly. It is no wonder that her bloom should attract the young "levite," Caponsacchi, known more for levity than for asceticism (9. 338–43). Mixing Horace with Scripture in his usual eclectic way, Bottini admonishes Guido not to blame Pompilia for her taste in lovers:

> "She laudably sees all,
> Searches the best out and selects the same."
>
> .   .   .   .
> 'Tis no ignoble object, husband! Doubt'st?
> When here comes tripping Flaccus with his phrase
> "Trust me, no miscreant singled from the mob,"
>
> .   .   .   .
>   . . . but a man of mark,
> A priest, dost hear? . . .
>
> .   .   .   .
> Was not the son of Jesse ruddy, sleek,
> Pleasant to look on, pleasant every way?
>   [1 Sam. 16:12, 18]
> Since well he smote the harp and sweetly sang,
> And danced till Abigail came out to see,
>   [2 Sam. 6:14–19]
> And seeing smiled and smiling ministered
> The raisin-cluster and the cake of figs,
> With ready meal refreshed the gifted youth,
> Till Nabal, who was absent shearing sheep,
> Felt heart sink, took to bed (discreetly done—
> They might have been beforehand with him else)
> And died—would Guido had behaved as well!
>   [1 Sam. 25:18 ff.]
>   (9. 336–66)

By this selective conflation of two passages in Samuel, Bottini produces a triumph of irony and innuendo. In the original, Abigail goes out to meet a sword-bearing David and his soldiers, offering his men figs and sweetmeats to conciliate him (1 Sam. 25:18 ff.). David dances not before an admiring Abigail but before the Ark of the Covenant, with Michal, captured daughter of Saul, secretly looking on; "and she de-

spised him in her heart" (2 Sam. 6:16). In neither passage
is there any hint of seduction. But Bottini unapologetically re-
writes Scripture to afford precedent for Caponsacchi's alleged
misconduct. If wooing another man's wife while he was away
shearing sheep was not reprehensible in David, why should it
be so in Caponsacchi, also a man of God, who called while
Guido was absent tending his vineyard at Vittiano, "where
husbandry required the master-mind"? (5. 1006–7; cf. 6.
518–19, 591–92.) The difference, the Fisc points out, is that
whereas Abigail's husband Nabal had the good taste to die,
Guido, returning from the villa to complicate affairs at home
(6. 647–48), churlishly went on living. By such talent as
Bottini's, canonical narratives are transformed into Boccaccian fictions.

The lawyer's transmuting skill is also seen in a descriptive
passage in which "our Saint George" is selected by the wise
Pompilia as the ablest dragon slayer:

> And should fair face accompany strong hand,
> The more complete equipment: nothing mars
> Work, else praiseworthy, like a bodily flaw
> I' the worker: as 'tis said Saint Paul himself
> Deplored the check o' the puny presence, still
> > [2 Cor. 10:10]
> Cheating his fulmination of its flash,
> Albeit the bolt therein went true to oak.
> Therefore the agent, as prescribed, she takes,—
> A priest, juvenile, potent, handsome too,—
> In all obedience.

> (9. 601–10)

With such loaded (Freudian?) interpolations as "fulmina-
tion" and the bolt going "true to oak," and the punning
substitution of "flash" for "flesh," one almost forgets the original intent of St. Paul's prescription, which is really a declaration of contempt for the body:

> But I beseech you, that I may not be bold when I am
> present with that confidence, wherewith I think to be
> bold against some, which think of us as if we walked

according to the flesh. For though we walk in the flesh,
we do not war after the flesh: (For the weapons of our
warfare are not carnal, but mighty through God to the
pulling down of strong holds;) . . . For though I should
boast somewhat more of our authority, . . . I should not
be ashamed: That I may not seem as if I would terrify
you by letters. For his letters, say they, are weighty and
powerful; but his bodily presence is weak, and his speech
contemptible. (2 Cor. 10:2–10)

Perhaps the chief irony here is that, whereas Bottini cites St.
Paul as sanction for Pompilia's choice of a virile soldier-lover,
Caponsacchi, as we know from his own speech, actually con-
ceives of his own warfare in terms similar to those of the
Pauline struggle to suppress the flesh in order that the spirit
may operate freely.

Having repeatedly degraded Pompilia's character through
the revision of scriptural passages, Bottini needs subsequently
to change her into an angelic being to intensify the contrast
with the devilish Guido. He hits upon the happy idea of
bestowing a Christlike blessing on Pompilia after she is
"saved" by the Convertite nuns: "Being healed, / Go blaze
abroad the matter, blessed one!" (9. 1213–14.) The echo is of
Jesus' enjoining the healed leper to tell no one of the miracle:
"But he went out and began to publish it much, and to blaze
abroad the matter" (Mark 1:45). Bottini goes on ceremo-
niously to absolve Pompilia of any taint of sin:

> Art thou sound forthwith? Speedily vacate
> The step by pool-side, leave Bethesda free
> [John 5:2–8]
> To patients plentifully posted round,
> Since the whole need not the physician! Brief,
> [Luke 5:31]
> She may betake her to her parents' place.
> Welcome her, father, with wide arms once more.
> [Luke 15:20]
> (9. 1215–20)

A leper cured, a Magdalene remade, a repentant prodigal
daughter of Eve, she returns, as if at Bottini's behest, to her
parents, there to present Guido with

> a babe,
> A son, an heir, a Franceschini last
> And best o' the stock!
>
> .   .   .   .
>
> An infant for the apple of his eye . . .
>   [Deut. 32:10]
>   (9. 1307–16)

With mock-messianic fervor, Bottini crowns Pompilia's prodigy while twitting Guido for his faithlessness. He adopts the
tone of the psalmist:

> Therefore be peace again: exult, ye hills!
> Ye vales rejoicingly break forth in song!
> *Incipe, parve puer*, begin, small boy,
> *Risu cognoscere patrem*, with a smile
> To recognize thy parent!
>   (9. 1372–76)

In a highly ironic echo of the jeering of the crowd-chorus at
Arezzo, Bottini transforms mirth into miracle, showing, in the
best ironist manner, how phraseology and tone of utterance
can act as a blind. Here, with renewed perversity, he seems to
praise Pompilia, but he does so without denying one jot of her
previously conceded sinfulness. He in fact compounds her
guilt by endowing her with an ambiguously conceived heir!

I I

Above this persistent comedy of misquoted and misapplied
Scripture presides the total thematic movement of the poem,
which embraces a series of religious antitheses or polarities:
law *vs.* Gospel, letter *vs.* spirit, old *vs.* new dispensation, old
vs. new Adam, fall *vs.* salvation. Religious and ethical ulti-
mates are held in conflict, in dialectical fashion, as the poem
progresses. Guido's ensuing second monologue notwithstand-

ing, there exists a progress, however erratic, toward a vision of grace in Book 10. The elemental drama of the Bible is felt everywhere in *The Ring and the Book:* reminders of man's temptation and fall, his propensity for violence and intrigue, his longing for love and aid, God's response in terms of grace incarnate, human sacrifice by way of atonement, and final redemption. In several of the monologues a single biblical theme is stressed. The idea of militant Christian witness after conversion, for example, dominates Caponsacchi's monologue, while the themes of the books immediately adjacent offer sharp contrasts. In the preceding one, Guido serves up an unlikely combination of Old Testament legalism and pseudo-Christian morality, and in the following one, Pompilia speaks in mystic tones of Christian submission and self-abnegation, her rescue by Caponsacchi being developed as a manifestation of spiritual affinity which, unlike the human love that is wrongly said to bind them, springs from their kinship in Christ.

Throughout the poem the development of the religious allusions accompanies and illustrates the movement of character and idea. In Books 2–4 such references occur relatively seldom and on a low level of significance, the most obvious instance being the repeated use of the Adam and Eve story as a mere domestic anecdote. Only in Guido's first monologue does a serious religious motif, the suffering and death of Christ, begin to be prominent, and then, ominously, it is used for perverted purposes, to identify himself as a latter-day martyr. By contrast, the emphasis in the ensuing books of Caponsacchi and Pompilia is upon the advent and motive power of the Holy Spirit. They employ religious figures and allusions reverently, as befits priest and Madonna-maiden. In renewed contrast, the two lawyers who follow them divest their biblical references of all spiritual significance and use them exclusively as convenient materials of argumentation. From these depths the Pope then restores Scripture through his solemnity of purpose and utterance; the metaphors and allusions for the most part lose their sharp definition and immediate human reference and take the form of symbols in a hazy, remote cosmic ambience. Finally, Guido in his condemned cell seizes upon the fund of

Christian allusion for the sake primarily of the wolf-sheep figures which emblematize his guilt-ridden and hypocritical nature.

However used, the principal themes of the fall, Incarnation, expiation, and resurrection, as concurrently developed through the poem, provide a metaphysical bridge from the old (Mosaic) dispensation, whose rule is stern justice, to the new (Christian) dispensation, whose law is mercy.

1. *The fall of man.* The moiling and bickering of late seventeenth-century Rome, exemplifying as it does "the primal curse / Which bids man love as well as make a lie" (1. 643–44; cf. Rev. 22:15 and 2 Thess. 2:11), reminds one constantly of the heavy toll of error and sin contracted in the Garden of Eden. Four parties to the marriage of Pompilia and Guido are portrayed as the original fallen man or woman, and the fifth, Paolo, as the serpent. Violante (Eve) is the first to fall, when she seduces Pietro (Adam) into believing she is to bear his child. She arranges Pompilia's marriage to Guido twelve years later "lest Eve's rule decline / Over this Adam of hers, whose cabbage-plot / Throve dubiously since turned fools'-paradise" (2. 253–55). (In Genesis 3:16–17, the ordained situation actually is the opposite: Eve's "desire shall be to thy husband, and he shall rule over thee.") When she revealed the marriage bargain to Pietro,

> Violante sobbed the sobs and prayed the prayers,
> And said the serpent tempted so she fell,
> Till Pietro had to clear his brow apace
> And make the best of matters.
>
> (3. 470–73)

In Half-Rome's version, the Eve and Adam roles belong also to the younger couple: "Pompilia, Eve-like, lured / Her Adam Guido to his fault and fall." (2. 168–69; cf. Gen. 3:6.) The idea of Pompilia as fallen Eve is well suited to the speakers' purposes. Tertium Quid, characteristically, extracts double advantage from it. In discussing Pompilia's hypothetical defense of her conduct he makes the identification and the accompanying point and then withdraws the identification for the sake of

redoubling the point. The cleverness of the maneuver is perhaps obscured by the more than usually elliptical terms in
which it is expressed:

> But then this is the wife's—Pompilia's tale—
> Eve's . . . no, not Eve's, since Eve, to speak the truth,
> Was hardly fallen (our candour might pronounce)
> So much of paradisal nature, Eve's,
> When simply saying in her own defence
> "The serpent tempted me and I did eat."
> Her daughters ever since prefer to urge
> "Adam so starved me I was fain accept
> The apple any serpent pushed my way."
> What an elaborate theory have we here,
> Ingeniously nursed up, pretentiously
> Brought forth, pushed forward amid trumpet-blast,
> To account for the thawing of an icicle.
>
> (4. 851–63)

In simpler language, "This," says Tertium Quid, "is Pompilia's tale. I might call it 'Eve's,' but Eve, being but newly
fallen, was not yet familiar with duplicity. Pompilia possesses
only so much of Eve's 'paradisal' (pre-fall) nature as to allow
her to use Eve's plea, 'The Serpent tempted me' (cf. Violante
above). But the daughters of Eve [women in general? wives?
fallen women? Tertium Quid leaves the identification open]
embellish the primal mother's story with one of their own: 'My
husband so starved me. . . .' " Pompilia, not so much Eve as a
daughter of Eve, is thus revealed to be splendidly sinful, not
least in her talent for inventing alibis. The suave irony of
Tertium Quid's succeeding argument is matched, at long
remove, by the Archbishop's far more slippery demonstration

> Know, daughter, circumstances make or mar
> Virginity,—'tis virtue or 'tis vice.
> That which was glory in the Mother of God
> Had been, for instance, damnable in Eve
> Created to be mother of mankind.
> Had Eve, in answer to her Maker's speech
> 'Be fruitful, multiply, replenish earth'—
> Pouted 'But I choose rather to remain
> Single'—why, she had spared herself forthwith

> Further probation by the apple and snake,
> Been pushed straight out of Paradise! For see—
> If motherhood be qualified impure,
> I catch you making God command Eve sin!
>
> (7. 756–68)

that it is Eve, not the Virgin, whom Pompilia should emulate: The final conversion of the Eve story for forensic ends, however, is Bottini's. In a clever argument already noticed (pp. 167–68) he likens Pompilia to Eve to explain why the seemingly ignorant girl might have had the gift of literacy and so be capable of writing the love letters attributed to her.

But of course it is Guido who is most representative of those who have fallen and choose to remain fallen, who "receiveth not the things of the spirit of God" (1 Cor. 2:14). To men like him there is allotted only the charitable Christian hope, shared by Pompilia and—much more faintly—the Pope, that by some miracle he may see and be saved. Ironically echoing Arcangeli's defense, the Pope maintains that Guido's culpability lies in his having carried to excess the normal sinfulness acquired in the Garden: "So has he exceeded man's due share / In man's fit licence, wrung by Adam's fall, / To sin and yet not surely die." (10. 179–81.) Guido will soon learn that the serpent's promise of immunity, quoted from Genesis 3:4, is a lie, for the Pope must, like God in the Garden, render judgment on the vengeful deed which led "Adam Guido to his fault and fall" (2. 169).

2. *The old and the new Adam.* The Pauline distinction between the man subject to the Mosaic law and the "new man" whose glory is in Christ is also given a variety of treatments ranging from the serious to the baldly comic. For Caponsacchi, the exemplar of the new Adam, the pentecostal infusion of Pompilia's holy spirit is a transforming experience: "By the invasion I lay passive to, / In rushed new things, the old were rapt away." (6. 947–48; cf. 2 Cor. 5:17 and Rev. 21:4, 5.) On a much diminished scale, Guido speaks also of regeneration as he sardonically describes the mercenary schemes of the Comparini, who

> Quit Rome and qualify for Arezzo, take
> The tone o' the new sphere that absorbed the old,

> Put away gossip Jack and goody Joan [Eph. 4:22–24]
> And go become familiar with the Great,
> Greatness to touch and taste and handle now,—
>   [Col. 2:21, 22]
> Why, then,—they found that all was vanity,
> Vexation, and what Solomon describes! [Eccles. *passim*]
>   (5. 518–24)

The "vanity" is, of course, that of human wishes, and the "vexation" the result of the cataclysmic discovery that Guido was not rich. The fifth line subtly reverses the meaning of the text in Colossians—"Touch not; taste not; handle not; which all are to perish with the using"—from spiritual restraint to secular license. In another allusion to the passage of Ephesians echoed above ("Put off . . . the old man, which is corrupt . . . and . . . put on the new man") Guido inverts the wording to speak for the unregenerate men in whom no Caponsacchi-like conversion has taken place: "They mutiny, mutter who knows what excuse? / In fine make up their minds to leave the new, / Stick to the old." (11. 1992–94.)

3. *Law and the Gospel.* Under the Christian dispensation, there are two sources of earthly authority: the codified, coercive laws by which man voluntarily limits his freedom of action, and the Gospel, which administers more gentle ethical and moral restraints. For dramatic purposes Browning converts the subordination of law to Gospel into outright opposition. Against those in the poem who argue for the mercy and saving grace of the Gospel are ranged the legalists who would base all ethics on a strict secular code. The latter are also the ironists, because they do not scruple to invoke Gospel, however misrepresented, to substantiate the judgments of law or, where law disobliges, to supplant them; and they are quick to detect any apparent conflict between law and Gospel. Some use appropriately modified texts to argue that the harshness of the Roman law should be made lenient. Others, on the contrary, find in the Gospel authority for the strict and literal application of the law.

Underneath Guido's Christian veneer is an unremitting legalism based on privilege, a code which in its severity is reminiscent of the old Hebraic laws, especially as regards marriage. He exploits the alleged conflict of religion and modern secular law, and the deficiencies of each, for all they are worth. He and his sympathizers often portray him as having been buffeted, to the point of becoming addled, from secular to church authorities and back again. When he appealed to the Pope for a judgment against Pompilia, the reply, according to the Other Half-Rome, was "Render Caesar what is Caesar's due" (3. 1477; cf. Matt. 22:21). Even when the two authorities momentarily concurred, it was not to provide him with the desired aid but to couch a perfunctory compliment in the familiar words—eminently inapplicable to Guido—of St. Matthew (25:21): "Religion and Law lean forward from their chairs, / 'Well done, thou good and faithful servant!'" (4. 1208–1209.) Good and faithful servant of law that he has always been, he maintains that if he has erred, then so has law; if he seeks a remedy, then law is bound to provide it. "Law renovates even Lazarus,—cures me! / Caesar thou seekest? To Caesar thou shalt go!" (5. 1174–75; cf. Luke 16:20 ff. and Acts 25:12.) Guido admits that there was a certain lack of bravery in his failing to kill his wife and her paramour on the spot, but

> Cowardice were misfortune and no crime!
> —Take it that way, since I am fallen so low
> I scarce dare brush the fly that blows my face,
> And thank the man who simply spits not there,—
> Unless the Court be generous, comprehend
> How one brought up at the very feet of law
> As I, awaits the grave Gamaliel's nod   [Acts 22:3]
> Ere he clench fist at outrage,—much less, stab!
> (5. 1101–8; cf. 8. 327–29)

Beneath the self-pity of this Aretine man of sorrows may be detected fine cunning; for though the grave Gamaliel of whom he intends his hearers to think represents the stringency of law, he would prefer the judgment of the same Gamaliel who in another place administered the birch, perhaps, but remitted capital punishment. "Refrain from these men [the apostles], and let them alone," Gamaliel said; and, continues Acts 5:40,

"To him they [the Sanhedrin] agreed: and when they had
called the apostles, and beaten them, they . . . let them go."

"I began life by hanging to the law, / To the law it is I hang
till life shall end," Guido tells the ecclesiastical court (5.
1750–51), echoing St. Matthew's "On these two command-
ments hang all the law and the prophets" (22:40) for the sake
of a desperate pun on his desperate situation: "Absolve, then,
me, law's mere executant!" (5. 2003.) This is a line of defense
which he owes, no doubt, to his lawyer, who later will be heard
crying, "Do you blame us that we turn law's instruments / Not
mere self-seekers,—mind the public weal, / Nor make the
private good our sole concern?" (8. 880–82.) In the ensuing
parable of a stolen purse recovered by Guido for the law,
Arcangeli borrows the form from Christ and, prompted by his
ever-suggestive stomach, the phraseology from Psalms 69:9
("For the zeal of thine house hath eaten me up"): "We are
the over-ready to help Law— / Zeal of her house hath eaten
us up: for which, / Can it be, Law intends to eat up us[?]" (8.
893–95.) Far from being punished, Arcangeli argues, the
luckless Guido should have been rewarded. If law refused, it
was up to religion to pay him:

> Law ducks to Gospel here:
> Why should Law gain the glory and pronounce
> A judgment shall immortalize the Pope?
> Yes: our self-abnegating policy
> Was Joab's—we would rouse our David's sloth,
> [2 Sam. 12:26–28]
> Bid him encamp against a city, sack
> A place whereto ourselves had long laid siege,
> Lest, taking it at last, it take our name
> And be not *Innocentinopolis.*
>
> (8. 1407–15)

But Pope Innocent rejected innocent Guido's appeal that he
appoint a special ecclesiastical court to hear the combined
suits engendered by Guido's marital difficulties (8. 1391 ff.).
"Hath not my [regularly constituted] Court a conscience?"
Arcangeli interprets the Pope as saying. "It is of age, / Ask
it!" (8. 1425–26.) Like the youth in the Gospel of St. John

(9:23) whose parents replied in that fashion when asked whether he had really been cured of blindness, the court can now (miraculously enough) see the light and therefore, according to the logic implicit in Arcangeli's use of the allusion, must acquit Guido.

4. *Adultery and its punishment.* The legal problem of the Franceschini case is tersely expressed in the Old Yellow Book's subtitle as Browning quotes it: "Wherein it is disputed if, and when, / Husbands may kill adulterous wives, yet 'scape / The customary forfeit." (1. 129–31.)

This issue of *honoris causa* is debated as fervently through the citation of Gospel as it is through that of law. Some speakers hold that the husband's honor demands punishment (cf. Exod. 20:14 and Lev. 20:10); others, inspired by Christ's example, urge forbearance (cf. John 8:7). Typifying the former, Half-Rome demands: "Who is it dares . . . / Deny God's word 'the faithless wife shall die?' / What, are we blind?" (2. 1477–79.) His Bible lesson concludes with this exhortation:

> Henceforward let none dare
> Stand, like a natural in the public way,
> Letting the very urchins twitch his beard
> And tweak his nose, to earn a nickname so,
> Of the male-Grissel or the modern Job! [Jas. 5:11]
>   (2. 1483–87)

Guido, supported by the Leviticus text that "the adulterous wife shall surely be put to death," pretends that he has been merciful in not exacting immediate revenge: "I did not take the license law's self gives / To slay both criminals o' the spot at the time, / But held my hand." (5. 1878–80.) But according to the Other Half-Rome, recalling the turn of the screw that brought blood issuing from the winepress in Revelation (14:20), Guido's lust for revenge was all-consuming: "Then did the winch o' the winepress of all hate, / . . . Take the last turn that screws out pure revenge / With a bright bubble at the brim beside." (3. 1542–45.) [6]

---

[6] Cf. Keats, "Ode to a Nightingale," line 17: "With beaded bubbles winking at the brim . . ."

In another passage, noteworthy like several others for the mental octave-reach by which Arcangeli brings together a rich sequence of allusions that govern the direction of his argument, he submits that Guido could not have known the proper punishment for his wife, in view of the conflicting laws:

> Under old dispensation, argue they,
> The doom of the adulterous wife was death,   [Lev. 20:10]
> Stoning by Moses' law. "Nay, stone her not,
> Put her away!" next legislates our Lord;   [John 8:4–5, 7]
> And last of all, "Nor yet divorce a wife!"   [Matt. 5:31–32]
> Ordains the Church, "she typifies ourself,   [Eph. 5:23]
> The Bride no fault shall cause to fall from Christ."
>   [Rev. 21:9–10]
> Then, as no jot nor tittle of the Law   [Matt. 5:18]
> Has passed away—which who presumes to doubt?
> As not one word of Christ is rendered vain—   [Luke 21:33]
> Which, could it be though heaven and earth should pass?
> —Where do I find my proper punishment
> For my adulterous wife, I humbly ask
> Of my infallible Pope,—who now remits
> Even the divorce allowed by Christ in lieu
> Of lapidation Moses licensed me?
> The Gospel checks the Law which throws the stone,
>   [Matt. 5:17]
> The Church tears the divorce-bill Gospel grants,
> The wife sins and enjoys impunity!
> What profits me the fulness of the days,   [Eph. 1:10]
> The final dispensation, I demand,
> Unless Law, Gospel and the Church subjoin
> "But who hath barred thee primitive revenge,
> Which, like fire damped and dammed up, burns more fierce?
> Use thou thy natural privilege of man,
> Else wert thou found like those old ingrate Jews,
> Despite the manna-banquet on the board,
> A-longing after melons, cucumbers
> And such like trash of Egypt left behind!" [Num. 11:4–6]

.   .   .   .

> Law, Gospel and the Church—from these we leap
> To the very last revealment. . . .

.   .   .   .

"Behold," quoth James, "we bridle in a horse
And turn his body as we would thereby!" [Jas. 3:3]
Yea, but we change the bit to suit the growth,
And rasp our colt's jaw with a rugged spike
We hasten to remit our managed steed
Who wheels round at persuasion of a touch.

(8. 697–739)

Guido, playing as he often does the role of patient beast of burden,[7] is now broken to the halter of the law; thus, the gentlest touch, admonition followed by acquittal, should be enough to correct his gait. In this medley of biblical echoes, the particular interest and the irony lie in the suppression of the verse preceding the one alluded to in the Epistle of St. James, which refers to a man blameless in his speech: "If any man offend not in word, the same is a perfect man, and able also to bridle the whole body. Behold, we put bits in the horses' mouths, that they may obey us." Guido's manifest inability to bridle tongue or body is later to become one of the Pope's grounds for condemning him to death.

Just as Arcangeli pleads in biblical terms for remission of harsh punishment for the wronged husband, so does Bottini, while tacitly admitting adultery, use the Bible to argue self-defense as exoneration of Pompilia. Here he represents the reaction of the sympathetic crowd to her exposure and defiance at Castelnuovo:

"This should be no wanton wife,
No conscience-stricken creature, caught i' the act,
And patiently awaiting our first stone: [8]
[John 8:3–5,7,10]
But a poor hard-pressed all-bewildered thing.

.   .   .   .

Even the blessed Magdalen mistook
Far less forgiveably: consult the place—

[7] For further instances see pp. 220–21. Guido's repeated appearance in this role adds dramatic emphasis to Tertium Quid's description of his turning into an enraged bull under the stress of his accumulated misfortunes and frustrations.

[8] One should not overlook the delicious humor—the crowd is dutifully conscious of the role Scripture has assigned it to play in this prospective reenactment of a biblical episode.

> Supposing him to be the gardener,
> 'Sir,' said she, and so following."   [John 20:15]
>   (9. 928–39)

As with most of the allusions conceived by the ironists, this has
a double edge. The stone-throwing, coupled with the name of
Magdalene, classes Pompilia with the company of fallen
women. The gardener in the biblical original is of course
Christ; but we remember also Guido's self-delineation as
Christ, and Bottini's comic treatment of Guido as gardener or
husbandman (9. 244–60, 294). The residual meaning of these
deftly managed associations is that as Christ forgave Magdalene for her mistake—and for her wantonness—so ought
Guido to have forgiven his errant wife for brandishing his
sword in her mistaken fear of him.

5. *Marriage and the church.* Typically, both saints and
sinners invoke Scripture to defend their respective attitudes
toward marriage. One text lends authority to both sides. Those
who look upon earthly marriage as a cumbrance to the spiritual life follow the words of St. Paul: "I say therefore to the
unmarried and widows, It is good for them if they abide
even as I" (1 Cor. 7:8). But Guido prefers the immediately
succeeding portion of "Paul's advice" (5. 413): "But if they
cannot contain, let them marry; for it is better to marry than
to burn." Those who, like Guido, hold fast to the old dispensation argue that marriage, far from having any spiritual import,
simply means that the wife belongs to her husband body and
soul; it is a knot, says Half-Rome, "which nothing cuts" except
the knife to which he none too subtly directs his auditor's
attention (2. 66–67). Nor does the supposedly romantic Other
Half-Rome see marriage as anything more than an earthly
union for procreation: " 'Tis in a child, man and wife grow
complete, / One flesh: God says so: let him do his work!" (3.
153–54; cf. Matt. 19:5.) It is Guido, naturally, who cites most
fully the biblical precedents for this view of marriage:

> "From the bride's soul what is it you expect?"
> Why, loyalty and obedience,—wish and will
>   [1 Cor. 14:34]

To settle and suit her fresh and plastic mind.

. . . .

Father and mother shall the woman leave, [cf. Gen. 2:24]
Cleave to the husband, be it for weal or woe.
                                        (5. 577–82)

Genesis thus improved (the canonical words are "Therefore
shall a man leave his father and his mother, and shall cleave
unto his wife: and they shall be one flesh") offers a perfect
text not only for proving the wife's sole obligation but for
getting rid of her bothersome parents.

Guido, enraged that his chattel-wife Pompilia "refused from
the beginning day / Either in body or soul to cleave to mine"
(5. 608–9), sues for divorce. The church answers,

Your plan for the divorce is all mistake.
It would hold, now, had you, taking thought to wed
Rachel of the blue eye and golden hair,
Found swarth-skinned Leah cumber couch next day:
                                [Gen. 29:16–18,25]
But Rachel, blue-eyed golden-haired aright,
Proving to be only Laban's child, not Lot's,
                                [Gen. 19:30–36]
Remains yours all the same for ever more.
                                        (5. 1309–15)

This clever joining of separate episodes (Laban's tricking
Jacob into marrying Leah instead of Rachel, and Lot's incest
with his two daughters) has the effect of making the church
say that the deception of which Guido was a victim is, unlike
Laban's, not covered by canon law. Guido loses on two counts:
the question is not the serious one of a substituted bed partner
but merely one of a mistake in parentage, and because Pompilia is not a daughter of Lot she is not guilty of sexual misconduct and so must remain united with her husband.

Given the circumstances of the poem, St. Paul's text in
Ephesians (5:23–24) provides an exceedingly apt metaphor:
"For the husband is the head of the wife, even as Christ is the
head of the Church. . . . Therefore as the Church is subject

unto Christ, so let the wives be to their own husbands in every thing." The ironists find in these words additional authority for making wife subservient to husband. Guido justifies his conduct toward Pompilia by what might be called the *ad ecclesiam* argument:

> My lords have chosen the happier part with Paul
> And neither marry nor burn,—yet priestliness
>   [1 Cor. 7:8–9]
> Can find a parallel to the marriage-bond
> In its own blessed special ordinance
> Whereof indeed was marriage made the type:
> The Church may show her insubordinate,
> As marriage her refractory.
>   (5. 723–29; cf. 5. 2044; 11. 1303) [9]

The literalists, however, see in Christ's example the great antetype of all marriage, that based on a heavenly union of compatible souls. The Pauline text, coupled with an associated theme from Revelation, informs Caponsacchi's thinking:

> My church: it seemed to say for the first time
> "But am not I the Bride, the mystic love [Rev. 21:9, 10]
> O' the Lamb, who took thy plighted troth, my priest[?]
>
> .   .   .   .
>
> This is a fleshly woman,—let the free
> Bestow their life-blood, thou art pulseless now!"
>   (6. 976–82)

Caponsacchi is already married to the church, through his priestly vows; it is his consciousness of this fact that enables him to withstand the temptation (he is by no means "pulseless") of the forged love letters. The court fails to understand that Caponsacchi's spiritual commitment to aid Pompilia is in no conflict with his priestly duty; in fact, for him the sincerest Christian witness may be symbolized by the silent helping hand.

[9] There is wicked innuendo in the first two lines, which no doubt allude both to the euphemistically named "nieces" Guido attributes to certain churchmen (e.g., 5. 266) and to Paolo and his colleagues being sleeping partners in a so-called peruke maker's shop (4. 439–51).

Pompilia's union with Caponsacchi, although invalid in earthly terms, is the only true one in her life. When, after her marriage to Guido, the priest Paolo gave her a moment's teaching on the obligations of the wedded state,

> [he] told me I was now a wife,
> Honoured indeed, since Christ thus weds the Church,
> And therefore turned he water into wine, [John 2:1–10]
> To show I should obey my spouse like Christ.
>
> (7. 447–50)

Paolo's sacramental legerdemain is intended to impress the ignorant Pompilia. (The implicit allusion to Christ's miracle at the wedding at Cana is wide of the mark: he turned the water into wine only at the behest of his mother, intending— unlike Paolo—no teaching thereby. But how is Pompilia to know?) Paolo's words supply illusory comfort when time passes after the wedding and nothing happens:

> When I saw nothing more, the next three weeks,
> Of Guido—"Nor the Church sees Christ" thought I:
> "Nothing is changed however, wine is wine
> And water only water in our house."   (7. 472–75)

But subsequent experience proves that earthly marriages bear little relationship to Christ's bond to the church, and that

> In heaven we have the real and true and sure.
> 'Tis there they neither marry nor are given
> In marriage but are as the angels: right,
> [Mark 12:25; Matt. 22:30]
> Oh how right that is, how like Jesus Christ
> To say that! [10] . . .

[10] This is perhaps the most bathetic sentence in the poem. But it is almost matched by several others, which are probably traceable to Browning's desire to portray Pompilia's simplicity through appropriate language. The flatness of her "How much good this has done! / This is a whole night's rest and how much more!" (6. 1333–34), "this Lorenzo seems / My own particular place, I always say" (7. 19–20), and "Let us leave God alone!" (7. 1759) considerably exceeds the license allowed to colloquialism in poetry. (The awesome incongruity—as it seems to us—of her "And this man, men call sinner? Jesus Christ!" [7. 1483] must be attributed not to Browning but to a relaxation of conventions of language which he could not have fore-

. . . .

Be as the angels rather, who, apart,
Know themselves into one, are found at length
Married, but marry never, no, nor give
In marriage; they are man and wife at once
When the true time is.

(7. 1826–37)

In Pompilia's scheme of values, marriage is so disembodied a
state that her husband would never recognize it. As for Guido,
marriage—the fleshly kind—is very much part of the Utopia
in which "Husbands [are] once more God's representative, /
Wives like the typical Spouse once more" (5. 2043–44). How
dim the Christ-church analogy has become! The implication
here is that husbands are latter-day Christs, and their wives the
church; but the inference to be drawn is not the spiritual bond
figured forth by the words of St. Paul, but the doctrine of
subservience.

6. *The life of Christ.* In the story told in the Old Yellow
Book, Browning found striking occasional similarities to that
of the Incarnation as reported in the New Testament.[11] The
terms are different, of course; a young woman, as Browning
interprets the case, acts the part of Christ as well as that of
Mary, and the Joseph of the Roman murder story is no husband but a priest accused of adultery. There is, furthermore,
an immense discrepancy in scope between the most crucial
event in the history of Western man and a domestic tragedy
played out to its grisly finale in seventeenth-century Rome. Yet
Browning clearly intended that the Franceschini case be read
as a latter-day story of Christian judgment and redemption. In
the Incarnation, God's love for man was revealed directly,

---

seen.) Pompilia's only rival in bathos is the Pope, whose maudlin
"stoop thou down, my child, / Give one good moment to the poor old
Pope" (10. 1005–6) remains as fixed in some readers' memories as his
more exalted utterances.

[11] For a discussion of this topic from a different viewpoint, see
William Whitla, *The Central Truth: The Incarnation in Robert
Browning's Poetry* (Toronto, 1963), pp. 115–41.

through the sacrifice of Jesus; in the Roman affair, it was
reflected in Pompilia's concern for her unborn child and by
Caponsacchi's rescue of her.

> What were it else but the first things made new,
> But repetition of the miracle,
> The divine instance of self-sacrifice
> That never ends and aye begins for man?
>
> (10. 1654–57)

It is against this background of implied resemblance—a
resemblance centered in spirit rather than in correspondence
of fact—that the manifold references to such manifestations of
God's providence as the Incarnation and the Crucifixion must
be read. The irony is deep and bitter. The figures in the poem
who are least susceptible to divine grace are the most likely to
exploit for crafty ends the power which the New Testament
narrative of the redemption has over the emotions of men.

Most of the allusions to Christ center on the Incarnation
and Christmastide, because, however blasphemous the parallel
may be, the ambiguous origin of Pompilia's babe Gaetano
recalls the mystic arrival of Christ in human form. In the poem
the theme of the Incarnation is announced with mordant sarcasm by Half-Rome, who, foreshadowing thus early the habit
of the speakers to come, fuses associated allusions into one
short passage. He refers to the miraculous rejuvenation and
subsequent pregnancy of both St. Elizabeth and Sarah, wife of
Abraham:

> Violante, 'twixt a smile and a blush,
> With touch of agitation proper too,
> Announced that, spite of her unpromising age,
> [Gen. 18:1–16]
> The miracle would in time be manifest,
> [Luke 1:5–25]
> An heir's birth was to happen: and it did.
>
> (2. 220–24)

The "miracle," as Half-Rome and Tertium Quid choose to
view it, is wrought by a discreet business transaction in which
the as yet unborn Pompilia is bought from a Roman prostitute.

The deal closed, Violante, like St. Elizabeth and the Virgin
Mary,

> Gains church in time for the *"Magnificat"*
>   [Luke 1:46 ff.]
> And gives forth "My reproof is taken away,
>   [Luke 1:25]
> And blessed shall mankind proclaim me now,"
> So that the officiating priest turns round
> To see who proffers the obstreperous praise.
>
>   (4. 195–99)

Pietro, like Joseph, is "enraptured-much / But puzzled-more
when told the wondrous news" (4. 200–201; cf. Matt.
1:19–20).[12]

The fact that the murders occurred during the Christmas
season provided Browning with a ready-made measure of the
enormity of Guido's crime:

> at a known name whispered through the door
> Of a lone villa on a Christmas night,
> It opened that the joyous hearts inside
> Might welcome as it were an angel-guest   [Heb. 13:2]
> Come in Christ's name to knock and enter, sup [Rev. 3:20]
> And satisfy the loving ones he saved;
> And so did welcome devils and their death.
>
>   (1. 393–99)

Guido does not shrink from the parallel. He deposes that, as a
wronged husband seeking the promised peace, his advent to
Rome was marked by his shriveled heart's endeavoring to

---

[12] A delightfully comic reversal occurs when Violante disowns
Pompilia, and Pietro, who now envisions his property reverting to
him, regards this as Good News indeed. Here, inferentially, he is the
pregnant St. Elizabeth, who on the salutation of Mary (Violante)
rejoices.

> Home went Violante and disbosomed all:
> And Pietro who, six months before, had borne
> Word after word of such a piece of news
> Like so much cold steel inched through his breast-blade,
> Now at its entry gave a leap for joy.
>   (3. 614–18; cf. Luke 1:40–42)

respond to the Christmas joy. In a vision (5. 1598–1606, quoted above, p. 50) the face of the Babe turned into that of the crucified Christ.

Like Guido, Pompilia is deeply aware of the parallels between the birth of Gaetano and that of Christ; but she evinces only the awe and wonder of the pious:

> There I lay, then, all my great fortnight long,
> As if it would continue, broaden out
> Happily more and more, and lead to heaven:
> Christmas before me,—was not that a chance?
> I never realized God's birth before—
> How he grew likest God in being born.
> This time I felt like Mary, had my babe
> Lying a little on my breast like hers.
> So all went on till, just four days ago—
> The night and the tap.
>
> (7. 1686–95)

That night, Pietro had just come home from his round of the churches that displayed the Nativity scene, awarding the prize to that at San Giovanni:

> There's the fold,
> And all the sheep together, big as cats!
> And such a shepherd, half the size of life,
> Starts up and hears the angel.   [Luke 2:8–9]
>
> (7. 263–66)

But when the tap comes at the door, it is not the angel of glad tidings, Caponsacchi, who stands outside; it is Guido, the angel of death.

Of the sympathetic witnesses, it is the Pope who feels most deeply the incongruity between the spiritual meaning of the Christmas season and the deed that has desecrated it:

> And thus they [Guido and his henchmen] break
> And blaze on us at Rome, Christ's Birthnight-eve!
> Oh angels that sang erst "On the earth, peace!
> To man, good will!"—such peace finds earth to-day!
>   [Luke 2:13–14]
> After the seventeen hundred years, so man

Wills good to man, so Guido makes complete
His murder!

(10. 786–92)

With the bitterness born of extreme disillusionment, the Pope
sees the murder as the type of anarchy loose in the world.

The journey toward Rome, interrupted at Castelnuovo, is a
recapitulation of the journey to Bethlehem. Pompilia, sick
with fatigue and like the Virgin "pure and pale" (6. 1411),
feels life quickening within her:

> That thrill of dawn's suffusion through my dark,
>   [cf. John 1:4]
> Which I perceive was promise of my child,
> The light his unborn face sent long before,—
> God's way of breaking the good news to flesh.
>   [Luke 2:10]
>   (7. 622–25)

The post house where she and her protector stop is the equivalent of the inn whose stable housed the Holy Family. And
Giuseppe Caponsacchi is a surrogate Joseph: "I paced the
passage, kept watch all night long. / I listened,—not one
movement, not one sigh. / 'Fear not: she sleeps so sound!'
they said." (6. 1418–20.)

The star of Christmas, a central symbol in the monologues
of both Pompilia and Caponsacchi which links their story still
more closely with that of the birth of Christ, has had its dark
counterpart in the "cloud of horror" which attends Guido's
journey to Rome (5. 1567–81). This cloud in turn has been
anticipated by the star of pestilence in Book 1 (544–49), which
finally will have its own counterpart in the lurid "wormwood
star" at the beginning of Book 12. Against so sinister a background, the promise of the star of Bethlehem shines ever
brighter as it becomes the symbol of Pompilia's own epiphany,
embodied in Caponsacchi: "I guessed there would be born a
star." (7. 1405; cf. Matt. 2:10.)

> So did the star rise, soon to lead my step,
> Lead on, nor pause before it should stand still
> Above the House o' the Babe,—my babe to be.
>   [Matt. 2:9]

. . . .

> No pause i' the leading and the light! I know,
> Next night there was a cloud came, and not he:
> But I prayed through the darkness till it broke
> And let him shine.
>
> (7. 1448–61)

The Pope also sees Caponsacchi's relation to the latter-day epiphany:

> Whatever love and faith we looked should spring
> At advent of the authoritative star,   [Matt. 2:2]
> Which yet lie sluggish, curdled at the source,—
> These have leapt forth profusely in old time,
> These still respond with promptitude to-day,
> At challenge of—what unacknowledged powers
> O' the air. . . . [?]   [Eph. 2:2]
>
> (10. 1547–53)

When Pompilia selects prayers to aid the mission, we become increasingly aware, with her, that her escape to Rome has religious significance. She asks Caponsacchi,

> —wherefore do you not read
> The service at this hour? Read Gabriel's song,
> The lesson, and then read the little prayer
> [Luke 1:26–35]
> To Raphael, proper for us travellers!
>
> (6. 1270–73) [13]

Something of both angels is in Caponsacchi: like Gabriel he keeps before him the blessedness of the flight, and like Raphael he protects her in her escape from the avenging Herod that is Guido.

For if the journey from Arezzo toward Rome recalls the journey upon which Christ was born, it also recalls the subsequent flight of the Holy Family into Egypt. Fearing that the tyrant would pursue and kill the newborn child, Pompilia

[13] The angel Raphael accompanied Tobias the son of Tobit to Rages of Media (see Tob. 5 ff.). Like Caponsacchi he was disguised.

gives thanks that "they took, two days after he was born, / My
babe away from me to be baptized / And hidden awhile, for
fear his foe should find" (7. 46–48). Bottini too is aware of
the likeness of Pompilia and Caponsacchi to the fleeing Holy
Family, and his description of the hegira, offered in connection
with his grandiose proposed painting, is clearly an ironist's
inversion of the theme as used by the literalists Pompilia and
Caponsacchi. After the sensuous manner of the Renaissance
painters, Bottini, the artist *manqué*, freely mixes paganism
and Christianity (as well as motherhood and virginity). Pompilia, described as a "Mother-Maid," is transformed into a
voluptuous Italian peasant girl, with "Marmoreal neck and
bosom uberous" (9. 55, 53).

Both literalists and ironists refer often to the Crucifixion, at
once a symbol of man's cruelty and of God's victory over evil
and death. Caponsacchi, angered by the court's levity, recalls
the story of the soldiers' casting lots for Christ's garments
(John 10:23–24) to convey his bitterness at the spectacle of
all Rome callously debating Pompilia's chastity while the
girl-saint herself lies dying (6. 51–59). The events on Calvary
provide Pompilia, too, with terms in which to express her
intuitions. Pondering Caponsacchi's motives in rescuing her,
she reasons that she must perforce pick the lesser of two evils:

> A thief [Caponsacchi] might save me from a murderer
>   [Guido].
> 'Twas a thief said the last kind word to Christ:
>   [Luke 23:42–43]
> Christ took the kindness and forgave the theft.
>   (6. 868–70)

Here, inferentially, the priest-"thief" is to share the fate of
crucifixion, and indeed Caponsacchi, as well as Pompilia, is
figuratively crucified by public opprobrium and misapprehension.

The Pope, rendering his judgment on the viability of the
Christian faith, sees in Pompilia's suffering the modern type of
Christ's agony on the cross:

> I can believe this dread machinery
> Of sin and sorrow, would confound me else,

Devised,—all pain, at most expenditure
Of pain by Who devised pain,—to evolve,
By new machinery in counterpart,
The moral qualities of man—how else?—   [Heb. 2:10]
To make him love in turn and be beloved,
Creative and self-sacrificing too,
And thus eventually God-like, (ay,
"I have said ye are Gods,"—shall it be said for nought?)
                              [Ps. 82:6]
                           (10. 1374–83)

When the Pope must judge Guido and weigh the effects of condemning him, the parallel is made more explicit. Here the Pope represents the "instinct of the world" urging him, as it did Pilate,

"Give thine own feelings play for once,—deal death?
Thou, whose own life winks o'er the socket-edge,
Wouldst thou it went out in such ugly snuff
As dooming sons to death, though justice bade?
Why, on a certain feast, Barabbas' self
Was set free not to cloud the general cheer. [John 18:40]
Neither shalt thou pollute thy Sabbath close!"
                           (10. 2051–57)

The Pope has an easy way out of the dilemma he is imagined to be in: by freeing Guido (Barabbas) he will clear himself with the populace, as Pilate did. But Pope Innocent is no Pontius Pilate.

I I I

Guido's insistence throughout both of his monologues on his Christlike qualities constitutes the most sustained single campaign of scriptural allusion in the poem. We have already traced most of its course (pp. 49–51, 72). But one aspect of his Christ-role, that of the suffering servant of mankind, is worth pursuing further, especially as it reaches out into other biblical contexts. From the start he cultivates the pose of the latter-day Christ who so loved the world (or Roman society) that he gave his own honor that it should not die, but have everlasting life. If he succeeds—and the stake is his very neck—it will be because he has persuaded his auditors to transfer their immanent sympathy for Christ to himself, substituting the divine image for his manifestly cruel (and by all accounts ugly) one.

With his customary effrontery, he trades on his ignominious history as a hanger-on of the church for far more than it is worth. At one point he maintains that, as a young churchman with noble blood, he held aloof from vulgar striving after perquisites. He was

> Ready to let the basket go its round   [Matt. 14:20]
> Even though my turn was come to help myself,
> Should Dives count on me at dinner-time.   [Luke 16:19]
>   (5. 280–82)

In this clever montage of allusions, the miraculously produced basket of bread and fishes (the perquisites of the clergy) is passed up by Christ's disciple Guido in favor of some choice tidbits from Dives' (the Pope's) sumptuous "feast," thrown, in the form of a sinecure, to the starving Lazarus-Guido. But this fancy is too rich for Guido, who is used, as he remarks elsewhere, to feeding on the east wind (5. 347; cf. Job 15:2), and his more usual means of describing his service to the church (viz., his participation in the scramble for preferment) is in terms of the suffering servant. In his exordium he says:

> Will my lords, in the plenitude of their light,
> Weigh well that all this trouble has come on me
> Through my persistent treading in the paths
> Where I was trained to go,—wearing that yoke
> My shoulder was predestined to receive[?]
>   (5. 122–26)

He has willingly "protruded nose / To halter, bent my back of docile beast", while others have "thrown their careless hoofs up" at the call of the church. But to no gain:

And now [I] am whealed, one wide wound all of me,
For being found at the eleventh hour o' the day
                                                        [Matt. 20:6]
Padding the mill-track.   [Judg. 16:21]
                                                        (5. 130–37)

In one rhetorical swoop, Guido has managed to liken himself
at once to Christ, to Samson,[14] and to the scriptural beast of
burden. The same metaphor embodies his last line of defense
in Book 11—that the church, itself plodding and oxlike, has
made him what he is, and that he is therefore not responsible
for his crimes:

Take your word on life's use? When I take his—
The muzzled ox that treadeth out the corn, [Deut. 25:4]
Gone blind in padding round and round one path,—
As to the taste of green grass in the field!
What do you know o' the world that's trodden flat
And salted sterile with your daily dung,
Leavened into a lump of loathsomeness?
                                                        (11. 1466–72)

Guido's vituperation here is ironical when we remember his
earlier clerical role of the muzzled ox; it is still more so if we
recall the biblical original, "Thou shalt not muzzle the ox when
he treadeth out the corn." The implication is that the church is
in some measure culpable for not having given its clerics
(including Guido) some of the "corn" or, in Guido's additional term, "the taste of green grass"—namely, a useful working knowledge of the world.[15]

[14] Cf. Arcangeli's paralleling of Guido to Samson grinding corn (8.
638–44).
[15] Another amusing agricultural image (one of many) is conceived by the Other Half-Rome, who depicts the Abate Paolo promot-
ing Guido's interests with the Comparini. The Count is one who, says
Paolo, has rejected all worldly interests,

Having, as one who puts his hand to the plough,   [Luke 9:62]
Renounced the over-vivid family-feel—
Poor brother Guido!
                                                        (3. 302–4)

As he proceeds, Guido's use of Scripture becomes ever more agile and eclectic. Sometimes he appears to have devised the ironies that ensue from his citing of a text; at other times, he seems unconscious of them and so is betrayed by his own ingenuity. At one point he recalls how he applied to his "fellows" for wisdom on how to get ahead in the church and was told of the peasant's son who "recoiled from muck, liked Latin more, / Stuck to his pen, and got to be a priest," later winning preferment that could support a "coach and six" by writing a tract against Molinos which his absent-minded superior published as his own. "Well, let me go, do likewise," Guido promptly decided (5. 193–209). In this context, the allusion to St. Luke (10:37) inverts the purport of the original, in which Christ advises the rich man to sell his goods and follow the church. Here Guido, having few goods, says he hoped (after a momentary consideration of "soldiership") to find both comfort and status, if not wealth, at Rome. In view of this hypocrisy, his next allusion is especially ironic: "Bidden qualify for Rome, I, having a field, / Went, sold it, laid the sum at Peter's foot." (5. 249–50.) The echo is of Acts 4:36–37: "And Joses, who by the apostles was surnamed Barnabas, . . . having land sold it, and brought the money, and laid it at the apostles' feet." Which is to say that Guido tried his best, with the small sum at his disposal, to buy his way into a sinecure at Rome within hailing distance of the Pope ("Peter"). Having failed, Guido must be content with being merely a vine-dresser on Peter's estate:

> Be not the vine but dig and dung its root,
>
> > [Luke 13:7–8]
>
> Be not a priest but gird up priesthood's loins.
>
> > [Luke 12:35]
> >
> > (5. 230–31) [16]

[16] "Then said he unto the dresser of his vineyard, . . . Cut it [the barren fig tree] down; why cumbereth it the ground? And he answering said unto him, Lord, let it alone this year also, till I shall dig about it, and dung it" (Luke 13:7–8). Cf. 10. 1967–69, where Guido is the vine which the vinedresser (the Pope) can save, and 11. 1865, where Guido is again the vine which "cumbers earth" but bears no fruit. The whole cluster of allusions to a single text shows Browning's

Lamenting the dearth of fortune at Rome, Guido now slips into
the role of "modern Job" with a bit of Moses on the side:

> And, although fed by the east-wind, fulsome-fine
>   [Job 15:2]
> With foretaste of the Land of Promise, still
> My gorge gave symptom it might play me false;
> Better not press it further,—be content
> With living and dying only a nobleman.
>
>   (5. 347–51)

Like Moses, Guido is willing to end his days without crossing
the Jordan to the Promised Land of preferment. He resolves to
return to Arezzo, where he is again forced into Job's plight:
that "plague-seed set to fester his sound flesh" (2. 629),
namely his wife Pompilia, is there to torment him.

> I felt this trouble flap my face,
> Already pricked with every shame could perch,—
>   [Job 2:7–8]
> When, with her parents, my wife plagued me too.
>   (5. 926–28)

But his Job-like torments are not ended even yet; a new gadfly,
his infant son, alights on Guido's face:

> This bastard then, a nest for him is made,
> As the manner is of vermin, in my flesh—
> Shall I let the filthy pest buzz, flap and sting,
> Busy at my vitals and, nor hand nor foot
> Lift, but let be, lie still and rot resigned?
> No, I appeal to God.
>
>   (5. 1537–42) [17]

Unlike Job, Guido fails to learn the will of God. Job may have
been proud and stubborn, but he also was able to recognize a
power greater than himself; Guido cannot, and his "appeal to
God" is therefore mere rhetoric.

---

genius for extracting totally different meanings from a relatively short
biblical passage torn from context and for playing off these meanings
against one another.

[17] Other accounts have Guido, Job-like, neck-deep in mire. See
below, pp. 251–52.

All such pious gestures are revealed for what they are in
Guido's second monologue, compact as it is of savage cynicism, accusation, and grim revealment of the villain beneath
the martyr. He takes a sadistic pleasure in watching his confessors recoil as he challenges one of them to follow Christ's
example: "Abate, gird your loins and wash my feet!" (11.
616; cf. John 13:4–14.) In a torrent of butt-ends of distorted
Scripture he cries:

Where's the obedience that shall edify?   [1 Cor. 8:1]
Why, they laugh frankly in the face of faith
And take the natural course,—this rends his hair
Because his child is taken to God's breast,
That gnashes teeth and raves at loss of trash   [Matt. 8:12]
Which rust corrupts and thieves break through and steal,
                                                 [Matt. 6:19]
And this, enabled to inherit earth
Through meekness, curses till your blood runs cold!
                                                 [Matt. 5:5]
Down they all drop to my low level . . .

  .   .   .   .

We have the prodigal son of heavenly sire,
Turning his nose up at the fatted calf,
Fain to fill belly with the husks we swine
Did eat by born depravity of taste!   [Luke 15:11–32]
                                                 (11. 749–63)

Borne on the succession of New Testament echoes comes anti-
thetical doctrine: man's natural state is apostasy and amorality,
the unredeemed life of the senses. Guido demands, as a natural
right, to be allowed to satiate his carnal appetite and then be
readmitted to Christian society:

       Grow out of man,
Glut the wolf-nature,—what remains but grow
Into the man again, be man indeed
And all man? Do I ring the changes right?
Deformed, transformed, reformed, informed, conformed!
                                                 (11. 2057–61)

But St. Paul's words offer sufficient commentary on this proposal: "And be not conformed to this world: but be ye transformed by the renewing of your mind" (Rom. 12:2). To the very last, Guido affects the saintliness he never possessed, and does it so convincingly as to impress the case-hardened letter writer who describes his execution:

> He begged forgiveness on the part of God,
> And fair construction of his act from men,
> Whose suffrage he entreated for his soul,
>
> . . . .
> . . . —then rose up, as brisk
> Knelt down again, bent head, adapted neck,
> And, with the name of Jesus on his lips,
> Received the fatal blow.
>
> (12. 174–89)

In his extremity he still was determined upon playing a sanctified role, in this case that of St. Stephen, who was stoned as he called upon God and said, "Lord Jesus, receive my spirit" (Acts 7:59). The performance won the sympathy of the crowd. "So died the man," writes the witness, "and so his end was peace." (12. 205) The epitaph is from Psalms 37:37: "Mark the perfect man, and behold the upright: for the end of that man is peace." It is fitting that Guido should be commemorated by words of Scripture which are, once more, misapplied.

Eight

"*How That Staunch Image Serves at Every Turn!*"

THE DRAMA OF METAPHOR

I

If the Bible means all things to all men in *The Ring and the Book*—or, more precisely, supplies them with effective language in which to press their various cases—metaphors provide an even greater fund of adaptable terms. The speakers practice the art of metaphor so lavishly as to render the poem, from one point of view, a dense network of association, analogy, and attribution—similitudes ranging from the explicit and plainly applicable to the hazily implicit. Guido is portrayed in some 106 different metaphorical roles, a number of which are assumed many times; Pompilia in approximately 113; and Caponsacchi in 59. Of these roles, 14 are at one time or another assumed by all three principal characters; among them are several (lamb, shepherd, serpent, St. Michael–St. George) which occur most frequently in the poem and are of major thematic significance. Thirty-five more are shared by two of the leading characters. It is a complicated and subtle system, with unlimited opportunity for contrast, irony, and cross-commentary; and here, if anywhere, is Browning the rival of Shakespeare as a master of dramatic and evocative language which helps define both the speaker and the person spoken about. It is in their figurative speech that the characters most extensively demonstrate the persuasive potential of language that is at once flexible, ambiguous, laden with emotional power, and available equally to the honest and the guileful. By the very nature of its action, irrespective of what

226

it *says*, metaphorical language further exemplifies the treachery of man's discourse.

Metaphors enable nearly all the speakers to express with greatest force what they see or wish others to see in the events and characters of the story, including themselves. They seek to replace the commonly observed actuality with something that is either different or more intense: to substitute for the external aspect of a person, his individual "norm" so to speak, a version that more nearly accords with their private interpretation or, at any rate, the interpretation they wish their listeners to adopt. Thanks to the power that figurative language shrewdly used has to compel assent, shadow acquires the plausibility of substance: metaphor tends to discredit the "real" and to urge the acceptance of appearance as "truth." Where, in these "strange disguisings whence even truth seems false" (2. 1411), does truth really lie? The tension and the uncertainty mount as the intricate pattern is developed, the overlaid conflict of opposing or variant figures of speech intensifying the basic conflict of character and viewpoint.

Fresh speakers and new contexts are ceaselessly calling forth familiar tropes in novel forms. These iterated images, like leading themes in a sonata or a symphony, are both dynamic and accretive: dynamic in that they pass through a long sequence of forms, never twice exactly the same (a continuing emblem, therefore, of the poem's theme of universal flux), and accretive in that with every appearance new meaning is added to the original metaphor, each fresh occurrence involving reminiscence of previous forms, applications, and contexts. The same process occurs with the referents—the protean characters who in the course of the poem assume so many scores of different guises. Every new metaphor involving previously introduced elements is in fact a separate creative event in which each constituent—the referent and the vehicle of the comparison—is somehow modified, its earlier meaning being either altered or strengthened, before it proceeds on its separate way to the next conjunction. Each element in a given metaphor contains within itself the history of all its previous uses.

Browning most often selects for his image themes figures whose long presence and manifold uses in Western thought have made them highly adaptable. The lamb, for instance, a capacious symbol of the kind of which we shall have much to say in this chapter, is widely and variously used both in Scripture and religious iconography and in the even older pastoral tradition, and consequently it can be used by the different characters in the poem for completely divergent purposes.[1] The strong if sometimes ambiguous associations these figures possess—the emotional heritage of many centuries—lend them additional force as they are applied to so many disparate situations; and, as we have seen is true also of the poem's biblical allusions, they are especially productive of ironies.

Browning's virtuosity is never more evident than in his invention and mastery of this structure of metaphor. To work out these hundreds upon hundreds of purposeful variations required not only unflagging attention to minute detail but a memory that could span thousands of intervening lines for the sake of providing the exactly suitable variation of an earlier figure at the exactly suitable moment. But perhaps most remarkable is the manner in which he integrated the system of images with the poem as a whole. Although the primary artistic purpose of the image-play is to expand characterization and illuminate motive, the metaphors have also a dramatic func-

---

[1] This "convertibility" (Henry James's term) which characterizes Browning's use of metaphor was, in fact, given warrant—if not actually inspired—by the tendency of Christian symbolism in general. Just as Christ is both the Good Shepherd and the spotless sheep, so the symbols themselves have multiple, and sometimes actually contradictory, significance. The lion may symbolize the evil spirit which seeks to devour its prey or it may, on the other hand, represent Christ, the lion of the tribe of Judah. The serpent may be the devil or a talisman against evil, or it may represent prudence, regeneration, eternity, wisdom, or goodness.

This may be as good a place as any to pay tribute to the versatile mountain which in the course of a single book (3) is moved by faith (489), bears mice (1322), and is made from a molehill (1483–84). It is too bad Mahomet could not have been worked in somehow.

tion: by the appropriate choice and modulation of figures during the various narrative movements Browning orchestrates the action itself. At the same time, sometimes explicitly, more often by indirection, he uses the figures to restate and clarify the dominant metaphysical and religious themes. And because the subjects of the figures are drawn from the whole range of human experience, in their totality they contribute to that intimate mingling of the comic and the tragic, the celestial and the earthly, the pathetic and the repulsive, which is among the poem's most distinctive qualities.

I I

A simple catalogue of the guises attributed to the leading characters reveals not only the great scope of the poem's figurative language but in particular the audacity with which many metaphors are misapplied by the various speakers. Since all three of the principals are described with exuberant variety by both accusers and defenders, each is bound to be characterized in conflicting terms.

We begin with Guido. Besides the numerous appearances he makes as a snake, fish, or amphibious monster such as leviathan or dragon—roles whose affinity is implied in the Pope's remark that the false "probity / He figures in, is falsehood *scale on scale*" (10. 513–14)—he is seen as all manner of beasts, birds, and insects, a typology appropriate enough in view of the folk belief that the devil can appear in animal disguises.[2] The inventory of Guido's roles, quite possibly not complete, runs as follows, the letters C and P identifying roles assumed on other occasions by Caponsacchi or Pompilia, and an asterisk designating roles assumed too often for their individual appearances to be listed. (Most of the latter are discussed in some detail in the following pages.)

[2] For a systematic analysis of the animal imagery of the poem as illustrative of the various speakers' moral natures, see Honan, *Browning's Characters*, pp. 180–88. Honan also studies the poem's color imagery (pp. 188–98).

gardener (7. 1001; 9. 294)

vineyard keeper (2. 812–15, 1392; 5. 230)

keeper of hen roost (2. 820 ff.; 11. 1423)

shepherd (C) (3. 1300–1306; 5. 893)

owner of pet lamb (5. 666)

herdsman (9. 244 ff.)

goat trainer (7. 609)

huntsman (6. 1288)

fowler, trap setter (10. 721 ff.)

spearman (9. 1418)

bishop (5. 733, 761)

priest (5. 861; 11. 978)

"tuneful singer" (5. 919–24)

"low-browed verger" (6. 669)

butcher, market man (3. 464; 7. 578)

gambler (5. 370–81)

(not a) physician (C) (7. 413–23)

(not an) angel (7. 266)

foolish virgin (2. 318–19)

artist (11. 1555)

actor (3. 1587–89; 5. 1440; 6. 1566–69)

warrior (5. 601–2)

God, Christ (C, P)*

Satan (P)*

Adam (2. 169; 4. 858)

Jacob (5. 1309–21)

Moses (?) (5. 348)

Samson (C, P) (3. 1467–68; 8. 638–55)

Philistine (2. 909)

Job (1. 963; 2. 629, 1487; 5. 1539)

David (C) (5. 2020)

Solomon (4. 328)

Potiphar (6. 1732)

Ahasuerus (11. 993–97)

Lucifer (C) (1. 623; 5. 1046)

Holofernes (?) (C ?) (9. 574)

Herod (7. 48; 9. 128)

Lazarus (5. 1174)

St. Peter (5. 969)

Barabbas (10. 2055)

Nabal (9. 363)

St. Michael (or not St. Michael) (C, P) (7. 390–93; 11. 2096–97)

Aristaeus (9. 1344)

Bellerophon (11. 1125)

male Griselda (2. 1487) [3]

Hercules (C) (3. 385–97; 9. 400)

Menelaus (2. 1003–6, 1020; 5. 1265; 6. 1747)

Perseus (C) (4. 1385)

Vulcan (3. 1450; 6. 1459; 9. 866)

Ulysses (C) (9. 626)

---

[3] Ironically, Pompilia, who is a true patient Griselda, is never cast in that role.

elephant (1. 234)
horse (P) (2. 391)
ox (C, P) (5. 125 ff.; 11. 1478)
wolf (C)*
werewolf (1. 612 ff.)
animal in den (10. 1462–63)
caged animal (10. 416)
dog (C, P) (2. 1062; 3. 1461; 4. 1200, 1206; 6. 1513; 7. 1086; 8. 1504–13; 11. 1332)
swine (C, P) (11. 762)
sheep, lamb (C, P) (2. 1090; 5. 1096; 11. 344)
fox (C, P) (3. 641; 4. 1095)
tiger cat (C, P) (1. 1296)
wildcat (3. 1324, 7. 1315)
cat (6. 426)
mouse (3. 415)
lynx (11. 917)
lion (or no lion) (C) (3. 534; 5. 798, 1096)
badger (2. 865)
ferret (3. 781)
bear (C) (6. 545)

bull (4. 1559 ff.)
owl (P) (7. 398)
bird (C, P) (7. 832)
dabchick (2. 296)
hawk (P) (3. 1537; 6. 109)
bird of prey (10. 587–88)
swan (P) (5. 658)
decoy bird (C, P) (4. 505–6)
rooster (5. 293)
bat (5. 360)
[gad]fly (C, P) (2. 503; 11. 1812)
[soldier] bee (P) (5. 2009–11)
spider (2. 1165; 6. 616)
snake, dragon, serpent (C, P)*
cockatrice (P) (6. 1950)
scorpion (P) (3. 1167)
worm, maggot (P) (3. 696)
soldier crab (10. 485–509)
fish, leviathan, sea monster (C, P)*
stockfish (4. 1147)

witches' brew ("sulphur, snake, and toad") (5. 636)
stone (P) (5. 96)
ice block (7. 1595)
butcher's block (P) (9. 406)
star (C) (1. 535–43)
solar system (2. 845)
skyrocket (12. 3–8)
pestilential cloud (1. 544–54)
wave in the sea and mist (11. 2352–55)

tree (C, P) (11. 2405)
grass ready for mowing (11. 148)
flame (11. 2064)
ship (C) (5. 1301–3; 11. 50–52)
plume on a horse's head (4. 415)
ornament on tail of a donkey (2. 300)
morsel on a dish (P) (4. 726–27)

Pompilia has two main recurrent roles, those of Madonna [4]
and a lamb. In addition, brandishing the sword of righteousness at Castelnuovo she assimilates all the heroic figures who
ever fought or tamed dragons in defense of the good: St.
Michael (with whom the Pope explicitly associates her [10.
1010–12]); St. George; the Madonna, who in art is sometimes
portrayed with her foot on the serpent of sin; and St. Margaret,
the special protectress of pregnant women, who is often represented in art leading a chained dragon or planting her foot on
one. Also noteworthy is the number of bird and plant guises
and masculine roles she is made momentarily to assume. (G
denotes roles also assumed by Guido, and C, as before, those
assumed also by Caponsacchi.)

saint (6. 175)	babe at baptism (5. 865–70)
Roman martyr (C) (6. 1185; 10. 1138)	playwright (C) (2. 1080)
	deacon (7. 732)
slave singer (11. 1418–20)	fury (8. 1059)
dying person (5. 862)	

Eve (2. 168; 4. 852; 7. 759; 9. 449 ff.)	Potiphar's wife (6. 1730)
	Abigail (9. 359)
Madonna*	Esther (11. 996)
Rachel (5. 1311 ff.)	Delilah (9. 515)

[4] Madonna allusions are most numerous in Pompilia's own monologue, but only once does she consciously associate herself with the
Madonna: "This time"—after the birth of her child—"I felt like Mary,
had my babe / Lying a little on my breast like hers." (7. 1692–93.) It
is worthy of remark that the other speakers usually couch the identification in terms of Mary the familiar figure in religious art rather than
the New Testament character. See, for example, 6. 406, 672–73, 911–15
(Caponsacchi's allusions to Raphael's Madonna), 1991–96; and 11.
2115 (another reference to Raphael). Bottini travesties this association by making Pompilia and her babe central figures in his imaginary
masterpiece of the Flight into Egypt (9. 126). Most of the rose and lily
images of the poem bear suggestions of the Madonna: books of
devotion refer to her as the rose of heaven or the mystic rose, and the
lily is her designated flower, associated especially with the Annunciation. An oblique allusion to Pompilia as a Madonna figure is the
repeated representation of her as a young girl at her "broider-frame"
(3. 263; 7. 483). In Christian art Mary is often portrayed teaching
girls in the temple to spin or embroider.

Samson (C, G) (2. 909)
Judith (9. 567 ff.)
Magdalene (9. 936)
Malchus (5. 967, 982)
Christ (C, G) (6. 59; 11. 981)
St. Michael (C, G) (6. 1603–4)
Satan (G) (2. 1159)
Amaryllis (9. 539)
Archimedes (9. 758)
Cleodolina (St. George's princess) (1. 587; 6. 1772; 7. 1324)

Corinna (5. 1359)
Dido (9. 655)
Hebe (9. 235)
Helen of Troy (2. 1003; 5. 1264; 6. 1747; 9. 624)
Hesione (9. 966)
Locusta (5. 811)
Medusa (4. 1385; 11. 1363 ff.)
Philomela (6. 582)
Phryne (9. 169)
Venus (3. 1452; 9. 527, 712, 867, 891)
[Eurydice] (4. 842–49)

horse (G) (11. 1362)
heifer, cow (7. 674; 9. 246 ff.; 11. 977, 989)
ox (C, G) (5. 428)
ass (C) (5. 428)
sheep, lamb (C, G)*
goat (7. 609)
swine (C, G) (2. 1137)
hare (C) (4. 919; 11. 1328–32)
fawn (6. 1286; 10. 918, 1463)
dog (C, G) (2. 637; 4. 611, 5. 88; 6. 813–14)
fox (C, G) (2. 866)
tiger cat (C, G) (11. 1716)
bird (C, G) (7. 888, 1246; 11. 1321)
bird in trap (3. 809–10)
decoy bird (C, G) (4. 505–6; 7. 678)
migratory bird (3. 1122)
fowl in coop or grange (2. 821–22; 3. 778 ff.)

chick (2. 839)
pullet (11. 1423)
(not a) swan (G) (5. 658–62)
(not a) pigeon (5. 701)
haggard hawk (G) (5. 703–10)
magpie (9. 455)
parrot (C) (9. 454)
owl, lure owl (G) (7. 678)
lark (3. 338)
cuckoo (3. 340)
partridge (C) (11. 1540)
(not a) pheasant (4. 738)
raven (12. 723–25)
crow (9. 455)
carrion crow (4. 738)
dove (3. 1533; 4. 1383; 5. 753; 6. 110; 7. 464, 992; 9. 1230; 12. 475 ff., 723–25)
finch (3. 217; 5. 715)
sparrow hawk (3. 336)
phoenix (C) (3. 335)

chimera's head (11. 1118–25)

fly, gadfly (C, G) (7. 1246)

bee (G) (7. 977)

snake, serpent (C, G) *

worm, tapeworm, maggot (G) *

cockatrice (G) (5. 657)

scorpion (G) (11. 1597)

fish (G) (2. 270)

minnow (2. 273, 323)

eel (9. 393 ff., 1417)

flower or weed (3. 5, 72, 84; 5. 1848; 7. 1002, 1516–27; 10. 1017, 1033)

rose, thorn (C) *

lily (3. 365; 4. 323)

plant graft, root (2. 627, 1189 ff.; 11. 1091–1108)

parasitic mistletoe (5. 813–14; 11. 2405)

furze sprig (11. 2177)

fig (7. 822)

apple (3. 384)

tree, bough (C, G) (3. 234; 5. 605; 6. 778, 1375; 7. 341; 9. 701; 10. 736)

flower garden (9. 290 ff.)

ruined building (7. 856–57)

besieged Troy (9. 843)

butcher's block (G) (9. 406)

stone (G) (7. 1005, 1117; 9. 408)

stream (7. 873; 11. 2052)

the moon (6. 1146; 9. 886)

pearl (11. 1209); pearl into sapphire into opal (9. 199–204)

paten borne by priest (6. 1620)

myrrh, nard (C) (9. 324–26)

candle flame (2. 503)

brand in flame (3. 1024)

painting (11. 2115)

leper rag (2. 632–33; 5. 809–11)

plague seed (2. 629)

bait, snare (6. 716–17)

angler's lure (2. 342, 1356; 4. 941–42)

food (6. 595–96)

morsel on dish (G) (4. 727; 5. 643)

bread (9. 321)

icicle (4. 863)

egg (3. 215; 5. 655)

Because Caponsacchi enters the story late, his part in the various narratives is not so long as Guido's and Pompilia's; and because he is a somewhat less controversial character, he does not appear in so many attributed roles as they do. He is primarily a St. George-Perseus figure,[5] but he is much else besides:

[5] Although there apparently are no explicit references to Caponsacchi as Perseus, it does not seem stretching things too far to include

angel (7. 1587, 1617–19)
Roman martyr (P) (6. 1185)
soldier saint (7. 1786)
Roman athlete (10. 1140–65)

physician (G) (2. 1206; 7. 1147)
playwright (P) (2. 1080)
drudging student (6. 2098)
shepherd (G) (5. 1197)

Christ (G, P) (2. 1159)
Joseph (son of Jacob and Rachel) (6. 1729)
St. Joseph (9. 125)
Samson (G, P) (9. 515)
David (G) (9. 356)
Holofernes ("or is it the Count?") (9. 573–74)
doubting Thomas (6. 1099)
St. Michael, St. George (G, P) *
Lucifer (G) (2. 167)

Apollos into Apollo (2. 794)
Hercules (G) (6. 1002 ff.; 9. 974)
Perseus (G) *
Mars (3. 1455; 6. 1459; 9. 867)
Myrtillus (9. 539)
[Orpheus] (4. 842–49)
Ovid (2. 1221 ff.)
Paris (2. 1006; 5. 1264; 6. 1747)
Ulysses (G) (9. 546)

lion (G) (3. 29)
wolf (G) (3. 786–87; 6. 1362)
fox (G, P) (2. 821–25, 838–40, 1146)
bear (G) (6. 631)
tiger cat (G, P) (11. 1716)
hare (P) (4. 919)
dog (G, P) (6. 100)
ox, beast of burden (G, P) (6. 993–94)
ass (P) (9. 1285)

swine (G, P) (6. 1723)
sheep, lamb (G, P) (3. 29; 7. 1588)
game (6. 640)
bird (G, P) (10. 1103)
decoy bird (G, P) (3. 783–84)
sentry crane (7. 1351)
phoenix (P) (9. 350)
partridge (P) (11. 1540)
parrot, popinjay (P) (3. 784–85)

---

the role, since it is closely cognate with that of St. George. Certainly "the Andromeda situation," as W. C. DeVane calls it, is frequently alluded to. DeVane counts some thirty references to the related St. George-Cleodolinda and Perseus-Andromeda myths of beleaguerment and rescue in the books favorable to Pompilia and Caponsacchi. See his "The Virgin and the Dragon," *Yale Review*, n.s., 37 (1947): 33–46, esp. pp. 41–45.

gadfly (G, P) (5. 912; 6. 616, 958)

firefly (7. 1521)

butterfly (9. 311)

grub into hornet (4. 1157–58)

serpent (G, P) (4. 859); serpent into eel into snake (9. 393–400)

leviathan (G) (10. 1102)

hollow rock (6. 72)

nard (P) (10. 1122–26)

south wind on a warm day (3. 1125–26)

the sun (7. 1524, 1595)

star (G) *

orb in [Guido's] solar system (2. 845)

tree swaying in wind (G, P) (9. 701)

rose, thorn (P) (10. 685, 1096)

ship (G) (6. 369–70)

liquor, wine (3. 414–15; 9. 1554)

puppet (1. 1019–21)

The minor characters, too, have their full share of shifting guises. Especially in Books 4, 5, and 11 (Tertium Quid and the two Guido speeches), where they are blamed for most of the mischief, Pietro and Violante are seen in roles as comic, grotesque, and inappropriate as any attributed to the protagonists. They are jointly a chimera (11. 1118–25), anglers (2. 1355 ff.; 4. 707–11), and brick walls (3. 233–41); they are barnyard birds (3. 339), field workers (2. 518), slugs (4. 117), ravens (4. 114), decoy birds (4. 505), gnats (4. 561), scullions (4. 730), crucified thieves (5. 532), monks (5. 729, 756), frightened mice (6. 425), a pair of plagues (11. 1128), geese (11. 1195), fighting cocks on a dunghill (11. 1209), insects (11. 1261–74), scorpions (11. 1594), earthworms (5. 1668), tapeworms (11. 1604), and shepherds (11. 1174). Violante, in addition, is Eve (2. 253; 3. 170), an old sheep (4. 123 ff.), a hag who turns into a serpent (5. 1649–68), an old dove (7. 464), the Virgin Mary and St. Elizabeth (4. 195–99), St. Anne (9. 124), Sarah (3. 172 ff.), Laomedon's wife (9. 968), an ass in a stall (11. 1142), and—a particular triumph of miscasting—Danaë (3. 439). Pietro is Adam (2. 254; 3. 169), a kite (7. 465), an ox in a butcher's shop (7. 578), a clown (11. 1153–55), St. Joachim (9. 123), the pregnant St. Elizabeth (3. 615–18), and Laomedon (9. 967).[6]

The various descriptions of Guido's mother are variations on a single theme. She has a monkey mien (1. 571), she is a dragon (2. 491), a "gaunt grey nightmare," a hag, and a she-leopard who placidly watches as her whelps feast on a fawn (these are the Pope's terms in his corrosive denunciation of her [10. 910–24]). Elsewhere the leopard's whelps, Paolo and Girolamo, are ducks on the Galilean pond (2. 293–95, 338–41) and, like churchmen in general (who in other places are cattle [5. 133, 239; 11. 1466 ff.]), they are roosters (4. 397–99) on the dungheap which is the church (2. 298). Paolo, additionally, has the face of a fox (1. 549; 10. 879) and is an iridescent serpent (3. 358–75), a mouse (3. 412), and a trapper (10. 892–93), while Girolamo is a moth (2. 503) and has the claws of a cat (1. 550). The lawyers are not only foxes (1. 215; 8. 302–5), a role shared by Pompilia, Caponsacchi, Guido, and Paolo, but also dogs (4. 44–48; 8. 303–5).[7] This last role too is shared by the three principals. At one time or another Guido, Pompilia, and Caponsacchi are deserted or

---

[6] He is also, in a manner of speaking, Walter Savage Landor. Violante describes Pietro's refusal to approve of Pompilia's marriage

> As if I put before him wholesome food
> Instead of broken victual,—he finds change
> I' the viands, never cares to reason why,
> But falls to blaming me, would fling the plate
> From window, scandalize the neighbourhood
>
> (7. 539–43)

—which was exactly the habit of the aged, irascible Landor, as Browning, who helped care for him in Florence, had good reason to know.

[7] Places as well as persons share in this universal metamorphosis. Contemporary Arezzo and Rome appear as the Garden of Eden, hell, Gaza (8. 640), and Troy (9. 966). The road from Arezzo to Rome figures as the route taken by the fleeing Joseph and Mary. Specific metaphorical sites likewise change inhabitants from time to time. The dungheap which is one of the most-used stage properties in this poem is populated by squabbling, ambitious clergymen-fowl (2. 298; 5. 293) and by those crowing game cocks the Comparini, who find a pearl (Pompilia) there (11. 1209–10; cf. 2. 558). Pompilia later blooms above the Roman dungheap as a "dewy-dear" rose (4. 246–47).

beaten dogs—an image normally, but not always, evocative of
sympathy. The three such references to Guido supply an instance of the same metaphor being used in the same context in
three different versions of the story, but each time with significant variations of intention and effect. When Pompilia and
Caponsacchi are taken to Rome after their arrest, Guido's
partisan Half-Rome sees "The husband trooping after, pit-
eously, / Tail between legs, no talk of triumph now" (2.
1061–62). The Other Half-Rome, presenting the sequel to that
situation, is much amused at Guido's well-earned discomfiture:
the municipal gaiety of Arezzo is refreshed by the spectacle of
the husband returning from Rome, who had "ne'er showed
teeth at all, / Whose bark had promised biting; but [who] just
sneaked / Back to his kennel, tail 'twixt legs, as 'twere" (3.
1459–61). Tertium Quid, however, argues that Guido deserves
compassion. Put yourselves in his place, he urges his elegant
auditors:

> Nought left you but a low appeal to law,
> "Coward" tied to your tail for compliment!
> Another consideration: have it your way!
> Admit the worst: his courage failed the Count,
> He's cowardly like the best o' the burgesses
> He's grown incorporate with,—a very cur,
> Kick him from out your circle by all means!
> Why, trundled down this reputable stair,
> Still, the Church-door lies wide to take him in,
> And the Court-porch also: in he sneaks to each,—
> "Yes, I have lost my honour and my wife,
> And, being moreover an ignoble hound,
> I dare not jeopardise my life for them!"
>
> (4. 1195–1207)

But whatever sympathy is extorted for Guido at this point
eventually dissolves in hilarity when Arcangeli identifies Guido's four accomplices as fleas and Guido therefore (by a
backward associational leap) as Tobit's dog, the implication
being that Guido, hurrying from Rome after the murder, is
slowed down by having to scratch the importunate fleas who
insist on being paid (8. 1503–13, quoted above, pp. 113–14).
Pompilia meanwhile implores Caponsacchi to take her to

Rome: "Take me as you would take a dog, I think, / Master-less left for strangers to maltreat." (6. 813–14.) Caponsacchi does so, and for his pains he too is converted into a dog by a court jealous of law's prerogatives: "A kind of culprit, over-zealous hound / Kicked for his pains to kennel." (6. 100–101.)

Each of the alleged lovers is said to have been a bird used to decoy the other. "The plume o' the popinjay" Caponsacchi is meant to lure the captive Pompilia into making a false move (3. 784–85); and Guido accuses Pompilia of being "A lure-owl posturing to attract birds" (7. 678). "Which bird o' the brace / Decoyed the other into clapnet?" pertinently demands Tertium Quid (4. 505–6).

If Guido is accurately called a hawk (3. 1537; 6. 109), he has company in his hawkhood, for, he says, Pompilia is one also:

> Pompilia was no pigeon, Venus' pet,
> That shuffled from between her pressing paps
> To sit on my rough shoulder,—but a hawk,
> I bought at a hawk's price and carried home
> To do hawk's service.

(5. 701–5) [8]

The same commodious habit of language enables Guido, the true scorpion (3. 1167), to attribute his evil qualities instead to the "three scorpions" Pompilia, Violante, and Pietro (11. 1594).

In Browning's casting, Guido, the villain, and Caponsacchi, the hero, share four quasi-human roles: Hercules, Samson, Lucifer, and Perseus. Guido, according to Bottini, performed the Herculean feat of killing the Lernaean hydra (9. 400–402) and, according to Violante, who presumably had it from Paolo, in his Herculean role he came to pluck the Hesperian apple, Pompilia (3. 384–85). Caponsacchi also thinks of himself as Hercules, who,

> i' the fabled garden, . . . had gone
> On great adventure, plucked in ignorance
> Hedge-fruit, and feasted to satiety,

[8] Guido is rather uncertain what he did purchase. A hundred lines earlier he had, by another analogy, bought, "timber and twig, a tree," with "the song o' the nightingale" thrown in (5. 605–6).

> Laughing at such high fame for hips and haws,
> And scorned the achievement.
>
> (6. 1002–6)

Later, Bottini credits him with a Herculean achievement, the rescue of Hesione (Pompilia), daughter of Laomedon (Pietro), from the "snorting orc" (Guido) (9. 966–76). The role of Samson first is Guido's, upholding his weighty house (3. 1467–68); later Guido's vengeance is likened to Samson's (8. 638–55). Subsequently Bottini assigns the role to Caponsacchi, who sinks into Delilah's (Pompilia's) snare (9. 515). Both Caponsacchi (2. 167) and Guido (5. 1046) are Lucifer. Guido is Perseus when he slays Medusa-Pompilia (4. 1385); Caponsacchi inferentially has the same role on the numerous occasions when allusion is made to the heroic rescue of an imperiled maiden.

But such enumerations convey only an inadequate notion of the variety and interplay of the metaphorical roles which occur in every one of the narrative books (2–11). A chart of the figures in Book 2 alone shows how often the principal characters change in appearance:

Line(s)	Guido	Pompilia	Caponsacchi
	Adam (which Pie-	Eve (which Vio-	Lucifer
167–69	tro becomes at 254)	lante becomes at 253)	
233		snake	
270		fish	
273–77	fish	minnow	
296	dab-chick		
300	ornament on tail of donkey		
318	foolish virgin		
321–23	fish ("gleam i' the gloom")	minnow	
327		rosebud	
342–43	hooked fish	fish bait (cf. 1356)	
391	beast of burden		
503	**fly**	**candle flame**	

Line(s)	Guido	Pompilia	Caponsacchi
627		plant graft	
629	[Job]	plague seed	
632–33		leper rag	
637		mongrel dog	
794–95		snake	Apollos → Apollo
821–25	grange keeper	fowl in grange	fox
838–40		chick	fox
865–66	badger	fox	
903		lamb	
909		Samson	
1003–6	[Menelaus]	Helen of Troy	Paris
1062	beaten dog		
1080		playwright	playwright
1090	sheep or wolf	sheep or wolf	
1137		swine	
1146			fox
1159	[Christ]	Satan	
1165	spider		
1189		plant	
1221			Ovid
1356–57	fish	gilded fly (lure)	
1434	monster		
1445		viper	
1487	"male Grissel, modern Job"		

I I I

Probably the best way to exhibit the chief uses Browning makes of his fund of adaptable imagery is to trace a few of the major image themes, not sequentially as they appear from book to book but in terms of their shifting applications. This necessarily limited discussion cannot reveal the full number or variety of images which are in some way related thematically to each of the main motifs, nor can it show the extent to which these motifs overlap. But it will at least lay the groundwork for more detailed future studies of Browning's technique.

1. *The snake-serpent-worm figures.* In their metaphors the speakers of the poem capitalize upon man's aversion to slimy,

crawling things as they do upon probably no other single human trait. The multitude of figures involving snakes and serpents is prepared for by the allusions to the Garden of Eden in the opening books, where it represents the innocent happiness of the Comparini's home before Paolo's appearance in search of a wife for his brother. Borrowing from Milton rather than Genesis, Browning makes the advent of Paolo, with his snakelike attributes and sinuous speech, one of the most vivid episodes in the poem. The Abate is a "Smooth-mannered soft-speeched sleek-cheeked" priest,

> giving now his great flap-hat a gloss
> With flat o' the hand between-whiles, soothing now
> The silk from out its creases o'er the calf,
> Setting the stocking clerical again,

who dissertates to Violante on the glory of the Franceschini, the while "never disengaging, once engaged, / The thin clear grey hold of his eyes on her." After this satisfactory interview, in a final serpentine gesture he "rise[s] up his whole height / (A certain purple gleam about the black)" and—inferentially—slithers forth (3. 250–376 *passim*).[9]

But of course it is brother Guido who is the principal snake of the piece. In that guileful role he is first encountered, suitably enough, under another name, "worm," a word Browning often uses in the archaic sense of any serpent, snake, or dragon: "Nor cranny whence, desperate and disgraced, / Stripped to the skin, he might be fain to crawl / Worm-like, and so away with his defeat." (3. 694–96.) Guido sarcastically quotes the Comparini as reporting that he sought "To lure and bind her [Pompilia] to so cursed a couch, / Such co-embrace with sulphur, snake and toad" (5. 635–36). Caponsacchi speaks of Guido as a member of a brood of vipers (6.

---

[9] Paolo the priest-snake is an interesting composite figure. In addition to the fairly obvious derivations from Milton's diabolic serpent, his fixating eyes suggest the Victorian mesmerist; and he may owe something also to the stock character of the Jesuit in Victorian religious novels, with his "bland smile," "insinuating voice," "diplomatic skill," and "noiseless velvet step"—terms used by Margaret Maison, *The Victorian Vision*, p. 172.

689), a "soft sly adder, endlong 'neath my tread" (6. 620).
He and Bottini—the one passionately, the other facetiously—
speak of Guido as the "dragon belching flame" which required
him to assume the role of St. George (6. 1776; 9. 600).
Climactically, Caponsacchi envisions Guido's fate as that of a
snake which,

> hatched on hill-top by mischance,
> Despite his wriggling, slips, slides, slidders down
> Hill-side, lies low and prostrate on the smooth
> Level of the outer place, lapsed in the vale.
>
> (6. 1924–27)

Pompilia sees her husband as a serpent "towering and
triumphant" (7. 1589; cf. 7. 1218). The irony, however, is
that the innocent girl-bride herself figures as a snake, or as
possessing serpentine attributes, oftener than does Guido. Her
defamers use the image repeatedly. Half-Rome imagines someone telling Pietro that his girl-baby will bring them disaster:

> "For love of you, for liking to your wife,
> I undertake to crush a snake I spy
> Settling itself i' the soft of both your breasts.
> Give me yon babe to strangle painlessly!"
>
> (2. 232–35; cf. 1. 814–18)

In the eyes of Half-Rome, too, Pompilia is the snake who
"writhed transfixed through all her spires" when Caponsacchi,
as Apollo, sent "his god-glance after his shot shaft" (2. 793–
95). True to her imputed nature, she is only scotch'd, not killed,
by Guido's assault. In the hospital, "Viper-like, very difficult to
slay," she "Writhes still through every ring of her," though,
according to old snake-lore, "at day's end die she must" (2.
1445–50). At Castelnuovo, according to Tertium Quid (quoting a hypothetical partisan of Pompilia—an example of the
speaker's technique of slipping a counteracting element into a
supposedly sympathetic reported speech), Pompilia "sprang"
at Guido "like a pythoness" (4. 1162). Pythoness was exactly
what Guido maintains he took her for; as he tells the court,

> scarce your back was turned,
> There was the reptile, that feigned death at first,

> Renewing its detested spire and spire
> Around me, rising to such heights of hate
> That, so far from mere purpose now to crush
> And coil itself on the remains of me,
> Body and mind, and there flesh fang content,
> Its aim is now to evoke life from death,
>
> (5. 1957–64)

—that is, by way of her son. Much later in the poem, Bottini, pursuing his peculiar strategy, argues that Guido was wrong; Pompilia was not a serpent but a tasty eel. Guido

> pleases to mistake the donor's gift,
> And spies—I know not what Lernaean snake
> I' the luscious Lenten creature, stamps forsooth
> The dainty in the dust.
>
> (9. 393, 399–402)

It was in this slippery role that, according to Bottini, she frustrated Guido's hope of giving her instant death (9. 1415–20, quoted above, p. 93).

Nevertheless, to Guido in his

> close fetid cell,
> Where the hot vapour of an agony,
> Struck into drops on the cold wall, runs down
> Horrible worms made out of sweat and tears—
>
> (1. 1286–89)

Pompilia remains an evil, slimy, lethal snake, her long hair suggestive of "black serpents" (11. 1365). Tertium Quid, significantly, sees Pompilia in the same terms, as a snake-haired Medusa slain by the heroic Guido-Perseus:

> He lifts her by the long dishevelled hair,
> Holds her away at arm's length with one hand,
> While the other tries if life come from the mouth—
> Looks out his whole heart's hate on the shut eyes.
>
> (4. 1385–88)

In Guido's own account, however, the leading serpent at the Comparini's home was not Pompilia but the asp Violante. When he and his accomplices burst in,

> the folds o' the thing,
> Twisting for help, involved the other two
> More or less serpent-like: . . . I was mad,
> Blind, stamped on all, the earth-worms with the asp,
> And ended so.
>
> (5. 1665–69)

Elsewhere he makes no such distinction. All three Comparini—Pietro, Violante, and Pompilia—were tapeworms in his vitals, of which the murders happily purged him:

> so, unbrokenly lay bare
> Each taenia that had sucked me dry of juice,
> At last outside me, not an inch of ring
> Left now to writhe about and root itself
> I' the heart all powerless for revenge!
>
> (11. 1603–7)

But worms do not always imply evil; the word also has the pathetic connotation of someone easily victimized. Even Guido's partisans, intent on fixing blame on Violante, concede that Pompilia was a "poor worm" with whom her foster-mother baited the hook to catch Guido and who, after the Comparini fled back to Rome, was left to "float or sink" (4. 708–11). But poor worms are not always passive. The Other Half-Rome exults in the remembrance that at Castelnuovo "this worm turned" (the worm in this passage is actually a dragon) and would have slain her tormentor on the spot had not her hands been seized (3. 1289–91); and Pompilia herself maintains that "a worm must turn / If it would have its wrong observed by God" (7. 1592–93). A worm not only turns; it turns into something. The Pope acclaims Pompilia's metamorphosis:

> There skulks crime
> Behind law called in to back cowardice!
> While out of the poor trampled worm the wife,
> Springs up a serpent!
>
> (10. 696–99)

"Serpent" itself, in the Pope's usage, is stripped of the malign connotations it regularly has elsewhere and emerges as the symbol of heroism in defense of a righteous cause.

One particular use of "worm," in the sense of a maggot which bores into or through a healthy organism, occurs so often as to constitute a minor motif. Like many of the figures involving snakes and serpents, it is suggestive of guilty concealment (the "mass of men," says the Pope, "slink / Worm-like into the mud" [10. 1892–94]) and of guile ("That is the fruit of all such wormy ways, / The indirect, the unapproved of God" [7. 669–70]). In addition, no doubt again because of the Eden association, it connotes inward corruption (the worm in the core of the apple), dissatisfaction, and potentiality of evil. Its recurrent use is foreshadowed ("germ" anticipating "worm") in the early mention of the "hidden germ of failure" which will frustrate Half-Rome's "feel after the vanished truth" (1. 847–50). Both Halves of Rome use the worm-germ figure to describe the same situation—the Comparini's desire for a child—but, of course, for different ends. Half-Rome stresses the crass financial consideration (if he has an heir, Pietro will possess outright the property of which he now enjoys only the usufruct): this was "the worm i' the core, the germ / O' the rottenness and ruin which arrived" (2. 209–10). The Other Half-Rome, on the contrary, attributes to the Comparini only a laudable desire to leave something of themselves behind:

> Not otherwise a fatal germ lurked here:
> "With mortals much must go, but something stays;
> Nothing will stay of our so happy selves."
> Out of the very ripeness of life's core
> A worm was bred—"Our life shall leave no fruit."
>
> (3. 143–47)

The yearly payment of the usufruct, the Other Half-Rome adds, was simply a "reminder of this gnawing want, / One special prick o' the maggot at the core" (3. 155–56).

After representing the Comparini's contentment, the "core" becomes the ripe apple of a church sinecure, the worm being momentarily replaced by a mouse:

> The brother, Abate Paolo, shrewder mouse,
> Had pricked for comfortable quarters, inched
> Into the core of Rome, and fattened so;

> But Guido, over-burly for rat's hole
> Suited to clerical slimness, starved outside.
>
> (3. 412–16)

Guido subsequently becomes, in his own account, the site of the (now restored) worm's depredations. When he receives news of the birth of Pompilia's baby, he asks,

> The worm which wormed its way from skin through flesh
> To the bone and there lay biting, did its best,
> What, it goes on to scrape at the bone's self,
> Will wind to inmost marrow and madden me?
>
> (5. 1485–88)

But Caponsacchi throws the image back at him, this time reshaped to allude to the deathless worm which adds to the tortures of the damned (Mark 9:44, 46, 48):

> Again
> Let the incarnate meanness, cheat and spy,
> Mean to the marrow of him, make his heart
> His food, anticipate hell's worm once more!
>
> (6. 603–6)

These shifts in reference and emphasis, as sinuous as the worm itself, remind us by implication of the characters' differing moral stature and values: with the Comparini, the worm (i.e., the worst evil that could befall them) is nothing more than the possibility of having no heir; to Guido, the worm is the gnawing parasitic annoyance of the Comparini (11. 1594–1607) and the living reproach of bastardy in Gaetano (5. 1485–1541).

2. *The devil-hell-quagmire figures.* Inseparable from the Garden of Eden and its catastrophic serpent is the hell from which corruption came. All the serpents and dragons already noticed are to some degree Satan symbols, but they are outnumbered by the direct references in the poem to hell and the devil. Many such allusions are nothing more than rhetorical commonplaces, the imprecations and epithets natural to a poem so permeated with evil. These, though contributing to

the general tone, have little structural or thematic value. But many more have a larger and more specific function, to stress beyond doubt Guido's diabolic nature.

The blasphemy inherent in Guido's frequent assumption of the role of Christ is intensified by the fact that he is more often—and truly—seen as the devil incarnate. Pompilia's scream when he confronts her at Castelnuovo, filling the room with noise and ruddy flame (3. 1151–52), typifies the loathing all the sympathetic figures of the poem have for him:

> "Away from between me and hell!"—she cried:
> "Hell for me, no embracing any more!
> I am God's, I love God, God—whose knees I clasp,
> Whose utterly most just award I take,
> But bear no more love-making devils: hence!"
> (6. 1528–32)

Even hell itself is to be preferred to a life tormented by Guido, who explicitly identifies himself with Satan when he defies the Cardinal and Abate to "exorcize the devil, for here he stands / And stiffens in the bristly nape of neck, / Daring you drive him hence!" (11. 555–57.) His family is a band of wolves and satyrs, hell-creatures unspeakably ravenous, cruel, and vile; the mother is "true novercal type [the wicked stepmother of legend], / Dragon and devil" (2. 490–91). Because of them, to Pompilia "earth was hell" (3. 14), and most of all their palace at Arezzo, "a fissure in the honest earth / Whence long ago had curled the vapour first, / Blown big by nether fires to appal day" (1. 559–61).[10] The most dreadful of the numerous images relating to her captivity portrays her as surrounded by the fires of hell. Ironically, the flames strain round her (4. 796, 842) just as Pietro's and Violante's lovingly protective arms had encircled her, the growing tree, in the preceding book (3. 230–32). Alternatively, she is goaded over the brink of hell (3. 726–27), a site later to be visited by the condemned Guido, "the incline, earth's edge that's next to hell!" (11. 2083.) That is where Caponsacchi imagines him in the long

---

[10] In the next book, however, the capricious fortunes of metaphor turn Arezzo, if not the palace itself, into the Garden of Eden (2. 167–69).

execration near the end of his monologue (6. 1921–54), and
where in turn the Pope sees him, pushed

> Up to the gulf which, where I gaze, begins
> From this world to the next,—gives way and way,
> Just on the edge over the awful dark:
> With nothing to arrest him but my feet.
>
> (10. 171–75)

But, like the serpent allusions noticed earlier, the images
and allusions of hellish significance are not employed to desig-
nate only Guido and his foul company of mother, brothers,
and paid accomplices (e.g., 1. 399; 10. 850). Guido uses them
to identify the Comparini as the true agents of craft and
villainy. In his doubtless prejudiced view it is Violante, not his
mother, who is a devilish hag, one "that brought hell / For a
dowry with her to her husband's house" (5. 1649–50). Tertium Quid, sharing Guido's opinion, declares the Comparini to
be scullions who concocted him a witches' brew of "brimstone,
pitch, vitriol and devil's-dung" and threw in, "for fiend's
arch-prank," the revelation that Pompilia was not their child
(4. 730–38; see below, p. 301). When they fled Arezzo, accordingly, it was from "a hell of [their] own lighting-up" (4.
603). There is stern justice, then, in Guido's actions in that
bloody Christmas season. Listening to the promptings of
"some song in the ear, some snatch / Of a legend, relic of
religion," he heeds the impulse

> to quench
> The antagonistic spark of hell and tread
> Satan and all his malice into dust,
> Declare to the world the one law, right is right.
>
> (5. 1571–78)

When he gains entrance to the home of the authors of his
variegated torture, his vengeance

> burst, like a mountain-wave
> That holds a monster in it, over the house,
> And wiped its filthy four walls free again
> With a wash of hell-fire,—father, mother, wife,
> Killed them all, bathed his name clean in their blood.
>
> (2. 1433–37)

The several allusions, noticed above, to the precipice of earth overlooking the gulf of hell belong to a group of images of salvation or extrication which can serve as a final capacious example of Browning's use of a single metaphorical idea for widely different purposes. Several times (illustrating the fated affinity of their thoughts) Pompilia and Caponsacchi independently employ such figures, if only by suggestion.[11] She alludes to her hope that "Some hand would interpose and save me—hand / Which proved to be my friend's hand" (7. 619–20); "I only could emerge one way from hell / By catching at the one hand held me, so / I caught at it and thereby stepped to heaven." (3. 1345–47; cf. 7. 1497–98.) Caponsacchi recalls how, sitting over his *Summa*, he thought of her in "need of a finger's help" (6. 497), and Tertium Quid, for the moment wholly faithful to the spirit of the rescue, notes how the priest broke through the circle of hell fire, crying,

> "This way,
> Out by me! Hesitate one moment more
> And the fire shuts out me and shuts in you!
> Here my hand holds you life out!" Whereupon
> She clasped the hand, which closed on hers and drew
> Pompilia out o' the circle now complete.
>
> (4. 844–49)

The idea is too useful for Guido to overlook. Seizing upon the Pope's image (10. 988–90) he tries to evoke sympathy for himself:

> And now what does this Vicar of the Lord,
> Shepherd o' the flock,—one of whose charge bleats sore
> For crook's help from the quag wherein it drowns?
> Law suffers him put forth the crumpled end,—
> His pleasure is to turn staff, use the point,

[11] As a group these images appear to assimilate two separate allusions. One is to the representation in early Christian art, when direct portrayal of God was forbidden, of the divine hand reaching from behind a cloud hiding his presence. (Caponsacchi thus is inferentially described as God's surrogate.) The other is to Orpheus' rescue of Eurydice from hell.

> And thrust the shuddering sheep he calls a wolf,
> Back and back, down and down to where hell gapes!
>
> (11. 400–406)

Thus, so late in the poem, an explicit connection is made between the burning sea of hell and the mundane "quag" or marsh of sin—two versions of the same figure whose relationship has been clearly implied throughout.

Guido has been in the swamp before, says Half-Rome, when, spurning "the old way trod when men were men" and dealt summarily, not diplomatically, with an errant wife, he

> preferred the new path,—for his pains,
> Stuck in a quagmire, floundered worse and worse
> Until he managed somehow scramble back
> Into the safe sure rutted road once more,
> Revenged his own wrong like a gentleman.
>
> (2. 1524–29)

But, by a transposition common in the closely linked monologues of Half-Rome and the Other Half-Rome, in the next book Pietro and Violante replace Guido in the quag, the new cast reflecting the shift of sympathy from speaker to speaker. Faced with Violante's *fait accompli*, the marriage of Pompilia, and swallowing the ruinous advice in respect to the marriage settlement offered by Paolo's patron the Cardinal, Pietro "closed eyes, / Jumped and was in the middle of the mire, / Money and all, just what should sink a man" (3. 493–95). Violante followed him, "And neck-deep in a minute there flounced they." Though "they touched bottom at Arezzo" (3. 520–21), they remained in the mire until the opportune hand indispensable to the figure—now not Caponsacchi's, but Violante's announcement that Pompilia was not her child—reached down and enabled them to "spring thereby / Out of the mud, on ten toes stand once more" (3. 620–21).

Now Browning puts Guido, a suffering Job, back into the quagmire and keeps him there—but varies the effect from appearance to appearance. First it is Guido himself who reports his position. Having endured the embarrassment proper to a husband whose wife is too free with her gaze, he must now cope with Caponsacchi:

> I,—chin deep in a marsh of misery,
> Struggling to extricate my name and fame
> And fortune from the marsh would drown them all,
> My face the sole unstrangled part of me,—
> I must have this new gad-fly in that face,
> Must free me from the attacking lover too!
>
> (5. 908–13)

In Caponsacchi's estimation, however, Guido deserves no sympathy: he is "Miserably caught / I' the quagmire of his own tricks, cheats and lies" (6. 1799–1800). Bottini finally reduces the image to an absurdity that stems from both its grotesquely inappropriate context and its latent farcicality. He explains Pompilia's surprising behavior at Castelnuovo by the proposition that a wife is obliged to follow her husband's lead. If he brings her a sword, she must wave it; if he prescribes the way she is to save him, she must obey.

> No question but who jumps into a quag
> Should stretch forth hand and pray one "Pull me out
> By the hand!" such were the customary cry:
> But Guido pleased to bid "Leave hand alone!
> Join both feet, rather, jump upon my head,
> I extricate myself by the rebound!"
> And dutifully as enjoined she jumped—
> Drew his own sword and menaced his own life,
> Anything to content a wilful spouse.
>
> (9. 915–23)

3. *The lamb-sheep-shepherd figures.* Here again Browning makes much use of the great range of effects afforded by images derived, on the one hand, from scriptural story and religious art and, on the other, from the inheritance of the folk mind. In either vocabulary, "lamb" usually suggests an animal that is guileless, soft, harmless, and defenseless. To her partisans, therefore, Pompilia is always a "lamb-like innocent" (2. 903), and the pathos of her story lies in her being sacrificed, first to her foster parents' ambition and then to her husband's—

owner's—cruelty and avarice. When Violante and Guido made
their bargain, she was as placid in her ignorance of impending
evil as

> yon lamb,
> Brought forth from basket and set out for sale,
> [Who] bears while they chaffer, wary market-man
> And voluble housewife, o'er it,—each in turn
> Patting the curly calm inconscious head,
> With the shambles ready round the corner there,
> When the talk's talked out and a bargain struck.
>
> (3. 462–68)

Pompilia recalls that

> Pietro cried "Withdraw, my child!
> She is not helpful to the sacrifice
> At this stage,—do you want the victim by
> While you discuss the value of her blood?"
>
> (7. 522–25)

The less sympathetic speakers' use of the image, however, is
inflected with sarcasm. Tertium Quid describes the Comparini's departure from Arezzo:

> These fools forgot their pet lamb, fed with flowers,
> Then 'ticed as usual by the bit of cake,
> Out of the bower into the butchery.
>
> .   .   .   .
>
> A pet lamb they have left in reach outside,
> Whose first bleat, when he plucks the wool away,
> Will strike the grinners grave.
>
> (4. 675–77, 665–67)

And Guido characteristically tries to convert the figure to his
own advantage by transferring sympathy from Pompilia, now
a *raucous* lamb, to himself, a *cornered* wolf:

> My lamblike wife could neither bark nor bite,
> She bleated, bleated, till for pity pure,
> The village roused it, ran with pole and prong
> To the rescue, and behold the wolf's at bay!
>
> (11. 2302–5)

The superficially uncomplicated and sympathetic image of the lamb, indeed, proves full of diverse significances convenient to the purposes of the various speakers. A lamb is valuable for its fleece—in Pompilian terms, her dowry: a possession which, along with the animal's attributes of timidity and defenselessness, especially qualifies it to be a prey and lure for men in the shape of beasts. The several uses made of this idea contribute to the general disagreement over who was schemer and who was victim in this drama of contested motives. Pietro rejoices that the disclosure of her illegitimacy will bring Pompilia back to him and Violante: "Ay, let him taste the teeth o' the trap, this fox, / Give us our lamb back, golden fleece and all, / Let her creep in and warm our breasts again!" (3. 641–43.) Guido insists that the Comparini were not victims but victimizers; it was he who was their prey. Pompilia did them "the blind service, lured / The lion to your pit-fall" (5. 797–98). Pompilia sees her lamb role in still another light, not as the Comparini's decoy for Guido but as Guido's suffering decoy for Caponsacchi:

> My husband used to seem to harm me, not . . .
> Not on pretence he punished sin of mine,
> Nor for sin's sake and lust of cruelty,
> But as I heard him bid a farming-man
> At the villa take a lamb once to the wood
> And there ill-treat it, meaning that the wolf
> Should hear its cries, and so come, quick be caught,
> Enticed to the trap.
>
> (6. 1357–64)

Nor, despite the received notion of lamblike innocence, is the lamb-in-human-form of this poem incapable of foxlike conduct. Guido, as pictured by the Other Half-Rome, realized only during the confrontation at Castelnuovo that the "restif lamb" he had once so fondly petted was in fact meditating mischief all the while she "silverly baaed gratitude" (3. 1300–1306; see above, pp. 107–8). Such a complaint, however, comes with remarkably ill grace from Guido, because he himself trades on the sympathy the lamb role evokes.

> Say I stand
> Convicted of the having been afraid,
> Proved a poltroon, no lion but a lamb,—
> Does that deprive me of my right of lamb
> And give my fleece and flesh to the first wolf?
>
> (5. 1094–98)

As he begins his long harangue in the condemned cell, it is he, not Pompilia, who is "a sheep / Destined ere dewfall to be butcher's-meat!" (11. 344–45.) But he goes on to substantiate the suspicion the reader has long held (with occasional direct confirmation, e.g., at 3. 991): Guido has been a wolf in sheep's clothing. The Pope, he says, calls him—a "shuddering sheep"—a wolf (11. 405); and though Guido bespatters the "self-styled shepherd" (11. 434) with invective, he admits the Pope is right. "There, let my sheepskin-garb, a curse on 't, go— / Leave my teeth free if I must show my shag!" (11. 443–44.) The inspiration for the masquerade had been the church's:

> you as good as bade me wear sheep's wool
> Over wolf's skin, suck blood and hide the noise
> By mimicry of something like a bleat,—
> Whence it comes that because, despite my care,
> Because I smack my tongue too loud for once,
> Drop baaing, here's the village up in arms!
> Have at the wolf's throat, you who hate the breed!
>
> (11. 824–30)

The dissociation of "sheep" and "lamb" from the conventional suggestion of hapless innocence and passivity occurs in other contexts as well. Bottini's assertion that Pompilia meant "no more harm than a frightened sheep" (9. 933) is unconvincing in the light of the record he has ascribed to her earlier. If she is frightened, she has failed to profit by her experience of the world—and her casual amours:

> lamb and lamb,
> How do they differ? Know one, you know all
> Manners of maidenhood: mere maiden she.
> And since all lambs are like in more than fleece,

> Prepare to find that, lamb-like, she too frisks—
> O' the weaker sex, my lords, the weaker sex!
>
> (9. 220–25)

It was with some reason, therefore, that after marriage Guido cried, "No more friskings o'er the foodful glebe[!]" (9. 246.)

Nor did Violante's behavior suggest sheeplike docility. She was, Tertium Quid argues, no passive victim of Guido's wiles,

> the harmless household sheep
> One ought not to see harassed in her age—
> Judge, by the way she bore adversity,
> O' the patient nature you ask pity for!
> How long, now, would the roughest marketman,
> Handling the creatures huddled to the knife,
> Harass a mutton ere she made a mouth
> Or menaced biting? Yet the poor sheep here,
> Violante, the old innocent burgess-wife,
> In her first difficulty showed great teeth [12]
> Fit to crunch up and swallow a good round crime.
>
> (4. 123–33)

There is the same confusion of false shepherds and true. As passages already quoted suggest, Guido does not hesitate to imply that he had been, Christlike, a shepherd to the Pompilia who "was once my lamb / And lay in my bosom" (5. 1639–40). Elsewhere he declares that Pietro, and by implication Violante also, was a "shepherd [who] crooks a sheep-like thing / And meaning to get wool, dislodges fleece / And finds the veritable wolf beneath" (11. 1174–76). There is plausibility, not unmixed with malice, in his earlier identification of Caponsacchi as a shepherd. The court, he says sarcastically, interpreted Caponsacchi's elopement as a discharge of his priestly function: "What did he else but act the precept out, / Leave, like a provident shepherd, his safe flock / To follow the single lamb and strayaway?" (5. 1196–98.)

---

[12] "Great teeth" suggests those of a carnivorous rather than a ruminant beast, thus removing Violante from the ordinary run of sheep and aligning her with Guido, the wolfish one. —It might be noted that Pompilia's child is called "Guido's lamb" (9. 1331): the role is handed down through three generations.

The archbishop who heartlessly turned Pompilia away was chosen, the Pope imagines himself telling him, "To do the shepherd's office, feed the sheep— / How of this lamb that panted at thy foot / While the wolf pressed on her within crook's reach?" (10. 988–90.) The one character in the poem to whom the role of shepherd rightly belongs, of course, is the Pope, who has been introduced as the "great guardian of the fold" in an extended dramatic image in the middle of Book 1 (648). Arcangeli makes the expected gesture of obeisance toward him as "the father of the flock" (8. 1437). But Guido reviles "this Vicar of the Lord, / Shepherd o' the flock" for refusing to save, indeed for wilfully sending down to hell, "the shuddering sheep he [correctly, as Guido goes on to admit] calls a wolf" (11. 400–405). Of all the hypocrites in the world, cries Guido, the Pope is the worst.

> Your self-styled shepherd thieves!
> A thief—and how thieves hate the wolves we know:
> Damage to theft, damage to thrift, all's one!
> The red hand is sworn foe of the black jaw!
> That's only natural, that's right enough:
> But why the wolf should compliment the thief
> With the shepherd's title, bark out life in thanks,
> And, spiteless, lick the prong that spits him,—eh,
> Cardinal?
>
> (11. 434–42)

By the time Guido finishes, the accustomed noble phrases and associations of "lamb" and "shepherd"—the church as "the Bride, the mystic love / O' the Lamb" (6. 977–78), or God himself as the shepherd who holds his sheep in his hand (10. 641)—have become befouled by indiscriminate or signally inappropriate use.

4. *The fish and sea monster figures.* Of the numerous sustained image themes in the poem, Guido's career as a metaphorical fish is by all odds the most entertaining. Inheriting the drained fortunes of his family, he was (according to himself) a pathetic stranded creature,

> born fish with gill and fin
> Fit for the deep sea, now left flap bare-backed

In slush and sand, a show to crawlers vile
Reared of the low-tide and aright therein.
The enviable youth with the old name,
Wide chest, stout arms, sound brow and pricking veins,
A heartful of desire, man's natural load,
A brainful of belief, the noble's lot,—
All this life, cramped and gasping, high and dry
I' the wave's retreat . . .

(5. 172–81)

He seemingly managed to refloat himself, however, because
the several sympathetic descriptions of the deal that resulted in
his marriage portray Guido as the unsuspecting fish that
gulped down the bait (Pompilia as worm, minnow, or gilded
fly) fixed on the hook [13] by the angler Violante (2. 270–77,
343; 4. 708–11; 5. 1400–1403). (The angler simile is noticeably absent from Book 3, which is generally pro-Comparini.)
Once caught, Guido was pulled to the shore and gutted. In
Tertium Quid's version, however, Guido is enlarged from an
ordinary fish into a "monster" (4. 711), and he then goes on
to become leviathan, the giant aquatic creature whose exact
form (crocodile, whale, or seagoing monster?) is left unsettled
in the Old Testament and in religious art—a windfall that
nicely suited Browning's purposes. In Guido's own eyes, he is
"leviathan[,] that king of pride" who has been hooked and
landed by the "three-fold cord" of the Comparini and Caponsacchi (5. 1504–5). Bottini, too, sees him "Deserted by each
charitable wave, / . . . left high and dry" (9. 374–75).[14]

[13] "Hook," used here and elsewhere in the piscatorial sense, also
suggests "hook knife," the vicious weapon Guido used to kill the
Comparini and Pompilia (2. 145–49). Insofar as Guido regarded
himself as a fish hooked by his enemies, his employment of such a
knife constituted a symbolic revenge.

[14] "High and dry" offers an instance of the way such phrases
sometimes associate two quite different and widely separated images,
enriching or otherwise modifying the later one by recalling the
former. "High and dry," explicitly associated with a stranded fish
here and in a passage previously quoted (5. 180), occurs also in
Guido's second speech:

What is this fact I feel persuaded of—
This something like a foothold in the sea,
Although Saint Peter's bark scuds, billow-borne,

Bottini's genius is responsible for the ludicrous momentary conversion of Guido into a "snorting orc," the "brute" that "came paddling" after the nude Hesione (Pompilia), chained to a crag (9. 965–88).

The normal (or intended) effect of the images of Guido stranded, hooked, or gutted is to evoke sympathy: his partisans, to say nothing of Guido himself, adopt them to convey his helplessness and lack of guile and the injustice of the disaster that has befallen him. But when used by others, the same situation calls for amusement rather than pity— satisfaction that the menacing, ugly, blundering, and, what is worse, greedy fish-monster has got his deserts. Once Guido-as-fish has been established in the poem's figurative pattern, moreover, the association produces several ironies. When Arcangeli, noting that the monogamous ideal is almost universal in animal creation, remarks that "Only cold-blooded fish lack instinct here" (8. 507), he inadvertently discredits his own client, the cold-blooded fish who has argued in Book 5 that it was natural instinct which led him to vindicate the principle of monogamous honor by killing his wife. Later, finishing the rough draft of his pleading, he cries,

> And, lo,
> Landed and stranded lies my very own,
> My miracle, my monster of defence—
> Leviathan into the nose whereof
> I have put fish-hook, pierced his jaw with thorn,
> And given him to my maidens for a play!
>
> (8. 1728–33)

The previous application of the metaphor to Guido permits the suspicion that Arcangeli has also hooked his client.[15] It is

---

> Leaves me to founder where it flung me first?
> Spite of your splashing, I am high and dry!
>
> (11. 2294–98)

Although in these lines Guido clearly is attempting to revive his analogy of himself with Christ, now walking on the waves, the "high and dry" suddenly introduces the former image of the beached fish. Guido's unlucky concluding choice of phrase torpedoes his own carefully shaped metaphor.

[15] If, as seems probable, Browning has Arcangeli pronouncing "fisc" as "fish" for the sake of a pun (Lamb had done so earlier, in

Bottini, however, who claims final credit for disposing of the aquatic monster. Looking back on the case after the execution, he remarks with his customary complacency,

> I had, as usual, the plain truth to plead,
> I always knew the clearness of the stream
> Would show the fish so thoroughly, child might prong
> The clumsy monster: with no mud to splash,
> Small credit to lynx-eye and lightning-spear!
>
> (12. 409–13)

Readers with long memories may recall that Bottini had already used the image with Guido as the spearman and Pompilia the wily eel (9. 1415–20; quoted above, p. 93). Recollection of the earlier set of referents enables us, as happens time and again in this poem, to discover in the passage an ironic secondary suggestion: is not Bottini unconsciously implying that, just as the spearman Guido stabbed his wife in literal truth, Bottini has stabbed her reputation?

In the Pope's monologue, the operation of metaphor (including the phenomenon just noted, the recurrence of previously-made associations in new contexts) results in Guido's being likened by way of his fish role to several other figures, with various results. That the truth about Guido is as much in dispute as the truth about the deposed Pope Formosus is driven home by Guido's fortuitous resemblance to Formosus, who was also a mutilated man, retrieved like a fish from the "queasy river" by the nets of the fisherfolk (10. 111–15). That "ΙΧΘΥΣ. . . means Fish / And very aptly symbolizes Christ" produces one more ironic association of Guido with Jesus (10. 89–90). The tradition that "the Pope is Fisherman / And seals with the Fisher's-signet" (10. 91–92) provides an additional reminder that it is he, the fisherman, who seals the fate of Guido, the fish. And the earlier associations of Guido with leviathan bring the two antagonists into ironic juxtaposition when the Pope images Caponsacchi as the same creature:

"The Two Races of Men"), the ensuing conjunction of metaphor and pun allows us to believe that the figure also applies to Bottini: "Giving my Fisc his finish," says Arcangeli at the end of the next sentence (8. 1745).

Faulty—and peradventure ours the fault
Who still misteach, mislead, throw hook and line
Thinking to land leviathan forsooth,
Tame the scaled neck, play with him as a bird,
And bind him for our maidens! Better bear
The King of Pride go wantoning awhile,
Unplagued by cord in nose and thorn in jaw,
Through deep to deep, followed by all that shine,
Churning the blackness hoary.

(10. 1100–1108)

5. *Images of trapping, captivity, and husbandry.* Throughout the poem there is naturally much talk of luring, snaring, and caging, as well as of the simple care of animals. Once more, the artfully indiscriminate use of figurative language deepens the pervasive confusion over the rights and wrongs of the case. Who in reality was the keeper and who the kept, who was the decoy and who the victim? The answers vary with the speaker and the import of his metaphors.

Guido several times is seen as a trapper, who "both laid the trap and fixed the lure / Over the pit should bury body and soul" (3. 1358–59)—with, to be sure, the assistance of his brother Paolo, who prudently steps back "While Guido brings the struggle to a close" (10. 891).[16] On the other hand, his partisans several times portray him metaphorically as a benevolent overseer. We have already noted his recurrent appear-

---

[16] Guido was, in literal fact, a birdcatcher; he recalls that, resigning himself to a humble life in the country at Vittiano, he had found solace in the thought that "one limes flocks of thrushes there" (5. 364), and in his second speech he remembers an episode in his youth when "young I was, and gay, / And wanting to trap fieldfares" (11. 928–29). The allusion to luring larks by looking-glass at 3. 338, when Paolo is urging Guido to find a wife, is therefore apt enough. Guido was also a poor but honest owner of vineyards, studying "how to wring / Half the due vintage from the worn-out vines / At the villa" (2. 814–16) and later receiving news of the baby's birth as he was "among his vines, it seems, / Doing his farm-work" (2. 1392–93). This circumstance is useful to his partisans, who by alluding to him metaphorically as a vineyard keeper (e.g., 5. 230–31) can turn to advantage the fact that in Christian symbolism the vine is sometimes the emblem of Christ and God is the husbandman (John 15:1–6).

ances as a shepherd. He is also, in his own account, a henwife, reasonable but firm (11. 1423), and, according to Bottini, a herdsman understandably bent upon keeping his "restive" heifer in line (9. 246–57). Most important, however, he is the keeper of a grange. Half-Rome describes him as hearing suspicious sounds:

> Up he jumps.
> Back to mind come those scratchings at the grange,
> Prints of the paw about the outhouse; rife
> In his head at once again are word and wink,
> *Mum* here and *budget* there, the smell o' the fox,
> The musk o' the gallant.
>
> (2. 820–25)

The nature of his guardianship and the desperation of his captive, however, are made clear only when the Other Half-Rome takes up the image:

> Accordingly did Guido set himself
> To worry up and down, across, around,
> The woman, hemmed in by her household-bars,—
> Chased her about the coop of daily life,
> Having first stopped each outlet thence save one
> Which, like bird with a ferret in her haunt,
> She needs must seize as sole way of escape.
>
> (3. 776–82)

For whatever purpose—as Violante's decoy for Guido or Guido's decoy for Caponsacchi, or for the gratification of Guido's lust for cruelty, depending on whom we hear—Pompilia is a captive. Arezzo is "the woman's trap and cage and torture-place" (1.502), where the Franceschini family, in an image suggestive of the witches' sabbath, "took hands / And danced about the captives in a ring" (1. 573–74).

By the poetic justice the convertible metaphors often provide in this poem, Guido in turn finds himself a captive beast. The Comparini relish the idea of his receiving the news of his wife's illegitimacy: "Ay, let him taste the teeth o' the trap, this fox" (3. 641). The springe which the Other Half-Rome imagines Pompilia saying someone set for her (3. 809–11; cf. 7. 1369) later becomes the springe which Guido alleges the Pope set to trap him (11. 113–15); and by a similar reversal the "outlet" she sought from her place of captivity (3. 780) becomes the "light at length / A cranny of escape" that Guido professes to see in the chance that the Pope will pardon him (11. 1771–72). Like the Pompilia-bird seen in the early books, he in turn patrols the cage of his cell, "eyes each outlet of the cirque, / The narrow penfold for probation, pines / After the good things just outside the grate" (10. 416–18). But the Pope is of no mind to rescue him.

6. *The rose and dove figures.* These images, which occur less frequently than figures of lambs and fish, for instance, provide a final example of Browning's adaptation of religious symbols for characterization and argument; and they also raise a point, implicit in what has been said so far, that deserves consideration. Once a given image, originally viable and with relatively stable significance, has been bandied about in the cross-purposes of the various speakers, what is left of it as a dependable conveyor of meaning?

The rose regularly is Pompilia. In earlier monologues she is seen only in earthly terms, as a rosebud which Guido snatches from the "prickly brake" to lend beauty to his dark house at Arezzo (2. 327), a "blossom at the briar's end, . . . the rose / Two jealous people fought for yesterday / And killed each other" (3. 77–79). She is also the symbol of purity in a world of evil, a "rose above the dungheap" of Roman libertinage and bastardy (4. 247). Her ultimate significance, however, is expressed by the Pope: "My flower, / My rose, I gather for the breast of God" (10. 1045–46). It is almost to be expected, then, that during his final diatribe Guido will degrade the figure—hitherto occupying but a line or two, now much elaborated—into a symbol of disappointed expectation and deceit. He is, he says, a man

> Who, tired i' the midway of my life, would stop
> And take my first refreshment in a rose:
> What's this coarse woolly hip, worn smooth of leaf,
> You counsel I go plant in garden-pot,
> Water with tears, manure with sweat and blood,[17]

[17] An echo of Keats's *Isabella*, stanzas 52–54.

In confidence the seed shall germinate
And, for its very best, some far-off day,
Grow big, and blow me out a dog-rose bell?
Why must your nephews begin breathing spice
O' the hundred-petalled Provence prodigy?
Nay, more and worse,—would such my root bear rose—
Prove really flower and favourite, not the kind
That's queen, but those three leaves that make one cup
And hold the hedge-bird's breakfast,—then indeed
The prize though poor would pay the care and toil!
Respect we Nature that makes least as most,
Marvellous in the minim! But this bud,
Bit through and burned black by the tempter's tooth,
This bloom whose best grace was the slug outside
And the wasp inside its bosom,—call you "rose?"

                                        (11. 1089–1108)

Similarly, Pompilia at first is a dove with the conventional attributes: maternal protectiveness, purity, and the helplessness and softness that make it, like the lamb, easy prey. (In Christian iconography the dove, symbol of the Holy Ghost, often occurs in pictures of the Annunciation; hence its association with Pompilia augments the suggestions of Madonna.) When Pompilia and Violante return in a rainstorm from the wedding ceremony, the unsuspecting Pietro laughs,

> Very near
> You made me brave the gutter's roaring sea
> To carry off from roost old dove and young,
> Trussed up in church, the cote, by me, the kite!
>
>   (7. 462–65)

Tertium Quid envisions Pompilia, when Guido and his accomplices burst into the Comparini's dwelling, rushing "here and there / Like a dove among lightnings in her brake" (4. 1382–83). And Caponsacchi demands of his judges whether they wish to free him "to break the blow, next hawk that swoops / On next dove" (6. 109–110). But "dove," like "rose," suffers eventual corruption: Bottini converts Pompilia into something approaching the soiled dove of Victorian sentimental euphemism. When she was returned to the Comparini, he says, Guido should have been "Proud that his dove which lay among the pots[18] / Hath mued those dingy feathers,—moulted now, / Shows silver bosom clothed with yellow gold" (9. 1230–32). This degradation is temporarily neutralized by Celestino, who in his sermon demands:

> Because Pompilia's purity prevails,
> Conclude you, all truth triumphs in the end?
> So might those old inhabitants of the ark,
> Witnessing haply their dove's safe return,
> Pronounce there was no danger all the while
> O' the deluge, to the creature's counterparts,
> Aught that beat wing i' the world, was white or soft,—
> And that the lark, the thrush, the culver too,
> Might equally have traversed air, found earth,
> And brought back olive-branch in unharmed bill.
> Methinks I hear the Patriarch's warning voice—
> "Though this one breast, by miracle, return,
> No wave rolls by, in all the waste, but bears
> Within it some dead dove-like thing as dear,
> Beauty made blank and harmlessness destroyed!"
>
> (12. 472–86)

But it is Bottini who finally disposes of Pompilia-as-dove in his swaggering assurance, deliberately echoing Celestino's Noah's-ark figure, that he will smear her reputation as the Convertites desire,

> And this foul-mouthed friar shall find
> His Noah's-dove that brought the olive back,
> Is turned into the other sooty scout,
> The raven, Noah first of all put forth the ark,
> And never came back, but ate carcasses!
>
> (12. 722–26)

[18] "Though ye have lien among the pots, yet shall ye be as the wings of a dove covered with silver, and her feathers with yellow gold" (Ps. 68:13). Whether or not "pots" is a mistranslation for "sheepfolds" (Cook, *Commentary*, p. 194) the suggestion of fleshpots is irresistible.

IV

But, vivid and suitable as many of its applications are, what is the eventual effect of this use of capacious, malleable, unstable imagery? Metaphorical language as a vehicle for the sure conveyance of meaning is put to a severe test by the uses to which Browning, inveterate dramatist and psychologist, puts it in this babel of conflicting testimony. On this question, the authors of the present book have divergent, though possibly not irreconcilable, opinions; and, considering the nature of the poem that is the subject of these pages, there could be no more appropriate procedure than for each in turn to state his view of the truth.

One effect is to weaken the force inherent in the central figure of speech and, indeed, to degrade the whole cluster over which it presides. We have already noticed what happens to "rose," "dove," and "lamb." When the sentimental and scriptural associations of "lamb" are joined by a host of other associations, including the great-toothed mutton that is Violante (4. 130–33) and the (non-metaphorical) smoking-hot fry that will regale little Giacinto's birthday guests, the resulting mixture and dispersal of meaning weakens the connotative force of "lamb" in its primary role. As usages multiply, clear-cut effect diminishes, so that what we have in many instances is the progressive corruption of a figure which entered the poem with positive, generally well-defined connotations. Bottini's travesties of some of the leading image themes, of course, assist the process. In the later books, few of the major metaphors retain their original strength or meaning; they have, for the most part, accumulated so many additional associations that their initial force is blunted or, sometimes, almost parodied. The protean quality of language has been amply demonstrated, but so has the weakness of language as a dependable means of communication. Metaphors, it turns out, are at the mercy of human motives, and after they have been subjected to as many conflicting demands as they are in the course of the ten monologues, they are shopworn and suspect.

What is true of the metaphors is true also of certain basic words that contain the poem's focal meanings. The degradation of "truth" has been discussed above (pp. 121–22). "Saint" is another example. Browning quotes a partisan of Pompilia as crying that Guido "slaughtered . . . a saint, / Martyr and miracle!" (1. 207–8.) But by the time Tertium Quid has got around to scoffing at "the pair of saints," as he says Pompilia and Caponsacchi are called by sympathizers whose heads are as soft as their hearts (4. 1044), "saint" has begun to be corrupted through both overuse and misuse, and when Arcangeli speaks of his son as "the saint o' the day" (8. 62–63), no resumption of the word in later, loftier contexts can wholly restore it to its original dignity. Significantly, the last appearance of "saint" occurs in connection with Guido: he "Died like a saint, poor devil!" (12. 420.) The final misapplication of the word accompanies the final misconception of Guido's nature—and, not incidentally, illustrates the way in which "devil," meanwhile, has lost the terrible force it earlier possessed and become a pale, innocuous, everyday epithet. "Martyr," likewise, is sullied by the sarcastic, facetious, or hypocritical uses made of it, as in Tertium Quid's allusion to Pompilia's "described martyrdom" (4. 1000) and Guido's to his own (5. 66). The similar fortune of "miracle" will be described in the next chapter.

On the contrary (maintains the author who takes a different view), far from becoming attenuated in meaning through diverse applications, the metaphors in *The Ring and the Book* gain strength, or at least resilience, through continued exercise. It would be poetic suicide, in a poem so long, to cause a given metaphor to recur again and again in roughly the same context and with the same tone. Even worse, a one-for-one correspondence between metaphor and subject would soon diminish the freshness and power of the metaphor itself—a power which is the result of an often surprising, often intellectually arresting, juxtaposition of unlike elements. By continually shifting the relation between metaphorical vehicle and subject, Browning is able to preserve this freshness.

There is, too, a discernible logic in Browning's plotting of metaphorical patterns. In two ways he supplies all-encompassing frames of value by which he preserves the integrity of metaphors, however recklessly they are abused by the various speakers. From the beginning he sets up a hierarchy of metaphor which closely corresponds to the traditional Christian typology, extending from angel to man to brute beast to vegetable to inanimate object. From this millennium-old hierarchy, each leading member of which possesses a particular moral significance, in the manner of medieval iconography, Browning draws the primary figurative roles his principal characters assume. Guido's prevailing roles—wolf, dog, serpent, fish—suggest bestiality, baseness, slipperiness. Pompilia's roles of lamb, bird, and flower all emblematize feminine virtue, as Caponsacchi's repeated appearance as a source of light—sun or star—defines his role in relation to her. Thanks to their deep-seated place in the symbolic vocabulary of Western thought, these primary metaphors have a durability and an explicitness which equip them to survive the semantic free-for-all into which they are cast. No amount of incongruous application can permanently affect their traditional core of meaning.

The second frame of value is a corollary to this. In Book 1 Browning tells us enough about the speakers to enable us to judge the direction and extent of the distortion to which leading figures of speech are subjected as they are bandied about from speaker to speaker and applied, seemingly without discrimination, to one character after another. Character norms are established as quickly as are the norms of the metaphors themselves, so that when, for instance, Bottini departs from the dominant application of the sacrificial-lamb figure to characterize Pompilia instead as a frisky spring lamb not averse to amorous adventure (above, p. 171) or Guido does so to emphasize her craftiness (pp. 107–8), we automatically make allowance for the agent of the misuse or the misapplication. We do not accept the remodeled metaphor at its intended face value. Its old value remains unaffected by the new coinage.

The very plan of the poem further protects metaphors from lasting devaluation. Those speakers who are most likely to distort the truth (Books 2–5, 8, 9, and 11) are to some extent counteracted by interspersed opposing speakers, whose tendency is to restore even the most ill-used metaphors to their proper signification. Thus, the Pope, in reaffirming Pompilia's whiteness, removes the stigma of the soiled-dove imagery used by Bottini. These *loci* of truth—Books 1, 6, 7, 10, and 12—preserve the balance by reminding us, through the speakers' usage, of the central application of a figure. By these various means, as a given metaphor vibrates through a whole spectrum of meaning in the course of the poem, Browning contrives recurrently to arrest the vibration at the normative point, in effect restoring the figure to useful life after each departure.

Nor are the metaphors applied as indiscriminately as at first appears, particularly when an individual instance is judged without reference to the total development of context and thematic argument. Close examination of context and application usually reveals that they are in fact employed with utter appropriateness. Abstractly, it is shocking to discover Guido representing himself as a latter-day Christ; but given Browning's initial assumptions about his moral nature, to say nothing of Guido's revelation of himself and the evidence we receive from other speakers, there is nothing surprising about it. It is his character that suffers from the blasphemous application, not the metaphor itself, for the absolute incongruity of the application keeps the metaphor's meaning intact. Conversely, Browning is at pains to prevent our regarding Caponsacchi as a Christ figure, because here the analogy would have a certain validity and yet would be essentially untrue. Despite superficial similarities (he mixes in the world, dines with sinners, undergoes temptation, and is self-sacrificing), the priest is unquestionably a soldier-saint, human not divine. To attribute Christlike qualities to him would not only distort his character as Browning intends to portray it: it would detract from the power of the analogy as Guido applies it to himself.

Although the shifts of meaning the basic images undergo in the poem are sometimes bewildering, they are not arbitrary; and although some of the metaphors are perhaps overused, they are kept from being shopworn by being given new or extended moral meaning in the course of their diverse applications. In the end, therefore, while Browning unquestionably succeeds in demonstrating the protean nature of linguistic symbols, the constant distortion, shifting, and misapplication serve only to strengthen, not corrupt or weaken, the primary meaning and long-established associational value of each metaphor.

So much for the authors' "discrepancy of judgments" (4. 1521), which the reader may adjudicate as he wishes. But—to echo Tertium Quid again—"let's see clearly from this point!" (4. 1214) At the beginning of this chapter, it was remarked that the action of metaphor in the poem seems to be a further hindrance to the achievement of truth; as the chief characters acquire role after role which casts them first on the side of the angels and then on the side of the devils, their true natures appear hopelessly obscured. Paradoxically, however, in the long run truth—of character at least—is gradually discovered by this means; it is an additional important way in which Browning works by indirection. For we, as readers with the whole poem before us, have a great advantage over the individual auditors in the poem who are the captive audience of one or another of the speakers and therefore hear but a single weighted version of the story. The truth is not accessible to them if (as we must assume in general) they are swayed by the image-making rhetoric of whichever person they hear. But it is accessible to us, because Browning gives us the means of comparing all the discrepant versions and discounting palpable bias wherever it appears. Able as we therefore are to distinguish the honest speakers from the dissembling ones, we can penetrate beneath the speaker's intention in each metaphor and so put a true valuation upon the image he chooses—and upon him. When Bottini types Pompilia as a lamb on the loose or as a restive heifer who kicks her driver, he moves her from her primary role (which we know is the true one) into a secondary role in which her animal instincts—sexual appetite, self-preservation—are implicitly emphasized. But these are instantly discounted, and the residual effect of the figure is to lay further stress upon Bottini's preoccupation with sex and his failure to perceive her true charac-

ter. He may succeed in blackening the dove Pompilia's feathers (to shift her role once more) but in the total allegory he
damns himself, and her whiteness is preserved.

Irrespective of the light a speaker's choice and shaping of
metaphors throw upon him, his image-making always throws
additional light on the character he describes. If the quality of
personality or moral bent implied by a metaphor is demonstra-
bly part of the character's makeup, the figure simply intensifies and more sharply defines that quality; and if the attributed
quality is patently misapplied, the very discrepancy between
what the character is said to be and what we know, on better
authority, he actually is, again helps define him more clearly.
Either way, the final effect of this continual representation of
character through variegated images is to come closer to
truth—but only because we, with the benefit of the broad view
denied to the auditors in the poem, can make the necessary
assessments and comparisons.

V

The repetitions-with-variations of the concurrent image
threads from book to book supply not only diversity but coherence. They are as important to the poem's eventual unity as
are the careful organization of structure, the progression, the
symmetry, and the contrast analyzed in chapter 2. For *The
Ring and the Book* is a triumph of close weaving. The warp
consists of the major characters, the woof of the many strands
of metaphor (snake, bird, lamb, and the rest) which denote
them. Although the two sets of threads are constantly changing
color—the characters assuming one guise after another, the
guises at the same time having fresh applications and altering
in aspect or detail to suit each new circumstance—they never
break, but instead run through the entire poem. Each of their
hundreds of intersections forms one of those points of strength
which in the aggregate prevent the poem's bulk from collaps-
ing into a huge formless mass.

It is not the well-established major motifs alone which contribute to this structural solidity. Cooperating with them is an intricate system of cross-references, echoes, and incidental repetitions of image or phrase which throw their tendrils across as many as half a dozen books. The notion of a gadfly or some other elusive annoyance (or hope) buzzing around one's head occurs at least nine times. At 1. 1275–76 it is the chance of continued life that tantalizes Guido; at 4. 561–63 the bothersome Comparini are "gnats"; at 5. 912, 1103, and 1537–40 Guido's various tribulations are presented respectively as gadflies attacking a drowning man, flies that blow in his face, and filthy pests that "buzz, flap and sting, / Busy at my vitals"; at 6. 1970 the inclination of Caponsacchi's judges to believe he was involved in a conventional liaison is a "vulgar fly" buzzing about their brains; at 9. 771 the gadfly is one of the "frivolous" accusations against Pompilia which Bottini delights in trying to swat; at 11. 1265–67 the Comparini (resuming the role they had in Tertium Quid's monologue) are a host of flies newly hatched in lusty June, buzzing Guido deaf and stinging him blind; and at 11. 2245–47 Guido is a damsel fly trying to save himself from extinction.

Other, less frequent, repetitions help hold the poem together. The dance of the "obscene ring" which is the Franceschini family (1. 570–82) later is taken up by the jeering citizens of Arezzo, "devils o' the dark" whom Pompilia allegedly sets loose in Guido's house "to cover her escape" (5. 1512–13; cf. 5. 1031–34). The locale and the diabolic nature of the dance remain, only the personnel changing. Another five books later, in the Pope's fierce judgment, though the dance itself is abandoned the Franceschini circle is reintroduced:

> Such I find Guido, midmost blotch of black
> Discernible in this group of clustered crimes
> Huddling together in the cave they call
> Their palace, outraged day thus penetrates.
>
> .   .   .   .
>
> All alike coloured, all descried akin
> By one and the same pitchy furnace stirred
> At the centre.
>
> (10. 868–878)

The principal motif of the rose is extended by the subtheme of the "blossom at the briar's end" of the Other Half-Rome (3. 77), the "bud [that] is born / At a wild briar's end" in Pompilia's speech (7. 302–3), and the Pope's "at least one blossom makes me proud at eve / Born 'mid the briers of my enclosure!" (10. 1033–34.) Three times is Molinism associated with the tares growing amidst the corn of the true religion (2. 175–76; 6. 151–52; 11. 2034–35). For a final example (many more could be cited), there is the blood-sweat-manure nexus which provides a pair of the numerous incidental connections between the speech of the Pope and both of Guido's monologues: "Ten years a gardener of the untoward ground, / I till," sighs the Pope, "—this earth, my sweat and blood manure / All the long day that barrenly grows dusk" (10. 1030–32); later he hears Guido's partisans urging him, "We pray thee dig about and dung and dress / Till he repent and bring forth fruit even yet." (10. 1968–69.) The latter image recalls the lines in Guido's first monologue in which he quotes his Aretine friends urging him to reject clerical celibacy for the sake of propagating new generations of Franceschini: "Be not the vine but dig and dung its root, / Be not a priest but gird up priesthood's loins." (5. 230–31.) And the former image of the Pope anticipates Guido in his second defense. "You counsel," he tells the Cardinal and Abate as representatives of the church, "I go plant in garden-pot, / Water with tears, manure with sweat and blood." (11. 1092–93.)

Sometimes the form of the image changes, but because the intent of the second clearly recalls the first, the connection is clear and provides an unspoken cross-commentary. Half-Rome sarcastically cites Pompilia's and Caponsacchi's declaration (relayed by "law") that

> in thought, word and deed,
> Innocent were they both from first to last
> As male-babe haply laid by female-babe
> At church on edge of the baptismal font
> Together for a minute, perfect-pure.
>
> (2. 1109–13)

Later Caponsacchi remembers his awed thoughts as he traveled through the night with the silent, pale Pompilia by his side:

> I have caught it, I conceive
> The mind o' the mystery: 'tis the way they wake
> And wait, two martyrs somewhere in a tomb
> Each by each as their blessing was to die.
>
> (6. 1183–86)

In the interim the figures laid side by side have changed from newborn babes to dead martyrs, but the juxtaposition of innocence and sacred ritual as a means of characterizing the love between Pompilia and Caponsacchi remains.

Less frequently, but with the same effect, allusions are repeated in the manner of metaphor strands, as we have already seen is the case with biblical echoes. Half-Rome likens Caponsacchi's relegation to that of the sentence laid upon the author of the *Ars Amatoria,* "a like sufferer in the cause" (2. 1221); Guido echoes the reference to Ovid when, quoting "friends' " letters, he characterizes Caponsacchi as "A brisk priest who is versed in Ovid's art / More than his *Summa*" (5. 1357–58). Later we find that Caponsacchi had his *Summa* open, though he did not necessarily read it (6. 484, 500), and that he wrote love poems ("a Marinesque Adoniad," which presumably is close enough to Ovid [6. 333]).

The two books of the poem which are most closely linked by many separate repeated figures are 2 (Half-Rome) and 3 (the Other Half-Rome). There are a score of such echoes, some conspicuous, some so incidental they are almost hidden. Not only do they bind the two related books more tightly together, but—at least as important—as a group they provide a key to the contrast of attitudes between the two speakers. They are, indeed, the principal means by which, in these first two narrative books, Browning differentiates the sympathies of the two onlookers and sets the argumentative pattern for the remainder of the poem. Drawing from a common fund of metaphor, symbolic perhaps of their common but limited fund of information respecting the Franceschini case, each speaker contrives an account of personality and events quite at variance with the other's.

The roster of these repeated figures, some of which have been quoted during the preceding discussion, includes: [19]

Figure	Book 2	Book 3
the garden of Eden	168–69, 253–54	169–71, 233–37
the turn of the screw	1376	1429, 1542–45
the rosebud	327	77, 874–76
Jove's banquet	441–42	386
the germ-worm in the core	209	143–47
the quagmire	1526	494, 519–20, 619–21
⎰ the fox in the grange	821–25	
⎱ the bird in the coop		778–81
the lily	303 (clerical preferment)	365 (Pompilia)
the casting of lot into lap	393	503–4
the dog with tail between legs	1062	1461
the stump in Eden	256	234–48 (turns into a tree)
⎰ the plant graft	627–28	
⎱ the slip from the Eden tree		234–35
the star	(of love) 1074 (of Caponsacchi)	846–51
⎧ the corrosive distilled "drop by drop"	1267–71	
⎨ the bitter medicine administered "dose by dose"		526
Guido as scorpion	1305–6	562, 1167
⎰ the plague seed or spots	629, 655	
⎱ leprosy		1383

By the same technique, Browning indicates sympathy between two speakers even at the remove of several books. Half-Rome's pro-Guido bias, for instance, is manifested in his anticipation of a number of figures Guido himself will later employ.

[19] Books 2 and 3 are further bound together, and the speakers' respective attitudes often differentiated, by an equal number of parallels, contrasts, and reversals involving not metaphors but literal details, suppressions, shifted emphases, and the like. The Molinos references at 2. 126 and 175–78 are balanced by the ones at 3. 34 and 95–104; the movement of the Comparini's fortune is down in 2 and up in 3; in Book 2 (1331–42) it is Pompilia's influential friends who take the initiative in removing her from the convent, in 3 (1500) it is the nuns who do so; the world laughs in Guido's face in 2 (826–40, 1238–62), but in Pietro's in 3 (396); both speakers invoke saints' legends to make the incredible credible (2. 1107–15; 3. 1050–51), and both quote self-appointed oracles who detect the Antichrist in the murders (2. 127; 3. 95). The list could be considerably extended. See below, p. 300 n. 11.

Half-Rome's image of ambitious clergymen as barnyard fowl
jostling one another on the church's dungheap (2. 298) is
picked up by Guido (5. 293–94). Both speakers picture Guido's disappointment over the decline of his family fortunes as
the bursting of soapsud bubbles (2. 454–56; 5. 449–51). In
both books, again, is found a collocation of three images—the
plant graft, the tree parasite, and the lazar rag. Half-Rome
asks:

> Left alone with Pompilia now, this graft
> So reputable on his ancient stock,
> This plague-seed set to fester his sound flesh,
> What did the Count? Revenge him on his wife?
> Unfasten at all risks to rid himself
> The noisome lazar-badge, fall foul of fate,
> And, careless whether the poor rag was ware
> O' the part it played, or helped unwittingly,
> Bid it go burn and leave his frayed flesh free?
>
> (2. 627–35)

From Guido's defender the associated ideas pass, suitably
altered, to Guido himself as he attributes these rather unlikely
words to Pompilia:

> "If, far from casting thus away the rag
> Smeared with the plague, his hand had chanced upon,
> Sewn to his pillow by Locusta's wile,—
> Far from abolishing, root, stem and branch,
> The misgrowth of infectious mistletoe
> Foisted into his stock for honest graft,—" . . .
>
> (5. 809–14)

And the notion of "plague," though divorced this time from
the lazar badge, is resumed by Guido in a further employment
of the tree-parasite idea:

> in the process you call "justice done"
> All along you have nipped away just inch
> By inch the creeping climbing length of plague
> Breaking my tree of life from root to branch.
>
> (5. 1948–51)

Guido's likening of his trials as a married man to a "cup of bitterness" filling "drop by drop" with sewage (5. 879–83) is prepared for by Half-Rome's lines,

> on Guido's wound
> Ever in due succession, drop by drop,
> Came slow distilment from the alembic here
> Set on to simmer by Canidian hate,
> Corrosives keeping the man's misery raw.
>
> (2. 1267–71)

To Half-Rome, the visitation of vengeance upon the house of the Comparini is "like a mountain-wave / That holds a monster in it" (2. 1433–34); to Guido, it is the impulse that results in the deed which is "one / Immeasurable everlasting wave of a need / To abolish that detested life" (5. 1662–64). Pompilia's writhing "through every ring of her" as she lies, a dying viper "very difficult to slay" (2. 1445–46), is recalled in Guido's description of the "writhings of the bargain" by which he obtained her (5. 511).[20]

But the most noteworthy instance of the way shared metaphors symbolize affinity is found in the books of Caponsacchi and Pompilia, when, beginning in each case with the dawn of spiritual understanding between wife and priest, the running imagery, suffusing the whole of the subsequent narrative, is of the confrontation and triumph of light over darkness. Speaking independently, physically apart from each other and under very different circumstances, Pompilia and Caponsacchi thereby reveal that they are bound together by a common interpretation of their experience; and the nature of the imagery

---

[20] Some of the non-metaphorical connections between Books 2 and 5 should also be noted. Both books, of course, lay much stress on Guido as the victim of other people's lies. Half-Rome's characterization of Guido as "the biter bit" (2. 597) is matched by Guido's embroidery on the theme of the cheater cheated (5. 551–66), or, as Browning puts it in a phrase extraordinarily unmelodious even for him, "dupes / To dupe the duper" (5. 1360–61). The Aretine crowd cries, in effect, "We knew it all along" at some length in both books (2. 922–30; 5. 1000–29). And the angel who advises Guido in Half-Rome's account (2. 1404) turns up, singing "Peace upon earth," in Guido's version of events (5. 1608–9).

they select, with its echoes of the Bible and suggestions of religious art, establishes what the nature of the experience was. Both, for example, describe their initial spiritual epiphany in the same terms: "Began a whiteness in the distance, waxed / Whiter and whiter . . . / The white I saw shine through her was her soul's" (6. 1139–42); "The glory of his nature . . . / Shot itself out in white light." (7. 921–22.) By skillful parallelism of metaphorical theme—Book 6, from line 922 onward, being complemented by Book 7, beginning at line 1222—Browning leaves no doubt that Pompilia and Caponsacchi were "one soul in bodies twain."

The resumption of the light metaphors by the Pope, first quoting the imagined voice of Euripides and then continuing the imagery in his own person (10. 1759–1830), implicitly but effectively relates the story of Pompilia and Caponsacchi to the great issues of faith and doubt canvassed in that passage. The images of light thus forge a strong link between a specific episode in time and place and the eternal, universal problems which that story illustrates. When, speaking of the divine precaution that man be spared the unendurable direct vision of eternal truth, the Pope says, "Sun-suffused, / A cloud may soothe the eye made blind by blaze" (10. 1644–45), one recalls Caponsacchi's declaration that after his first sight of Pompilia, her gaze "Burnt to my brain, as sunbeam thro' shut eyes" (6. 435). The repetition of this metaphorical idea, a favorite of Browning's, epitomizes at a stroke the poem's ultimate symbolism: Pompilia, the essence of purity, the beloved of God, is to Caponsacchi what the sunburst of absolute truth—the matter of religious faith—is to mortal man at large.

The sustained light imagery of Books 6 and 7 has still other effects. Almost as if they were upon a stage, from the moment hero and heroine recognize their spiritual affinity the scene is illuminated and they are enveloped in a kind of radiant nimbus, whatever the cruel nature of the events that now involve them. And the fact that their two versions of the recognition and subsequent flight are alike in their dominant imagery points up the larger circumstance that here, alone among the various accounts, is essential agreement, and truth. Pompilia's and Caponsacchi's stories, bathed in light, are contrasted with the four shadowy versions that have preceded it, not least with Guido's own, which is marked by a dark nimbus, a "cloud of horror" (5. 1569–70).

Individual sequences and single occurrences of light imagery in the books of the two lovers have their own artistic interest. Pompilia's simple but audacious "so / Do new stars bud while I but search for old" (7. 1567–68)—a miraculous union of heaven and earth, the splendid and the small—is shortly followed by her vivid impressionistic-metaphysical figure of the experience at Castelnuovo, when Caponsacchi

> Carried me in, that tragical red eve,
> And laid me where I next returned to life
> In the other red of morning, two red plates
> That crushed together, crushed the time between,
> And are since then a solid fire to me.
>
> (7. 1580–84)

In Caponsacchi's monologue occurs a series of variations on a single basic image. In its first appearance, it symbolizes on an elementary level the contrast between purity and evil. Canon Conti remarks to his fellow priest when they see Pompilia and Guido at the theater: " 'Is not she fair? 'Tis my new cousin,' said he: / 'The fellow lurking there i' the black o' the box / Is Guido, the old scapegrace.' " (6. 413–15.) Soon afterward, the background for Pompilia's radiance changes from square theater box to the page of an opened book: ". . . when the page o' the Summa preached its best, / Her smile kept glowing out of it." (6. 500–501.) Two hundred lines later, the same essential pattern is conceived differently. Again there is the square background framing a human image, but the earlier contrast of degrees of (implied) whiteness is replaced by an absolute contrast of black against white. Caponsacchi beholds the radiant Pompilia at her window, "Framed in its black square length, with lamp in hand" (6. 702–3). In the pattern's next appearance it dissolves back to the book, this time, however, retaining the black-and-white contrast. "So, I went home. . . . / . . . I opened book,—Aquinas blazed / With one black name only on the white page." (6. 1022–26.) The alternation is completed five hundred lines later, when the full-length

framing of a figure is repeated, this time more elaborately and
again (in the last lines) with lurid change of color. The scene
is Castelnuovo:

> Up we all went together, in they broke
> O' the chamber late my chapel. There she lay,
> Composed as when I laid her, that last eve,
> O' the couch, still breathless, motionless, sleep's self,
> Wax-white, seraphic, saturate with the sun
> O' the morning that now flooded from the front
> And filled the window with a light like blood.
> "Behind the poisoner, the adulteress,
> —And feigning sleep too! Seize, bind!"—Guido hissed.
> She started up, stood erect, face to face
> With the husband: back he fell, was buttressed there
> By the window all a-flame with morning-red,
> He the black figure, the opprobrious blur
> Against all peace and joy and light and life.
>
> (6. 1514–27)

The examples in this chapter—a mere selection of what can
be found once one is prepared to acknowledge Browning's
almost unlimited resourcefulness—are enough to prove the
point: one can speak, without fancifulness or exaggeration, of
the drama that resides in the poem's metaphorical content
alone. Inextricably associated though it is with characterization, structure, and meaning, it has in addition an independent
existence. Beneath the surface drama of the ill-fated marriage
and its fatal consequence, and beneath the psychological
drama of good, morally uncertain, and evil men and women, is
the pulsing action of the poem's images, with its own rich store
of conflicts, reversals, transformations, and—above all—
ironies.

Nine

"The Tragic Stage"

COMEDY AND THE CROWD, MIRACLES AND MOLINISM

I

Traditional criticism has not done full justice to Browning's humor, which embraces farce and satire, ribaldry and sophistical wit. The truth is that it is this gift above all which renders his characteristic art, most particularly the art of *The Ring and the Book*, Shakespearean rather than Shelleyan in essential quality. We have already noticed his characters' sly misuse of language, especially in metaphors, allusions, and rhetorical devices; their equally inventive casuistry; and the countless ironic inversions, variations, and other kinds of imperfect parallels which allow Browning to turn to humorous use the repetition made necessary by the poem's size and scheme. As these instances suggest, the humor in *The Ring and the Book* is generated to a considerable extent by certain of its themes, the illustration of which (the pitfalls of human discourse, for instance) is typically seriocomic. The comedy, indeed, is true commentary. Far from being gratuitous or incongruous, it is integral to the whole fabric. The juxtaposition of the humorous with the serious matter is a part of the poem's elemental conflict. The tragedy is the more poignant for the occasional broad comedy; conversely, the comedy is often darkened by cynicism or macabre desperation. Implicit in Browning is the assumption—the same which underlay the original Greek conception of drama—that tragedy and comedy are not separate or opposed but part of the continuum of life. The comedians in *The Ring and the Book* tend to fill in the ground between the angels and the devils who wage the true conflict; their humor thrusts the angelic or diabolic natures of the principals into greater prominence (an effect magnified in the case of Guido, who is both comedian and devil) and underscores by contrast the seriousness of Browning's purpose.

Nowhere, however, is criticism in greater peril of overreaching itself than when it attempts to find a comprehensive artistic or philosophical rationale for the spirit of comedy in a work of art. Especially when we deal with a poem like this, so massive in dimension and so lofty, even solemn, in stated purpose, the urge for analysis gives way to simple gratitude that humor does abound in its pages, regardless of any theoretical justification. And a great many of the comic touches can be adequately explained on such obvious grounds as Browning's awareness that a full measure of comic relief was needed if readers' attention and acceptance were to be sustained to the end; his desire to supply an additional bond between the timeless spiritual argument and the common human life to which it is applied; and, finally, his irrepressible *joie de rire*.

Browning's innate exuberance sometimes was stronger than his ability to make best use of it. Although he had the common Victorian relish for puns, he seldom exhibited the brilliance of verbal wit that often marked the work of humorists like Hood, Barham, and Praed, whose influence is apparent in the comic passages of his earlier work. The normal level of his word play in *The Ring and the Book* is typified by Half-Rome's assertion that had not the guards pinioned Pompilia when she was waving the sword at Castelnuovo, "she had finished you my tale / With a flourish of red all round it, pinked her man / Prettily" (2. 1037–39). As if recognizing that his puns were more labored than inspired, Browning allotted most of the deliberate ones to Bottini, whom they suited. Omitting even more dismal examples, we remember his "Silence become historiographer, / And thou—thine own Cornelius *Tacit*us!" (9. 884–85) and his pun on "core"-"cor" (and conceivably on "parsimonious"-"persimmon") in

Pompilia will not have the old year end
Without a present shall ring in the new—
Bestows upon her parsimonious lord

An infant for the apple of his eye,
Core of his heart [Lat. *cor*], and crown completing life,
The *summum bonum* of the earthly lot!

(9. 1313–18)

Of greater interest in this passage, illustrating a facet of
Browning's humor that is seldom noticed because his received
reputation does not provide for it, is the implicit naughtiness.
Bottini, arguing that the baby Gaetano was Pompilia's Christmas present to her "parsimonious lord," who had given her
nothing, encourages the inference that Guido's parsimony was
not limited to the Christmas season. If so, the conclusion to be
drawn is that Pompilia's child was not a present from him in
the first place.

Bottini's oration, as we have observed, is laden with similar
sexual innuendoes. Otherwise the speakers most given to such
sly references are Tertium Quid and Guido. The former speaks
of a high-born lady who was caught *in flagrante* "with a negro
page" because, she maintained, her husband took her too
much for granted and protected her innocence even to the
extent of "curtaining Correggio carefully / Lest I be taught
that Leda had two legs" (4. 888–89)—which, we may believe
both Tertium Quid and his clerical auditors well know, is not
the point. Again, Tertium Quid, speaking of Pietro's miraculous begetting of a daughter, remarks "How orisons and works
of charity / . . . Had borne fruit in the Autumn of his life,—
/ They, or the Orvieto in a double dose." (4. 202–6.) [1]

[1] Other instances of Tertium Quid's talent in this line are mentioned on pp. 143–45 above. It is not only in the humorous vein that
Browning defies the proprieties of Victorian society. The passage in
which Pompilia describes her refusal to cleave to her husband, her
flight to the Archbishop, and the Archbishop's exasperated lecture on
her wifely duty (7. 721–846) involves an unusually frank expression
of the necessity of sex education for girls:

God's Bread! [says the Archbishop]
The poor Count has to manage a mere child
Whose parents leave untaught the simplest things
Their duty was and privilege to teach,—
Goodwives' instruction, gossips' lore: they laugh
And leave the Count the task,—or leave it me!

(7. 798–803)

Guido, also cognizant of the liberal sexual morality of Roman society, has his own thrusts to make. Outrageous though the suggestion may be, it is unmistakable: his reference to "My father's lacquey's son" who became a fashionable Roman physician and "Salved the last Pope his certain obstinate sore" (5. 299–301) imputes venereal disease to Innocent XII's predecessor. In its context, his allusion to "the Monk / Who fancied Francis' manna meant roast quails" has a mischievous secondary significance, because "quail" also means "prostitute"; why should not the monk also claim "sweet society" and a "pretty piece of virtue" such as the deacon enjoyed (5. 737–58)?

In another vein one remembers, too, Guido's self-portrait as a hypothetical courtly lover, serenading his Pompilia, "provençal roses in his shoe, / Plume to his cap, and trio of guitars / At casement, with a bravo close beside" (5. 673–75)—a prodigy of unlikelihood; the inexpensive civility of the official who as a favor assigns Guido, son of a man who once paid him liberally for a legal service, to the New Prisons ("Anything for an old friend!" [5. 333]); and the letter that mockingly speaks in answer to Guido's "smiled" thoughts (5. 1467). Sometimes the humor stems from palpable understatement, as in the Venetian observer's remark that Guido, awaiting execution, had a "natural sense of injury" (12. 127). And sometimes it derives from spectacular incongruity, as when Guido, likening himself in his condemned cell to succulent grass about to be mown, alludes to himself as "juicy me" (11. 148).

Besides sharing contemporary humorists' propensity for word play, Browning had something of their taste for comedy springing from the horrific and the brutal. Some of the action and a number of the characters and circumstances in *The Ring and the Book* are staples of Gothic romance: the moldering ancestral home at Arezzo and its sinister inhabitants, the haggard witch of a mother and the childless, evil Count; the sadistic treatment of an innocent girl; the torture racks and subtle priests and machinery of disguises and forged letters. But in the poem, the intrinsic horror of the corrupt Franceschini household and the sensationalism of the multiple murders are accompanied by a grim humor that occasionally suggests the mock-Gothic mode of such early Victorian wits as Barham

and Hood. Most typical, perhaps, of this junction of the grue-
some and the comic is Guido's fancy of exhibiting the evidence of his wife's adultery by splitting open the lovers' skulls
with mattock, pitchfork, or axe and inserting therein, as a sort
of epistolary cock's comb, the letters that passed between the
two, "each package in its proper place,— / Bidding, who
pitied, undistend the skulls" and read the incriminating contents (2. 1488–1503).

In the same manner, Guido offers another instance of what
should have happened had he acted in accordance with his
best interests. He regrets that instead of merely threatening
Pompilia when he observed her encouraging Caponsacchi's
attentions, he had not quietly sliced off her ring finger to the
first joint, promising a like amputation for each subsequent
offense.

> had I done so,
> Why, there had followed a quick sharp scream, some pain,
> Much calling for plaister, damage to the dress,
> A somewhat sulky countenance next day,
> Perhaps reproaches,—but reflections too!
>
> (5. 962–66)

This passage is inevitably recalled when, almost three hundred
lines later, Guido berates the court for its light sentence on the
lovers.

> Word for word, there's your judgment! Read it, lords,
> Re-utter your deliberate penalty
> For the crime yourselves establish! Your award—
> Who chop a man's right-hand off at the wrist
> For tracing with forefinger words in wine
> O' the table of a drinking-booth that bear
> Interpretation as they mocked the Church!
> —Who brand a woman black between the breasts
> For sinning by connection with a Jew:
> While for the Jew's self—pudency be dumb!
>
> (5. 1226–35) [2]

[2] The amputation motif appears again in the history of the dispute
over Formosus, as quoted by the Pope. The reigning pontiff, Stephen,
decreed that Formosus' body be stripped of its robes and haled to the
market place, where "Let the town-hangman chop from his right hand
/ Those same three fingers which he blessed withal" (10. 84–85).

What a world of trouble I would have saved you, he implies, had I emulated you in a trifling way by cutting off a portion of one of Pompilia's fingers! But I did not; the crime I sought thus to forestall was committed; and now your featherweight punishment is a mockery of justice.

With these examples, however, the humor darkens: woven into this sequence of superficially incidental passages is a thread of grimness. What seem at first glance to be mere comic or grotesque fancies shade off into the tragic. The violence present in the cruel Comparini murders is reflected in a general depravity among men. Mutilation, both of body and of spirit, reminds us how much nearer we are to the brutes than to the angels.

One of the most notable instances of Browning's ability to create a continuous underlying vein of comedy while carrying on the poem's serious business is the lawyers' verbal duel of culinary images. (The very names he found in the Old Yellow Book assisted him: an eminent Italian judge of older days was named Farinacci [8. 148], and one of the judges involved in the Franceschini case itself was Tommati [8. 219].) Arcangeli besprinkles his monologue with food figures as he spreads fine and tosses flat the "pulp that makes the pancake" of his brief (8. 66–67). His choice of words is dictated, however unconsciously, by suggestions of food and eating: "dry bare bones, no scrap to pick" (258); "rub some life / Into one's choppy fingers this cold day" (278–79); "Guido must be all goose-flesh in his hole, / Despite the prison-straw: bad Carnival [popular etymology: 'Farewell to flesh!'] / For captives! no sliced fry for him, poor Count!" (282–84.) The infant Hyacinth tries "his milk-teeth on some crusty case" (12); elsewhere a motive is described as "the only [one] they could masticate, / Milk for babes, not strong meat which men require" (1619–20). When his brief is finished, "Done!" Arcangeli cries, as if drawing a roast from the oven (1728). "Law is the pork substratum of the fry, / Goose-foot and cocks-comb are Latinity," he asserts, adding for good measure a culinary-legal pun, "We'll garnish law with idiom, never fear!" (152–55.) Hard upon his apprehension that the cook at home has stewed, not roasted, the festive porcupine ("I cannot stay

much longer stewing here [;] / Our stomach . . . I mean, our
soul—is stirred within" [1385–86]) he likens the "several
matters in dispute" to "a mushroom-growth" (1399–1401).
"Figment" (431) is echoed in "a fico [fig] for your aggravations, Fisc!" (1113.) Elsewhere "Saint Ambrose makes a comment with much fruit" (678), and another authority provides
a "fructuous sample" (822); "the chalice teems with noonday
wine" (694); Guido's revenge plot is "a round sound egg"
(1067); Molinism's canker has "eaten to the bone" (1073);
and "the last faint sands of life" are "frittered gold"
(1438)—the last image reminding us of our introduction to
Arcangeli in Book 1 (1158–59), where his wheezing laugh
was likened to the sound of fritters frying somewhere inside
him. Shall we, he demands in one more instance of linguistic
fatality, "break public peace, / . . . trouble order with our
broils?" (8. 1270–71.)

Arcangeli's gustatory preoccupation, it is evident, gave
Browning much opportunity for punning. He made the most of
windfalls—the fact, for instance, that the Bottini's title was
"Fisc," allowing a pun on "fish" (cf. p. 259, n. 15). Immediately after the second occurrence of the "Fisc" play ("Giving
my Fisc his finish" [1745]: the fish pun being perhaps under-
lined by "finish" [finnish?]) comes "where's my fry[?]"
(1746), alluding to both of his consuming delights, dinner
and—again the fishy suggestion is present—offspring. Earlier,
an implicit likening of the world at large to the kitchen where
the birthday feast is (he hopes) in preparation—"our low and
mundane sphere" full of "smoke and noise"—leads to the
lines "In a low noisy smoky world like ours / Where Adam's
sin made peccable his seed" (1431–36): an obvious pun on
"peccable," which thereby converts Adam into "the father of
the flock" of hungry barnyard fowl, and the symbolic seed of
human generation into their feed.[3]

[3] It is probably fairer to Browning to remove certain other sus-
pected plays on words to the decent subordination of a footnote:
"JAM *satis*" (8. 1748), "man*sue*tude" (658), "*Manna*ia" (670),
"falls *plumb*" (75), "carp" (1009), "*perch*ed" (9), "leak" (255,
256), "Law *ducks* to Gospel here" (1407), "cornu*ti*" (784), and the
"*Corne*lian" law (572: "Gracchus' law," mentioned in the same line,

Arcangeli is as proficient a user of folk sayings, parables, illustrations, and allusions as any other character in *The Ring and the Book;* and in his monologue the choice is most especially suited to the man. The "ingrate Jews" of Scripture, "Despite the manna-banquet on the board," are pictured "A-longing after melons, cucumbers / And such like trash of Egypt left behind" (722–25). He alludes to Jupiter's threat to "devour poor Priam raw" (896). From the New Testament he adopts, not without amendment, a parable about "A lad hath here / Seven barley loaves and two small fishes" (1201–2). "Enough," he declares, sagely but somewhat unconvincingly if we read his table habits aright, "is good as a feast" (834). "We fathers can but care," he observes (borrowing from Eccles. 11:1), "but cast / Our bread upon the waters!" (1462–63.) To him, the essence of piteous primitiveness is the fact that the first men were, like pigs, an "acorn-eating race" (733). He finds in the law books of Sicilian decisions the fate of a false wife who after being slain was "half-devoured by dogs" (816). And when dogs are hungry, their hunger is transmitted to their fleas (1507).

While Arcangeli's preoccupation is with eating, Bottini's sometimes quite deliberate intention is to bait the eater. Never, apparently, on easy personal terms with his rival, and now additionally annoyed that he was not invited to the birthday feast (9. 984–85), Bottini lards his oration with *ad hominem* images, puns, quips, and parables. He regards Arcangeli as a

> gross pamperer o' the flesh
> And niggard in the spirit's nourishment,
> Whose feeding hath offuscated his wit
> Rather than law,—he never had, to lose—
> Let not such advocate object to me
> I leave my proper function of attack!
> "What's this to Bacchus?"—(in the classic phrase,
> Well used, for once) he hiccups probably.
>
> (9. 1399–1406)

was also a corn law). Sometimes Latin words, used without punning intent, reveal Arcangeli's preoccupation in the same way as does his choice of English words: *"insulse,"* for example (173), literally means "unsalted."

The bacchic hiccuping implies an aspect of Arcangeli's inclinations not seen in his own speech, where the talk is almost entirely of solid food. Bottini chose earlier to ascribe the peculiar logic of Arcangeli's opening statement to his loving "good cheer" too well, and he quoted to the absent Arcangeli the opinion of the celebrated papal physician, Tozzi, that the best way to break a habit is to taper off gradually—advice Pompilia and Caponsacchi might have been following if, as Bottini postulates, they saw each other frequently after they were sentenced in Rome (9. 1266–80). The inference to be drawn from Bottini's aspersions on Arcangeli's habits is that he is himself a paragon of abstinence; but reasonable doubt is cast upon this supposition by his final example, in which he envisions himself stopping in at a wine shop and eclectically sampling the quality of the merchandise—"Strong, weak, sweet, sour, home-made or foreign drink" (9. 1547). Perhaps with Bottini, as with Guido, the true words come last.

In any case, the apocryphal exemplum of Peter, John, Judas, and the solitary starveling chicken obviously is specially chosen for Arcangeli's ears, not least the appetizing description of the fowl as "duly brown, both back and breast, / Hissing in harmony with the cricket's chirp, / Grilled to a point" (9. 1092–94).

A number of Bottini's images and implicitly metaphorical terms are direct echoes of Arcangeli's. His "Does every hazel-sheath disclose a nut?" (9. 563) recalls Arcangeli's similar expression for emptiness, "fluff, / Nutshell and naught" (8. 57–58), and his allusion to "each frittered nerve / O' the much-enduring man" (Guido as Ulysses [9. 625–26]) resumes the "frittered gold" of 8. 1438. Elsewhere we are reminded of Arcangeli's "chop" (9. 1037), "corn" (1238), "fruit" (1338), "figment" (475), "lamb" (220, 223–24, 1331), and "fish"—here a "sickly" one (512). Like Arcangeli, Bottini uses the imagery of cutting and carving (33, 35); his allusion to Authority (the Aretine officials) flinging "a bone at banquet's end" to Innocence (Pompilia) (1110–12) suggests Arcangeli's "flinging the breast-blade" in his—Bottini's—own face (8. 1577). In addition, Bottini inferentially reminds his rival of one or two articles of food he left

out, "herb" (9. 287) and "eel" (393, 1417). His expansion of
the earlier reference to "eel" seems especially designed to
needle Arcangeli: a "luscious Lenten creature," as he describes it,

> six foot length,
> And not an inch too long for that same pie
> (Master Arcangeli has heard of such)
> Whose succulence makes fasting bearable.
>
> (394–97)

Conscious of Arcangeli's shadowy presence, Bottini tends
naturally to couch abstract ideas in alimentary terms. Rome is
a "city nutritive of arts" (19) and a painter's preliminary
studies "may nourish eye" (30). Arcangeli, at the beginning
of his monologue, had proposed to "triturate . . . / To
smooth Papinianian [4] pulp" the "crusty case" of Guido
Franceschini (8. 12–14)—pulverizing it, that is, to a consist-
ency suitable to a child whose milk teeth have barely emerged.
Now Bottini applies to the process of artistic creation the same
metaphorical idea by which Arcangeli described his proposed
treatment of legal arguments: Arcangeli's trituration becomes
Bottini's enzyme action. The results of the painter's studies,
says the latter, are

> life
> Fed by digestion, not raw food itself,
> No gobbets but smooth comfortable chyme
> Secreted from each snapped-up crudity.
>
> (9. 95–98)

Bottini's own temperament and tastes, amply exhibited in
his choice of argument and example, are additionally revealed

---

[4] "Papinianian" is one of Browning's feats of multiple allusiveness.
The first syllable suggests baby food as well as the familiar diminutive
of "father"; as Cook (*Commentary,* p. 164) points out, Aemilius
Paullus Papinianus, mentioned by Gibbon, was an eminent Roman
jurist of the second century A.D.; and, as he does not point out, Denis
Papin, the seventeenth-century French physicist, invented a "diges-
ter" (obliquely referred to in "the patent truth-extracting process" of
1. 1114) by which extracts could be made from animal and vegetable
substances. All four allusions, of course, are perfectly apropos here.

by his choice of particular foods for allusive purposes when
Arcangeli is not dominating his thoughts. As might be expected of one who delights to pluck the fruits of biblical and
classical story, they are Mediterranean or Levantine in association, and literary as well; and, to pursue their implication a
bit further, it may be that Bottini has the sweet tooth that
Arcangeli, essentially a carnivore, lacks. Cups are quaffed
(313, 1260), Abigail serves David "the raisin-cluster and the
cake of figs" (361), and it is not impossible to suspect in his
use of "candid" (475) a pun on "candied." [5] The apple,
evidently not a staple of Arcangeli's diet, recommends itself to
Bottini's vocabulary by virtue, no doubt, of its associations
with the gardens of Eden and the Hesperides (450, 700,
1157). He explains Pompilia's possibly having learned to
write on the ground that she "hunger[ed] after fellowship,"
just as Eve's hunger for the apple led to knowledge ("especially how to read and write") and as "the move o' the maw,"
according to Persius, impels birds to speak (451–58). And,
dependably enough, the sexual attractions and rewards attributed to Pompilia—who "caters for a generous taste"
(513)—are repeatedly figured in terms of food and the per-
fume associated with spice. Her bountiful charms are no mere
"household-bread," easily consumed, but an inexhaustible
"lump of spice," "morsel of myrrh" (321–26; context quoted
above, pp. 173–74). In an interesting compounding of value,
simple kisses are "nectared" (532, 711), the wifely gift of body
is "sweets" (334), and something else, the supreme reward for
services rendered, is "a super-sweet [that] makes kiss seem
cold!" (534)

All this is entertaining if uncomplicated comedy, a long-
sustained farce of language. The lawyers' gastronomical imagery both characterizes them, defining their obsessions and
their limitations, and functions as an elementary kind of wit
combat supporting the more sophisticated clash of their legal-

[5] Again the modesty of small type may be invoked for an assortment of possible hovering puns: "[mag]pie" (9. 455), "reverse the
peal!" (521), "SALT*em*" (679), "*nuga*tory" (871), "*ef*FIGI*em*"
(1397), and—almost certainly intentional—Bottini's concluding "I
shall have to prune and pare and print" (1575).

istic minds. It also supplies an Arcangelic counterpart for
Bottini's lascivious preoccupation: the cerebra of both men are
at the mercy of their respective visceral drives—and, Browning would add, so much for the pretensions of the proud, pure
intellect as a sure way to truth. Nowhere in the poem is the
vulnerability of reason to men's appetites more extensively
argued. But the cuisine comedy has still another function.
Especially in the imagery of Arcangeli, one hears the ominous
sound of a knife being sharpened under the guise of metaphor
(". . . thereby whet our courage if 'twere blunt" [8. 1086];
"A common hack-block to try edge of jokes" [1670]), and
sees a well roasted bird being dissected:

> I spare that bone [a legal point] to Spreti and reserve
> Myself the juicier breast of argument—
> Flinging the breast-blade i' the face o' the Fisc,
> Who furnished me the tid-bit.
>
> (1575–78)

Pompilia, we remember, is frequently imaged as a bird. She is,
indeed, to borrow Hamlet's phrase, two dishes to one table, for
she is just as often a lamb, and a lamb has been trotting to the
slaughter throughout Arcangeli's speech. With this awareness,
our view of the food motif inescapably darkens; for Pompilia's
fame, we realize, is in the hands of men whose first allegiance
is to their animal senses.

I I

As the upshot of this lengthy exchange of food imagery
shows, supplementing earlier evidence, the principal bond between comedy and tragedy in the poem is irony. A still more
extensive illustration is found in the role of the crowd-chorus
and the critical significance of its error: it thinks it is witnessing a titillating farce or a melodrama, but what it actually
beholds is a miracle.

The chorus is so ubiquitous that it has almost the role of a
major character. Unlike its Greek prototype, however, it is not
an authoritative, perceptive commentator, interpreting the
play's essential meaning to the audience. On the contrary, it is
itself made up of spectators much in need of enlightenment.

Although it is vocal enough, it says nothing to the real point. Its blindness, its perversity, its invariable habit of responding to first appearances constitute its true commentary. From the beginning of the drama to the end, scene after scene evokes "Arezzo's banter, Rome's buffoonery" (2. 1303)—the amused reaction of the people in the street as they glimpse, and instantly interpret to their own satisfaction, the successive tribulations and crises undergone by Guido and the Comparini.

This crowd is of ancient lineage; its forebears were violently divided in opinion, "according as the deed addressed their sense" (10. 98), when Pope Formosus' corpse was cast into the Tiber. In Arezzo, as the Franceschini story began, its members were "crawlers vile / Reared of the low-tide and aright therein" gloating over the spectacle of the beached sea monster Guido, whose family fortunes had declined to penury (5. 172–75). In Rome, the neighborhood loafers "heartily laughed" in Pietro's "fool's-face" when he sought information on Guido's supposed wealth, and proceeded to tell him the worst: "a Count,—ay: / But a cross i' the poke to bless the Countship? No!" (3. 396–401.) Back in Arezzo, the local idlers derived much enjoyment from the Comparini's indignant account of the state of affairs *chez* Franceschini, which, they had discovered the hard way, was no figment of "neighbours' envy" and "gossips' malice" (3. 441–42) but all too real:

> Violante up and down was voluble
> In whatsoever pair of ears would perk
> From goody, gossip, cater-cousin and sib,
> Curious to peep at the inside of things
> And catch in the act pretentious poverty
> At its wits' end to keep appearance up,
> Make both ends meet,—nothing the vulgar loves
> Like what this couple pitched them [6] right and left.
> (2. 511–18)

---

[6] Pitched with a dung fork? If there is one image motif in the poem which can fairly be called obsessive, it is that of dung-ordure-manure, whose applications range from the stirring of a jakes with a broken sword (5. 1490–92) to the flinging of ordure in one's

When the Comparini transferred their activities to Rome,
Guido was "made a laughing-stock abroad" as well as "A
proverb for the market-place at home" (2. 625–26). It was "to
amuse the world," as Half-Rome puts it, that "these kindly
ones," by revealing Pompilia's illegitimacy, "stripped her
naked" (2. 653–54). After a lapse of time, the Aretines had a
new public entertainment, the alleged "passage of arms and
wits" between Pompilia and Caponsacchi (2. 812); and their
subsequent words and winks, their ominous *"Mum* here and
budget there" (2. 823–24) aroused Guido's suspicions.

> "Friends [says Half-Rome], there's falseness here!"
> The proper help of friends in such a strait
> Is waggery, the world over. Laugh him free
> O' the regular jealous-fit that's incident
> To all old husbands that wed brisk young wives,
> And he'll go duly docile all his days.
> "Somebody courts your wife, Count? Where and when?
> How and why? Mere horn-madness: have a care!
> Your lady loves her own room, sticks to it,
> Locks herself in for hours, you say yourself.
> And—what, it's Caponsacchi means you harm?
> The Canon? We caress him, he's the world's,
> A man of such acceptance,—never dream,
> Though he were fifty times the fox you fear,
> He'd risk his brush for your particular chick,
> When the wide town's his hen-roost! Fie o' the fool!"
> So they dispensed their comfort of a kind.
>
> (2. 825–41)

Undismayed when their reassuring words were disproved by
the elopement, they "crowded round him to condole" and, in

---

face (6. 700; 7. 1620; 11. 1217, 1268). Several, typified by the
description of Violante's confessor at St. Peter's as a "poor repugnant
Penitentiary / Set at this gully-hole o' the world's discharge / To help
the frightfullest of filth have vent" (3. 572–74), derive their repulsive-
ness from the idea of sewage en masse. There are more than a score of
such images, metaphorical and nonmetaphorical, some occurring naturally in agricultural contexts but others introduced with obvious care
to intensify the notion of undeserved insult and ignominy.

their magnanimity, allowed that Guido was a better prophet
than they:

> "Ah," quote a gossip, "well I mind me now,
> The Count did always say he thought he felt
> He feared as if this very chance might fall!
> And when a man of fifty finds his corns
> Ache and his joints throb, and foresees a storm,
> Though neighbours laugh and say the sky is clear,
> Let us henceforth believe him weatherwise!"
>
> (2. 921–28)

The crowd went on to supply a groaning Guido with the full
details of his wife's liaison and elopement, a delicious scene
described by Half-Rome in the passage following the one just
quoted (2. 931–51) and later by Guido himself, who fails to
appreciate its humor:

> (By this time the admiring neighbourhood
> Joined chorus round me while I rubbed my eyes)
> " 'Tis months since their intelligence began,—
> A comedy the town was privy to,—
> He wrote and she wrote, she spoke, he replied,
> And going in and out your house last night
> Was easy work for one . . . to be plain with you . . .
> Accustomed to do both, at dusk and dawn
> When you were absent,—at the villa, you know,
> Where husbandry [7] required the master-mind.
> Did not you know? Why, we all knew, you see!"
> And presently, bit by bit, the full and true
> Particulars of the tale were volunteered
> With all the breathless zeal of friendship.
>
> (5. 998–1011: there are twenty lines more)

---

[7] This feeble pun presumably would have done no more to alleviate
Guido's misery than the pair Tertium Quid attributes to his "friends"
as they recalled the birth of a son to Pompilia: ". . . then did there
befall / The luckiest of conceivable events, / Most pregnant with
impunity for him." (4. 1345–47.)

For a moment a new chorus took over: the onlookers at the Castelnuovo inn who burst into her room [8] and then watched in amazement the pale young girl's menacing use of her husband's sword. As they heard her accusations,

> the popular tide soon turned,
> The favour of the very *sbirri*, straight
> Ebbed from the husband, set toward his wife,
> People cried "Hands off, pay a priest respect!"
> And "persecuting fiend" and "martyred saint"
> Began to lead a measure from lip to lip.
>
> (2. 1043–48)

Eight months later, Roman "town-talk" had a new feast of gossip, the birth of Pompilia's child. "Square's jest, street's jeer" was that "he's the priest's bastard," no son of Guido (5. 1529–31). Then, swiftly, came tragedy; and now Guido finds himself before a solemn tribunal composed of the same ecclesiastics who earlier had shared the crowd's merriment over the misfortunes that had left him a stranded fish (5. 180–82). Later in his first defense, his anger overruling his diplomacy, he accuses his judges of truckling to the mob (5. 1855–57).

As he considers Guido's appeal, the Pope is equally aware of the crowd. Nearing the end of his long meditation, he reflects on the pressure of popular sympathy which urges him to remit Guido's sentence. "Our tears on tremble," he seems to hear the crowd crying,

---

[8] Bottini, speaking nominally in her behalf, stresses the untoward publicity of the discovery scene at Castelnuovo. As usual his argument goes astray, though perhaps not accidentally:

> Is 't by the rough way she shall be reclaimed?
> Who bursts upon her chambered privacy?
> What crowd profanes the chaste *cubiculum?*
> What outcries and lewd laughter, scurril gibe
> And ribald jest to scare the ministrant
> Good angels that commerce with souls in sleep?
>
> (9. 854–59)

If for "ministrant good angels" we substitute what the context obviously calls for—incubi, the male demons of folklore who impregnate sleeping women—we must add to the disguise of Caponsacchi-as-cavalier this further metamorphosis, which of course perfectly suits Bottini's interpretation of what happened in the inn room.

"hearts
Big with a benediction, wait the word
Shall circulate thro' the city in a trice,
Set every window flaring, give each man
O' the mob his torch to wave for gratitude.
Pronounce it, for our breath and patience fail!"

(10. 2092–97)

The Pope, however, dedicated instrument of divine judgment that he is, is not swayed, "for a voice other than yours," he imagines himself telling the mob, "Quickens my spirit" (10. 2098–99).

When the Cardinal and the Abate visit the prisoner in his cell, Guido not unnaturally accuses them of having come to extort a confession. They are, he maintains, fearful of "the tongue of Rome" gabbling about the condemnation and execution of a man who may have been innocent, and they therefore hope he will exculpate them (11. 420–32). Recognizing the capriciousness of the mob, he speaks of "The popular sympathy that's round me now" but which would break, bubble-like, if he struggled to live (11. 1810–15). No:

The mob's in love, I'll wager, to a man,
With my poor young good beauteous murdered wife:
For hearts require instruction how to beat,
And eyes, on warrant of the story, wax
Wanton at portraiture in white and black
Of dead Pompilia gracing ballad-sheet,[9]
Which, had she died unmurdered and unsung,

[9] A reminder of Guido's description, in his first monologue, of his reaction when a letter came to him from Rome after Pompilia and Caponsacchi had received their sentences. The bad news it undoubtedly contained, he speculated with a smile, might include a report that to while away his enforced leisure Caponsacchi had composed

A rattling ballad-rhyme which, bawled
At tavern-doors, wakes rapture everywhere,
And helps cheap wine down throat this Christmas time,
Beating the bagpipes.

(5. 1450–55)

The ballad of "Guido the gulled" (2. 375)?

Would never turn though she paced street as bare
As the mad penitent ladies do in France.

(11. 1823–31)

We last see the Roman populace as it watches Guido's beheading. To the end, it remains one of the chief focuses of the
poem's theme of ambiguity, of erroneous interpretation. Why
was the site of the execution shifted from the usual place, "the
out-o'-the-way old quarter by the Bridge," to the more easily
accessible People's Square? Because, avers the Venetian "man
of rank" who describes the event in a letter, the authorities
meant to throw "a conciliatory sop / To the mob; it gave one
holiday the more" (12. 106–9). But we know that the Pope,
who gave the order, had in mind no concession to the power of
the touchy rabble but an example to their betters (10.
2109–13).

In addition to its chief manifestations, as the populace of
Rome or Arezzo at large, the chorus takes several other forms.
It is directly represented, of course, by the speakers Half-
Rome and the Other Half-Rome. Sometimes the chorus is the
more restricted circles who are called—not always accurately
—"Guido's friends" (either his partisans among the people
at large, or the special few who commiserated with him or
advised him, as in 5. 1241–54).[10] Sometimes it is Caponsacchi's clerical friends, men whose twitting infuriated him in
precisely the same way that Guido was enraged by his friends'
facetiousness (6. 1740–53). Sometimes, again, it is Pompilia's
sympathizers, as they are alluded to in Tertium Quid's painstaking differentiation between one set of partisans and another.

Whatever specific identities it assumes, the crowd-chorus
posessses several unmistakable and fixed traits. It has, says
Browning,

---

[10] His least helpful advisers were those who suggested that the only
way out of his multiplying troubles was for him to go hang himself (5.
1280). Paolo, not unscathed by his brother's misfortunes, withstood
"a brief temptation to go jump / And join the fishes in the Tiber" (5.
1367–68) and found the most prudent means of escape was to sell his
property and decamp to parts unknown.

> chronic greediness
> For scandal, love of lying vanity,
> And appetite to swallow crude reports
> That bring annoyance to their betters.
>
> (12. 789–92)

Not paradoxically, one of its most dependable characteristics is its fickleness, as is illustrated not only by its switch from Guido's side to Pompilia's at Castelnuovo but by the *volte-face* of Pietro's Roman neighbors, who had shared his "cheery days and festive nights" before his disenchanting sojourn at Arezzo but who, upon his return, greeted him with "Just as we foretold," gave him "the dregs o' the cup, / Scraps of the trencher," and "let him share the mat with the mastiff, he / Who lived large and kept open house so long" (3. 540–48). It is always liberal with advice, rarely with help. It enjoins caution upon Pietro, who by temperament is especially vulnerable to outside counsel (3. 490–92), and offers free advice to Guido, not always with tact:

> Guide, guardian, benefactor,—fee, faw, fum,
> The fact is you are forty-five years old,
> Nor very comely even for that age:
> Girls must have boys.
>
> (5. 585–88; cf. 11. 1058–71)

Later the crowd urges him to kill Pompilia as the only adequate revenge for her offense against his honor; yet when he does so, he is met by the cry, "So rash? / . . . so little reverence for the law?" (5. 1068–86.)

The crowd therefore is a true agent of the plot, because it provides a motivation, if only an alleged one, for Guido's deeds. He finds rationale for his actions in the sheer force of public opinion, ill-informed and changeable though it may be. It was the crowd which kept his sense of injury alive and which finally goaded him to take vengeance. He and his sympathizers refer time after time, bitterly and at length, to the humiliation and the bad advice he suffered from his fellow Aretines. When the Archbishop thrice delivered the screaming Pompilia back home,

Judge [says Half-Rome] if that husband warmed him in
   the face
Of friends or frowned on foes as heretofore!
Judge if he missed the natural grin of folk,
Or lacked the customary compliment
Of cap and bells, the luckless husband's fit!

                                                                (2. 883–87)

Pompilia's reputed availability and the hints of Caponsacchi's
proximity—"the smell o' the fox, / The musk o' the gal-
lant"—were the obvious cue for "waggery" (2. 824–27). And
on his return to Arezzo after delivering the fugitive lovers to
the Roman court, Guido

Was welcomed by the city turned upside down
In a chorus of inquiry. "What, back—you?
And no wife? Left her with the Penitents?
Ah, being young and pretty, 'twere a shame
To have her whipped in public: leave the job
To the priests who understand!"

                                                                (2. 1238–43)

Half-Rome, in short, makes the dryly misnamed "chorus of
inquiry" a genuine cross for Guido to bear. "Ask yourself," he
demands, "had you borne a baiting thus?" (2. 1261.) [11]
   Tertium Quid, with his accurate sense of the tribulations
which would most evoke sympathy in an aristocratic audience,
includes the crowd's ridicule in his recital of Guido's, or his

[11] The Other Half-Rome's handling of the same point is a good
measure of the distance that separates him from Half-Rome. To him,
though the "chorus of inquiry" is admittedly a "plague" (3. 1444),
the sting is removed; in his version, the tale of Guido's misfortunes is
merely amusing, like a story in Boccaccio. Guido only got what he
deserved. But the most dramatic evidence of the Other Half-Rome's
attitude, as contrasted with Half-Rome's, occurs in his account of how
the Aretines regarded Pompilia before the elopement. To him, in a
laconic reference strikingly different from his customary jocular allusions to the chorus, the Aretine gossip, far from being waggery, is
"the news that buzzed / Of how the little solitary wife / Wept and
looked out of window all day long" (3. 859–61). Lack of elaboration
and the unexpected focusing on Pompilia rather than on Guido lend
poignant eloquence to the lines. Compare Half-Rome's Byronic picture of Pompilia at the window (2. 809–11; quoted above, p. 8).

"friends'," imaginary defense (4. 599–602, 657–62, 902, etc.) and—even more significantly, as additional evidence that he is a crypto-Guidonian—alludes three times *in propria persona* to the Count's public humiliation. Without recourse to the subterfuge of attributing the opinion to others, he speaks of the Comparini having to

> write, print, publish all abroad
> The straitnesses of Guido's household life—
> The petty nothings we bear privately
> But break down under when fools flock around.
>
> (4. 642–45)

As he warms to his unacknowledged apologia for Guido, Tertium Quid becomes more and more impassioned. The Comparini, he says, were

> two ghastly scullions [who] concoct mess
> With brimstone, pitch, vitriol and devil's-dung—
> Throw in abuse o' the man, his body and soul,
> Kith, kin and generation, shake all slab
> At Rome, Arezzo, for the world to nose,
> Then end by publishing, for fiend's arch-prank,

that Pompilia, the meat in his dish, was "never a pheasant but a carrion-crow" (4. 730–38). In his concluding enumeration of the ingredients that poisoned Guido's cup, Tertium Quid joins undeserved notoriety with the "cheat" of Pompilia's illegitimacy and the Comparini's robbery. Guido was

> Rendered anon the laughing-stock o' the world
> By the story, true or false, of his wife's birth,—
> The last seal publicly apposed to shame
> By the open flight of wife and priest.
>
> (4. 1490–96)

It was a long drawn out series of trials that would have taxed the patience of a David or a Samson. Guido got it, he says, from both sides, "my friends that joke, / My foes that jeer"—"gibe and jest, those stones that Shimei flung!" (5. 1900–1901, 2020.) "When he found himself, i' the public place, / Destined to make the common people sport," amplifies Arcangeli, he "pulled down pillar, roof, and death and all." (8. 645–51.) [12] In his stress on the crowd's ridicule Guido seeks not only to identify himself with the various Jobs of the world but, more important, to liken his suffering once again to that of Christ, who also, in his agony, was mocked by a populace that knew not what it beheld. [13]

I I I

To the crowd at Arezzo and Rome, as to several speakers who insistently repeat the analogy, the Franceschini affair was a spectacle—more particularly, a domestic comedy. The many theatrical allusions in *The Ring and the Book* suggest that to the onlookers, and occasionally to the participants themselves, the events are somehow detached from real life; they take place in public view, but as on a stage separated from the audience. Above all, to the spectators they are mere entertainment, with no moral or spiritual significance. The "divers scenes," as a letter Guido receives from Rome puts it,

> tickle rib
> And teaze eye till the tears come, so we laugh;
> Nor wants the shock at the inn its comic force,
> And then the letters and poetry—*merum sal!*
>
> (5. 1361–65)

[12] Perhaps the most memorable of all the images Guido uses to describe his humiliation is one describing his return after the fiasco at Castelnuovo:

> Step
> By step, across the pelting, did I reach
> Arezzo, underwent the archway's grin,
> Traversed the length of sarcasm in the street.
>
> (5. 1265–68)

This image with its quasi-metaphysical flavor adapts an idea earlier used by the Other Half-Rome in the same connection. The Count, he said, "Found the world's face an universal grin / At this last best of the Hundred Merry Tales" (3. 1445–46).

[13] Guido's exploitation of this aspect of his *via crucis* contrasts with the use that the Pope, however vainly, urges him to make of it. For all its propensity to err, says the Pope, the crowd with its "furnace-coals . . . of public scorn" gave Guido an additional chance to realize his own error and repent (10. 709–13).

Half-Rome sees the series of events as a farce with the classic complement of five acts (2. 622, 1078); the Other Half-Rome, forbearing because of his sympathy for Pompilia to call it a farce, terms it simply a play (3. 1338) climaxed by the bringing of Mannaia on the stage (3. 1489). By a clever and appropriate linkage, only a little more than two hundred lines later (at the opening of the next monologue), the grim instrument of avenging justice is replaced by another, more specifically theatrical machine:

> Law's a machine from which, to please the mob,
> Truth the divinity must needs descend
> And clear things at the play's fifth act—aha!
> Hammer into their noddles who was who
> And what was what.
>
> (4. 15–19)

Guido recurrently, but with little amusement, likens the episodes to scenes in a play. The "admiring neighbourhood," he says, watched the amorous transactions of Pompilia and Caponsacchi as "a comedy" (5. 998–1001), a view he himself had sarcastically taken, according to Pompilia, of her withholding herself from his bed: "We have been man and wife six months almost: / How long is this your comedy to last?" (7. 744–45.) [14] His circumstances were all too close to those in the plays which had educated him in the realities of married life and married deception:

> I have known a score of plays,
> Were listened to and laughed at in my time
> As like the everyday-life on all sides,
> Wherein the husband, mad as a March hare,
> Suspected all the world contrived his shame;
> What did the wife? The wife kissed both eyes blind,
> Explained away ambiguous circumstance,
> And while she held him captive by the hand,

[14] In ironic contrast with the ghastly non-comedy of Guido's and Pompilia's domestic life, Guido's lawyer anticipates the amiable play-acting which will be a feature of his boy's birthday party, "Rogue Hyacinth" portraying "Don father that defends the Count" (8. 1752–58).

> Crowned his head,—you know what's the mockery,—
> By half her body behind the curtain. That's
> Nature now! . . .
>
> .   .   .   .
>
> All those eyes of all husbands in all plays,
> At stare like one expanded peacock-tail,
> Are laughed at for pretending to be keen
> While horn-blind.
>
> (11. 897–916)

And so the playbill and the critics' opinions continue. Caponsacchi brands Guido's accusations at Castelnuovo a splendid, mirthful, ludicrous lie worthy of Molière's tastes (6. 1485–87). Bottini, sharing Caponsacchi's judgment, though not the furious spirit in which it was uttered, delights in the same scene as a "spectacle" (9. 850).[15]

All the leading characters are portrayed, either explicitly or by implication, as actors in a play. Pompilia is "a gamesome wife / Able to act Corinna without book" to Caponsacchi's Ovid (5. 1358–59), an actress who knew her cue (4. 1160) and "to the last . . . played her part" (9. 1415). She and Caponsacchi, in Guido's jaundiced account, acted stock roles at Castelnuovo:

> They never tried to put on mask at all:
> Two avowed lovers forcibly torn apart,
> Upbraid the tyrant as in a playhouse scene,
> Ay, and with proper clapping and applause
> From the audience that enjoys the bold and free.
>
> (5. 1127–31)

This was the climactic scene of the comedy which, according to Half-Rome, the two had written (2. 1080), the script consisting mainly, one gathers, of their love letters.[16] Pietro and

---

[15] The term is also applied to the display of the Comparini's corpses (1. 873) in the "church which had served as theatre" for Pompilia's baptism and marriage (2. 51)—the scuffling of the morbid crowd now providing "a show [which] repaid your pains" (2. 98)—and to the execution of Guido and his accomplices (1. 352; 12. 102, 309).

[16] In the theatrical analogies of the poem, as in so many of the others, doubt prevails: which is real life, which is the representation?

Violante are "waggish parents who played dupes / To dupe
the duper" (5. 1360–61) in the familiar classic mode, and
Pietro is "Pantaloon," a clown out of season who flaunts "his
tom-fool tawdry just the same / As if Ash-Wednesday were
mid-Carnival!" (11. 1153–55.) Guido, as seen by Caponsacchi when the dramatic conflict at Arezzo grew more taut,

> wiping brow
> And getting him a countenance, was fast
> Losing his fear, beginning to strut free
> O' the stage of his exploit, snuff here, sniff there.
>
> (6. 1566–69)

And Guido in retrospect casts himself, awaiting new developments in the ensuing "morose December," as "one [who] has
chosen his part and knows his cue" (5. 1436–40). Left alone
on the Roman stage by the departure of Paolo, he spent a
whole week "in study of his part" (3. 1587–88) before proceeding to the kill. (This version of his activity is the Other
Half-Rome's; Guido's story is that he was praying [5.
1582–87].)

The advocates are histrionic by profession as well as by
natural bent. Arcangeli looks to "the world's stage
. . .—whereon a man should play / The man in public, vigi-
lant for law, / Zealous for truth, a credit to his kind" (8.
1770–72), and Bottini's whole monologue, performed in solitude but assuming an immense crowd, is a bravura piece of
acting. Even the Pope is a member of the cast. He "knows his
cue," Guido says (11. 341), and the Pope has confirmed the
figure in advance:

> Still, I stand here, not off the stage though close
> On the exit: and my last act, as my first,
> I owe the scene, and Him who armed me thus
> With Paul's sword as with Peter's key. I smite
> With my whole strength once more, then end my part,

who are the actors, who the authors, who the audience? Pompilia and
Caponsacchi are once seen as spectators at a real play—on the
occasion of their first sight of each other (6. 393 ff.).

Ending, so far as man may, this offence.
And when I raise my arm, what plucks my sleeve?

(10. 1954–60)

Although there are some exceptions, such as this last
speech, the dominant tendency of these theatrical allusions
suggests that the events of the poem are a spectacle to be
enjoyed either for their farcicality or for their melodrama.
But, once more, their quality is subject to change according to
one's point of view—or the whim of the actors or the story
line. Such, in any event, is Tertium Quid's argument, when he
likens the progress of the Franceschini play to developments in
a Punch and Judy show: [17]

You've seen the puppets, of Place Navona, play,—
Punch and his mate,—how threats pass, blows are dealt,
And a crisis comes: the crowd or clap or hiss
Accordingly as disposed for man or wife—
When down the actors duck awhile perdue,
Donning what novel rag-and-feather trim
Best suits the next adventure, new effect:
And,—by the time the mob is on the move,
With something like a judgment *pro* and *con*,—
There's a whistle, up again the actors pop
In t'other tatter with fresh-tinseled staves,
To re-engage in one last worst fight more
Shall show, what you thought tragedy was farce.

(4. 1282–94)

This is among the most breathtaking of the poem's perversi-
ties. For the whole point is that what the crowd thought farce
was actually tragedy. "The blood," as Half-Rome perceptively
observed, "Gave the broad farce an all too brutal air" (2.
1460–61); after the first act, "The stealing sombre element
comes in / Till all is black or blood-red in the piece." (2.
623–24.) The darkening of the stage as the drama progressed
went unnoticed by the crowd.

[17] In the prologue, Browning describes Caponsacchi's (pre-
Pompilian) moral uncertainty in terms of puppetry (1. 1019–22,
quoted above, p. 90).

Yet Browning and the characters who speak for him allow us no doubt of the play's true nature. Browning in his own person describes the part Caponsacchi played on the Aretine stage as "a spectacle for angels" (1. 504), and the entire Franceschini story as a "tragic piece" (1. 523), an "old woe" that takes the stage and, under Browning's direction, "Act[s] itself o'er anew for men to judge" (1. 824–25). The Pope too sees the spiritual ordeal and triumph of Pompilia and Caponsacchi as "a spectacle" which has made an unmarked shrine of the window where she waited and holy ground of the street where he walked (10. 664–69).[18] Just as "This one earth, out of all the multitude / Of peopled worlds" was chosen by God "For stage and scene of Thy transcendent act" (10. 1335–38)—the *theatrum mundi*—so the town of Arezzo, of all earthly locales, was chosen to witness a new enactment of divine grace. The Pope's speculations on the nature and mood of the drama which will succeed in the next age are framed in an extended metaphor of masque and antimasque which will be discussed in the following chapter (pp. 358–59). And in the poem's last major use of theatrical imagery, the Pope's echo-voice, Fra Celestino, with prophetic urgency suggestive of Savonarola, preaches the meaning of the morality play that has been performed before the eyes of unbelieving Rome:

> Be . . . instructed, you!
> And preferably ponder, ere ye pass,
> Each incident of this strange human play
> Privily acted on a theatre,
> Was deemed secure from every gaze but God's,—
> Till, of a sudden, earthquake lays wall low
> And lets the world see the wild work inside,
> And how, in petrifaction of surprise,

---

[18] Whatever its eventual fate, the memory of the fleeing pair was still vivid at Castelnuovo when Guido passed through on his way to Arezzo after he had delivered the eloped couple to the law. "The fugitives / Had risen to the heroic stature." "The bench they sat on," "the board / They took the meal at," the "garden-ground / They leaned across the gate of" were, if not precisely shrines, certainly the objects of considerable local awe (5. 1259–63).

The actors stand,—raised arm and planted foot,—[19]
Mouth as it made, eye as it evidenced,
Despairing shriek, triumphant hate,—transfixed,
Both he who takes and she who yields the life.

(12. 542–53)

Far from attending a performance of inconsequential farce,
the crowd, as Celestino goes on to say, has witnessed a display
of celestial grandeur: God's truth on earth saved by God's
intervention. And thereby hang several ironies. In one sense it
is the spectators, not the actors they watch with so much
laughter, who are the comedians. But in a deeper sense, they
are really not comedians at all; their "unquenchable universal
mirth" (9. 868) is a sign of their lamentable human impercep-
tivity, and man's frailties are, at base, not comic but ineffably
tragic. Nowhere else in the poem, indeed, is the proclivity for
error which is man's "primal curse" more impressively demonstrated than in the crowd's enthusiastic clinging to nonessen-
tials, its belief in appearances, its prejudices—especially in the
reduction of its emotions from sympathy to empathy, from
pity to maudlin grief; and the diminution of all to the casual
theatergoer's narrow gamut of reaction, which reaches only
from guffaws to sentimental tears.

A third irony, dramatic rather than philosophical in its
import, is that, apart from Guido, it is the very exemplars of
the crowd, Half-Rome, the Other Half-Rome, and (if we may
be so bold) the haughty Tertium Quid, who wax most indignant over what the crowd does. Laying heavy stress upon its
mindless delight over Guido's misfortunes, its blithe disregard
of suffering, the speakers by their condemnatory tone in effect
dissociate themselves from the very mass to which they belong.
The blind ridicule the blind. And so, far from being only a
comic element, the crowd is a further emblem of one of the
poem's deepest meanings. In failing to realize that they are
witnessing a latter-day reenactment of Christ's self-sacrifice

---

[19] This stock histrionic attitude suggests, of course, the arm
raised with sword to defend the right—as Pompilia's had been in a
literal sense and Caponsacchi's figuratively—and the foot planted,
like St. Michael's, on the snake Satan.

and love, these onlookers fail to recognize the potential source of their own deliverance.[20]

To these generalizations there is one exception. The men and women who represent the populace-at-large at Pompilia's bedside are so deeply affected by her sanctity that the scales, in effect, fall from their eyes. "Busy helpful ministrants / As varied in their calling as their mind, / Temper and age," they all respond in their respective fashions; their "Small separate sympathies," negligible in themselves, combine into "something very much":

> As if the bystanders gave each his straw,
> All he had, though a trifle in itself,
> Which, plaited all together, made a Cross
> Fit to die looking on and praying with,
> Just as well as if ivory or gold.
>
> (1. 1088–99) [21]

These people have an advantage none of the other onlookers possess: they see the martyred girl, and, seeing, find that belief which eludes the rest.

[20] As J. M. Cohen points out (*Robert Browning* [London, 1952], p. 122), the situation is like that in pictures of the procession to Calvary, where "crowds rush hither and thither about their own business," wholly oblivious to the spiritual drama occurring in their midst. One such picture is Breughel's "Die Kreuztragung Christi," in which Christ, bearing the cross, is a figure almost swallowed up in the busy mob. Caponsacchi bitterly reminds the judges that in "an old book, you should con / For strange adventures, applicable yet, / 'Tis stuffed with" there is record of the way "a multitude of worthy folk" looked on while soldiers threw dice "For the coat of One murdered an hour ago!" (6. 49–59; cf. 10. 1524–30, quoted below, pp. 331–32.) The crowd's complete neglect of the transcendental meaning of Christ's sacrifice as it watches the soldiers gaming has its exact parallel, Caponsacchi says, in the present situation.

[21] This devotional cross of straw is not a mere incidental detail; it has thematic relevance. Once again Browning stresses that genuine Christian faith may be fashioned from humble everyday materials. And a little later we find that in his austere apartment the Pope sits beneath "one lathen crucifix" (1. 1239); symbolically the difference between high and low—the vicar of Christ and the poor watchers at Pompilia's bedside—is erased. In the presence of a miracle, all believing Christians are made equal.

I V

Some few among them realize they are witnessing the last stage of a miracle.[22] For miracle is precisely what Browning interprets the Pompilia-Caponsacchi "spectacle" to have been; and the blindness and waywardness not only of the crowd at large but of individual men and women are further demonstrated by the vicissitudes which the miracle—both the concept and the actual event—suffers throughout the poem. Because the possibility of miraculous occurrences is ever present in their minds, conditioned as much by superstition as by Scripture, the people persist in seeking and identifying miracles where they have not occurred; conversely they fail to recognize them when they do happen. They vulgarize the very idea of the miraculous almost beyond the possibility of redemption.

The debasement of word and notion alike begins at the very outset. One of Pompilia's defenders identifies her, perceptively enough, we subsequently learn, as "a saint, / Martyr and miracle"; but here the terms are mere rhetoric, and the description is at once turned inside out by a Guido-partisan: "A miracle, ay—of lust and impudence" (1. 207–10). In the first half of the poem several so-called miracles are reported: Violante's conceiving a child at her advanced age (2. 223); Pompilia's being filched from her strumpet mother and grafted to the Comparini tree, there to grow luxuriantly (3. 241); and her persistence in living after the "masterpiece" of stabbing she has undergone (1. 1079; 3. 7, 34, 1641; 4. 1439; cf. also 11. 1690). Because her survival is "miraculous" she is thought to possess curative powers, even though palsied old Monna Baldi is trundled from the bedside before she can benefit (3. 51–57).

[22] But there was to be a miraculous epilogue, for what else was Browning's discovery of the Old Yellow Book in the midst of an assortment of Florentine junk but a predestinate miracle? (1. 40–41) The fate of the murder case's records up to that moment had recapitulated that of the Pompilia-Caponsacchi story even as it was being enacted; both the miracle and the documents that recorded it were lost in the debris of everyday life.

The whole theological question of the improbability inherent in miracles has its secular reflection in the debate whether or not Pompilia and Caponsacchi, young and attracted to each other, could possibly have been innocent of wrongdoing. "Difficult to believe, yet possible," says Half-Rome, skeptically quoting "law," "as witness Joseph, the friend's patron-saint." (2. 1114–15.) The Other Half-Rome, Pompilia's defender, finds Caponsacchi's story of his resisting the "over-luscious honey-clot" of the love letters a tale which "frankly outsoars faith" (3. 904–6), but finally decides that the version of events which alleges their complete innocence must be believed, however difficult belief may be: "How do you say? It were improbable; / So is the legend of my patron-saint." (3. 1050–51.) Guido, of course, has another opinion, as phrased by Tertium Quid:

> "It would indeed have been miraculous
> Had such a confidency sprung to birth
> With no more fanning from acquaintanceship
> Than here avowed by my wife and this priest.
> Only, it did not: you must substitute
> The old stale unromantic way of fault,
> The commonplace adventure, mere intrigue
> In the prose form with the unpoetic tricks."
>
> (4. 1013–20)

But in his second defense Guido is eager enough to adopt and elaborate the argument from miracles. If the belief that Pompilia and Caponsacchi were lovers was a lie, it was at least as credible to Guido as miracles are to his auditors. Equally credible, he asserts, is his own version of events. Five times in fifteen lines—not all of them quoted here—the word "plausible" drives the point home:

> "Saint Somebody-or-other raised the dead:"
> Did he? How do you come to know as much?
> "Know it, what need? The story's plausible,
> Avouched for by a martyrologist,
> And why should good men sup on cheese and leeks
> On such a saint's day, if there were no saint?"

> I praise the wisdom of these fools, and straight
> Tell them my story—"plausible, but false!"
>
> (11. 866–73)

Guido here is putting the Cardinal and the Abate on the spot:
he assumes that their belief in biblical miracles is mere form,
part of the general hypocrisy he attributes to the men of his
time. He would force them to concede that if they cling to
belief (or pretended belief) in events that are both unauthenti-
cated and patently contrary to physical law, they must grant
his honest belief in events that are, alas, all too familiar in
human habit and therefore far more "plausible."

To Pompilia and Caponsacchi, in contrast, the true miracle
is the fact of each other's existence at the moment when most
needed. Caponsacchi says that, just as a Raphael Madonna
might miraculously raise her painted hand and fix her face
upon him, so "Pompilia spoke, and I at once received, /
Accepted my own fact, my miracle / Self-authorised and
self-explained" (6. 912–20). Vacillating in the cold later light
of caution, he allows himself to think that "God, who created
her, will save her too / Some new way, by one miracle the
more, / Without me" (6. 1031–33); but in the end, he embraces his predestined part in the miraculous story, for he
cannot forget Pompilia's words:

> If it be truth,—why should I doubt it truth?—
> You serve God specially, as priests are bound,
> And care about me, stranger as I am,
> So far as wish my good,—that miracle
> I take to intimate He wills you serve
> By saving me,—what else can He direct?
>
> (7. 1428–33)

This was the conjoined private miracle of the wife and the
priest. But the development of the theme of miracles is accompanied by a grotesque variation supplied by the riddle of who
fathered Pompilia's child. Guido refuses to believe the baby is
his, yet he cunningly leaves the question open: "Or say, by
some mad miracle of chance, / Is he indeed my flesh and
blood, this babe?" (5. 1506–7.) His allowing the possibility

enables him to deliver a magnificent compliment to the court's apparently limitless powers. Concluding his first defense, he asserts that man's law, as represented by present company, transcends the law of nature and can negate even the stigma of illegitimacy: "Give me—for last, best gift, my son again, / Whom law makes mine,—I take him at your word, / Mine be he, by miraculous mercy, lords!" (5. 2026–28.) To Pompilia, however, the "miraculous mercy" has been visited in quite another way. Far from designating which of the two men begot her child, she declares, "No father . . . he ever knew at all, / Nor ever had—no, never had, I say!" (7. 91–92.) "My babe," she insists near the end of her dying speech,

> nor was, nor is, nor yet shall be
> Count Guido Franceschini's child at all—
> Only his mother's, born of love not hate!
> So shall I have my rights in after-time.
> It seems absurd, impossible to-day;
> So seems so much else not explained but known.
>
> (7. 1762–67)

In explaining the seemingly impossible lack of a father for her baby, Pompilia offers a standard theological solution to the problem of miracles in general: they are phenomena which, though not rationally explicable, must be accepted as articles of faith.

Her assertion that her child had no father gives Bottini the opening for one of his most outrageous exercises of forensic ingenuity. Gaetano's origin, he says, was indeed a miracle. Nature, resenting the "taunts upon her sloth" occasioned by Pompilia's non-production of a child to Guido, roused herself to a supreme feat, like the one Aristaeus witnessed, in Virgil's *Georgics*, when swarms of bees emerged from the carcasses of the animals he had sacrificed to the gods:

> And lo, a new birth filled the air with joy,
> Sprung from the bowels of the generous steed!
> Just so a son and heir rejoiced the Count!
> Spontaneous generation, need I prove
> Were facile feat to Nature at a pinch?

Let whoso doubts, steep horsehair certain weeks,
In water, there will be produced a snake;
A second product of the horse, which horse
Happens to be the representative—
Now that I think on 't—of Arezzo's self
The very city our conception blessed!
Is not a prancing horse the City-arms?

(9. 1339–58)

In so expert and unlovely a manner does Bottini reduce the doctrine of the Virgin Birth to its pseudoscientific counterpart, the ancient theory, freshly discredited in Browning's time, of spontaneous generation.[23] The "bowels" which in the Virgilian story—and in the cognate story of Samson and the slain lion (Judg. 14:5–8)—are simply the entrails of a decaying carcass become, in Bottini's version, the intestines of living horses; for the theory of spontaneous generation held that life could be produced from any putrescent matter, including horse dung. Bottini's chain of reasoning is plain, multiply fallacious though it may be. Spontaneous generation is possible in nature, as is witnessed by such unimpeachable authorities as Virgil and the author of the book of Judges. Therefore parthenogenesis, which is a kind of spontaneous generation, is also possible. Therefore the doctrine of the Virgin Birth has scientific validity. And therefore it was possible for Pompilia, the Virgin Mary's modern analogue, to have conceived a child without a father. To disbelieve this to be disbelieve—heretically—in the Virgin Birth. Whether or not Bottini's argument compels assent, it is rendered even more memorable by the innuendo he manages to convey in the process. Thanks to the lucky circumstance that a horse appears on the municipal arms of Arezzo,

---

[23] The discreditation was largely the work of Louis Pasteur, whose discovery of the micro-organism of fermentation, communicated to the Académie des Sciences in a series of reports (1860), won him the academy's prize for "well-constructed experiments [which] should throw new light on the question of spontaneous generation." On April 7, 1864, his dramatic and well-publicized lecture at the Sorbonne on abiogenesis was heard by a packed and fashionable audience which included savants, philosophers, ladies, priests—and novelists like Dumas *père* and George Sand.

and with the aid of a pun on "conception," he manages to suggest that the whole town may have participated in fathering Pompilia's child.

To such a deplorable depth of ridiculousness, not to say obscenity, has the Christian concept of God's miraculous intervention been degraded by the time the Pope speaks. The Pope resuscitates the true meaning of "miracle" in the context of the poem's events. If Caponsacchi, with his human frailties, cannot measure up to "the other rose, the gold, / We grave to imitate God's miracle," this "warrior-priest" is nonetheless a "good rose in its degree" (10. 1095–98).[24] But Caponsacchi's act of selfless devotion in Pompilia's behalf is not the miracle that is destined to remain in our view. It may state the truth as far as the Pope and Browning are concerned; but the world is still in the hands of the evil and the misguided, who subvert the idea of miracles to their own uses.[25] In his second speech, Guido fancies himself, a confessed pagan, as a miracle worker, converting the present hypocritical Rome into a seat of genuine Christian faith:

> Come, thus I wave a wand and bring to pass
> In a moment, in the twinkle of an eye,
> What but that—feigning everywhere grows fact,
> Professors turn possessors, realize
> The faith they play with as a fancy now,
> And bid it operate, have full effect

[24] The allusion is to the golden rose, emblematic of the Godhead, the body and soul of the Redeemer, which certain popes gave to monarchs to whom they were indebted (Cook, *Commentary*, p. 216). Browning's differentiation between the gold rose and the "good rose in its degree" is based on color. Pompilia is golden, the soul of the miracle; Caponsacchi is of natural (red?) color, as befits the body or the physical agent of the miracle.

[25] As, for example, the use of belief in miracles to rationalize craven inaction where justice and mercy require vigorous measures. Bottini reports that the Governor, the Archbishop, and the rest of Pompilia's "friends" to whom she appealed for aid "Shook heads and waited for a miracle, / Or went their way, left Virtue to her fate" (9. 991–94). Caponsacchi, as we saw above (p. 312), was tempted to use the same excuse.

On every circumstance of life, to-day,
In Rome,—faith's flow set free at fountain-head!

(11. 587–94)

This prodigy, we find a moment later, might just as easily be
supplanted by the second coming of atheism. It may, says
Guido, be as viable a force as faith.

Before I work the wonder, there's no man
Woman or child in Rome, faith's fountain-head,
But might, if each were minded, realize
Conversely unbelief, faith's opposite—
Set it to work on life unflinchingly,
Yet give no symptom of an outward change:

.   .   .   .

What saintly act is done in Rome to-day
But might be prompted by the devil[?]

(11. 596–607)

Guido's rhetorical question is answered in the poem's last
scene and last irony, where the devil—Guido himself—not
merely prompts but actually performs a saintly act in the form
of a supposed miracle. "Now," writes the visitor to Rome who
describes the events attending Guido's execution,

did a beggar by Saint Agnes, lame
From his youth up, recover use of leg,
Through prayer of Guido as he glanced that way:
So that the crowd near crammed his hat with coin.

(12. 159–62)

Whereas in popular conviction Pompilia has fallen short of
producing a true miracle, Guido, her husband and murderer,
succeeds on his way to the scaffold.

It is that feat, rather than the story of Pompilia and Caponsacchi as an evidence of divine grace, which is finally recognized by the multitude as the miraculous part of the poem's
chain of events. The true miracle has occurred virtually unnoticed—seen as such, to their varying degrees of awareness,
only by Pompilia, Caponsacchi, the Pope, and the watchers by

Pompilia's bedside—and then it has quickly been obscured by a fresh pseudomiracle, a "cure" that men, relying on the evidence of their senses rather than of their souls, instantly accept for what it seems to be. In that little four-line episode is captured the inveterate confusion of physical and spiritual values which, to Browning, characterized his own age's debate over miracles. A further epitome is found in two earlier lines: "O faith where art thou flown from out the world? / Already on what an age of doubt we fall!" The words, we feel, must be the Pope's, for they are the clearest and most concise summary possible of the mood of his entire speech. But they are, in fact, Bottini's (9. 1327–28), alluding to the controversy over Gaetano's paternity. Bottini has reduced the problem of miracles to its narrowest dimensions: here it applies merely to a small domestic issue of ephemeral concern in the Rome and Arezzo of 1698. It will be the Pope's task to re-expand the problem to its proper magnitude—to restore the scale of values which has been shattered by the persistent reductions, throughout the poem, of matters of supreme moment to the level of comparative trivia, and so finally to reveal, in Chesterton's phrase, the overwhelming significance of the insignificant.

For the whole conflict between scientific knowledge and the desire to believe scriptural reports of rationally incredible events is implicitly shadowed forth in the poem's tragicomic treatment of miracles and what pass for miracles. In *The Ring and the Book* they symbolize all obstacles to Christian belief. Doubt takes the specific form of refusal to recognize or accept the manifestations of God's providence.

The supreme miracle, assent to the truth of which is the crucial act of faith a Christian must perform, is of course the Incarnation. To Browning the Franceschini story is an equivalent of the story of the Incarnation, not in substance (though we have noted several incidental resemblances) but in purpose and effect. Just as the Gospels gather the materials relating to the life and teachings of God incarnate in man, so the Old Yellow Book gathers materials relating to another sequence of events also demonstrative of God's love; and *The Ring and the Book* is an attempt to do for those historical facts what Browning regards it as indispensable to do for the Bible, whose

effectiveness and credibility, as history, have also declined
with the passage of years.

> The act, over and ended, falls and fades:
> What was once seen, grows what is now described,
> Then talked of, told about, a tinge the less
> In every fresh transmission.
>
> (12. 13–16)

In this poem Browning presents to his age an illustration,
composed of modern, secular materials, of how it may be
possible to revitalize the Bible and its spiritual message without demanding assent to the literal truth of miracles. The
poem

> Makes new beginning, starts the dead alive,
> Completes the incomplete and saves the thing.
> Man's breath were vain to light a virgin wick,—
> Half-burned-out, all but quite-quenched wicks o' the lamp
> Stationed for temple-service on this earth,
> These indeed let him breathe on and relume!
>
> (1. 733–38)

The sordid events involved in the Roman murder case, "an
episode in burgess-life," as Tertium Quid depreciates it (4.
64–65), contain the same powerful message to the human race
as does the story of the Incarnation, but because they are
realistic they are adapted to men's changed powers of comprehension and more limited powers of assent. The lessons of
Christian faith can be learned as well from everyday instances
as from spectacular supernatural events and deeds—far more
easily, in fact, since the supernatural is discredited in our
modern age. The teachings of the miraculous, Caponsacchi
realizes, are found

> not alone
> In the main current of the general life,
> But small experiences of every day,
> Concerns of the particular hearth and home.

Men "learn not only by a comet's rush / But a rose's birth" (6.
2090–95). In Pompilia's story are found the same evidences
of God's will for man and of man's obligation to God as are

discovered in saints' legends (referred to more than once in
the poem) and in the chronicles of "battle, earthquake, famine, plague" that Caponsacchi pictures a crooning monk as
transcribing from parchment (6. 216–18). Each is a different
kind of narrative, but each is susceptible of the same kind of
religious interpretation.

The Franceschini story, *pace* Bottini and his generative
horse dung, contains no element that requires suspension of
belief in physical law. Furthermore, it is thoroughly vouched
for by historical documents, so that there can be no question
that the events it relates did happen at the time and place
specified. (This is undoubtedly another reason why Browning
in Book 1 lays such heavy stress on his fidelity to "facts":
here, he implies, is a miracle whose authenticity is beyond
challenge.) What, then, is miraculous about it? Simply this:
although it involves no violation of physical law, its "repetition of the miracle, / The divine instance of self-sacrifice /
That never ends and aye begins for man" (10. 1655–57) is so
uncommon, given the state of society in 1698 (or 1864–68),
that it is as truly miraculous as, say, walking upon the waters,
multiplying the loaves and fishes, or raising a man from the
dead—indeed, more so. In earlier ages it was wondrous physical events which brought God's message to men and challenged their faith; in modern times it is moral miracles,
episodes strikingly at variance with man's inveterately self-
regarding habits, that serve the same ends. The terms of the
miracle, in brief, have been adjusted to new conditions.

This is the kind of miracle, Browning implies, which alone
has validity in a skeptical, materialistic age. The old kind has
lost its power to persuade. Guido, the type of the skeptic, tells
of relics that worked wonders "in a crazy land / At a fabulous
epoch":

> "Here's a shred
> Of saintly flesh, a scrap of blessed bone,
> Raised King Cophetua, who was dead, to life
> In Mesopotamy twelve centuries since,
> Such was its virtue!"—twangs the Sacristan,
> Holding the shrine-box up, with hands like feet
> Because of gout in every finger-joint:

Does he bethink him to reduce one knob,
Allay one twinge by touching what he vaunts?
I think he half uncrooks fist to catch fee,
But, for the grace, the quality of cure,—
Cophetua was the man put that to proof!

(11. 565–78)

Like the arthritic cleric, the church depends for its existence upon outworn modes of inspiring belief. But the Guido who so derides this exploitation of spurious miracles is himself incapable of perceiving a genuine miracle even when it touches him close. The idea of miracles, we have seen, is meaningful and useful to him only insofar as he can employ it to persuade his judges to believe his own version of events. Otherwise his attitude toward improbable or impossible events is that of the naturalist in Browning's time. Arguing in his second speech that his is an age of hypocrisy and mistaken motives, he illustrates at length the difference that possession or lack of religious faith makes in the interpretation of unexpected events (see below, pp. 347–50). Ironically, while the examples he offers there are wholly imaginary, his own incompetence and negligence supply two authentic instances of the same point. Both involve the forestalling of death in order that justice be served. Pompilia's survival despite her grievous wounds is regarded by her sympathizers as a "miracle." Guido, however, has a bitter naturalistic explanation: it was his own bungling hand that prevented her instant death. He had gained considerable knowledge of anatomy from his fencing master, information he displays at length in his second defense (11. 285–311); but it failed him when the time came to make effective use of it at the Comparini's. As a result, Pompilia was left to "Tell her own story her own way, and turn / My plausibility to nothingness" (11. 1676–87), and he was deprived of a perfect alibi—that he had caught Pompilia with Caponsacchi at the Comparini's house and they had fought him like tiger cats (11. 1712–20).

Only hours afterwards, Guido blundered again when he forgot his exit permit, an oversight which resulted in a delay at the Tuscan frontier and his consequent capture before he

could reach safety in his own town.[26] This too is looked upon
by the truly perceptive speakers of the poem as miraculous or
providential. The Pope stresses the unlikelihood of Guido's
overlooking such a precaution:

> Why, the first urchin tells you, to leave Rome,
> Get horses, you must show the warrant, just
> The banal scrap, clerk's scribble, a fair word buys,
> Or foul one, if a ducat sweeten word,—
> And straight authority will back demand,
> Give you the pick o' the post-house!—in such wise,
> The resident at Rome for thirty years,
> Guido, instructs a stranger! And himself
> Forgets just this poor paper scrap, wherewith
> Armed, every door he knocks at opens wide
> To save him.
>
> (10. 818–28)

Guido, however, attributes the fatal incident not to personal
negligence but to hard luck. At any other time, he could have
bribed the post master (confiding that he and his blood-
stained companions had been "mauling who was malapert")
and immediately received horses and clearance:

> Yet I try the trick,
> Double the bribe, call myself Duke for Count,
> And say the dead man only was a Jew,
> And for my pains find I am dealing just
> With the one scrupulous fellow in all Rome.
>
> (11. 1629–37)

To the Pope, this piece of what Guido regards as wretched
fortune (the odds being extravagantly long against encounter-
ing an uncorruptible official, given the current moral condition

[26] A final illustration of the poem's abundance both of symmetry
and of irony: Guido's downfall lies in his inability to reach the safety
of Arezzo, just as Caponsacchi and Pompilia, heading in the opposite
direction, had earlier sought and failed to reach the safety of Rome.
In the one case, the fugitives, Guido and his accomplices, are success-
fully pursued by the arm of true vengeance, the law; in the other, the
fugitives were the prey of one who falsely claimed revenge, Guido
himself.

of Rome) is a case of divine intervention. For as the Pope says, though "Guido the astute . . . / . . . curses the omission . . . / More than the murder," the accident spared his life: the delay (or their fatigue?) prevented his accomplices' fulfilling their plan to kill him for the money he owed them (10. 852–62). Instead of being sent spinning down to hell, therefore, he was saved not only to be accountable to earthly judges for his sins but—possibly—to repent: "So may the truth be flashed out by one blow, / And Guido see, one instant, and be saved." (10. 2126–27.)

V

If the eagerness to interpret all unusual events as miracles, at the same time overlooking true miracles, exemplifies one way in which human nature manages to divert itself from truth, the Roman populace's near-obsession with Molinism illustrates another. Miracles and Molinism, in effect, symbolize two different sources of faith: supernatural events and the inner light. And if the whole notion of miracles and what they stand for is degraded by the people of *The Ring and the Book,* the principle behind Molinism is no less misapprehended and abused.

Browning's partial misrepresentation of historical Molinism need not concern us here. It is enough simply to define this seventeenth-century heresy as the belief that contemplation of God is the sole requisite for salvation. Such quietism was at once alien to the activist Browning, implying as it did that virtuous conduct and the valiant snatching of belief from the jaws of doubt are supererogatory, and attractive to him in that it rejected dogma, ritual, and other external grounds and expressions of faith in favor of private illumination. In the poem Browning avails himself of the notoriety of the Molinist sect in Pope Innocent's Rome in a number of ways, all germane to his artistic and philosophical purposes as we have so far viewed them.[27]

[27] For fuller treatments of the subject see William Coyle, "Molinos: 'The Subject of the Day' in *The Ring and the Book,*" *PMLA,* 67 (1952): 308–14; Robert Langbaum, *The Poetry of Experience* (New York, 1957), pp. 128–31; and Cook's *Commentary,* app. 8.

He well describes the casual manner in which the people
adopt Molinism as the controversial "subject of the day" (6.
360), utterly careless of its true import. The Molinists, he
says,

> 'Gainst whom the cry went, like a frowsy tune,
> Tickling men's ears—[were] the sect for a quarter of an hour
> I' the teeth of the world which, clown-like, loves to chew
> Be it but a straw twixt work and whistling-while,
> Taste some vituperation, bite away,
> Whether at marjoram-sprig or garlic-clove,
> Aught it may sport with, spoil, and then spit forth.
>
> (1. 308–14)

"Molinism" to the Romans and Aretines is an all-purpose
smear word, a verbal gesture which one can load with whatever degree of calumny one desires, especially with the aid of
associated terms. Thus the Other Half-Rome links Molinists
with "churls" (3. 989), and Bottini links them with Jews and
Turks—all three groups being fit subjects for the anatomist's
knife (9. 32–33). Guido, emphasizing with a topical allusion
his complaint over Pompilia's unsatisfactory development into
adulthood, twice suggests that to grow up a Molinist is to meet
a bad end (5. 870; 11. 2039), and the Aretine archbishop,
reprimanding Pompilia for her refusal to cleave to her husband and therefore her implicit assumption that God com-
manded Eve to sin, accuses her—however improbably—of "A
blasphemy so like these Molinists', / I must suspect you dip
into their books" (7. 768–70). Caponsacchi's superiors similarly detect Molinism in the canon's new habit of staying away
from countesses young and old and going to "play truant in
church all day long." (Caponsacchi's reply is rapier-quick:
"Sir, what if I turned Christian?") (6. 471–74.) To Luca
Cini, the aged prophet-in-the-street who is given to seeing
apocalyptic signs, "Molinos' doctrine," joined with the triple
murder, is a symbol of the ultimate wickedness which presages
the approach of doomsday (2. 125–27), an opinion shared by
an attendant at Pompilia's bed (3. 93–104). Neither of these
oracles is wholly wrong, for they recognize the presence of
something supernatural, prophetic, or at least illustrative in

the case; but like that of the miracle-mongers, their superstitious eagerness to see omens prevents their comprehending the true meaning of what they witness.

Devoid of specific ideological significance as it is replete with emotional force, the popular notion of Molinism is a convenient device, however irrelevant, for making a rhetorical point, as Arcangeli twice demonstrates (8. 1072, 1330) and Bottini once (9. 564). Adopting "Molinism" as a simple synonym for heresy or mere heterodoxy of any sort also enables Bottini to picture Peter, John, and Judas as on the trail of "some Molinism i' the bud" (9. 1046); and, predictably, he dismisses Celestino's sermon as "Molinism simple and pure!" (12. 650–51.) Both lawyers brand as Molinists the straw men they set up to demolish with their superior arguments; if the arguments fail, the evil name will nevertheless persuade (8. 695; 9. 1497–98). Writing tracts against Molinism is a good way to court advancement in the church (2. 174–80; 5. 203, 223). When the Other Half-Rome wishes to convey the full enormity of Guido's evil, he says that the experience of it was reserved not for the sinful, "Not you, not I, not even Molinos' self" but for the innocent Pompilia, who therefore deserved no less a reward than sainthood (3. 109–11). Subsequently, in one more of the poem's ironic inversions, we hear Guido claiming to be the victim of Pompilia the torturer, with whose exquisite kind of cruelty he urges his judges "try persuade / The next refractory Molinist" (5. 1041–43).

But Molinism provides more than an incidental gloss on the crowd, the speakers, and the subsidiary themes of the poem. In certain passages the word refers not so much to either historical Molinism or heresy in general as to critics and enemies of the Roman church in 1698. Guido recommends that his ecclesiastical judges "take note" of the inconsistency of their judgments "before the Molinists do" (5. 1238). Bottini pompously conceives of his voice warning the Molinists that Rome "is built upon a rock nor shall / Their powers prevail against her!" (9. 724–27.) And the Pope hears the voice of Roman opinion warning him that by sacrificing a count and exonerating Caponsacchi he is paving the way for Molinos, the successor and spiritual coadjutor of "the Luthers and the Calvins"

(10. 2065). The simple equation of Molinism with heterodoxy allows the elastic term also to represent skeptical naturalistic thought, as in the Other Half-Rome's remark concerning Pompilia's surviving long enough to forgive her husband and murderer: "A miracle, so tell your Molinists!" (3. 34.)

Seen against the poem's whole argument, the many allusions to Molinism have at least three related functions. One is markedly ironic. No matter that, as the various speakers' discrepant applications of the term show, they do not understand what it means; sufficient that they can use it as a symbol of all that they, right thinkers every one, despise and fear, confident that their auditors share their opinions and react to the mere sound of the word as they are intended to do. They worry far more about a "heresy" they do not trouble to comprehend than about the true Christian faith which would help them grasp the ultimate significance of the Franceschini affair. This, Browning would seem to imply, is one of the dangers to which his own time has succumbed: in their restless and needless search for tenable grounds of religious belief the people of the nineteenth century look in the wrong places, fear the wrong things, and apply to false and futile ends the emotional energy they should devote to positive Christian faith and action.

At the same time, the Pope sets an example which few follow, Browning intimates, either in 1698 or in the 1860's. He is, as has often been observed, the only speaker in the poem who has a measure of tolerance and sympathy for the Molinist heretics—he, the Supreme Pontiff, who of all people should be most rigorous in opposition to these supposed enemies of the Roman church. " 'Leave them alone,' bade he, 'those Molinists! / Who may have other light than we perceive, / Or why is it the whole world hates them thus?' " (1. 315–17.) Like the Molinists, "at peril of their body and their soul," is it necessary for us to deny "recognized truths" in obedience "to some truth / Unrecognized yet, but perceptible?" (10. 1868–71.) The Molinists, misguided though they seem, may in reality be true prophets, revealing the inadequacy and obsolescence of our present dogmatic religion and pointing to a future rejection of outworn beliefs in favor of a new and more vital "other light"—that of inner conviction.

For what most concerns the Pope is the "torpor of assurance" which lies so heavy upon "our creed" (10. 1853). This easy complacency, that the battle is won and man knows all he needs to know and believes all he needs to believe, is the true enemy of faith. Molinism, notwithstanding all the speakers and listeners who shudder at mere mention of the word, is not the fearsome enemy without, the "wild beast" that prowls just outside the Christian camp (10. 1857). On the contrary, the real peril to Christianity is within: it is the assumption among the orthodox that their creed is both right and unassailable and that all dissent is wrong. The only justifiable attitude toward dissent is that of the Pope: the Molinists *may* be right. Only by listening to heresies, Browning says, and where necessary formulating a response to their errors, can the vitality of religious faith be maintained and strengthened. Supine acquiescence in a creed is spiritual death.[28]

We have come a long way in this chapter, from simple comedy to matters of high seriousness. From the incidental, often farcical characterization of individual men (the lawyers) we have moved through the half-comic, half-tragic delineation of the shortsightedness and perversity of men as a race (the crowd) to the problems of knowledge and faith which are the ultimate concern of the poem yet which only the Pope is competent to define and articulate. This movement is neither fortuitous nor unfitting, because it is the tendency of the poem itself. The inseparability of the comedy from the philosophical content shows, once more, how closely Browning wove his artistic pattern. And the adjacent themes of miracles and Molinism are threads which have brought us to a final consideration of the poem's meaning.

[28] Although Browning and John Stuart Mill shared few philosophical or religious views, the similarity of Browning's conviction to Mill's statement of the same principle in secular terms (*On Liberty* [1859], chap. 2) deserves more notice than it seems to have received.

Ten

"Suffice the Eye and Save the Soul Beside"

THE POEM'S ULTIMATE MEANING

I

Whatever opinions the Romans of 1698 actually entertained on the subjects of miracles and Molinism, the convictions and anxieties Browning attributed to them were one important means by which *The Ring and the Book* became a tract for his own times. If it was not strictly true to history, it was true to Browning's conception of the Victorian religious dilemma. By using a story laid in Rome at the end of the seventeenth century to utter his views on crucial issues of an age of doubt such as his own—one which, he suggests, was foreshadowed in the time of Guido and Innocent XII—he once more achieved his constant purpose of setting topicalities at a historical distance and, hence, of commenting upon them indirectly rather than directly. The ultimate effect is to present those problems *sub specie aeternitatis*. How can we know? How and what can we believe? What should be our guide to right conduct? These fundamental questions, Browning's treatment implies, are both historical and immediately contemporary; and they are also ageless.

The epistemological problem, dealt with implicitly throughout the poem, is given immediately topical illustration by the several references to the doctrine of papal infallibility, which was much debated in the very years when Browning was composing *The Ring and the Book* and was promulgated shortly after the poem's fourth and final volume appeared.[1]

---

[1] Pope Pius IX had initiated the modern phase of the movement toward promulgation of papal infallibility in his first major utterance,

Controversial as the doctrine was within the church—its acceptance as an article of faith had long been urged by the Jesuits and the ultramontanes and opposed by the Gallicans—it was of course anathema to Protestants. Irrespective of what the historical Pope Innocent might have thought of it, for the purposes of the poem infallibility was already dogma in the Rome of 1698. One of Guido's mentors reports the failure to get the Pope

> To set aside procedures, sit himself
> And summarily use prerogative,
> Afford us the infallible finger's tact
> To disentwine your tangle of affairs,
>
> (5. 1348–51)

and his lawyer pays due respect—privately tinged with irony —to "my infallible Pope" (8. 710), whose infallible judgment, as events turn out, will lead him to condemn Guido. Bottini denies the doctrine by maintaining that it is instead antiquity which is "our one infallible guide" (9. 183). This infallible guide in Bottini's hands proves Pompilia the lightest of light women.

Calmly questioning that part of his church's doctrine which relates most directly to himself, the Pope is disturbed by the assumption that a human being can be immune from error, even though he occupies Peter's throne. Reviewing the fluctua-

---

the encyclical *Qui pluribus* of November, 1846. The dogma was given weighty reiteration in December, 1854, when, in proclaiming the doctrine of the Immaculate Conception of the Blessed Virgin Mary before a concourse of prelates in St. Peter's, he acknowledged as authorities only "that of our Lord Jesus Christ and the Blessed Apostles Peter and Paul and . . . our own." This and other decrees collected in the *Syllabus of Errors* (1864), together with the address of the Bishops at Whitsuntide, 1862—"thou are the center of Unity, thou art the Divine Light prepared by the Divine Wisdom for the Nations, thou art the rock, thou art the very foundation of the Church"—made the decision of the Vatican Council of 1869–70 (the infallibility decree *Pastor aeternus*) a mere formal ratification of a *fait accompli*. For the outlines of the story, see Lord Acton, "The Vatican Council," *North British Review*, 53 (1870): 183–229. Probably the best-known single contemporary discussion of infallibility was that in the final chapter of Newman's *Apologia*.

tion of papal opinion regarding Formosus—holy man or fraud?—he asks, "Which of the judgments was infallible? / Which of my predecessors spoke for God?" (10. 150–51.) The idea of infallibility by virtue of office cannot accommodate contradictory decisions. As for himself, the Pope, Antonio Pignatelli that was, humbly enrolls himself among men; fallibility therefore is his inescapable lot. In handing down judgment on Guido he may err, but he will use such wisdom as he has:

> I shall face Guido's ghost nor blench a jot.
> "God who set me to judge thee, meted out
> So much of judging faculty, no more:
> Ask Him if I was slack in use thereof!"
>
> (10. 263–66)

He is aware, moreover, that whatever decision he renders will be secured by intuition and lifelong moral practice, not by a faculty peculiar to his office:

> eyes grow sharp by use,
> I find the truth, dispart the shine from shade,
> As a mere man may, with no special touch
> O' the lynx-gift in each ordinary orb.
>
> (10. 1241–44)

Such confidence as he possesses is derived from his faith in the beneficent God who transmits a modicum of his infinite wisdom to man:

> Yet my poor spark had for its source, the sun;
> Thither I sent the great looks which compel
> Light from its fount: all that I do and am
> Comes from the truth, or seen or else surmised,
> Remembered or divined, as mere man may:
> I know just so, nor otherwise.
>
> (10. 1284–89)

Browning thus uses a contemporary issue to draw together and additionally illustrate several of the poem's chief themes. The idea of infallibility seems to be introduced expressly in order that its ensuing discreditation can give further scope to the familiar principles that man is a creature born to error and that all human knowledge is relative. The Pope's awareness of these facts, however, does not prevent his delivering an absolute judgment on the Franceschini case. Where moral imperatives are involved, to hesitate or hedge is to be craven.

Fallible or not, the divinely bestowed gift of insight the Pope possesses is intuitive, not rational. One should not overlook in this connection two more limited groups of allusions, both obliquely referring to specific sources of Victorian religious perplexity, in which Browning additionally denies the primacy of reason as an instrument for discovering truth. As some of his other poems of the 1860's and the earlier *Christmas Eve* (1850) show, Browning was deeply troubled by two notable contemporary manifestations of rationalism and naturalism, the higher criticism of the Bible and natural theology.

From one viewpoint *The Ring and the Book* veritably epitomizes the problem of the higher criticism, which, because it reduced the supposedly inspired word of God to a fortuitous collection of historical documents, seemed to pose a grave threat to Christian faith. The poem's subject, like that of the Gospels, is a sequence of events in time and place which are shown to possess a spiritual meaning that transcends time. Like the nineteenth-century "scientific" critics in their treatment of the Bible, those in the poem who watch the Franceschini story unfold insist upon interpreting it in purely naturalistic terms, thereby neglecting the numinous truth it represents. This response on the part of the crowd, the first three speakers, and the lawyers emblematizes what Browning deplores in the liberal or skeptical attitude toward the Bible in his own time. The brain, bent upon applying rational tests and explanations to the nonrational, inhibits the action of the soul.

The principal statement of this idea is the Pope's. He sweeps aside the difficulties that would later be grist for the higher critics' mill, not only the problem of miracles but historical and scientific inconsistencies and contradictions of all sorts, everything in the content and provenance of the Scriptures that disturbs the reason. It is of little moment to him whether the biblical stories are literal history or myth:

> whether a fact,
> Absolute, abstract, independent truth,
> Historic, not reduced to suit man's mind,—
> Or only truth reverberate, changed, made pass
> A spectrum into mind, the narrow eye,—
> The same and not the same, else unconceived—
> Though quite conceivable to the next grade
> Above it in intelligence,—as truth
> Easy to man were blindness to the beast
> By parity of procedure,—the same truth
> In a new form, but changed in either case:
> What matter so the intelligence be filled?
>
> (10. 1387–98)

"Nor," he goes on to say,

> do I much perplex me with aught hard,
> Dubious in the transmitting of the tale,—
> No, nor with certain riddles set to solve.
> This life is training and a passage; pass,—
> Still, we march over some flat obstacle
> We made give way before us; solid truth
> In front of it, were motion for the world?
> The moral sense grows but by exercise.
>
> (10. 1407–14)

So too with the seeming discrepancies and improbabilities in the story of Caponsacchi and Pompilia: to regard it not as a routine case of adultery but as a witness of God's love, despite the difficulties such an interpretation presents to the reason, is a formidable challenge to faith. Instead of welcoming the Word, men indulge their skepticism by questioning the received tale of the chaste Pompilia just as their descendants in the middle of the nineteenth century were to convert the Son of God into a mere noteworthy figure in the history of the Jews. "Why," exclaims the Pope in bitterness,

> scripture yields no parallel for this!
> The soldiers only threw dice for Christ's coat;
> We want another legend of the Twelve
> Disputing if it was Christ's coat at all,

> Claiming as prize the woof of price—for why?
> The Master was a thief, purloined the same,
> Or paid for it out of the common bag!
>
> (10. 1524–30) [2]

The Pope's attitude toward what men require or reject as "evidences of Christianity" was clearly foreshadowed by that which Browning's figure of the dying St. John expresses in "A Death in the Desert" (1864). The similarity of these two imagined characters, who utter prophetic wisdom from the shadow of extreme old age, is not, however, limited to their ideas. For in both structure and strategy *The Ring and the Book* seems to allude to one particular concern of the higher critics, the problem of the Synoptic Gospels and the relation of the fourth Gospel to them. With its interpretive and transcendental viewpoint, the book of the Pope is to the preceding derivative and partial books of "witness" (the two Halves of Rome and their aristocratic successor) what the fourth Gospel, traditionally but mistakenly attributed to St. John, is to the other three.

Though the three Synoptic Gospels present similar portraits of Jesus, each has its special biases and doctrinal emphases.

---

[2] Two other allusions to the assumptions, methods, and results of scientific criticism of the Bible seem unmistakable. Bottini, introducing his apocryphal parable of Peter, John, and Judas, calls it

> a tale —
> A case in point—what though an apologue
> Grace by tradition,—possibly a fact?
> Tradition must precede all scripture, words
> Serve as our warrant ere our books can be:
> So, to tradition back we needs must go
> For any fact's authority.
>
> (9. 1019–25)

Thus he in effect reverses the Pope's criterion for scriptural authority; to the latter, assent must come first. Guido later refers to the belief that much of the New Testament represents a mere restating, in fresh terms, of old truths:

> Christ's gospel changes names, not things,
> Renews the obsolete, does nothing more!
> Our fire-new gospel is retinkered law,
> Our mercy, justice,—Jove's rechristened God.
>
> (11. 362–65)

Mark's simple account is designed to show God triumphant over his opposition. Matthew, derived from Mark, delineates Jesus fully in order to point out the many ways in which he fulfilled the Old Testament prophecies and supplanted the old laws with his own. Luke's gospel emphasizes God as deliverer. In contrast to these stands the fourth Gospel, emphasizing as it does the mystic spirituality of Christ as coequal with God, and Christ's power to give everlasting life to the faithful. Facts are here subordinated to the feelings and transcendent insights of one who possesses esoteric knowledge presumably vouchsafed only to members of the inner circle.

The Synoptic Gospels differ in detail and organization as well as in overall emphasis. Each omits some crucial details contained in another: Matthew omits the story of Jairus' daughter found in Mark, who in turn omits the death of John the Baptist found in Matthew. Both Matthew and Luke treat of the birth and youth of Christ, omitted entirely in Mark; but these two accounts differ sharply in certain particulars. The only detailed narrative of Christ's last journey on the way to Emmaus is found in Luke; Luke on the other hand omits a few incidents in Galilee reported by both Matthew and Mark. Luke's story of the Passion departs considerably from Mark's. Sometimes there are palpable contradictions: Matthew and Luke cannot be reconciled on the genealogy of Jesus, and Matthew and Mark disagree on the number of blind men from Jericho healed by Jesus, as they do also on the petition of the mother of James and John (in Mark, the sons do the pleading).

These are precisely the kinds of differences that set each of the several narratives of the Franceschini case in *The Ring and the Book* apart from the rest. Browning may well have intended the manifold dissimilarities among the various speakers' versions to illustrate the point the nineteenth-century higher critics made about the authors of the Synoptic Gospels—that each has a bias which is revealed by his emphases, suppressions, innovations, transpositions, and other manipulations of "fact," and that the truth, whole and unalloyed, cannot be found in any one account. In poem as in New Testament, there is the same problem of reconciliation. The Pope's judg-

ment on the successive accounts of the same events in the
Franceschini documents is equally applicable to the Synoptic
Gospels: "Truth, nowhere, lies yet everywhere in these— /
Not absolutely in a portion, yet / Evolvable from the whole."
(10. 228–30.)

Like the author of the fourth Gospel, the Pope comes to
terms with the disagreements of the earlier speakers by dispensing with a consecutive recital of events and rising above
historic circumstance to seek and deliver the story's ultimate
religious significance. To both the Pope and the man once
identified as St. John, the conflicts of detail which so concern
the literal-minded are of no great importance. The question,
What actually happened? is irrelevant; the true issue is, What
do the reported events mean? The Pope, like St. John before
him, therefore is not a narrator but an interpreter, not a
historian but a philosopher and prophet.

Like the higher criticism, natural theology—the attempt to
discover proof of God's existence and evidence of his purposes
in physical creation and the nature of man—used the weapons
of empiricism for ends Browning looked upon as inimical to
true belief. In "Caliban upon Setebos" (1864) he had already
satirized that branch of religious thought, which to many
Victorians had the effect not merely of supplementing but of
actually replacing revelation as a prop of faith. The Pope also
disparages natural theology. In man's search for assurance of
God's supreme strength, intelligence, and beneficence, says the
Pontiff, he appeals to the testimony of creation.

> Conjecture of the worker by the work:
> Is there strength there?—enough: intelligence?
> Ample: but goodness in a like degree?
> Not to the human eye in the present state,
> This isoscele deficient in the base.
>
> (10. 1361–65)

This lack of material evidence of divine love forces the Pope,
on man's behalf, to return to revelation, which supplies
it:

> What lacks, then, of perfection fit for God
> But just the instance which this tale supplies

> Of love without a limit? So is strength,
> So is intelligence; then love is so,
> Unlimited in its self-sacrifice:
> Then is the tale true and God shows complete.
>
> (10. 1366–71)

But recourse to the Bible (or to the miracle of Pompilia) involves confronting difficulties in the interpretation and transmission of the tale. Everywhere one turns, there are obstacles to faith.

Natural theology as such, however, is glanced at only incidentally. It simply adds to the poem's metaphysical and moral argument a small further discreditation of reason as an instrument of knowledge and of ethical decision. Although the human intellect has its uses, says the Pope, the qualities embodied in Pompilia—purity, forbearance, unshakable faith in God—are jewels infinitely more precious than reason and learning:

> Everywhere
> I see in the world the intellect of man,
> That sword, the energy his subtle spear,
> The knowledge which defends him like a shield—
> Everywhere; but they make not up, I think,
> The marvel of a soul like thine, earth's flower
> She holds up to the softened gaze of God!
>
> (10. 1012–18)

And judicious reasoning is always in peril of being subverted by preconception and bias; it becomes, in Browning's concise phrase, "instinctive theorizing whence a fact / Looks to the eye as the eye likes the look" (1. 863–64). Hence, in the hierarchy of ways to knowledge, reason ranks below intuition, in which (given purity of purpose and dedication to the search for God's truth) the spiritual eye penetrates surfaces to discern the meaning within.

I I

Intuition, however named and defined, is invoked by both sinners and saints in explanation of their—and others'—conduct. An unerring indication of their moral character is their choice of the "law" they profess to be moved by: is it nature's or God's?

Leslie Stephen once remarked, "Nature is a word contrived in order to introduce as many equivocations as possible into all the theories, political, legal, artistic or literary, into which it enters." [3] The familiar admonition "Follow nature" could be interpreted in two ways. It could mean either "Follow reason"—the faculty through which nature allegedly spoke, as in Guido's argument—or "Follow the promptings of the heart," the natural moral sense, celebrated by the Cambridge Platonists, which guided Pompilia and Caponsacchi. Browning, as we might expect, makes full use of these equivocations. "Follow nature" is as ambiguous and adaptable an idea in the mouths of the various speakers in *The Ring and the Book* as it was in the actual thought of the seventeenth and eighteenth centuries. "What do they," Half-Rome quotes the Roman court as demanding when it assesses Caponsacchi's and Pompilia's conduct, "but obey the natural law?" (2.1103.) But later Half-Rome, in his own person, invokes the same principle in defense of Guido: "Who is it dares impugn the natural law? / Deny God's word 'the faithless wife shall die?' " (2. 1477–78.)

Guido bases his self-justification on the power and legitimacy of the amalgam of instincts and impulses he glibly categorizes as "natural law." The terms in which natural law is urged as a defense of his actions provide an insight into the status of the idea in Guido's time (as Browning, at any rate, interpreted history) as well as a vehicle for Browning's com-

[3] Quoted by Basil Willey, *The Eighteenth-Century Background* (London, 1940), p. 10. The discussion in the following paragraphs of nature as a leading concept in the historical milieu of the poem is heavily indebted (even for a few phrases) to this luminous book.

The very equivocation and instability of the idea of natural law are, from Browning's viewpoint, additional counts against it. It is an ideological victim of flux, its definition and authority constantly susceptible to change; therefore it cannot provide a true staff for man to lean upon. Once again human knowledge and judgment are revealed to be subject to an instrument which is itself invalidated by ambiguity and changeableness.

mentary on its application to ethics in the middle of the nineteenth century. In earlier Christian centuries, the law of nature inherited from classic pagan thought became the law of God, or at least that part of God's law which is made known through reason. But even so early, the concept was ambiguous: "nature" could refer either to man's prelapsarian state—the golden age of primal innocence—or to his fallen condition in modern times. In Guido's age, the end of the seventeenth century, natural law became a liberating rather than a regulating principle, and, as his use of it amply reveals, it was seized upon as a license for the indulgence of unregenerate impulse and thus as a rationalization for self-seeking, predatory, ruthless conduct. The law of nature was read, by those who wished to do so, not as the law of God but as the law of the jungle.

Against this anarchic and atheistic interpretation of natural law was posed the one which Browning adopted. In his condemnation of Guido's argument from natural instinct and reason and his own contrasted use of the argument from grace and conscience to defend the actions of the sympathetic characters, Browning shows himself aligned with Bishop Butler, whose influence upon his thinking has never, perhaps, been sufficiently realized. "Brutes, indeed," as Professor Willey summarizes Butler, "act according to their natures in following the determination of instinct and environment. But man, in addition to passions and affections, possesses the 'principle of reflection' or conscience, the faculty which approves and disapproves and recognizes the higher and the lower." [4]

The assertion of the ascendancy of emotion over reason as the governing "natural" principle of human conduct was to be the gradual work of the eighteenth century, eroding the rationalism personified by Guido. In this respect, Pompilia and Caponsacchi may be said to foreshadow the coming age of romanticism, although their consultation of their emotions was prompted far more by specifically religious motives than would be true of the typical eighteenth-century man or woman of romantic sensibility. But it is Guido, not the lovers, who

[4] *Ibid.*, p. 86.

provides the chief means by which Browning uses the intellectual situation on the eve of the eighteenth century to decry the power of naturalistic, rationalistic thought in his own era.[5] Like Guido, liberal Victorian thinkers tended to substitute "nature"—now defined as the totality of the mechanical laws that govern the universe and the human race—for a transcendental personal God. Browning's attitude is well summed up in the implied significance of an assertion of Guido and a response by the Pope thousands of lines later. "I appeal to God," cries Guido, "—what says Himself, / How lessons Nature when I look to learn?" (5. 1542–43.) The deistic identification of God with nature—or, more accurately, the assumption that nature is what was formerly named God—is evident enough; [6] and the Pope tersely rebukes it. "What I call God," he says, "fools call Nature." (10. 1072–73.)

The poem's philosophical tension on this vital subject is supplied by the conflict of views on the relation between nature and God and the subjection of man to natural law. The children of darkness, typified by Guido, either differentiate between God and nature—maintaining that nature's law is by no means necessarily in harmony with God's, which indeed it may supersede when desirable—or, as in the preceding quotation, demote God to the sum of the impersonal forces controlling the universe. The children of light, on the other hand, place nature within God's realm and under his command; through it men may receive his message.

There is a similar conflict of interpretation in respect to instinct, the irrational force that determines, and can be used *ex post facto* to extenuate, men's deeds: how wide is its acceptable power, and does it derive from nature outside God, or from nature under God? The range of man's "permissible

---

[5] Some of the views Browning expresses in *The Ring and the Book* are strikingly similar to those of the guiding spirits of the Broad Church movement. His response to the problem of miracles suggests that of Thomas Arnold, and his attitude toward the higher criticism was anticipated by both Arnold and Coleridge.

[6] By themselves, the lines could be read another way: God and Nature are not synonymous but are separate entities—Guido appeals to each in turn. But elsewhere (5. 1171) he explicitly identifies them: he is, he says, "confident in Nature,—which is God."

impulse," as the Pope calls it, runs "from the mere liking of the eye and ear, / To the true longing of the heart that loves." Each level of creation has its own appropriate gamut; the brute's appetites are brutish in comparison with man's permissible ones, but since they fitly belong to him, they are not to be deplored (10. 537–41). Guido's great sin, however, is that he cultivates and gives way to the "low instinct, base pretension," an obsession with "the vile of life" (5. 511–12) which is a betrayal of his human state, and above all of his Christian heritage. As he says, he is a pagan, appropriately enough for a native of a town that flourished long before the birth of Christianity—"a primitive religionist— / As should the aboriginary be / I boast myself, Etruscan, Aretine" (11. 1917–19). As moral aboriginary, he occasionally resembles Browning's most famous representation of man-as-beast, the decidedly pre-Etruscan and amphibious Caliban. Guido is a believer in "natural caprice" (11. 1437), an arbitrary determinant of action which he attributes to the Cardinal and the Abate, just as the Caliban of the islands had attributed it to Setebos, the naturalist's god, whom he imitated: "You favour one, / Brow-beat another, leave alone a third." (11. 1435–36.) He identifies himself, in Caliban's very accents, with all propitiators of a vengeful deity who restrict their worship to self-interest: "Why should we do our duty past the due? / When the sky darkens, Jove is wroth,—say prayer! / When the sun shines and Jove is glad,—sing psalm!" (11. 1949–51.) And like Caliban when the moment of reckoning comes, Guido frantically tries to recant all his previous blasphemies: "All was folly—I laughed and mocked!" (11. 2417.) His ultimate appeal to Abate, Cardinal, Christ, Maria, God, and Pompilia recalls Caliban's craven desperate resolve to "love" (actually to placate) Setebos—for the sake of his own skin.

As the very incarnation of "the natural man" (1. 961), Guido invokes instinct both to justify his thirst for the blood of summary vengeance—a cover-up, as the Pope observes, for the even blacker appetite of greed—and to rationalize what is really cowardice. He can urge, in specious apology for his evil character and deeds, "So was I made, a weak thing that gave way / To truth, to impulse only strong since true, / And hated, lusted, used guile, forwent faith." (10. 357–59.) But the Pope, who ascribes these words to him, finds in them no excuse. We have seen that Guido pleads the promptings of instinct to justify his murder of Pompilia and the Comparini, man's law and God's having (he says) both failed him; and, in fact, popular sentiment largely agreed with him that had he killed the fugitive wife and priest when he surprised them at Castel-nuovo, he would have been exonerated on the ground that "nature must have her way" and that "the power o' the pulse" cannot be denied (4. 1133, 1146). Having eventually done the deed and been condemned to death for it, Guido puts the plea of instinct to another use. He defends his first defense, so to speak, on the ground that, now that he has emerged from his purgatory and "Health is returned, and sanity of soul / No-wise indifferent to the body's harm," he finds "the instinct bids me save my life" (5. 1740–42), a plea reduplicated in his second speech.

Arcangeli adopts the same argument from instinct in his formal pleading. He deduces man's obligation to act as man (i.e., to avenge marital dishonor) from the natural law which governs the rest of creation (8. 531–40, quoted above, pp. 156–57). Moreover,

> Revelation old and new admits
> The natural man may effervesce in ire,
> O'er flood earth, o'er froth heaven with foamy rage,
> At the first puncture to his self-respect.
>
> (8. 684–87)

In Christian law, however, "defense of honor" does not cover the punishment of an erring wife. On the contrary, "Law, Gospel and the Church" (8. 718) specifically forbid it. Natural law, happily, comes to the rescue. "But who," Arcangeli represents all three as urging the frustrated Guido, "hath barred thee primitive revenge, / Which, like fire damped and dammed up, burns more fierce? / Use thou thy natural privilege of man." (8. 719–21.)

Laden though it is with ambiguity and potentiality for evil, the exercise of natural instinct as a guide to human choice has, Guido claims, the sanction of the church. He admits that he has transgressed man's law, which according to his view originated in a kind of *contrat social* to keep the race's hedonistic impulses within bounds (11. 515–45). But he maintains that the church invited him to exercise his "proper manly instinct" in its company: "We'll compass joy by concert; take with us / The regular irregular way i' the wood." (11. 799–802.) Rather than force him either openly to indulge or to renounce his instincts, it encouraged him to conceal them, "sheep's wool / Over wolf's skin" (11. 824–25). The church, he implies, thus recognized the presence of animal passions (which Guido euphemizes as "The inexorable need in man for life" [11. 1980; cf. 11. 2011, 2419]), even though, unlike the pagan religion, it officially deplored them.

>   —blame yourselves
> For this eruption of the pent-up soul
> You prisoned first and played with afterward!
> "Deny myself" meant simply pleasure you,
> The sacred and superior, save the mark!
> You,—whose stupidity and insolence
> I must defer to, soothe at every turn,—
> Whose swine-like snuffling greed and grunting lust
> I had to wink at or help gratify,—
> While the same passions,—dared they perk in me,
> Me, the immeasurably marked, by God,
> Master of the whole world of such as you,—
> I, boast such passions? 'Twas "Suppress them straight! ["]
> .   .   .   .
> My nature, when the outrage was too gross,
> Widened itself an outlet over-wide
> By way of answer?—sought its own relief
> With more of fire and brimstone than you wished?
> All your own doing: preachers, blame yourselves!
>   (11. 1493–1517)

But once he has fully indulged his passions he can still claim readmittance to the human race:

> Let me turn wolf, be whole, and sate, for once,—
> Wallow in what is now a wolfishness

Coerced too much by the humanity
That's half of me as well! Grow out of man,
Glut the wolf-nature,—what remains but grow
Into the man again, be man indeed
And all man?

(11. 2054–60)

Insinuating and blunt by turns, Guido's defense of his wolfish
actions contains its own rebuttal. In this second speech of his,
the natural law adduced in his behalf by his lawyer turns out
to be a feral ethic in which the distinction between good and
evil is erased and satisfaction of the vilest passions of man's
animal nature is the be-all and end-all of existence.

Meanwhile Bottini is busy citing the natural law also, except
that now, instead of justifying satisfaction of dishonor, it
requires the wife to manifest "The proper piety to lord and
king / And husband" (9. 252–54). But this is merely the
other side of the same coin, because inferentially a wife's
unnatural neglect of this duty also would warrant her husband's taking stern action: she suffers in either case. More
generally, Bottini attributes all of Pompilia's alleged wantonness to her obeying what he takes to be the natural law of her
sex. Far from being found reprobate, she should be applauded
for following her feminine instincts, especially that of self-
preservation. But having done so, she ran afoul of the principle of *honoris causa;* which means at the very least, if we are
to believe both Arcangeli and Bottini, that there are separate
and irreconcilable "natural laws" for husbands and for wives,
and furthermore that the law even for one sex contains inherent
contradictions—for a woman cannot indulge her supposedly
"natural" bent for promiscuity and at the same time conform
to the "natural" requirement that she be true to her husband.
As an ethical concept the law of nature, however defined, is
shown to be a highly convenient and flexible device whereby
men circumvent the laws of society and of God.

All this vicious recommendation of instinct as a guide to
conduct, especially as it is imputed to the church itself, is
recognized for what it is when we hear expressed "the true
instinct"—the adjective must be stressed—"of an old good
man / Who happens to hate darkness and love light" (12.

593–94). Whatever the errors of the churchmen beneath him, the Pope is guided by an instinct which is simply the representation of God's will made evident within man. So with the natural law whose moral authority and imperatives have been so recklessly twisted by the poem's casuists. The substitution of "nature's law," properly understood, for "God" is a matter only of terminology, to accommodate the needs of a new day, just as science provides a new means of formulating men's response to, and explanation of, natural phenomena. The idea of law, says the Pope, replaces animism, which served at an earlier stage of society:

> To the child, the sea is angry, for it roars;
> Frost bites, else why the tooth-like fret on face?
> Man makes acoustics deal with the sea's wrath,
> Explains the choppy cheek by chymic law,—
> To both, remains one and the same effect
> On drum of ear and root of nose, change cause
> Never so thoroughly: so our heart be struck,
> What care I,—by God's gloved hand or the bare?
>   (10. 1399–1406)

In the new vocabulary of moral forces, "Warmth / By law, and light by rule" have superseded the "unacknowledged powers / O' the air," the "uncommissioned meteors" not comprehended by law and rule that once stirred men to virtuous action, and still occasionally do (10. 1552–54). For Caponsacchi saw such a meteor. When he put to the test *his* "instinct of the natural man" (10. 1582), unlike Guido he heard and heeded the voice of God. The moving story of his hesitation when Pompilia's beauty and plight called to him shows the self-protective instinct (not to be equated with Guido's outright cowardice) at war with intuitive recognition of his duty to risk all in her service. Thought, as he says (6. 937–46), was of no use to him; he abandoned it as positively as did Tertium Quid, on Guido's behalf, when Guido's murderous instincts came to the fore (4. 1521–42). But the selfish instincts that had tempted him to have nothing to do with Pompilia's peril were left behind "when at the last we did rush each on each, / By no chance but because God willed it so— / [and] The spark of truth was struck from out our souls" (6. 1812–14). But the struggle was not ended when that impulse of elective affinity leaped the gap. The Pope, profoundly cognizant of the natural needs of men, realizes that Pompilia's physical presence may have induced further temptation.

> In thought, word and deed,
> How throughout all thy warfare thou wast pure,
> I find it easy to believe: and if
> At any fateful moment of the strange
> Adventure, the strong passion of that strait,
> Fear and surprise, may have revealed too much,—
> As when a thundrous midnight, with black air
> That burns, rain-drops that blister, breaks a spell,
> Draws out the excessive virtue of some sheathed
> Shut unsuspected flower that hoards and hides
> Immensity of sweetness,—so, perchance,
> Might the surprise and fear release too much
> The perfect beauty of the body and soul
> Thou savedst in thy passion for God's sake,
> He who is Pity: was the trial sore?
> Temptation sharp? Thank God a second time!
> Why comes temptation but for man to meet
> And master and make crouch beneath his foot,
> And so be pedestalled in triumph?
>
> (10. 1168–86)

The difference between Caponsacchi's response to temptation and Guido's was, quite simply, dictated by the difference between man and beast. The test of man's moral sense is the ability to reject those instincts which serve self-interest of whatever kind and to heed instead those which lead to selfless and, if necessary, heroic deeds. Both Caponsacchi and Guido took positive action as the result of consulting instinct, but the deed of one was chivalric, while that of the other was villainous.

The former deed, moreover, was a sign of healthy growth, while the latter was evidence of moral stagnation. Man, says the Pope, is not irrevocably confined to one state of being by

the assumption that he is made of mortal elements impervious
to change:

> the fault, the obduracy to good,
> Lies not with the impracticable stuff
> Whence man is made, his very nature's fault,
> As if it were of ice, the moon may gild
> Not melt, or stone, 'twas meant the sun should warm
> Not make bear flowers,—nor ice nor stone to blame:
> But it can melt, that ice, and bloom, that stone,
> Impassible to rule of day and night!
>
> (10. 1538–45)

Caponsacchi's ice melts, his stone blooms; and he thereby
proves his manhood. Guido, however, like the bastard Edmund
in *King Lear*, is committed to nature, which does not change;
he therefore boasts that he is "changeless." But to Browning
the boast is, in fact, self-condemnation, for moral growth,
which Guido renounces, is the very principle of human life.
Guido's invocation of natural law to explain and justify his
conduct is as fallacious as it is fatalistic.

The harmony of God's law with nature's, rightly interpreted, is most specifically illustrated in Pompilia's decision to
leave Arezzo for Rome: "The strange and passionate precipi-
tance / Of maiden startled into motherhood / Which changes
body and soul by nature's law." (3. 1530–32.) Although it is
the combined promptings of psychological and external nature
which move her, she discovers that these are actually God's
voice sounding through his creation.

> A broad yellow sun-beam was let fall
> From heaven to earth,—a sudden·drawbridge lay,
> Along which marched a myriad merry motes,
> Mocking the flies that crossed them and recrossed
> In rival dance, companions new-born too.
> On the house-eaves, a dripping shag of weed
> Shook diamonds on each dull grey lattice-square,
> As first one, then another bird leapt by,
> And light was off, and lo was back again,
> Always with one voice,—where are two such joys?—
> The blessed building-sparrow! I stepped forth,

Stood on the terrace,—o'er the roofs, such sky!
My heart sang, "I too am to go away,
I too have something I must care about,
Carry away with me to Rome, to Rome!
The bird brings hither sticks and hairs and wool,
And nowhere else i' the world; what fly breaks rank,
Falls out of the procession that befits,
From window here to window there, with all
The world to choose,—so well he knows his course?
I have my purpose and my motive too,
My march to Rome, like any bird or fly!"

                                        (7. 1225–46) [7]

This is a far cry from the instincts Guido ascribes to her—
those of calculated behavior designed to aggravate her husband's wounds ("This worst offence of not offending more
. . . / I'll not believe but instinct wrought in this" [11.
1342–43]) and of seeking aid by bleating "till for pity pure, /
The village roused" (11. 2302–4). Nor is it any closer to the
version of Pompilia's instinctive behavior conjured up by the
lascivious Bottini. But neither man could conceive of anything
higher.

I I I

In his dual and historically compatible role of natural man
and rational man, Guido ascribes his unbelief, along with his
other unadmirable moral and intellectual qualities, to the age
at large. Although the claim has already received support in

[7] Additional evidence of the rightness of Pompilia's instinctive
response is found in the fact that the swallow (here, the sparrow)
nesting in the eaves after wintering in the mud is a medieval and
Renaissance symbol of the Incarnation. She too is affected by the
mystic sense of birth, or rebirth, manifested by the bird's activity.
Directly opposed to this passage and the earlier one (3. 1527–38)
suggestive of the Annunciation are those in which Guido credits to
"instinct" his "love of life" which prompts him to resist execution. In
the one case, instinct speaks in behalf of a life barely begun, and
therefore to be protected at all costs; in the other, it is invoked in
behalf of a life fifty years old and sinful beyond reach of
redemption.

the Pope's vehement denunciation of the new breed of "educated man" (10. 1976) represented by the worldly higher clergy and secular intellectuals of Tertium Quid's breed, at the same time the Pope has denied its universal application: the rank and file of Christians suffer illness of another, though hardly less disturbing, sort. Whatever the validity of Guido's argument, he is an extreme exemplar of a doubting, naturalistic age, the logical product of rigorous atheism and pragmatism. And through him, both as a representative and as a commentator, are expressed Browning's deep misgivings about the state of belief in modern times. With appropriate allowance for changed conditions but with close correspondence of essentials, Guido's exemplification and description of an unbelieving, hypocritical Rome is Browning's indictment of the Europe, and particularly, one assumes, the England of 1864–68. In this respect, Guido is, in both senses of the term, a prophetic figure.

In his second monologue Guido endeavors at considerable length to discredit contemporary Christianity as a source of moral imperatives, alleging that faith is now merely a hypocritical posture and therefore has no force to govern men's actions, notably his own. The truth, he tells his would-be confessors, is that for all significant purposes Christianity is dead.

> I say, if ever was such faith at all
> Born in the world, by your community
> Suffered to live its little tick of time,
> 'Tis dead of age now, ludicrously dead;
> Honour its ashes, if you be discreet,
> In epitaph only!
>
> (11. 558–63)

In this Rome, so-called believers actually are but feigning faith; if they became admitted nonbelievers, their characters and actions would undergo no essential change.

> Why should things change because men disbelieve?
> What's incompatible, in the whited tomb,
> With bones and rottenness one inch below?
> What saintly act is done in Rome to-day

> But might be prompted by the devil,—"is"
> I say not,—"has been, and again may be."
>
> (11. 602–7)

The presence or absence of true faith affects merely the attributed motives and the practical consequences of an act, not its nature. Suppose two cases. In one, a papal guard suddenly flings down his halberd, dashes along the corridor, and disrupts the Pope's interview with an ambassador. In the other, a papal official, awaiting an audience with the Pope, with equal suddenness bursts from the Vatican and rushes home. If, says Guido, I now waved a wand and miraculously turned Rome into a society of true believers, these two mysterious, decisive actions could be explained as sudden visitations of faith. The halberdier has been "convinced of sin" and the Pope, seizing the occasion (this in itself is part of the "miracle"), with perfect Christian forbearance at the interruption suspends his conference "Till he secure that prize, outweighs the world, / A soul, relieve the sentry of his qualm!" (11. 636–37.) The waiting Referendary, similarly, has been inspired by a "master-stroke of argument" that will destroy Molinism forever; in his zeal, he rushes home to write it all down, leaving "who likes / Go pacify the Pope: there's Christ to serve!" (11. 638–47.) These acts produce upon uncomprehending beholders the same predictable effect—the appearance, at least, of insubordination or lack of diplomacy—and are therefore deemed culpable because nothing materially profitable results. The spiritual rewards gained from true Christian witness are lost upon the world; thus, these "miracles" of true faith have proved abortive.[8]

[8] There seems to be a flaw in Guido's argument. He says that his hypothetical miracle, the conversion of Rome to genuine Christian faith, affects everyone:

> feigning *everywhere* grows fact,
> Professors turn possessors, realise
> The faith they play with as a fancy now,
> And bid it operate, have *full* effect
> On *every* circumstance of life.
>
> (11. 589–93; italics supplied)

One would suppose that this total conversion would result in all Rome's being blessed with spiritual insight, the ability instantly to perceive the true motives behind deeds, especially when those motives

Moreover, says Guido, the same actions can be explained just as adequately without assuming they are motivated by faith. Revoke the "miracle" and restore the Rome we know. The halberdier acts as he does because he suspects a Gunpowder Plot underneath the Vatican pavement; the Referendary races home because he has just remembered he left his jewel case unlocked.

> Which means,
> That both these, each in his degree, would do
> Just that,—for a comparative nothing's sake,
> And thereby gain approval and reward,—
> Which, done for what Christ says is worth the world,
> Procures the doer curses, cuffs and kicks.
>
> (11. 663–68)

Any action conceivably is motivated either by moral or religious impulse or by pragmatic self-interest; but it wins the applause and rewards of the world only when its results are materially evident and beneficial to the doer—when, that is to say, they can be understood and appreciated by the run of men. An altruistic, or at least spiritually motivated, act may produce bad results (in the eyes of the world) and therefore be condemned; a selfish act may produce good results and therefore be praised. In either case, there is a crucial discrepancy between appearance and reality, or, more accurately, between intention and execution. The prudent way of life is to take account of this discrepancy and, in the Benthamite manner, calculate the probable consequence of an act, regardless of its motive.

Guido directs at his listeners, the Cardinal and the Abate, a further series of examples designed to show that human motives and responses are deeply tinged by self-interest. Either man, he says, would unhesitatingly rescue a friend in danger of being poisoned—so long as he is a respectable guest; but

---

are religious. Yet, in the examples Guido supplies, none of the onlookers seems the wiser for his freshly acquired Christianity; actions are as freely misinterpreted as ever. Only the doers of the deeds have been affected by the new order; nor has this order affected the "rewards" they can expect for their conduct.

neither would perform the more Christian act of saving a
thief's soul from hellfire. And, he goes on to argue, circumstances affect results. Warning a friend at Mass that his wine
cask is leaking will, under ordinary circumstances, win the
friend's gratitude; but if a bishop is in attendance at that same
Mass, the friend will brusquely bid the informant go and turn
off the tap himself. The better part of ethics is discrimination.
"He and you know the relative worth of things, / What is
permissible or inopportune." (11. 693–94.)

To win the rewards of this life, Guido continues, often
demands hypocrisy. The great majority of sane people, inside
and outside the church, are unbelievers; their pretense of faith
is mere politic sham. They know that faith, being merely a
convenience and a guise, is inadequate in crises. At such
times, even self-styled believers must act according to their
hedonistic and egocentric nature. Christian faith cannot sustain a life, because it is too easily (or necessarily) abandoned
when occasion requires; and it contains an element of doubt
which Guido cannot risk.

> Therefore, I descend
> To the next faith with no dubiety—
> Faith in the present life, made last as long
> And prove as full of pleasure as may hap,
> Whatever pain it cause the world.
>
> (11. 723–27)

Pure hedonism, like unbelief, has the advantage over Christianity in that it can be held to consistently and is not susceptible to doubt. "Entire faith, or else complete unbelief,— /
Aught between has my loathing and contempt." (11.
730–31.) [9] For this reason Guido urges that the race revert to
its primitive paganism, which suits the convenience of men far
better than does Christianity with its persistent but irrelevant
difficulties of belief. For what is Christianity, after all, but

[9] Cf. the cry of Gigadibs, the skeptical journalist: "Whole faith, or
none!" ("Bishop Blougram's Apology," line 598.) Bishop Blougram's
systematic, casuistical, and fundamentally pragmatic demolition of
this demand offers an interesting contrast to the way in which Browning deals with Guido's similar position in this poem.

remodeled paganism, new in name and with the distracting element of doubt added, but unchanged in self-serving spirit?

> So, the living truth
> Revealed to strike Pan dead, ducks low at last,
> Prays leave to hold its own and live good days
> Provided it go masque grotesquely, called
> Christian not Pagan?

(11. 1973–77)

While Guido's pleading is of course undercut by his unconcealed private motive of exempting himself from the judgment of Christian morality, all that he urges against the Christian religion must be read in remembrance of what the Pope has already said, especially in response to the long argument the Pontiff fancies he hears Euripides making (10. 1666–1789). Here the cultivated pagan past speaks, in the grave accents of classical discourse. In my age, says Euripides, there was no promise of salvation or immortality, none of the supernatural sanction which underlies Christianity. Yet even in a fatalistic culture I laid emphasis upon virtue; the moral ideals I and my fellow stoics advocated were to become essentially those of St. Paul, only the terms differing. In its ethical nature Christianity differs little from the Greek religion, which had neither God nor Christ. And my age had the advantage over Christianity in that we could see more clearly, were less racked with doubt and misgiving.

Thus Euripides by clear implication poses the same question Guido raises in an entirely different spirit: Why not a return to paganism? The tragedian's own statement of the case is infinitely more attractive than Guido's. It is, in its basic principles, a recognizable argument for the kind of ethical, man-centered religion which, at the moment *The Ring and the Book* was being written and published, was urged by the Comtists and, at considerable distance from them, by Matthew Arnold.

The extensive association of natural law with men's baser appetites and impulses in connection with the arguments for and against Guido (and Bottini's "for" Pompilia) has pre-

pared an answer the Pope can make: namely, that Christianity
provides a higher, nobler alternative to naturalism—that by its
very character it seeks to raise man above the level of the
brute. But Euripides anticipates this. My age, he says, was also
a naturalistic one. "I saw that there are, first and above all, /
The hidden forces, blind necessities, / Named Nature, but the
thing's self unconceived." (10. 1733–35.) Christianity has
conceived "the thing's self" and called it God:

> The beings so contrarious that seemed gods,
> Prove just His operation manifold
> And multiform, translated, as must be,
> Into intelligible shape so far
> As suits our sense and sets us free to feel.
>
> (10. 1766–70)

But Euripides' age was as well equipped to rise above naturalistic ethics as would be a later age with its concept of one God.
Although the lack of any promise of eternal reward invited
men to "live brutishly" (10. 1701), Euripides readily
"Adopted virtue as my rule of life, / Waived all reward, and
loved for loving's sake" (10. 1710–11).

Reasonable where Guido will be cynical and reckless, Euripides demands of the Pope: Where, then, is Christianity's
gain? Is Christianity in truth anything more than what Guido
will call it, "retinkered" natural—pagan—law? (11. 364)
The Pope replies only obliquely; the succeeding passage is
more addressed, by anticipation, to Guido's description of his
age as one of rampant unbelief and crass values than to Euripides' advocacy of an enlightened ethical naturalism, an Ar-
noldian "religion of humanity." For it is Guido and all he
stands for that is the most urgent problem in 1698, a problem
epitomized, once its implications are understood, by Guido's
picture of the millennium that will be brought about if his life
is spared:

> And when, in times made better through your brave
> Decision now,—might but Utopia be!—
> Rome rife with honest women and strong men,
> Manners reformed, old habits back once more,
> Customs that recognize the standard worth,—

> The wholesome household rule in force again,
> Husbands once more God's representative,
> Wives like the typical Spouse once more, and Priests
> No longer men of Belial, with no aim
> At leading silly women captive, but
> Of rising to such duties as yours now.
>
> (5. 2037–47)

Utopia, in short, will be achieved not by the creation of the heavenly city of the Christian philosophers but merely by restoring the Roman *status quo ante*, when, as Guido interprets history, pagan hedonism ruled and conditions were specifically framed to suit husbands' comfort. This grotesque reduction of values is not Guido's alone; it is expressed also by the "new tribunal now / Higher than God's—the educated man's" (10. 1975–76), which recommends Guido's acquittal (though it stops short of urging the papal blessing) on the ground that "the main prop" of society "was, is, and shall prove / —Supremacy of husband over wife!" (10. 2033–34.) The argument that marital honor is "the supreme good" proves, therefore, to typify all the values of a generation of nominal Christians. Guido is the representative "votarist of the mode," the modernist of skeptical, if not outright atheistic tendencies, who now crowns the age-long succession of "brute-beast . . . Pagan, Gentile, Jew, / . . . Christian" (8. 860–61). Upon such matters as the private needs of the world's Guidos, nothing higher, are focused the ethical concerns of "the spirit of culture," of "civilization"—a society in the course of becoming secularized, aspiring to a "golden age" when "Christianity and Pope" will be replaced by "Civilization and the Emperor" (10. 2016, 2027–29).

The tone of that golden age, if and when it comes, will be set by men such as Guido and his brothers, who "like the lowest of life's appetites,"

> live for greed, ambition, lust, revenge;
> Attain these ends by force, guile: hypocrite,
> To-day, perchance to-morrow recognized
> The rational man, the type of commonsense.
>
> (10. 1933–40)

There promises to be a "multitude" of these new men, who

> will fall, perchance,
> Quite through the crumbling truth subjacent late,
> Sink to the next discoverable base,
> Rest upon human nature, take their stand
> On what is fact, the lust and pride of life!

(10. 1887–91)

Guido himself may die, but the fact that his type exists at all, not to say flourishes, is enough to cast the future of Christian society into the gravest doubt. For Browning considers him to be not merely "the rational man," the man whose "stand on what is fact" reaches down into the Caliban mire, but the very symbol of Antichrist, that arch-deceiver who "denieth the Father and the Son" (1 John 2:22). Browning of course does not conceive of Count Guido Franceschini as having the proportions of the Antichrist described in the Epistles of John and in Revelation. Guido is a human being, satanic enough, but not an apocalyptic visitation. As a portent, however, he is terrible enough to appall men of good will, for his denial of the fundamental Christian truth embodies the spirit of Antichrist operative in late seventeenth-century Rome and, by extension, mid-nineteenth-century England.[10]

Is an accurate forecast of the future to be read in the generation of Guido, naturalistic in thought, rejecting scriptural authority, reliant solely on human power and self-regarding instinct? In the dialectic of time, the Pope implies, it is quite probable that they will next be supreme. This dark augury is substantiated from another source, the responses which the Franceschini case elicited from mankind at large as

[10] The ordinary people whose opinions are quoted by Half-Rome and the Other Half-Rome glimpse the truth. Old Luca Cini exclaims that in the Comparini murders "the world's wickedness seals up the sum: / . . . Antichrist's surely come" (2. 125–27), and an attendant at Pompilia's bedside also detects the advent of Antichrist (3. 94–96). But, as usual, the idea veers off in the wrong direction. Although they identify Guido's crime as symptomatic of the coming of Antichrist, they associate the wickedness, however illogically, with "Molinos' doctrine" and fail to realize that the fulfilment of Revelation's prophecy is foreshadowed in Guido himself.

represented by the spectators at Arezzo and Rome, by the two Halves of Rome and Tertium Quid and the lawyers. The controversial characters and events of the affair have tested afresh man's ability to come to grips with the obvious imperfection and elusiveness of truth—and to profit from the struggle. The Pope, echoing a refrain heard throughout Browning's poetry, asserts that the inescapable element of doubt in life is to be welcomed because it challenges man's will and exercises his moral faculty.

> Solid truth
> In front of it, were motion for the world?
> The moral sense grows but by exercise.
>
> .   .   .   .
>
> Neither does this astonish at the end,
> That, whereas I can so receive and trust,
> Men, made with hearts and souls the same as mine,
> Reject and disbelieve,—subordinate
> The future to the present,—sin, nor fear.
> This I refer still to the foremost fact,
> Life is probation and this earth no goal
> But starting-point of man: compel him strive,
> Which means, in man, as good as reach the goal,—
> Why institute that race, his life, at all?
>
> (10. 1412–14, 1429–38)

In fact, man truly lives only when there is a healthy element of uncertainty against which he must contend; doubt is the prime conditioner of the moral muscles.

But the Pope deplores man's failure to rise to this latest renewal of the perennial challenge, the manifold dubieties of the Franceschini case. And because, for anyone who was moved to see, the case involved a fresh enactment of the salvation story, the almost universal inertia amounted to a willful rejection of divine grace. Far from asserting his adventurous strength by seizing the opportunity to vigorously pursue truth through the endless thickets of error, man has once more proved himself content to remain enslaved to "the primal curse / Which bids man love as well as make a lie" (1. 643–44). The sheer perversity of the human addiction to falsehood, which nearly always overrules the equally inherent but weaker yearning for truth, chills the Pope's heart, especially in face of the fact that the supreme truth has been made known and its pricelessness declared in Scripture. "What does the world, told truth, but lie the more?" (10. 672.) With considerable reason does Celestino declare in his sermon that the world "hates white," the white equally of truth and of goodness (12. 573). The text of his sermon is drawn from Romans 3:4, "Let God be true, and every man / A liar" (12. 453–54):

> if you rather be disposed to see
> In the result of the long trial here,—
> This dealing doom to guilt and doling praise
> To innocency,—any proof that truth
> May look for vindication from the world,
> Much will you have misread the signs, I say.
>
> .   .   .   .
>
> Because Pompilia's purity prevails,
> Conclude you, all truth triumphs in the end?
>
> (12. 459–73)

The sequence of statements in the poem's closing books, to which these despairing words provide a climax, must give pause to readers who, clinging to the old notion that Browning was a congenital and indefatigable optimist, expect to find there a predominantly hopeful assessment of man's prospects. Guido's second speech, the manifesto of a Godless way of life, is enclosed by separate but equally bleak estimates—the Pope's and Celestino's—of the human appetite for truth. Nor do the incidental events reported in Book 12 contain any suggestion that a new birth of Christian spirit is about to occur in the wake of Guido's execution. Although it is true that the cause of righteousness and justice wins a victory of sorts when Guido is sent to a hell of his own making, the dark atmosphere of the poem's close, with the taint of the wormwood star corrupting all, forbids our reading the poem optimistically.

Yet while the procession returning from Guido's execution may seem irrevocably headed for the gateway to the new age of Voltaire and Hume, the prospect Browning surveys through the Pope's eyes is not irrevocably black. For the very fact that the new age promises to be one of widespread and profound doubt may prove in the end to be man's salvation. The moral malaise of late seventeenth-century Rome, as the Pope sees it, is traceable to the prevalent overassurance in religious thought, which is the converse of doubt. Lacking the stern challenge it had in the earliest Christian centuries when the new faith had to fend off the enemies that surrounded it, the religious spirit has subsided from passion to complacency: "We have got too familiar with the light." (10. 1793.) Or, as St. John puts it in "A Death in the Desert," a lamp surfeited with oil is soon extinguished. Consequently, the moral sense which depends for its vitality upon the health of religious faith has grown fat and pursy. Worldly satisfactions are too easily won. "The politic, the thrifty way" (10. 1834), neither encumbered nor directed by religious sanction but paying off well enough, has become the mode of modern ethics. "Is it not," demands the Pope, "this ignoble confidence, / Cowardly hardihood, that dulls and damps, / Makes the old heroism impossible?" (10. 1847–49.)

Because the result may be a renewal of man's spiritual energy and an elevation of his moral sights, the Pope welcomes the signs of a coming age of questioning, an age prefigured, as we noted at the end of the preceding chapter, by the Molinists, who threaten to "shake / This torpor of assurance from our creed, / Re-introduce the doubt discarded" when Christianity ceased to be beleaguered by its first enemies (10. 1852–54).

> As we broke up that old faith of the world,
> Have we, next age, to break up this the new—
> Faith, in the thing, grown faith in the report—
> Whence need to bravely disbelieve report
> Through increased faith in thing reports belie?
>
> (10. 1863–67)

"Faith in the report," the Bible as history, will lose its conviction and therefore its moral effectiveness; and so men will have to return to first Christian principles, to "faith in the thing," the spiritual truths—not the vulnerable historical ones—shadowed forth in the biblical story. The way back to that faith will lie not through reliance upon a scriptural tradition which no longer compels belief, but through personal illumination such as the Molinists strive for—assent generated from within. "Man's God," the portrait offered in revelation, must be replaced by "God's God," "the living face" seen by the soul (10. 1872–73). For the impotent letter of Christianity must be substituted its revitalized spirit.

This is the urgency which confronts the race as one age gives way to a new. "The impatient antimasque," says the Pope, "treads close on kibe / O' the very masque's self it will mock." (10. 1903–4.) The onward movement of society, symbolized in the extended figure of a dance—a familiar Renaissance trope for the progress of universal order—will present the dancers with a clear choice. The one alternative is exemplified by Guido, the other by Caponsacchi. The Pope's hopefulness, such as it is, of course resides not in Guido, bidding mankind follow him back along the well-posted road to paganism, but in Caponsacchi, "the first experimentalist / In the new order of things" (10. 1909–10), a man whose path is unmarked by any received, formulated philosophy or by any allegiance to mere institutions—and a man shortly to become the sole survivor of the poem's three figures who have been visited by divine grace. Unwilling to conform to the no longer persuasive "standing ordinance" and "customary law" of the church (10. 1068–71), he says in effect, "I know the right place by foot's feel, / I took it and tread firm there." (10. 1885–86.)

> his own mere impulse guides the man—
> Happily sometimes, since ourselves admit
> He has danced, in gaiety of heart, i' the main
> The right step in the maze we bade him foot.
> What if his heart has prompted to break loose
> And mar the measure? Why, we must submit
> And thank the chance that brought him safely through.
> Will he repeat the prodigy? Perhaps.
> Can he teach others how to quit themselves,
> Prove why this step was right, while that were wrong?
> How should he? "Ask your hearts as I asked mine,

And get discreetly through the morrice [11] so;
If your hearts misdirect you,—quit the stage,
And make amends,—be there amends to make."
Such is, for the Augustine that was once,
This Canon Caponsacchi we see now.

(10. 1913–28)

Upon the spread of the spirit typified by Caponsacchi, a sort of honest moral empiricism, depends man's hope.

The grace that visited Caponsacchi when Pompilia called to him, Browning maintains, is symbolic of the redemption that can come to all humanity if it heeds the voice of Christ. Before he was drawn into Pompilia's crisis, Caponsacchi's faith was perfunctory, a matter of words, not burning conviction; and when faced with the problem of whether to act or not to act, he wavered. But soon his vacillation was resolved, not by mortal love, he says, but by faith, "The feeling that there's God, he reigns and rules / Out of this low world" (6. 1194–95). And so with mankind.

For even under the regime of skepticism and materialism, man's will remains free and he can save his soul, if he wishes, through decisive action that rends the chains of custom. The glory of Pompilia, says the Pope, is that she could

> rise from law to law,
> The old to the new, promoted at one cry
> O' the trump of God to the new service, not
> To longer bear, but henceforth fight, be found
> Sublime in new impatience with the foe!
> Endure man and obey God: plant firm foot
> On neck of man, tread man into the hell
> Meet for him, and obey God all the more!
> Oh child that didst despise thy life so much
> When it seemed only thine to keep or lose,
> How the fine ear felt fall the first low word
> "Value life, and preserve life for My sake!"
> Thou didst . . . how shall I say? . . . receive so long
> The standing ordinance of God on earth,
> What wonder if the novel claim had clashed

[11] Does Browning's choice of this spelling suggest a pun on "morass," thus linking the figure with the quagmire motif?

With old requirement, seemed to supersede
Too much the customary law?

(10. 1055–71)

Just as Pompilia turned from the "old" law of obedience and
passivity to the "new" law of action in behalf of a sacred cause
(the preservation of a new life), so mankind must abandon its
torpid, mechanical adherence to the "standing ordinance" and
"customary law" of received religion and heed "the novel
claim": the need, even at the cost of transgression, to take
militant action in behalf of God's kingdom on earth. Although
Pompilia's faith was never in question, it did not operate in any
positive way until she was confronted by the crisis of her pregnancy. Then her passiveness gave way to unquestioning action: her faith came alive.

Much older, much less tempted by the vanities of the world
than Caponsacchi, the Pope undergoes no such trial as does
the priest. Although he is sadly aware of the existence of
doubt, he never hesitates, at least within our sight. His stead-
fast decisiveness throughout his monologue substantiates all
he says concerning the necessity of doubt as a moral strength-
ener. Supposedly he has himself doubted in the past (else how
could he speak with so much understanding?) but his faith has
been victorious. Hence his unhesitating condemnation of
Guido; and Browning never allows us to question the complete
justice of that verdict.

To Browning, the decisiveness of Caponsacchi, Pompilia,
and the Pope is symbolic of the way modern man must respond to the challenge of imperfect knowledge if his soul is to
be saved. Whereas Guido uses what he takes to be the preva-
lence of doubt in the world as a rationalization for evil deeds,
the Pope welcomes the prospect of its spreading as a stimulus
to brave action.

Difficulties of belief such as those presented by miracles or
by conflicting versions of historical events are significant only
insofar as they bear upon conduct. It is not so much what men
believe as what they do, especially by way of responding to
doubt, that is the crucial consideration. But, Guido's knotty
argument to the contrary notwithstanding, belief and action
cannot be separated, for to Browning, the tireless activist,

belief itself is a form of activity; action divorced from belief is sterile, and belief which neither occasions action nor results from it is meaningless.

This is the final statement of *The Ring and the Book*. Toward it all the poem's principal themes have pointed—the ceaseless conflict of testimony, the equally discrepant interpretations of character and motive, the constant reminders that appearance frequently is more plausible than reality and that language is oftener a vehicle of falsehood than of truth. The search for truth in the midst of deceit and illusion, for stability in the midst of flux, turns out to be the search for the principles of right conduct. In human affairs the pervasive curse of doubt can be countered only by the vigorous response of a soul inspired by Christian teaching. The link between knowledge and morality, therefore, is faith manifested in virtuous action: the faith in things unseen, but tested on the pulse, which can serve as the basis of the ethical life.

The Pope in this poem, like the author of the fourth Gospel and Browning's created figure of St. John, applies his wisdom to a tangle of controverted and ambiguous events and emerges with prophecy. And on the wide canvas of *The Ring and the Book*, Browning as artist emulates the Pope and St. John by employing his superior gift of imagination to do what he is persuaded all men should do according to their capacity. With the events of the Franceschini case, as with the events narrated of Christ, it is incumbent upon men to look behind appearances and contested motives, to find the symbolic, transcendental meaning behind deeds. In this story of Pompilia and Caponsacchi, hidden for a century and a half in the records of a forgotten trial, God "showed for once / How He would have the world go white" (10. 680–81). To resuscitate such a shining instance of sacrificial love and to give it immediate meaning to an age desperately in need of such examples and all too unwilling or unable to discover them is, in Browning's view, a poetic mission of the noblest order. *The Ring and the Book* is the memorial of Browning's four years' dedication to his ideal of art as a religious exercise.

> Art, wherein man nowise speaks to men,
> Only to mankind,—Art may tell a truth

Obliquely, do the thing shall breed the thought,
Nor wrong the thought, missing the mediate word.
So may you paint your picture, twice show truth,
Beyond mere imagery on the wall,—
So, note by note, bring music from your mind,
Deeper than ever the Andante dived,—
So write a book shall mean, beyond the facts,
Suffice the eye and save the soul beside.

(12. 854–63)

Bibliographical Note

A full record of what was written on *The Ring and the Book* down to 1950 is found in *Robert Browning: A Bibliography, 1830–1950*, ed. L. N. Broughton, C. S. Northup, and Robert Pearsall (Ithaca, N.Y., 1953). This bibliography is extended through May, 1965, in *The Browning Critics*, ed. Boyd Litzinger and K. L. Knickerbocker (Louisville, Ky., 1965), pp. 391–417. Recent material is also listed in two annual compilations, the Victorian Bibliography in *Modern Philology* (to 1957) and *Victorian Studies* (1958——) and the MLA International Bibliography in *PMLA*.

For a record of the various editions of the poem, see the Broughton-Northup-Pearsall bibliography, items A73–A90. The text of the first edition, followed in the present book, is available in, *inter alia*, the Everyman edition (London, 1911) and the one-volume Oxford edition (London, 1912). The former, though unfortunately flawed by a number of typographical errors, has the advantage of being currently in print. Browning's revised text is found in Vols. 5–6 of *The Works of Robert Browning*, ed. F. G. Kenyon (London, 1912), and in the edition in the Norton Library (New York, 1961), which was printed from the plates of the Fireside Edition (Boston, 1899).

There are two indispensable aids to serious study of the poem: A. K. Cook's *A Commentary upon Browning's "The Ring and the Book"* (London, 1920), which contains the fullest annotation available as well as a number of valuable appendices, and chapter 5 of William C. DeVane's *A Browning Handbook*, 2d ed. (New York, 1955), with a digest of the history of the poem's composition and of its sources.

Charles W. Hodell's facsimile reproduction and translation of *The Old Yellow Book* (Washington, D.C., 1908) is the basic tool for any work involving comparison of *The Ring and the Book* with its sources. The long essay "The Making of a Great Poem" appended to the volume is a perceptive account of just how Browning worked as he transmuted the dross of the Roman legal documents into the gold of English verse. The later translation and commentary by a Philadelphia lawyer, John Marshall Gest (Boston, 1925), is distinguished by a minute, immensely learned analysis of the legal aspects of the Franceschini case; it has little relevance to any literary study of the poem, but Judge Gest's deep distress and indignation over Browning's treatment of the lawyers make the book unintentionally amusing reading. Additional documents relating to the case are reproduced and translated by E. H. Yarrill in the *Baylor Bulletin*, 42 (1939), no. 4, and by Beatrice Corrigan in her *Curious Annals: New Documents Relating to Browning's Roman Murder Story* (Toronto, 1956).

All the old "standard" critical volumes on Browning— Herford's, Dowden's, Chesterton's, Phelps's, and the rest— contain passages of some length on the poem, but these normally are not very penetrating, and they are confined, in any event, to broad generalities. Henry James's essay, "The Novel in 'The Ring and the Book,' " read before the Royal Society of Literature on May 7, 1912, first published in the *Quarterly Review* in the same year, and later included in his *Notes on Novelists* (New York, 1914), is a classic of enthusiastic appreciation, but it tells us more about James's view of the art of the novel than it does about the poem. Robert Langbaum's *"The Ring and the Book:* A Relativist Poem" (*PMLA*, 71 [1956]: 131–54, reprinted as chapter 8 of his *The Poetry of Experience* [New York, 1957]) is probably the most intelligent modern commentary on any single aspect of the poem; it should be read alongside the present volume, which does not attempt to cover the same ground. Other fairly recent discussions worth consulting are E. D. H. Johnson, "Browning's Pluralistic Universe: A Reading of *The Ring and the Book*," *University of Toronto Quarterly*, 31 (1961): 20–41; the passage (pp. 148–53) in J. Hillis Miller, *The Disappearance of God* (Cambridge, Mass., 1963); and Barton R. Friedman, "To Tell the Sun from the Druid Fire: Imagery of Good and Evil in *The Ring and the Book*," *Studies in English Literature*, 6 (1966): 693–708, which appeared after our manuscript was completed. A few other modern treatments are mentioned in our footnotes.

The fullest source for Browning's own view of *The Ring and the Book*—particularly his vigorous defense of his purposes against a lady's objections to the poem's sordidness and emphasis on evil—is *Robert Browning and Julia Wedgwood: A Broken Friendship as Revealed by Their Letters*, ed. Richard Curle (New York, 1937).

Index